Springer
Berlin
Heidelberg
New York
Barcelona
Hong Kong
London
Milan
Paris
Singapore
Tokyo

Springer Series in Information Sciences

Editors: Thomas S. Huang   Teuvo Kohonen   Manfred R. Schroeder

Volumes 1–29 are listed at the end of the book.

Manfred R. Schroeder

Computer Speech

Recognition, Compression, Synthesis

With Introductions to Hearing and Signal Analysis
and a Glossary of Speech and Computer Terms

With 78 Figures

Springer

Professor Dr. Manfred R. Schroeder

Drittes Physikalisches Institut
Universität Göttingen
Bürgerstrasse 42–44,
D-37073 Göttingen, Germany

Series Editors:
Professor Thomas S. Huang

Department of Electrical Engineering and Coordinated Science Laboratory,
University of Illinois, Urbana, IL 61801, USA

Professor Teuvo Kohonen

Helsinki University of Technology, Neural Networks Research Centre, Rakentajanaukio 2 C,
FIN-02150 Espoo, Finland

Professor Dr. Manfred R. Schroeder

Drittes Physikalisches Institut, Universität Göttingen, Bürgerstrasse 42-44,
D-37073 Göttingen, Germany

ISSN 0720-678X
ISBN 3-540-64397-4 Springer-Verlag Berlin Heidelberg New York

Library of Congress Cataloging-in-Publication Data applied for.
Die Deutsche Bibliothek – CIP-Einheitsaufnahme

Schroeder, Manfred R.:
Computer speech: recognition, compression, synthesis; with introductions to hearing and signal analysis
and a glossary of speech and computer terms / Manfred R. Schroeder. – Berlin; Heidelberg; New York;
Barcelona; Hong Kong; London; Milan; Paris; Singapore; Tokyo: Springer, 1999
(Springer series in information sciences; 35)
ISBN 3-540-64397-4

The use of general descriptive names, registered names, trademarks, etc. in this publication does not imply, even
in the absence of a specific statement, that such names are exempt from the relevant protective laws and
regulations and therefore free for general use.

Typesetting: Data conversion by Satztechnik Katharina Steingraeber, Heidelberg
Cover design: *design & production* GmbH, Heidelberg
SPIN: 10676879   56/3144 - 5 4 3 2 1 0 - Printed on acid-free paper

To Anny

Marion, Julian, Alexander

Marion, Uwe

Julia, Lilly, Nora, Nicola

Preface

World economies are increasingly driven by research, knowledge, information, and technology – with no small part being played by computer speech:

- automatic speech recognition and speaker authentication,
- speech compression for mobile phones, voice security and Internet "real audio,"
- speech synthesis and computer dialogue systems.

According to the London *Economist* information technology represents "a change even more far-reaching than the harnessing of electrical power a century ago . . . Where once greater distance made communications progressively more expensive and complicated, now distance is increasingly irrelevant."[1]

Natural speech, predominant in human communication since prehistoric times, has acquired a brash new kin: synthetic or *computer speech*. While people continue to use speech liberally, many of us are increasingly exposed to speech manufactured and understood by computers, compressed or otherwise modified by digital signal processors or microchips. This evolution, driven by innumerable technical advances, has been described in a profusion of scientific papers and research monographs aimed at the professional specialist. The present volume, by contrast, is aimed at a larger audience: all those generally curious about computer speech and all it portends for our future at home and in the workplace. I have therefore kept the technical details in the first chapters to a minimum and relegated any unavoidable "mathematics" to the end of the book.

Considering the importance of hearing for speech compression, speech synthesis (and even recognition), I have included a brief overview of hearing, both monaural and binaural.

I have also added a compact review of signal analysis because of its relevance for speech processing.

For the benefit of readers new to speech and computers I have added a glossary of terms from these fields. I have also augmented the numbered references by a list of books for general reading, selected journals, and major meetings on speech.

---

[1] Frances Cairncross, *The Economist*, 13 September 1997. Quoted from *The New York Review of Books*, 26 March 1998 (p.29). But see also Thomas K. Landauer, *The Trouble with Computers* (MIT Press, Cambridge, MA 1995).

Progress in any field does not arise in a vacuum but happens in a manifestly human environment. But many scientists, Carl Friedrich Gauss, the "Prince of Mathematicians" foremost among them, take great pride in obliterating in their publications any trace of how success was achieved. From this view, with all due respect for the great Gauss, I beg to differ. Of course, in mathematics, the "conjecture – lemma – theorem – proof" cycle will always remain the mainstay of progress. But I believe that much is to be gained – and not only for the nonspecialist – by putting scientific advances in a personal context.

Some Personal Recollections

This book has its genesis in a visit by a Bonn linguist to the University of Göttingen in Germany shortly before Christmas 1951. The noted speech scientist had been invited to give a talk at the General Physics Colloquium, not on the usual nuts-and-bolts exploits in physics, but on Shannon's communication theory and its potential importance for human language, written or spoken.

After the distinguished guest had safely departed, most of the physicists present professed "not to have understood a word." During the ensuing departmental Christmas party the chairman, the reigning theoretical physicist, asked me how I had liked the lecture. When I admitted that (although far from having understood everything) I was deeply impressed, the professor's answer was a disapproving stare. How could anything be interesting, he seemed to be saying, that did not partake of Planck's quantum of energy or general relativistic covariance.

I was working on concert hall acoustics at the time, using microwave cavities as a convenient model for acoustic enclosures. I was soon astounded by the chaotic distribution of the resonances that my measurements revealed – even for relatively small deviations from perfect geometric symmetry of the cavity: I had stumbled on the very same probability distribution that also governs the energy levels of complex atomic nuclei and that Eugene Wigner in Princeton had already promulgated in 1935. But at that time and for decades thereafter few (if any) physicists appreciated its general import.

Now, 60 years later, the Wigner distribution is recognized as a universal tell-tale sign of "non-integrable" dynamical systems with chaotic behavior. But, of course, chaos hadn't been "invented" yet and I for one didn't know enough nuclear physics – too much like chemistry I thought – to see the connection. Nor, I think it is safe to say, did atomic physicists know enough about concert halls or microwave cavities to appreciate the common thread. Interestingly, the Wigner distribution also raises its head in – of all things – number theory, where it describes the distribution of the (interesting) zeros of the Riemann zeta-function.

Be that as it may, my thesis advisor was much impressed by my progress and suggested that I go to America, the "microwave country." The thought had crossed my mind and it did sound interesting. So I applied for a Fulbright Fellowship – and failed flat out. My academic grades were good, my English was passable but, the Fulbright commission concluded, I was not politically active enough. They were looking for foreign students who, upon their return from the States, could be expected to "spread the gospel" about democracy, the American Way of Life and so forth. But I, it seemed, was mostly interested in physics, mathematics, languages, photography, tennis and – perish the thought – dancing.

During my thesis on the statistical interference of normal modes in microwave cavities and concert halls, I discovered the work of S. O. Rice on random noise, which explained a lot about sound transmission in concert halls.[2]

Now Rice, I knew, was with Bell and so was Shannon. So after my Fulbright failure I went to my professor and asked him for a recommendation for Bell Laboratories. But he told me that Bell didn't take any foreigners. In fact, in 1938 he had backed one of his better students (who was eager to leave Germany) but Bell declined. (I still wonder what was behind that rejection.)

Then, in early 1954, James Fisk (later president of Bell Laboratories) and William Shockley (of transistor fame) traveled to Germany (Fisk had studied in Heidelberg) to look for young talent for Bell. When I heard about this, I immediately went again to my professor telling him that Bell was not only accepting foreigners but they were actively *looking* for them. This time around the kind professor promised a recommendation and just three weeks later I received an invitation from Bell for an employment interview in London.

An Unusual Interview

The venue of the interview was the lobby of the Dorchester Hotel. After explicating my thesis work, I asked the recruiter to tell me a bit about the Bell System. "Well, there was AT&T, the parent company, Western Electric, the manufacturing arm, Bell Laboratories, and 23 operating companies: New York Telephone, New Jersey Bell, Southern Bell..." when, in the middle of this recitation, he stopped short and, with his eyes, followed an elegant young lady (an incognito *countess*?) traversing the long lobby. After a minute

---

[2] It transpired that such transmission functions were basically random noise, albeit in the frequency domain, and that room acousticians, for years, had measured nothing but different samples of the same random noise in their quest for a formula to pinpoint acoustic quality. Within a limited cohort of acousticians I became quite wellknown for this work although it was just an application of Rice's theory. But it did establish a new area of research in acoustics (and later microwaves and coherent optics): *random wave fields*, with many interesting applications: acoustic feedback stability of hands-free telephones and public address systems, fading in mobile communications and laser speckle statistics.

or two, without losing a beat, he continued "yes, and there is Southwestern Bell, Pacific Telephone, ..."[3]

Everything went well during the interview, and I soon received an offer of employment. The monthly salary was \$640 – five times as much as a young Ph.D. could have made at Siemens (500 Marks). But, of course, at Bell I would have worked for nothing.

On September 30, 1954, arriving in New York, I stepped off the *Andrea Doria* (still afloat then) and into a chauffeured limousine which took me and my future director and supervisor to one of the best restaurants in the area. I couldn't read the menu (mostly in French) – except for the word *Bratwurst*. So, with champagne corks popping and sparkling desserts going off at neighboring tables, everybody in our party had *Bratwurst* and *Löwenbräu* beer (my future bosses were obviously very polite people) – I wonder how many immigrants were ever received in such style.

Arriving at the Murray Hill Labs, I was put on the payroll and given a dollar bill as compensation for all my future inventions. (When I retired 33 years later I had garnered 45 U.S. patents and innumerable foreign filings, but the fact that I had earned less than 3 cents for every invention never bothered me.)

Once securely ensconced at Murray Hill, I was encouraged to continue my work on random wave fields but – in typical youthful hubris – I thought I had solved all relevant problems and I elected to delve into speech. Speech, after all, meant language – always a love of mine – and possibly relevant to the telephone business.

The Bachelor and the Hoboken Police

William H. Doherty, my first Executive Director at Bell, introduced me to one and all as "Dr. Schroeder, who just joined us from Germany – and he is a bachelor." I was 28 then but apparently already getting a bit old for a single Catholic male. (I later had to disappoint Bill by marrying in an interdenominational ceremony – at the Chapel of the Riverside Church on the Hudson – my wife being Orthodox.)

When one night, carrying a camera with a very long lens, I was arrested by dockworkers on the Hoboken piers (believing they had caught a foreign spy),

---

[3] Twenty-five years later, to the day, on April 25, 1979, I went back to the Dorchester. At the far end of the lobby there was a kind of hat-check counter with an elderly lady behind it. I went up to her and asked "Could it be that on this day, 25 years ago, on April 25, 1954, a Sunday, a young woman might have appeared from the door behind you – it was about 2 p.m. – crossed the lobby and then exited by the revolving door?" She must have thought I was from Scotland Yard or something. But, unflustered, she answered "Oh yes, of course, at 2 p.m. we had a change of shifts then. This entrance was for service personnel – *chambermaids* and so forth." I asked her, "How do you know this?" And she said, "I have been here for 30 years."

he vouchsafed for me that I was just taking pictures of the full moon rising over the New York skyline across the Hudson. (The dockworkers had called the Hoboken police, who, however, were completely sidetracked by my collection of photographs of beautiful models. The dock hands were apparently not satisfied with this result of their "citizen arrest" and the incident was raised again years later during my naturalization proceedings when Doherty, now assistant to the President, rescued me once more.)

Acknowledgments

In my career in speech I am indebted to many people, not least the "noted linguist" noted above: the late Werner Meyer-Eppler, who sparked my interest in Shannon's communication theory and linguistics.

Professor Erwin Meyer was the professor who rescued me from the clutches of German industry with a scholarship for my Ph.D. And it was he who wrote the recommendation that propelled me first to London and then on to New York and Murray Hill.

Winston Kock was the polite director who had received me in such style in New York.

Bell People

Starting out in a new field is never easy but I learned a lot – much by osmosis – from the speech pioneers at Bell: Ralph Miller, my first supervisor, Harold Barney of formant-frequency fame, Homer Dudley, the inventor of the vocoder, Hugh Dunn, who had built an early electrical model of the vocal tract, Warren Tyrrel, inventor of the microwave Magic Tee, and the kindly Floyd Harvey, who was assigned to "teach me the ropes."

Within a year or two after my arrival at Murray Hill a crew of contemporaries appeared on the speech scene at Bell: the Swiss physicist Erich Weibel, the mathematician Henry Kramer (originally from Düsseldorf), Hank McDonald, the instrumentation genius, and Max Mathews who taught us all that working with analog circuits was basically solving mathematical equations and that this could be done much better on a "digital computer" an idea that I took up with a vengeance, soon simulating sound transmission in concert halls with computer running times a thousand times real time.[4]

I must make special mention here of Ben Logan ("Tex" to the country music community) with whom I worked very closely for many years and who taught me electrical engineering. I will never forget when, reading an article bemoaning the poor sound quality of artificial reverberators, I turned to Ben

---

[4] When the first artificially reverberated music emerged from the digital-to-analog converter, the computer people thought that this was a prank, that I had hidden a tape recorder behind their racks.

(literally – we were sharing an office) asking him whether there were *allpass* filters with an exponentially decaying impulse response. Ben's answer was yes and the allpass reverberator was born.

At about the same time, shortly after the Hungarian revolution – on December 31, 1956, to be exact – Bela Julesz, arriving through Camp Killmer, New Jersey, knocked on our door and was immediately admitted. Bela became a lifelong friend and limitless source of intellectual stimulation.

Later the acoustics department was merged with the "vision" people which brought me into contact with the psychologist Georg Sperling, Leon Harmon ("Einstein's technical aide" and jack-of-many-trades), the superlative John L. Kelly, Jr., who had given Shannon's concept of information rate a new meaning (in a gambling context). Kelly, with Lou Gerstman, digitally simulated the first terminal-analog speech synthesizer.

Of the people I encountered at Bell perhaps the most noteworthy was Ed David who had the inspiration to persuade our immediate superiors, Vice President for Research William O. Baker, and John R. Pierce, of satellite communication fame, to establish, at Bell Laboratories, a broadly based research group in human communication – complementing the usual engineers, physicists and mathematicians by psychologists, physiologists and linguists. It is in this environment that I got to know many outstanding people from a broad range of scientific disciplines: Peter Denes, the linguist from England, who introduced online computing in speech research, Gerald Harris from nuclear physics (who showed that the threshold of hearing was just above the molecular Brownian noise in the inner ear), the psychologists Newman Guttman, Thomas Landauer, and Lynn Streeter, and the physiologists Willem van Bergeijk, Larry Frischkopf, Bob Capranica, and Åke Flok from Sweden.

Ed David also inaugurated a visiting scholar program with MIT and Harvard which brought to Murray Hill such luminaries as the neural-network pioneers and authors of "A Logical Calculus Immanent in Nervous Activity," Walter Pitts (typically delivering his lectures from a crouching position), and Warren McCulloch, the noted linguists Roman Jacobson, Morris Halle, Gunnar Fant, Ken Stevens, and Arthur House; also Walter Rosenblith and the inimitable Jerry Lettvin (the latter with a live demonstration of "what the frog's eye tells the frog's brain").

On the social side, Ed and his charming wife Ann acted as my chaperones (sometimes too stringently, I felt) in converting me from a peccable European to a good American. (Ed also showed me how to boil lobster and the secrets of properly grilling steak.) And Ann, hailing from Atlanta, taught all of us newcomers the essence of a gracious social life.

In 1956, Ed was my best man when I married Anny Menschik in New York. Later he and Newman Guttman acted as sponsors for my U.S. citizenship.

At the Labs I also profited much from my close associations with the resident mathematicians: the critical but always helpful David Slepian, Ron Graham, Dick Hamming, who taught me how totally counterintuitive higher dimensional spaces are, Jessie MacWilliams, who introduced me to primitive polynomials, Ed Gilbert, who solved an important integral equation on reverberation for me, Aaron Wyner, Neil Sloane, who worked with me on a data compression scheme involving new permutation codes, Andrew Odlyzko, Henry Landau, Leopold Flatto, Hans Witsenhausen, Larry Shepp, and Jeff Lagarias, who infused dynamical systems (chaos and fractals) with number theory.

Elwyn Berlekamp, an early friend, supplied the mathematical underpinnings for my proposal to use Hadamard smearing in frame difference picture coding.

Ingrid Daubechies, now at Princeton, initiated me into the world of wavelets and redressed my Flemish at the Bell Labs Dutch Table.

I also knew, albeit in a more cursory manner, the "old guard": Hendrik Bode and Serge Schellkunoff, with whom I shared an interest in microwaves. The fatherly Harry Nyquist and I worked together for a while on underwater sound problems. Claude Shannon once came to my office with a funny little trumpet wanting to know whether I could compute its resonances. David Hagelbarger introduced me to several of his "machinations," including Shannon's outguessing machine.

The Bell mathematician with whom I had the most frequent contacts for over 30 years was John W. Tukey, one of the sharpest minds around, who split his time between Bell and the Princeton Statistics Department. Tukey, who seemed to thrive on half a dozen glasses of skim milk for lunch, was the first human parallel processor I have known: during staff meetings he would regularly work out some statistical problem while hardly ever missing a word said during the discussion. He is of course best known for his (re)invention, with IBM's Jim Cooley, of the fast Fourier transform, which changed the topography of digital signal processing (never mind that Gauss had the FFT 150 years earlier). Tukey was also a great wordsmith: he coined the terms *bit* and *cepstrum*, (the Fourier transform of the logarithm of the Fourier transform). But some of his cookier coinages, like quefrency (for cepstral frequency) and saphe (for cepstral phase) didn't catch on.

Henry Pollak, who directed mathematics research during my tenure as director of acoustics and speech research, was an unstinting source of mathematical talent for our down-to-earth problems in speech and hearing. (But his devotion to administrative detail never rubbed off on my more nonchalant style of management.)

Of all the people I worked with at Bell only one was a bona-fide speech researcher *before* joining us: Jim Flanagan, whose thesis at MIT was concerned with the measurement and perception of formant frequencies. Jim served as one of the department heads who reported to me during one of the most fertile periods in speech research at Bell, an epoch to which Jim contributed mightily.

Three other department heads who added greatly to the prestige of acoustics at Bell Labs were Peter Denes, author (with Elliot Pinson) of the *Speech Chain*, Bob Wallace (inventor of the tetrode transistor and several ingenious directional microphones for conference telephony) and Warren Mason (holder of over 200 U.S. patents). Warren in turn was aided by Orson Anderson (who invented compression bonding), and Bob Thurston and Herb McSkimmin, wizards of ultrasonic precision measurements.

A physicist by training, I also enjoyed friendly relations with a few of the physicists at Bell, notably Sid Millman (long in charge of AT&T's University Relations and co-editor of the Bell System History), Conyers Herring, with whom I shared an interest in Russian, Phil Anderson, who was our guest when the Göttingen Academy awarded him the Heinemann Preis, Stan Geschwind, and the laser pioneer Jim Gordon, whom my wife Anny knew from Columbia, Al Clogston, inventor of end-fire arrays, Rudi Kompfner, inventor of the traveling wave tube, Arno Penzias and R.W. Wilson, discoverers of the Big Bang radiation, Bill Pfann of zone refining fame, Walter Brattain, inventor of the point-contact transistor whom I didn't get to know until an *Institut de la Vie* meeting in Paris in 1976, and Phil Platzman and Horst Störmer, co-discoverer of the fractional Hall effect, who, for many years, kept me supplied with my favorite engagements calendar that includes the consumer price index for the last 50 years and a chart of vintage wines.

I also kept in touch with several psychologists, notably Roger Shepard, whose work on scaling I greatly admired, Saul Sternberg, Ernie and Carol Rothkopf, Joe Kruskal and Doug Carroll, whose multidimensional preference algorithms came in very handy when I became interested in the subjective quality of sounds and concert halls.

Attorneys Harry Hart and Al Hirsch steered my patents from rough design to legal perfection, often adding their own innovations.

Atal et al.

My sojourn at Bell was blessed with an abundance of new talent, Bishnu Atal foremost among them. I had heard about Bishnu from my old ally in room acoustics, Dick Bolt of Bolt, Beranek, and Newman in Cambridge, Massachusetts. I don't recall why BBN would or could not hire Bishnu but, even without a Ph.D., he sounded too good to miss. I therefore wrote Bishnu and called him at the Indian Institute of Science in Bangalore. This was in 1961, before satellite communication, and while everything was crisp and clear up to New Delhi, communication completely fell apart beyond Poona, India. I had started our "conversation" with the rhetorical question whether he had already received my letter. Sorry to say, after forty-five minutes of misunderstandings and repetitions (some with the help of telephone operators in White Plains (New York), London, New Delhi, and Poona) that question was still unanswered. So I finally gave up and said "I enjoyed talking to you. I will confirm all this by letter." (It is only fair to add that the telephone company – fully aware of the non-communication – charged us only for three minutes connection time.)

In due course Bishnu arrived at Murray Hill, and the stage was set for a close and enduring collaboration, first in hearing and room acoustics and before too long in speech. Simultaneously, Bishnu worked on his Ph.D. from Brooklyn Polytechnical Institute (with a thesis on speaker recognition).

The 1960s also saw the advent of such outstanding researchers as Mike Noll, with whom I explored visual perception of four-dimensional spaces and who later advanced to an office in the White House, Gerhard Sessler from Germany, Hiroya Fujisaki, Sadaoki Furui, and Osamu Fujimura from Tokyo; Mohan Sondhi who came via Canada, Cecil Coker, Paul Mermelstein, Harry Levitt, Aaron Rosenberg, Noriko Umeda, Jont Allen, Dave Berkeley, Allen Gersho, Gary Elko, Jim West, Roger Golden, Oded Ghitza, Naftali Tishby, and Joseph Hall, with whom, in the 1970s, after a long slumber, I revived hearing research at Bell.

I also enjoyed many instructive encounters with yet another generation of linguists at Bell: Mark Liberman, Ken Church, and Ken Silverman.[5] Dan Kahn and Marian Macchi, with whom I once worked a bit on poles, zeros and nasals, later developed the speech synthesis program Orator^{TM} at Bellcore.

Bell Laboratories has benefitted greatly from the cooperative program in electrical engineering with MIT. Under the auspices of this program, I met some of my most able students, notably Dick Hause, who explored single-sideband modulation and infinite clipping, and Tom Crystal, with whom I worked on time-domain vocoders.

The prolific Larry Rabiner worked with us on digital circuits and binaural hearing from 1962 to 1964. In 1967 he joined Bell Labs as a full-time researcher and before too long rose on the corporate ladder to Department Head, Director and Vice President before he left for (stayed with?) AT&T.

I cannot complete this account without mentioning the expert programming help I received from Carol McClellan and Lorinda Landgraf Cherry, who

---

[5] Silverman, an Australian linguist, once got tripped up on the German word for emergency, *Not*, when he found himself trapped inside a burning building in Austria. Every door he approached repulsed him with a forbidding *verboten* sign saying NOTAUSGANG – not exit? My increasingly frantic friend, desperately seeking *Ausgangs*, knew enough Latin and German (besides his native English) to properly decode *aus-gang* as *ex-it*. But in the heat of the emergency, he never succeeded in severing the Gordian knot: *Not* is not *not*. Eventually Silverman tried a "not exit" and escaped!

Fig. 1. The author with Lorinda Cherry and Marion and Senator Javitz at the opening of the exhibition *Some New Beginning – Experiments in Art and Technology* at the Brooklyn Museum in November 1968. The wall-size poster in the background is a computer graphic by the author and was programmed by Ms. Cherry. It combines an image of the museum with the program of the exhibit.

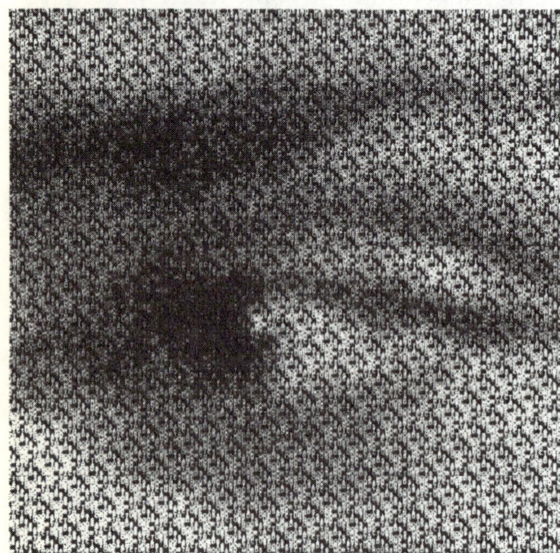

Fig. 2. *One Picture is Worth a Thousand Words.* A computer graphic by the author programmed by Suzanne Hanauer. This image won First Prize at the International Computer Art Exhibition in Las Vegas in 1969.

programmed the poster for Marion Javitz's and Billy Klüver's[6] avantgarde art show *Experiments in Art and Technology* at the Brooklyn Museum, see Fig. 1, and Sue Hanauer who realized the image *One Picture is Worth a Thousand Words* for me that won First Prize at the International Computer Art Competition in 1969 in Las Vegas, see Fig. 2. Sue also programmed my number-theoretic *Prime Spectrum* which – unbeknownst to me – required shutting down the Murray Hill Computer Center to press the last bit of core memory into service for the required 1024-by-1024 fast Fourier transform, see Fig. 3. (Yes, in the 1960s, even one of the world's larger computer centers didn't have as much memory as today's lowly laptops.) Sue later moved to Israel and became chief systems programmer for El Al airlines.

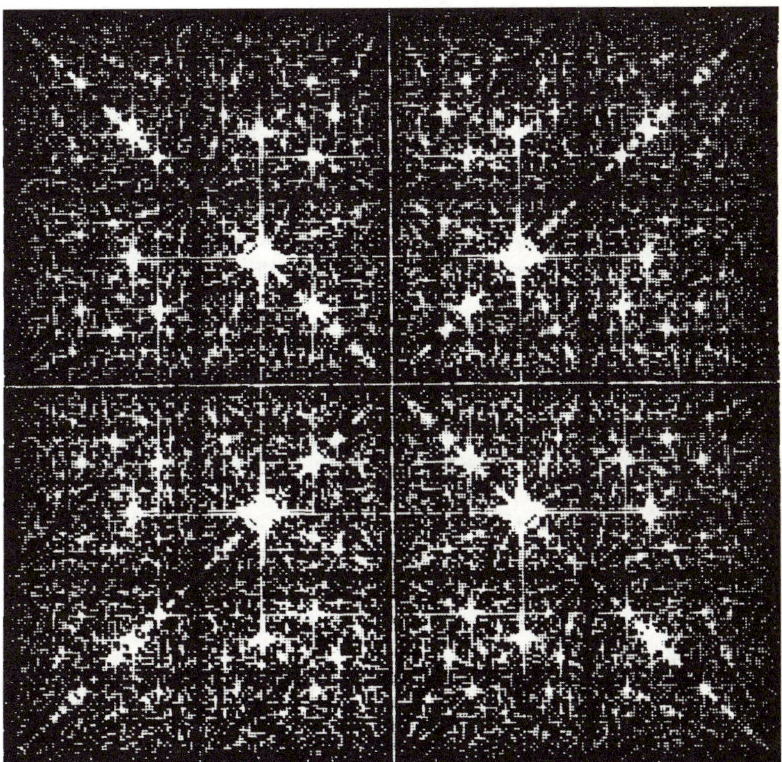

Fig. 3. *Prime Spectrum.* Another computer graphic by the author with Sue Hanauer. The image, originally containing 1024×1024 points, shows the Fourier transform of the distribution of the relative primes. It was calculated by a fast Fourier transform and (in 1969) required shutting down the Bell Laboratories computer center to marshal the necessary core memory.

---

[6] The Swede Klüver is now "immortalized" as the hapless depression-era "American" farmer in the new Franklin Delano Roosevelt Memorial in Washington.

Among the many other associates at Bell Labs whom I remember with gratitude are Chapin Cutler, whose work on self-steering arrays for satellite communication inspired my invention of "volume focussing" acoustic arrays, and Ernie Kretzmer, from whom I first heard about predictive coding for video, and John Limb. With Bob Lucky, a genius with words, I shared an early interest in automatic echo cancellation for satellite links. Jim Kaiser, of Fourier window fame and one of my tutors in electrical engineering, became a lifelong friend.

Students and Professors at Göttingen

In Göttingen my closest friend was and is Manfred Eigen whom I first met as a student in 1947. Manfred was interested in very fast chemical reactions. He had the brilliant idea that one could measure their reaction rates by disturbing the chemical equilibrium by high-frequency sound. And, as Manfred soon discovered, such ultrasonic measurements were already being made at the *Institut für Schwingungsphysik* (swinging physics?) next door.

Manfred's discovery had a large impact in molecular biology by elucidating the very fast reactions that sustain life. The work in the physics department was an outgrowth of earlier efforts to measure sound absorption in sea water (in connection with anti-submarine warfare). Thus a warlike endeavor became life science.

I also recall with gratitude my teachers in physics and mathematics at Göttingen: Richard Becker, Arnold Schmidt ("Hilbert's last assistant"), Wilhelm Magnus and Franz Rellich. Magnus was the politest person I have ever met.[7] Rellich once spent an hour with me in 1952 on the generalization of a theorem by Hermann Weyl (on the asymptotic density of eigenvalues of certain linear operators). When I thanked him he said, "Do you know that you are the first physicist to consult with a mathematician [in Göttingen] since 1933." (Before the wholesale dismantling of German science by the Nazis, Göttingen mathematicians, led by David Hilbert and Richard Courant, had enjoyed close contacts with their friends in physics, especially Max Born and Werner Heisenberg.)

Another close personal and professional friend at Göttingen was the late Otto Creutzfeldt with whom I shared my students at the Max Planck Institute for Biophysical Chemistry.

After my move to Germany I was again favored with many first-rate collaborators, especially Heinrich Kuttruff, Wolfgang Eisenmenger, who pioneered phonon spectroscopy at Holmdel, and Karl Joachim Ebeling, who began his work on solid-state lasers there. All three joined me at Bell for one or several summers.

---

[7] See my tribute "More on Magnus" in the Mathematical Intelligencer **18**, No.1, page 7 (1996).

Other Bell visitors from Göttingen include Wolfgang Möller, see Fig. 1.2, Sönke Mehrgardt, and Andreas Steingrube.

Dieter Gottlob, Karl Friedrich Siebrasse, Herbert Alrutz and Ulrich Eysholdt elucidated the main ingredients of good concert hall acoustics by digital testing and simulated digital modifications of existing halls. The late Tino Gramss, who held postdoc positions at CalTech and the Santa Fe Institute, became a close personal friend.

Lars Kindermann converted my number theoretic *Baroque Integers* into "fractal music" that, to me, sounded much like Bach. But when I got too many frowns from my German listeners, I started likening the music to Domenico Scarlatti, following the suggestion of an Italian audience in Naples.

Inga Holube never tired of telling me that our work on advanced hearing aids was actually useful so that I finally relented and got a pair for my own failing ears.

My greatest gratitude goes to Birger Kollmeier, Armin Kohlrausch, and Hans Werner Strube without whose help I could not have run speech and hearing research at Göttingen. I also thank Dr. Strube for the expert treatise on vocal tract acoustics, which forms Appendix A of this book.

Friends in Other Places

While Murray Hill and Göttingen were my main abodes (for 18 years in time-sharing mode) my interest in speech, hearing, and music brought me into fruitful contact with many of the leading researchers in these fields: Al Liberman, Frank Cooper, Eugene Peterson, and Cathy Harris at Haskins Laboratories in New York; Ira Hirsch from the Central Institute for the Deaf; Irwin Pollack from the University of Michigan; Thomas Stockham from Utah, who restored scratchy old Gigli recordings, Diana Deutsch from San Diego, whose auditory paradoxes are breathtaking; Walter Lawrence (of "what did you say before that" fame), John Holmes, Donald McKay, Ted Evans, Christopher Longuet-Higgins, Brian Moore, and Roy Patterson from England; Gunnar Fant, Sven Öhman, Björn Lindblom, and Johan Sundberg from Sweden; the incomparable Jan Schouten, founder of the Instituut voor Perceptie Onderzoek, the late Nico Franssen, Rainier Plomp, Willem Levelt, Egbert de Boer, Victor Peutz, Luis Pols, Guido Smoorenburg, Dirk Duifhuis, and Adrianus Houtsma from the Netherlands; Ludmila Chistovich, Valery Kozhevnikov and their daughter Irena from Russia;[8] Vern Knudson, Leo Beranek, Cyril Harris,

---

[8] One cold winter night, arriving at Leningrad airport and finding none of my friends to meet me and not even knowing where I was staying, I turned to the KGB operative on duty (always easy to spot, even when disguised as a tourist) explaining in basic Russian, "I Dr. Schroeder from Federal Republic. – All-Union Conference on Acoustics. – Which hotel?" Whereupon the man replied, without batting an eye, "You – Oktyabraskaya Gostinitsa." And sure enough, when I made my way by taxi to the Hotel October, all my friends were there, surprised that I had already arrived.

Maa Dah You, the late Ted Shultz, Bill Hartmann; Peter Ladefoged, Vicky Fromkin, Arthur House; Werner Endres from the German Federal Communications Central Laboratories, and Eberhard Zwicker, Hugo Fastl, and Ernst Terhardt from the Technical University of Munich.

My special gratitude goes to my Japanese friends, foremost the gracious Hiroya Fujisaki; we met on several continents and I was privileged to spend some time with him as a visiting professor at Tokyo University. I fondly remember the kind Sadaoki Furui under whose auspices I spent a very fruitful period at the Human Interface Laboratory of NTT and where I worked closely with Miki Tohyama. Osamu Fujimura is a long-standing and close friend whom I had the privilege of knowing both at MIT and Bell Labs. Of all my Japanese friends, the one closest to me in (mathematical) spirit is no doubt Fumitada Itakura whose partial-correlation analysis I have always admired. Yoichi Ando was a close associate in architectural acoustics who spent a year and several additional stays at Göttingen University as a Humboldt Fellow. I also remember with great gratitude Professors Miura, Saito, and Suzuki.

At MIT's Lincoln Laboratory Ben Gold and Charlie Rader became early friends. Charlie and J. H. McClellan showed me the way with their *Number Theory in Digital Signal Processing* for my own *Number Theory in Science and Communication*.

At Prometheus ("Professional Consultants to the Scientific Community") I learned a lot from such outstanding mathematicians as Jim Byrnes, John Benedetto and Harold S. Shapiro, whose Rudin–Shapiro polynomials helped me with the peak-factor problem in speech synthesis. Donald Newman's decimated Morse–Thue sequences inspired my *Baroque Integers* melodies.

The late Dennis Klatt, Jim Cooley, Bill Lang, and Benoît Mandelbrot were early friends from IBM. I first met Bill, who was then at the Naval Postgraduate School in Monterrey, at the First International Congress on Acoustics in Delft, Holland, in 1953. He and his Swedish wife Asta have been friends ever since.

My first encounter with Benoît's work was his analysis of word frequencies in natural and artificial languages, which touched upon my own interests in computer speech synthesis and recognition. Mandelbrot's monumental monograph *The Fractal Geometry of Nature* influenced me immeasurably, as it did so many other people.

John Horton Conway taught me several mathematical tricks, such as quickly calculating the days of the week in any century. He once stepped by my office to help me express a friends age in days by Euler's totient function.

Music

Working with Pierre Boulez on the establishment at the Centre Pompidou in Paris of the Intstitut de Recherche et de Coordination Acoustique/Musique

(IRCAM) was one of my more memorable labors. (But when I wanted to impress Pierre – who had absolute pitch – with a concert hall simulation at Göttingen, his first comment was "your tape recorders run at the wrong speed.") Luciano Berio and Gerald Bennet are other members of the original IRCAM "équipe" that I remember with fondness.

I also recall with affection the genial Hermann Scherchen whose avant-garde electro-acoustic laboratory in Gravesano on Lake Lugano in Italian Switzerland pioneered the fusion of music and modern technology. (But when once given a demonstration of computer music he whispered into my ear "Aber Musik ist das nicht!")

Leopold Stokowski came to Murray Hill when he was worried about the precious acoustics of Carnegie Hall after a proposal to install a huge (gift) organ behind the stage. (The solution: an acoustically impervious lead curtain covering the unloved gift when not in use.)

Other noted conductors I was privileged to work with were Joseph Kripps (when, in the fall of 1963, the San Francisco War Memorial Opera House was converted into a concert hall), George Szell[9] and Leonard Bernstein. Bernstein once asked me to translate the comments about Philharmonic Hall made by a German acoustician (Heinrich Keilholz, who didn't speak English) for the benefit of William Schuman and other Lincoln Center officials. (Bernstein himself was of course conversant with German.) Suddenly, everybody in attendance exploded in laughter. What had happened? Keilholz had said one sentence in English and I had translated it for everybody into German. I was obviously in a translating mode: one language in, the other out. (I often don't know what language I speak. Once at an international conference held in Göttingen, I was interrupted:"Manfred, your talk was announced in English." "Yes, and what am I speaking?" Well, talking in my own lecture hall, I was giving my talk in German. The majority wanted me to go on in German but I later repeated the talk in English.)

My closest friends among musicians are Jean-Claude Risset, whose musical paradoxes inspired my own work on self-similar melodies, and John Chowning who turned my artificial reverberators into sounds swirling through three-dimensional space.

---

[9] Szell had an intense dislike of Philharmonic Hall at Lincoln Center in New York. He called the new hall, which he threatened to boycott in favor of Carnegie Hall, a bank on the outside, a movie theatre on the inside, illuminated by "schwangere Frösche mit beleuchtetem Bauchnabel." We once went together to a concert by Erich Leinsdorf conducting the Boston Symphony. He was enthusiastic about Leinsdorf's violins (I had never heard him enthusiastic about anything before) but agreed that the acoustics of the hall was abominable. After the intermission I led Szell to seat A15 on what was then the "Second Terrace," which our measurements had shown to have much better acoustics. Szell agreed. But then we had to vacate the good seats for the legitimate ticket holders. We therefore sat down on the floor next to the wall. I felt that the acoustics on the floor was really superb but didn't dare say anything. I was therefore much pleased when the crouching Szell pronounced the acoustics on the floor likewise excellent.

I also thank Laura Bianchini and Michelangelo Lupone for their hospitality during my sojourns in Rome, allowing me to sample their enticing compositions. Giuseppe Di Giugno's impact on electronic music will long reverberate.

I was also privileged to have known some outstanding modern composers, notably Györgi Ligeti, Milton Babbitt, James Tenney, and John Cage, for whom I once played my own electronic music (produced by a frequency shifter with feedback through a reverberant space).

Cronkite and Company

It is amazing how the lowly field of acoustics has catapulted me into the presence of such celebrities as Alfred P. Sloan. (I think he had a hearing problem, but he also reminisced with evident nostalgia about his "good old days" at the helm of General Motors.) Another memorable encounter was with Walter Cronkite and his boss at CBS, William S. Paley. (Again the subject was hearing, Cronkite's I think, but this was never explicitly stated.)

Watergate

Acoustics (and language) even got me involved in Watergate (albeit ever so slightly and, I hasten to add, on the innocent side). Rose Mary Woods, President Nixon's secretary, was using a German (*Uher*) tape recorder when she produced that famous 18-minute gap in one of the President's recordings and Judge Sirica naturally wanted to know whether such an erasure could happen accidentally by just "leaning over" the recorder. But the machine's instructions, alas, were in German...

Heidelberg and New York

I thank Dr. Helmut Lotsch, Managing Editor at Springer Verlag in Heidelberg, with whom I savored a long and fruitful cooperation. I am happy to contribute the present volume as a token of my appreciation before his mandatory retirement.

I also thank Thomas von Foerster of the American Institute of Physics and Springer New York and Dr. H.J. Kölsch, Heidelberg, for their wise rede.

Adelheid Duhm reigned supremely over the production process. Dr. Angela Lahee purged the syntax of original sin.

Murray Hill and Göttingen

Martina Sharp at Murray Hill and Karin in der Beek in Göttingen excelled, as always, in their typing from very rough drafts. Gisela Kirschmann-Schröder prepared the illustrations with her customary skill. Jobst von Behr deflected me from serious error; Wolfgang Schröter suggested the Glossary; Gerhard König ruled the References. Holger Quast brought the manuscript up to Springer standards and made numerous valuable suggestions.

Finally I thank William Oliver Baker and John Robinson Pierce who fostered a research climate at Bell Laboratories in which my career in speech could flourish.

Göttingen and Berkeley Heights   *Manfred Schroeder*
February 1999

Also by Manfred Schroeder

Fractals, Chaos, Power Laws: Minutes from an Infinite Paradise
(W.H. Freeman, New York 1992)

Number Theory in Science and Communication
Springer Series in Information Sciences, Vol. 17, Third Edition (Springer, Berlin Heidelberg 1997)

Speech and Speaker Recognition (Ed.)
Bibliotheca Phonetica, Vol. 12 (S. Karger, Basel 1985)

Contents

1. Introduction

Language was created by Nature – like Vision or Digestion.

Epicurus (341–270 BC)

Language ability is a gift of God – except for Chinese,
which is the invention of a wise man.

Gottfried Wilhelm von Leibnitz (1646–1716)

Where does language come from? Did God create it, or is it a result of natural selection and fitful adaptation, as Epicurus held? Does language languish, once conceived, or does it grow and decay like living "matter"? And what did Leibnitz have in mind when calling Chinese an invention of a wise man? Was he alluding to the fact that Chinese is a tonal language and as such perhaps easier to recognize?? Whatever the answers, language lets us live the lives we love and like to talk about.

In this introductory chapter we shall explore some of the possibilities of language that were neither created by God nor foreseen by Nature: linguistic signals fashioned not by human tongues but manufactured by machines. And we shall likewise ponder speech signals perceived by machines rather than the human ear. Let us take a look at some "ancient" history of our subject.

1.1 Speech: Natural and Artificial

Language – both written and spoken – is the primary means of communication between humans. Written language and the richness of spoken idioms distinguish the human species from all other forms of life: language is the very essence of humanness and humanity.

Yet, human communication by language is beset by many obstacles, from the simple misunderstanding within a single dialect to the "untranslatable" slang between different languages and cultures. Illiteracy, much more common than naively assumed, is one of the great banes of civilization. For the hard-of-hearing, the deaf, the speechless, and the deaf-mute, spoken language communication is impaired or impossible. But even for the sound listener, the screaming of an overhead plane, the noisy restaurant, the roar from a nearby highway, lawn mower, or leaf blower – or the chatter of a cocktail party in full swing – can make normal speech perception difficult if not hopeless.

The large distances covered by modern trade and travel demand new means of rapid and reliable communication. The traveler – on the road, in the air, on a train – calls for new methods of mobile communication that offer maximum convenience and privacy without cluttering up scarce "air" space. While optical fibers offer ever more communication capacity, the usable radio frequency spectrum for wireless communication by mobile phones is limited.

Many of the problems of spoken language communication – both ancient and those engendered by modern mores and technology – are amenable to amelioration by emerging strategies of *speech processing:* the transformations of speech signals for more efficient storage and transmission, for enhanced intelligibility and ease of assimilation. These new departures in spoken language processing should be based on a thorough understanding of how humans speak and how they *hear* the sounds that impinge on their ears – and how they *absorb* the intended message.

On the technical side, it is the emergence of fast algorithms, such as the Fast Fourier Transform, and the tiny transistor and its latter-day descendants, the integrated circuit and computer chip, that have made sophisticated signal processing a present reality. Modern computers and digital signal processors can do good things to speech that would have taken many bays of analog equipment not too long ago. And the future holds further advances at the ready: digital hearing aids that not only amplify speech but suppress unwanted sounds; voice synthesizers that actually sound human; public-address systems that work; better book-reading aids for the blind; error-free automatic speech transcription (the voice-typewriter or "electronic" secretary); and reliable speaker verification for access to confidential data and limited resources (such as one's own bank account).

Many of these modern miracles can trace their ancestry to an invention made in 1928.

1.2 Voice Coders

In 1928 a new transatlantic telegraph cable was installed between Britain and the United States. Its frequency bandwidth was an unheard-of 100 Hertz, an order of magnitude wider than previous cables. Still its bandwidth was 30 times narrower than that required for the transmission of intelligible telephone speech. Yet this did not deter an engineer at Bell Telephone Laboratories in New York named Homer Dudley from thinking about sending speech under the Atlantic. Dudley reasoned that speech is produced by the sluggish motions of the tongue and the lips and that meager information should easily fit within the capacity of the new cable.

Unfortunately Dudley's idea foundered as soon as it was born because neither he nor anyone else knew how to extract tongue and lip positions from a running speech signal. These "articulator" positions change the resonances of the human vocal tract and these resonances, in turn, determine the frequency content, the *sound*, of the speech signal. After all, that is how humans hear and distinguish different speech sounds, like the "ah" in the word *bar*, or "ee" in *beer*. But the frequency content, called the *spectrum* – as opposed to the articulator positions – *can* be easily measured. Dudley therefore suggested transmitting this spectrum information across the Atlantic, rather than the speech signal itself, and reconstruct a replica of the original speech at the other end. The spectral description should easily fit into the new cable. The resulting invention, first described in his Lab notebook in October 1928, was called *Vocoder* (coined from *Voice coder*) by Dudley [1.1].

The Vocoder is the grandfather of modern speech and audio compression without which spoken language transmission on the Internet (think of Internet telephony and live broadcasts over the World Wide Web) would be impossible.

Of course it was not easy to build the first Vocoder and its manually operated cousin, the . *Voder*. With their profusion of resistors, capacitors, inductances, and vacuum tubes (there were no transistors then, let alone integrated circuits) these early speech coders were truly monstrous. Nevertheless, the monsters were eventually built and demonstrated to great public acclaim at the New York World Fair in 1939. An electric speaking machine!

The Vocoder was first drafted into service during World War II in the secret telephone link between British Prime Minister Winston Churchill in London and President Roosevelt in the White House in Washington – and Allied military headquarters on five continents. The vocoder allowed enough compression of the speech signal so that it could be digitized by as few as 1551 bits per second and subsequently encrypted by what professional spooks call a "one-time-pad," most secure method of encryption.[1]

This was the actual beginning of the digital speech age, but it was kept under wraps until thirty years after the war for reasons of military secrecy. For more details of this epic story, the reader is referred to the eyewitness account by Ralph L. Miller, one of the few surviving participants [1.2].

The vocoder has spawned many other methods of speech compression, not least Linear Predictive Coding (LPC), which has enriched not only speech compression but speech recognition and voice synthesis from written text.

---

[1] The secret key was obtained from thermal (Johnson) noise – not from some algorithmic noise generator, which might have been broken. The random bits extracted from the thermal noise were recorded on phonograph disks that were hand-carried between the continents. Synchronizing these disks was one of the many technical problems that had to be surmounted.

Compression is crucial for "real audio" on the World Wide Web and voice security for the Internet. Speech recognition and synthesis are ever more ubiquitous in all kinds of verbal information services. Information that one can *listen* to with one's ears instead of having to be read by eye is a mode of communicating that is a lot less dangerous for the driver on the road or the surgeon at the operating table – to mention just two of the innumerable applications.

Since the vocoder separates the excitation signal (the glottal puffs of air) from the transfer function (the vocal tract) all kinds of games can be and have been played, like "head switching" (see Sect. 1.10) and changing a male voice into a female (Sect. 1.11). Some pranksters have even used the noise from a sputtering and stalling Volkswagen engine as an excitation signal and having the VW whimper "I am out of gas ... I am dying." Cute effects can be achieved by using organ music as an excitation signal and having the organ preach and admonish the congregation in no uncertain tones – a kind of virtuous reality.

1.3 Voiceprints for Combat and for Fighting Crime

The linguistically important elements in a speech signal can be represented visually to the human eye. Such a graphical rendition of speech is called a *speech spectrogram* or, somewhat misleadingly, "voice print." Sound spectrograms portray the energy in an audio signal, shown as different shades of gray or color, as a function of frequency and time, see Fig. 1.1. The temporal resolution of the underlying Fourier analysis is about 10 ms – like that of humans listening to speech. The corresponding frequency resolution is roughly 100 Hz. For better spectral resolution, the temporal window can be increased in duration. Phase information is discarded in the spectrogram. Thus, speech spectrograms show the linguistically important information of an utterance: what was said and, to an extent, who said it.

In addition to the gray or color scale, contours of equal energy can be superimposed on the spectrograms. This makes them look vaguely like a fingerprint (hence the term *voiceprint*), but their practical usefulness is thereby hardly enhanced. Figure 1.2 shows an image composed entirely of contour lines. Adorning the cover of a book on speech recognition, this picture was once mistaken, by a prominent speech scientist, as a voice print [1.3].

In principle, trained people should be able to "read" sound spectrograms. But in practice this has proved difficult, especially on a real-time basis. This is unfortunate because a running sound spectrogram, displayed on a video screen, would have given the deaf a measure of speech communication beyond lip reading and tactile sensors. This effort, alas, has failed, but not for want of exertion. Still, as a tool in speech research, the sound spectrograph – originally an analog device, but now often implemented on computers – has proved of great value.

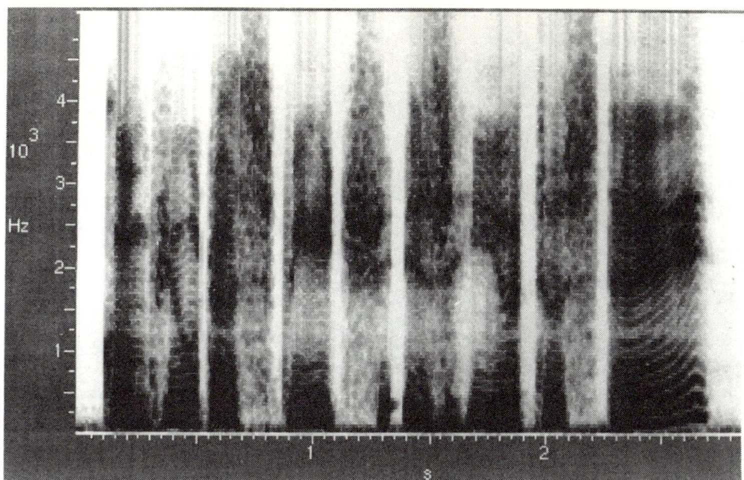

Fig. 1.1. Speech spectrogram or "voice print" of the utterance "computer speech?" by a male speaker. Time, in seconds, runs from left to right. Frequency, in Hertz, runs vertically. Increasing spectral intensity is indicated by increasing degrees of blackness. The dark areas are the formants or resonances of the vocal tract. The striations, visible especially at the end of the utterance (around 2.5 s), are the fundamental frequency and its harmonics. They are seen to be rising as appropriate for a question ("computer speech?"). Such spectrograms contain much of the linguistic information in a speech signal but are difficult to "read" and controversial for identifying voices from a large group of speakers. The designation "voice print" is therefore misleading

In addition to identifying sounds, speech spectrograms can be used to identify individual speakers from a limited pool of potential voices. In fact, sound spectrographs were originally developed in the United States during World War II to analyze radio voice communication by the enemy. One aim was to identify individual radio operators at the division level and to infer from their movements on the other side of the front line impending offensive actions by the opposing forces. The famous Battle of the Bulge was thus signalled long before its starting date (16 December, 1944).[2]

In forensic applications, voiceprints are especially useful in *eliminating* a suspect because, with a given vocal apparatus, some suspects could not possibly have produced the recorded utterance. But the general applicability of voiceprints in criminal trials remains doubtful [1.4].

---

[2] Another piece of evidence was the sudden change of secret radio codes preceding this last-gasp German offensive. The new code, however, was almost instantly cracked by the Allies because one German commander couldn't decipher the new code and asked for a retransmission in the old – already broken – code. The retransmission opened the door to what is known in the deciphering community as a "known clear-text" attack.

Fig. 1.2. Sometimes speech spectrograms are adorned by contour lines of equal spectral intensity to make them look more like fingerprints. This figure was once misread by a leading speech scientist as such a contour spectrogram. However the contours in this computer graphic represent lines of equal *optical* intensity in the likeness of a bearded young man (the programmer Wolfgang Möller). To properly see the subject it helps to view it from a large distance. – This computer generated image, called "Eikonal Portrait," is an example of the efforts by the author and his colleagues at Bell laboratories, especially the late Leon Harmon, to create images that show different things at different viewing distances

By contrast, voiceprints have been spectacularly successful in supplying clues for sorting out the causes of several man-made disasters. One fateful case was the collision of two airliners over the Grand Canyon in 1956. The last words recorded from one of the planes, uttered in a screaming voice just before the crash, were "We're going in...". Apparently, the screamer had just noticed the other plane closing in. But which member of the crew was it? Although the utterance was utterly unnatural in pitch, analysis of the spectrogram revealed that the speaker had an unusually long vocal tract, as betrayed by his resonance frequencies being noticeably lower than those produced by a normal vocal tract of 170-mm length. Thus, the speaker was probably an exceptionally "big" person. And there was, in fact, such a person on that plane – the copilot. From his position in the cockpit, investigators could infer the direction from which the other plane was probably approaching – a crucial piece of evidence in the reconstruction of the disaster.

Another tragic case in which the voiceprint of a last message was instrumental in pinpointing the cause of the calamity was the fire in an Apollo space capsule that cost the lives of three American astronauts during a training run on the ground. Here the last recorded message, again screamed in a terrified voice, began with the words *"Fire!* We are burning up...". Which of the three astronauts was the speaker? – because it was he who had presumably first seen the fire. Because of the highly unnatural, screaming quality of the signal (the pitch was above 400 Hz), the voice could not be identified by human listeners familiar with the voices of the astronauts. But comparisons of the voiceprint with voiceprints of the normal voices revealed the identity of the screamer. He was sitting not in the middle between his two mates but off to one side – the side where, in all likelihood, the fire had started. This pinpointing of the location of the fire's origin was an important clue in NASA's investigation and a subsequent improved design of the space capsule (including, incidentally, the elimination of pure oxygen for breathing).

Beyond portraying human voices, sound spectrograph have been successfully employed in the analysis of a wide variety of acoustic signals, including animal sounds. In such applications it is important to "tailor" frequency range and resolution of the spectrograph to the information-bearing characteristics of the signal. Thus, to analyze the infrasound (fractions of a Hertz) from the launching of a space vehicle in Florida near New York, the rocket rumble should be recorded (on an FM tape recorder) and translated up in frequency, by speeding up the playback of the tape so that the signal falls into the audio range. In other applications, frequency shifting may be preferable.

The importance of selecting the proper time and frequency *resolution* is illustrated by the following near snafu. One of my doctoral students at the Max Planck Institute in Göttingen, working with guinea fowl *(Numida meleagris)*, was unable to elicit the expected motion responses of the birds (head turning etc.) with synthetic sound stimuli which were closely patterned on their natural utterances. The synthetic calls sounded exactly like the natural ones – and looked the same on a spectrogram. But the birds wouldn't budge.

I suspected that, perhaps, the time resolution of the spectrograph (designed for human speech) was too low. Indeed, spectrograms of the bird's natural calls at greatly reduced tape speeds revealed temporal detail in the 100-μs range that had been completely obscured by the 10-ms time resolution of the spectrograph (and was inaudible to human listeners). Resynthesizing the calls with due attention to fine temporal detail made the birds respond just as they did to their own natural calls. In fact, it turned out that considerable liberty could be taken with the *frequency* content of the calls as long as the temporal structure was preserved. Thus, it seems that guinea fowl, and perhaps many other species, have a much greater time resolution – and use it – compared to mammalian monaural systems. (The human *binaural* system also resolves time differences in the 10 to 100-μs range. Otherwise the localization error in the horizontal plane would be uncomfortably large for survival.)

1.4 The Electronic Secretary

Automatic speech recognition has been the dream of many a manager. Think of a machine that automatically executes every spoken command or transcribes your dictated letters without typographical errors, misunderstandings or other distractions. And what a boon speech understanding by machines would be for all kinds of information services. But except for rather specialized tasks with a limited vocabulary, like airline and train travel information, progress has been slow. In fact, some recorded dialogues between humans and machines have been nothing less than hilarious for their unintended humor brought about by total mutual misunderstandings between machine and human – such as the machine, not being able to understand a certain word, responding over and over again "please repeat"; and the human, instead of simply repeating the word, saying something like "OK, I will repeat..." which threw the uncomprehending machine completely off course.[3]

It is clear that for automatic speech understanding to become more generally useful, machines have to assimilate a lot more syntax, i.e. how spoken sentences are constructed. (Perhaps a *sin tax* would help, too.) They also have to absorb the idiosynchrosies of different individual speakers, often requiring long training sessions.

Even more difficult, machines have to learn a lot more about the subjects that people talk about. Much like human listeners, to properly understand speech, machines have to know the different *meanings* of words and the subtle semantics that underlies most human discourse. But this is something very difficult to teach to dumb and mum machines. Humans, from day one of their lives (maybe even before birth) learn a lot of things acoustic by "osmosis", so to speak, that are difficult to formalize and put into the kind of algorithms that machines prefer as their food for "thought".

1.5 The Human Voice as a Key

A task closely related to speech understanding is *speaker verification*. Applications range from controlling access to restricted resources, off-limit areas or confidential files (such as medical or criminal records). Banking by phone, using one's voice for identification instead of the signature on a check, is another potential application.[4]

Voice recognition is also important in military chains of spoken, non-lethal commands. (Was it really my boss, General Halftrack, or some subordinate sergeant who called me with an urgent order for new golf clubs for the Strategic Weapons Reserve?) Automatic speaker verification for such applications,

---

[3] This account reminds me of the fable of the first-time PC user who returned his machine to the manufacturer because it lacked an ANY key and he was therefore unable to execute the installation instruction "hit any key."

[4] Representatives of the American Bankers Association once told the author that absolute certainty of identification by voice was not necessary and that even with signed checks many errors occurred, including cashing checks with false signatures or no signatures at all, costing American banks large amounts of money.

in which false alarms and misses have no catastrophic consequences, hold considerable promise.

1.6 Clipped Speech

Nonlinear distortions of speech signals, such as peak clipping in overloaded amplifiers, lowers the quality of speech signals without, however, affecting the intelligibility much. In fact, as J.C.R. Licklider (one of the progenitors of the Internet) has taught us, "infinite peak clipping," i.e. reducing the speech signal to just two amplitude levels, see Fig. 1.3, results in a square-wave like signal that sounds horribly distorted but, to everyone's surprise, is still quite intelligible [1.5]. How is this possible?

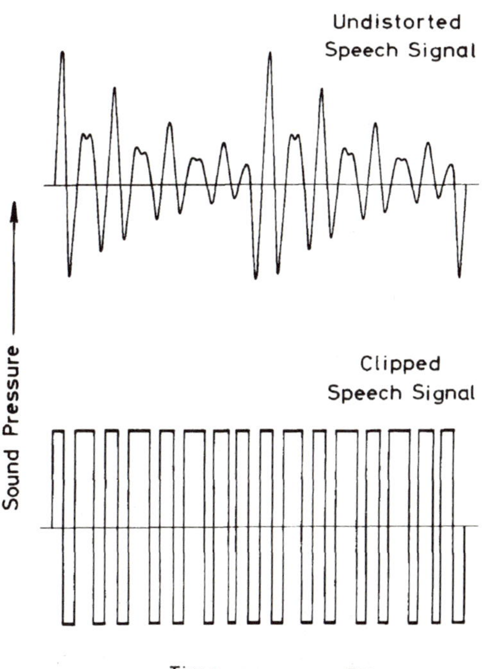

Fig. **1.3.** *Top:* The waveform of an undistorted speech signal. *Bottom:* the corresponding infinitely clipped signal. Although sounding highly distorted, infinitely clipped speech signals remain surprisingly intelligible

The seemingly obvious answer was that most of the information content of a speech signal must reside in its *zero-crossings* because the zero-crossings are the only parts of the signal that are preserved by infinite clipping. (Mathematically, infinite clipping corresponds to taking the algebraic sign and with zero defined as the output for a zero input.)

However, this theory is contradicted by the fact that many operations that displace the zeros have little or no effect on intelligibility. For example, manipulating the phase of the signal by putting it through an allpass filter with limited group delay distortion makes little perceptual difference. Differentiating the signal before infinite clipping even *enhances* its intelligibility. Frequency shifting the signal to higher frequencies, above 20 kHz say, before clipping and then frequency-shifting down again results in a further increase of intelligibility and even improves the quality.

What is going on? As is well-known, human speech perception is based on the time-varying spectrum of the signal. Nonlinear distortion generates additional frequency components ("spectral clutter") but does not destroy the spectral prominences (formants) *and their movements* that our ears rely on in decoding the signal. That is the reason for the relatively high intelligibility of infinitely clipped speech – not the preservation of the zero-crossings.[5]

Allpass filtering can even eliminate perceptual distortion completely! This was demonstrated by the author by putting speech signals through allpass reverberators and applying (approximate) inverse filtering after infinite clipping [1.6]. If the reverberation process has an impulse response that is time-inverted compared to ordinary reverberation (i.e. echo intensity *increases* with increasing delay) speech becomes not only unintelligible but, at reverberation times exceeding 2 s, does not even sound like speech anymore.

Such "negative" reverberation is observed in the deep ocean for sound transmission over long distances (several thousand kilometers). The strongest sound, traveling in a straight line at constant depth, is the slowest ray and arrives *after* all the weaker rays. Evolution has enabled us to "live with" normal reverberation, such as occurs in caves and dense forests, but our ancestors never encountered time-inverted reverberation in the course of evolution and nature apparently didn't bother to tell us how to suppress it.

Infinite clipping of this curious sounding signal makes it sound even more curious. But, to the great surprise of some life-long speech experts, a completely *undistorted* signal was recovered after inverse filtering. Apparently, the inverse *allpass* filtering converts the signal-correlated distortion (perceived as nonlinear distortion) into an uncorrelated noise (perceived as an *additive* background noise).[6]

---

[5] Differentiating and frequency-shifting increases the number of zero-crossings, resulting in less in-band spectral clutter. Representing a speech signal $s(t)$ as the product of its Hilbert envelope $a(t)$ and a phase factor $\cos\phi(t)$, infinite clipping after frequency shifting is equivalent to dividing the signal $s(t)$ by its envelope $a(t)$. This suggests that phase filtering to reduce the variability of $a(t)$ (the signal's "peak factor") will result in less audible distortion. This is indeed so: signals with a nearly constant $a(t)$ suffer less from clipping.

[6] To further analyze this astounding effect, one may decompose the input–output step function inherent in infinitive clipping into a linear part and a remainder with no linear component. Inverse filtering the linear part gives the *undistorted* signal whereas the remainder is converted into an added Gauss-like noise.

If this explanation is correct, then distorting the signal by a *symmetric* input–output function which has no linear component, such as full-wave rectifying or squaring the signal, should give complete "rubbish" in combination with *allpass*

1.7 Frequency Division

The misleading observation that the information of a speech signal resides in its zero-crossings has spawned some interesting ideas for speech compression. These schemes fall under the generic label *frequency division* [1.7]. In a typical frequency-division bandwidth compressor, the signal is filtered into several adjacent frequency bands, such as formant frequency regions for speech. In each channel the "carrier" frequency is halved (e.g. by eliminating every other zero-crossing and smooth interpolation). The resulting signal is centered on half the original carrier frequency but does not in general have half the original bandwidth. (In fact, for an FM broadcast signal, halving the carrier frequency will not reduce its bandwidth. It will simply move to a different location on the radio dial, still emitting the same program.) Nevertheless, the frequency-halved signal is sent through a bandpass filter with half the original bandwidth. Thus, a total bandwidth compression by a factor 2 is achieved. At the synthesis end all received frequencies are doubled, for example by full-wave rectification (taking the absolute value) and smoothing. This is, roughly, how the so-called Vobanc works [1.8]. The resulting speech signal is intelligible but somewhat marred by "burbling" sounds.

For each harmonic having its own filter channel (with a bandwidth of 100 Hz or less), the distortion of a frequency compressor can be made practically inaudible. This idea, dubbed *Harmonic Compressor*, see Fig. 1.4 was first tested by B. F. Logan and the author by *digital simulation* in 1962 using a block-diagram compiler [1.9]. The demonstration was in fact the first large-scale application of digital speech processing, comprising the simulation of 160 (Hamming-type) bandpass filters: 40 filters for separating the signal into adjacent frequency bands, 40 filters to remove the distortion from halving the bandwidth at the transmitter, 40 more filters for channel separation at the receiver and a final set of 40 filters for reducing the distortion inherent in frequency doubling. In spite of a very efficient filter design, the running time on an IBM 7090 computer was 530 times real time. But that was a small price to pay for a successful test that would have been prohibitive with analog circuits.

The output of the analyzer, when speeded up by a factor 2 (by means of a two-speed tape recorder, for example), constitutes time-compressed speech with little audible distortion. The design of such a time compressor was made available by Bell Laboratories to the American Foundation for the Blind who had the compressor built for use in their recorded-book program for the blind.

---

reverberation and inverse filtering – which it does: the result is unintelligible noise that is not even speech-like.

Implicit in these observations is a method to reduce the audible effects of nonlinear distortion: Randomize the phase angles of the signal by a linear filter that has an inverse before applying it to the nonlinear device. Inverse filter the distorted signal. If high-frequency emphasis is used before distortion, the noise power can be reduced by lowpass filtering.

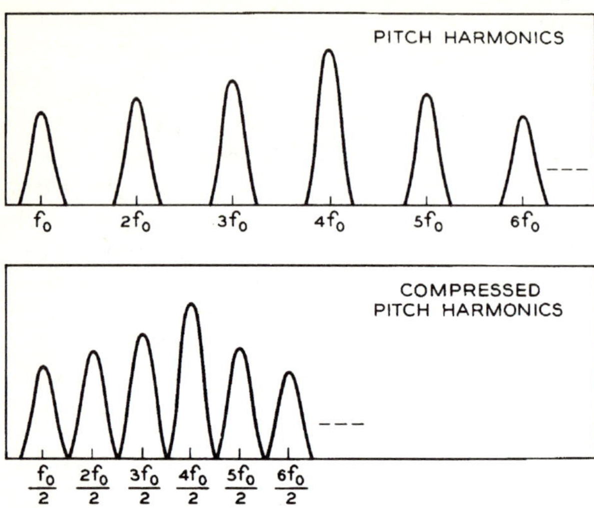

Fig. 1.4. *Top:* the spectrum of the fundamental frequency f_0 and its harmonics of a vowel sound. *Bottom:* the "compressed harmonics" after the frequency gaps between the harmonics have been eliminated. The resulting signal can be transmitted over half the original bandwidth. By recording the frequency-compressed signal and playing it back at twice the speed, speech can be accelerated by a factor 2. Such a speech accelerator has been made available for the book-reading program of the American Foundation for the Blind. – By the inverse process ("harmonic expansion") speech can be slowed down with interesting applications in foreign-language acquisition and studies of aphasic patients

With this technique, blind people could "read" books at nearly the rate of sighted people.

1.8 The First Circle of Hell: Speech in the Soviet Union

The success of frequency division by a factor 2 soon led to schemes attempting to compress the bandwidth by a factor 4 or more. Marcou and Daguet in France claimed a compression factor of 8 [1.7]. But careful analysis revealed that their signal was intelligible only because their filters were not sharp enough. *Bona fide* bandlimiting (with sufficiently steep roll-off bandpass filters) destroyed the usefulness of the signal.

Alexander Solzhenitsyn must have known all this when he wrote his *First Circle of Hell*. The action takes place in a *sharaga*, a Soviet speech research laboratory peopled by political prisoners *(zeks)*. One of the lab's aims, dictated by Stalin personally, was to develop reliable voiceprinting so his security forces (NKVD, later KGB) could better identify dissidents and other critics of the regime from monitored phone calls. Another aim of the laboratory was speech compression so that speech signals could be digitally encrypted for secure transmission over existing telephone lines in the Soviet Empire.

Apart from channel-vocoder techniques, frequency division schemes were vigorously pursued at the Soviet laboratory. After "successful" demonstration of 4:1 frequency compression, prisoner Rubin moved on to a compression factor of 8. To test its viability, he summons fellow workers walking by his lab and reads to them, over his compressor, the first paragraph of the latest lead story from the Communist Party newspaper *Pravda*. Then he asks the listeners whether they were able to understand the text. The answer invariably is *da*. So Rubin decides to move on to a frequency compression ratio of 16:1.

To understand the supreme irony of Solzhenitsyn's description, one has to know that useful frequency compression by a factor 8 is completely fictitious and to try 16:1 is outrageous. Of course, Solzhenitsyn knows that; he was a *zek* himself, working in just such a laboratory (as punishment for daring to criticize comrade Stalin's leadership during World War II).

But the irony goes deeper. As anyone who has ever glanced at a lead article in Pravda knows, the information content in the first 10 lines or so is practically nil, most articles beginning with the exact same words: "the Presidium of the Central Committee of the Communist Party of the Union of Soviet Socialist Republics [i.e. the *Politburo*] and the Council of Ministers of the USSR...". Of course, Rubin is not *consciously* engaged in deceiving his superiors; he is simply a victim of self-deception, a common cause of being led astray by speech researchers – and of course not just speech researchers. Rubin has no doubts that his compressor produces intelligible speech – much as I once "proved" the usefulness of a correlation vocoder by *counting* (from 1 to 10) over my new vocoder and asking innocent listeners whether they understood (answer: yes!) [1.10]. Of course, counting can be decoded by the human ear just from the *rhythm* of the utterance. (More formal tests conducted later revealed a surprisingly low intelligibility of the device – surprising perhaps only to the self-deceived inventor).

1.9 Linking Fast Trains to the Telephone Network

Special speech communication needs sometimes require unorthodox solutions. A case in point is the first public telephone link (in the 1960s) between a high-speed passenger train, running between New York and Washington, and fixed "ground" stations. Maintaining a constant telephone connection with a fast-running train requires a lot of signalling and switching between different "ground" stations along the track. In the original system there was no frequency space available for a separate signalling channel; the signalling had to be done "in band", simultaneously with the ongoing conversation. But how can such fast, inband signalling be done without interfering with the speech signal?

Here an insight into the psychophysics of speech perception, originally gained with vocoders and particularly formant vocoders, came to the rescue: while the human ear is quite sensitive to the accurate center frequency locations of the formants ("resonances") of a vowel sound, it is surprisingly tolerant to formant *bandwidth*. Formant bandwidths may be increased by a factor three or more, from 100 Hz to 300 Hz, say, without such a drastic spectral change making much of an audible difference. This auditory tolerance to increased bandwidth implies that the ear cannot accurately "measure" the decay rate of formant waveforms. Speaking in the time domain (as people usually do), the time constant for the decay of a formant can be decreased by a factor three or more, from 10 ms to 3 ms, say, without undue subjective distortion.

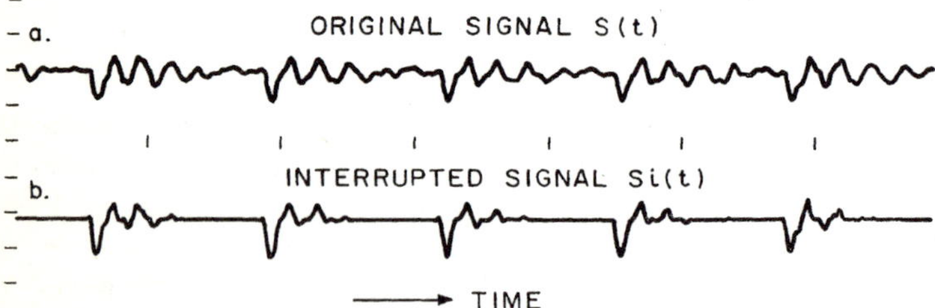

Fig. 1.5. *Top:* voiced speech signal. *Bottom:* the same speech signal with a reduced envelope. Amazingly, the reduced-envelope signal, although highly distorted, retains a good degree of naturalness. The time gaps created by this kind of center clipping can be utilized to transmit other information, such as signaling information in a telephone system for high-speed trains

Another way of speeding up the decay of a formant in a speech signal is to modify its envelope by subtracting an adjustable bias from it, setting the diminished envelope equal to zero if it falls below the bias. (This operation is equivalent to center clipping of the *envelope*, rather than the signal itself.) The result of this envelope modification is a pitch-synchronous gating in which the low-amplitude parts of each pitch period are softly set to zero, thereby creating time gaps in the signal, see Fig. 1.5. As long as these time gaps do not exceed about one third of the pitch period, the gating, if done properly, is hardly audible. The resulting "silent" time slots can be used to transmit other information, such as switching signals [1.11].

1.10 Digital Decapitation

Which is more characteristic of an individual speaker: the shape of his or her vocal *tract* and the motions of the articulators; or the characteristics of the vocal *source*? Certainly, the main difference between male and female speech is the fundamental frequency, those of males being typically lower in pitch than those of females. But within a given gender, is pitch still more important than the vocal tract and articulatory motions?

There is some circumstantial evidence favoring both alternatives. The importance of pitch patterns is emphasized by the following observation. I see a group of people talking to each other on a noisy street corner in New York City but I do not understand a word; there is too much traffic noise. But even through the din of traffic, I can hear the pitch patterns – and they are clearly Italian. (Later, on approaching the group, I discover they are actually speaking *English* with an Italian accent.)

Evidence for the importance of articulatory motions again comes from foreign and regional accents. Articulatory motion patterns are "frozen in" at an early age (around 10 years) and are hard if not impossible to break in later life. Apart from pitch patterns, this is how we recognize the voice of a friend or guess the place of birth and early life of an unknown speaker.[7]

To investigate the relative importance of pitch patterns and articulatory dynamics in characterizing an individual voice, John Pierce and Joan E. Miller separated the two effects by "cutting off peoples' heads," so to speak, and switching them around. All this was of course done on the computer [1.12], by means of digital simulation; no laws – local or otherwise – were violated. Miller and Pierce digitized speech signals from several speakers and, on a digital computer, made a *pitch-synchronous* spectral analysis of the utterances. The required pitch detection was done by hand by inspecting waveform printouts. The pitch patterns from one speaker were then combined with the results of the spectral analyses of the other speaker. The synthetic speech signal therefore contained elements of two different speakers: the pitch from Ronald, say, and the vocal tract (including the lips) from George.

Naive (phonetically untrained) subjects then compared these synthetic voices with the natural ones, and for each synthetic signal had to make an identification with a natural speaker. To the surprise of some bystanders, the majority of the identifications were made on the basis of the vocal tract – not the pitch.

This interesting pilot study did not systematically explore all possible parameters that characterize an individual voice, and there is room for considerable future research here.

---

[7] Of course, articulatory motions are not the only movements that characterize an individual. One can often recognize an acquaintance from behind by his gait and a skier from the style of his turns. Skiing, dancing (and the playing of musical instruments) should be learned at an early age – just like walking. In fact, walking without stumbling or falling down, seemingly so simple, is such a complicated task that only persons with the highest degree of neural plasticity, namely babies, can learn it efficiently.

1.11 Man into Woman and Back

The "head switching" experiment just described also bears on an exercise in speech synthesis in which the gender of the speaker is changed at will. In a first attempt to change a male into a female voice by digital manipulation, Bishnu Atal and I simply raised the pitch by one octave. The resulting "female" sounded suspiciously like a high-pitched male, confirming the age-old adage that there is more to the inequality between the sexes than pitch of voice.

In a second attempt, we increased the formant frequencies by a constant factor to account for the shorter vocal tract of many females. But even this proved insufficient for a bona-fide female. We finally changed the individual formant frequencies independently with an algorithm that made allowance for other gender dissimilarities such as thinner cheek walls. The resulting synthetic voice was judged as clearly female by all listeners not familiar with the experiment. Yet, to the experimenters themselves, there remained a vestige of maleness, a soupçon of something deceptive.

Recently, in addition to transmuting a male voice into female one, *fusion* of male and female into a single voice has been achieved – with pretty artistic consequences: for the sound track of the 1995 film *Farinelli-Il Castrato* the voice of the countertenor Derek Lee Ragin was "married" by computer to that of the soprano Ewa Mallas-Godlewka – best men: P. Depalle, G. Garcia, X. Rodet of IRCAM, Paris.

1.12 Reading Aids for the Blind

One of the earliest motivations for synthesizing speech from printed text were reading aids for the blind. Optical character recognition of fixed (or even mixed) type fonts has been possible for some time. Optical scanners are becoming ever more popular. But the conversion of graphemes (printed letters) to phonemes (spoken sounds) and natural sounding sentences is still difficult. There are problems at the lexical, syntactic, and semantic levels: The pronunciation of a word or phrase often depends on its prominence, its grammatical function, and its intended meaning. The selection of the proper prosody (intonation, segment durations, and stress patterns) is likewise dependent on syntax and semantics. Thus, the purely *algorithmic* synthesis of natural sounding speech from written text (without human "fine tuning") remains an active field of linguistic research.

1.13 High-Speed Recorded Books

Another effort to help the blind in gaining access to printed texts is the recorded book program of the American Foundation for the Blind (AFB).

The AFB and the Library of Congress have long had programs in which trained speakers (radio announcers and actors) record books on magnetic tape so that the blind can *listen* to the books they can't read. But there is a remaining handicap: reading aloud takes twice as long or longer than silent reading. To close this gap, as already mentioned, Bell Laboratories has made available to the AFB a technique that speeds up spoken utterances by a factor two without loss in speech quality [1.9].

1.14 Spectral Compression for the Hard-of-Hearing

Speech analysis and resynthesis allows a wide range of *spectral* modifications in addition to the time compression and expansion just mentioned. High-frequency components that are difficult to hear, especially by older people, can be transposed in frequency to lower frequencies where they can be better heard. But learning to understand such recorded speech is difficult and may require special training [1.13].

1.15 Restoration of Helium Speech

Spectral compression is also required for the restoration of the "Donald Duck"-like speech of divers who, to avoid the "bends," breathe a mixture of oxygen and helium (rather than the nitrogen in ambient air). Since the velocity of sound in helium (being a lighter gas) is considerably greater than in nitrogen, the resonances of the vocal tract are shifted upward in frequency resulting in a strange and often unintelligible "quack-quack." Spectral compression puts the resonances back in their proper place [1.14].

1.16 Noise Suppression

A major aim of speech processing is the suppression of unwanted noises. Many noises have a broadband continuous spectrum, as opposed to voiced speech signals which have their energy concentrated near the harmonics of the fundamental frequency (pitch). Thus, a *comb filter*, tracking the fundamental frequency and its harmonics, can reject much of a continuous-spectrum noise. Improvements in signal-to-noise ratio of 20 dB and more were realized in this manner by the author as early as 1956. However, the remaining noise has the same harmonic structure (and pitch-like sound) as the speech signal itself so that the *human* auditory processor can no longer exploit the spectral distinction between voiced speech and noise.

Another approach to noise suppression relies on spectral analysis and synthesis: an estimate of the noise spectrum (obtained during silent speech

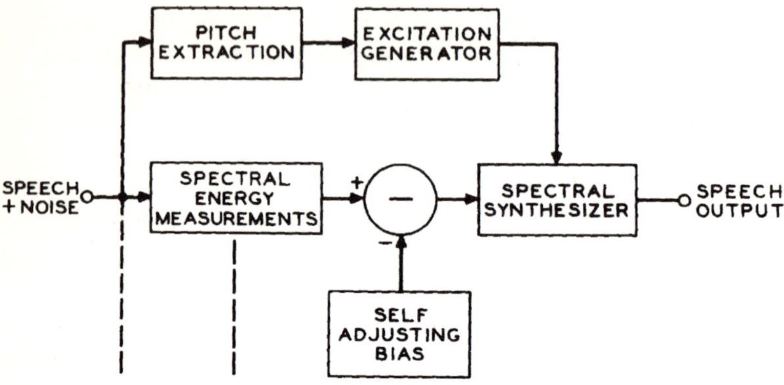

Fig. 1.6. Noise reduction by spectral analysis of the signal and subtraction of the estimated noise level in each of 10 to 20 frequency channels. The noise spectrum is estimated during silent intervals in the speech signal. For voiced speech signals a reliable pich extractor is needed

intervals) is *subtracted* from the noisy speech spectrum, see Fig. 1.6. The resulting "cleansed" spectrum is used in the resynthesis of a noise-free speech signal. However, since the noise spectrum is never exactly known, the resulting speech suffers from spectral distortion [1.15].

The application of this resynthesis method requires the accurate extraction of the fundamental frequency from the noisy speech signal. Luckily, the *cepstrum* method, originally developed to distinguish underground nuclear explosions from earthquakes,[8] can cope with speech signals with signal-to-noise ratios near 0 dB.

---

[8] Underground explosions, such as those set off by nuclear weapons tests, generate *compressional* waves which travel faster than the *shear* waves emanating from earthquakes. Thus, the travel times (delay patterns) with which these waves arrive at the seismic recording stations contain important clues to distinguish nuclear from natural events. To measure these delay differences accurately, J. W. Tukey and B. P. Bogert invented the "cepstrum" (a neologism coined by Tukey). The cepstrum is defined as the Fourier transform of the *logarithm* of the power spectrum of a signal. (Without the logarithm, one would obtain the autocorrelation function with its known difficulties of disentangling delays and resonances.)

When I first heard about the cepstrum, I realized its potential for accurately measuring the delay pattern of the vocal cord motions, i.e. the fundamental frequency of speech, without interference from the resonances of the vocal tract.

1.17 Slow Speed for Better Comprehension

A device similar to that for speeding up speech (see Sect. 1.7) can slow it down by a factor of two or more. The resulting slow speech is helpful in foreign language acquisition (think of a fast foreign speaker), for communicating with the mentally retarded and for speech therapy for aphasiacs.

1.18 Multiband Hearing Aids and Binaural Speech Processors

For a "flat" (frequency-independent) hearing loss, simple amplification of all speech frequencies would compensate for the auditory damage. But most hearing impairments, be they inner-ear (sensorineural) in origin or poor sound conduction in the middle ear, show an increasing loss with increasing frequency. Thus, high frequencies have to be amplified more than low frequencies. The limited amplitude range ("recruitment") that usually accompanies hearing loss requires amplitude *compression* to avoid overloading the ear. This fitting of the speech spectrum into the available perceptual "window" in the amplitude–frequency plane requires *multi-channel* hearing aids with independent amplitude compression in each frequency channel.

Further improvements for listeners with residual hearing in both ears can be expected from binaural hearing aids that allow the listener to suppress noise from directions not coincident with the direction of the desired speech source.

Even greater enhancements of speech understanding may be possible with binaural signal processors ("cocktail-party processors") that suppress unwanted noises by sophisticated algorithms implemented on wearable integrated circuits ("chips") [1.16].

Yet, with all the advances – real or impending – in the art of hearing aids, there remains one major obstacle to achieve good hearing for hearing impaired people: *upward spread of masking.* In a quiet environment, even a high-frequency hearing loss of 60 dB is not fatal for speech understanding. But in the presence of intense low-frequency disturbing sounds, the middle and high frequencies, which are crucial for proper speech perception, are totally *masked,* i.e. made inaudible.

Unfortunately, masking engendered by low-frequency noise prevails in many places, not least in packed restaurants that lack sufficient sound absorption (carpets, curtains, and acoustic tiles). Such eateries could be made quieter by smaller tables (or larger distances *between* tables) thereby improving the "signal-to-noise" ratio (i.e. the loudness of the voices of people at the *same* table relative to those at surrounding tables).

1.19 Improving Public Address Systems

Another evil for the hard-of-hearing are public-address systems whose low-frequency ("bass") amplification has not been sufficiently turned down compared to the high-frequency ("treble") setting. Since reverberation times in churches and lecture halls are generally longer at low frequencies, any low frequencies radiated into such enclosures play havoc with speech intelligibility because of reverberation in combination with upward spread of masking. This is particularly true for strong vowels (such as /a/) preceding weak consonants (like /f/ or /s/).

To counteract this masking effect of reverberation, W. Meyer-Eppler has suggested a speech-activated switch that "kicks in" extra gain for weak high-frequency sounds. Unfortunately, the switching did more harm than good to speech intelligibility. (But this was in the 1950s using crude analog circuits. Perhaps a modern "soft" switch based on digital processing would do better.)

The stable gain of public address systems can also be raised by frequency shifting; see the following section.

1.20 Raising Intelligibility in Reverberant Spaces

Of all room-acoustical parameters, reverberation time is the most important. It is defined as the time interval during which the sound energy in an enclosure (without new sound input) decays by a factor of one million, i.e. by 60 dB. Good concert halls have reverberation times around two seconds, and somewhat longer for frequencies below 250 Hz.

It used to be said that a reverberation time of one second was ideal for speech intelligibility in a lecture hall. In reality, the ideal is *no* reverberation at all. In fact, any echoes with delays exceeding 50 ms, i.e. those not integrated with the primary sound by the human auditory system, are deleterious. Of course, reducing the sound absorption in a given hall will raise the sound intensity for a fixed input power level. But the benefits in intensity or loudness are more than offset by the ill effects of increased reverberation.

However, sound intensity can be increased without adding reverberation by well-designed public-address systems that radiate only mid- and high-frequency sound *aimed at the audience* (by directional loudspeaker columns) where it is quickly absorbed by clothing and hair.[9]

---

[9] To focus the sound into the required horizontal-fan pattern, the loudspeaker columns ("broadside" arrays in antenna lingo) have to be vertically positioned, with a slight tilt toward the audience if they are located (as they should be) somewhat above head level. Amusingly, in the Göttingen *Stadthalle* the loudspeaker columns are oriented horizontally (to better hide them inside a large central chandelier). The predictable result: good speech intelligibility only at the few seats in the directions of the center normal of the three columns employed. – Apparently, people will go to any length (and width) to be unintelligible!

To conceal the location of the electroacoustic sound sources and to enhance the illusion that the sound emanates from the speaker's lips, the sound from the loudspeakers should be delayed by about 10 ms. This exploits the *Haas effect* which permits the sound intensity to be raised by some 10 dB without affecting the perceived direction of the sound. The first large-scale Haas-effect public-address system was installed in London's St. Paul's Cathedral. It employed multiple speaker columns with increasing delays. Its resounding success led to worldwide clones.

To reduce the incidence of acoustic feedback ("sing around"), I suggested frequency-shifting the speech signal by about 5 Hertz. This puts the energy at the peaks of the transmission response (where the feedback leads to instability) into the valleys of the response (where the excess energy is rendered harmless) [1.17].

The first field application of frequency-shifting took place during the 1963 AT&T shareowner's meeting in Chicago, attended by 23 000 eager investors. The frequency shifting (realized by a simple single-sideband modulation method) allowed an extra gain of about 6 dB. But the most important advantage, according to Bell Laboratories' sound engineers who operated the system, was the "soft-failure" behavior of the system with frequency shifting: instead of going from stable to unstable ("screeching") within a fraction of a decibel of extra gain, the frequency-shifted system offered a 4-dB range (beyond the 6-dB extra gain) over which the system became *progressively* unstable (signalled by a 5-Hz pulsating modulation).

With the advent of integrated circuits and the promise of elaborate signal processing, sophisticated *dereverberation* schemes have been suggested and tested [1.18]. These go far beyond the simple enhancement of weak unvoiced sounds as originally proposed.

1.21 Conclusion

Analysis and synthesis of speech signals, made possible by a better understanding of human speech production and perception – and implemented with the aid of ever more powerful digital signal processing devices – has enhanced human speech communication and enlarged its reach. In the remainder of the book some of these themes will be taken up again in greater depth.

2. A Brief History of Speech

Descended from monkeys? My dear, let us hope that it is not true!
But if it is true, let us hope that it not become widely known!

The wife of the bishop of Worcester,
hearing of Darwin's Theory of Evolution

In the Beginning was the Word.

St. John 1.1

Nothing could be more succinct about the power of words than John's opening phrase of his gospel. The word reigned supreme at the creation and – for better or worse – has never lost its potency up to the present.

By comparison, the scientific study of speech has had but a very brief history. The following is a casual chronicle of some of the highlights of this history, from von Kempelen's speaking machines to neural networks and wavelets.

2.1 Animal Talk

Sound communication – from love calls to warning cries – plays a pivotal role in the animal kingdom and the survival of species. Although animals do not "speak" in the human sense of the word (except in cartoons and fairy tales), their vocabulary of whoops, yells and roars often shows a remarkable variety, finely tuned to their specific needs. True, many a mynah bird or parrot produces acoustically respectable speech sounds, but it is doubtful – to say the least – that they know what they are saying, see however Fig. 2.1.[1] Along

---

[1] I once sent an associate named Perry to a local pet shop to record the voice of a mynah bird also called Perry. Their "conversation" started out on the worst

Fig. 2.1. Parrots among themselves (when nobody seems to be listening) – overheard by Leo Cullum of *The New Yorker*

with the ability to produce meaningful sounds, some species, including humans, developed the art of acoustic deception: think of the popular comedian emulating the voice of a vaunted president; the resourceful hunter imitating a bird call or stag roar; or certain cunning animals that ensnare a juicy prey (or partner) by forged sound signatures.

Often the emphasis is on disguise rather than imitation: the wily kidnapper making his extortionist call; the foreign spy camouflaging his true identity; or the ravenous wolf softening his voice by ingesting chalk to better masquerade as mother goat in a well-known fairy tale.

2.2 Wolfgang Ritter von Kempelen

With this pervasive precedent in acoustic simulation (and dissimulation), it is perhaps small wonder that man would one day attempt to fabricate human speech by machine.

---

possible note when associate Perry thought his leg was being pulled when the bird introduced himself with "My name is Perry, what's yours?" Next the noisome bird uttered "Merry Christmas," whereupon the human Perry tried to convince his feathered namesake that is was almost Easter.... Before too long, their exchange was marked by utter confusion!

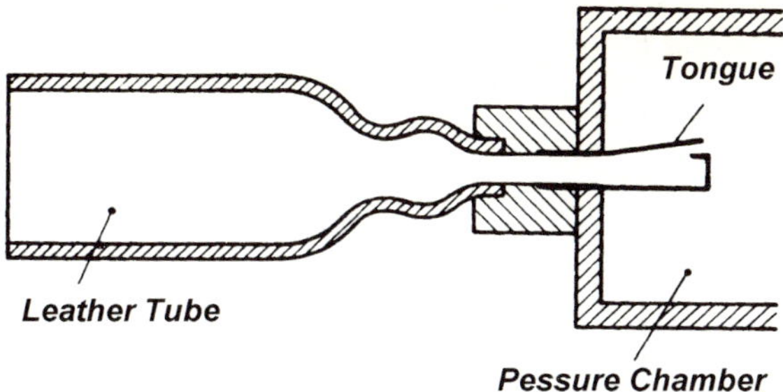

Fig. 2.2. Wolfgang Ritter von Kempelen's 1769 speaking machine, as reconstructed by Sir Charles Wheatstone, comprising a pressure chamber (the "lung"), a vibrating reed (the "tongue"), and a leather tube (the "vocal tract"). Von Kempelen's contraption produced respectable vowel sounds but was widely disbelieved when exhibited throughout Europe: in a singular piece of poor timing, the Hungarian count had just demonstrated a "chess playing machine" that was exposed as fraudulent

While today talking computers are ever more widely heard (and perhaps abhorred), the first speaking "chip" was not etched in silicon but carved out of wood. More than 200 years ago, in 1769, Wolfgang Ritter von Kempelen, a Hungarian nobleman, began work on a mechanical speaking machine that is reported to have produced respectable speech sounds [2.1]. In 1791, after 20 years of hard labor, von Kempelen published a book in which he described his observations on human speech production and his experiments with his speaking machine [2.2]. The essential parts of the machine were a pressure chamber for the lungs, a vibrating metal reed to act as the vocal cords, and a pliable leather tube for the vocal tract, see Fig. 2.2. By manipulating the shape of the tube, von Kempelen could produce many different vowels. For brief presentations these artificial vowels reportedly sounded quite realistic. For the production of plosive speech sounds, von Kempelen employed a model of the vocal tract that included a hinged tongue and movable lips, see Fig. 2.3.

While before von Kempelen the larynx was considered central to speech production, his simple and successful demonstration drew the attention of 19th-century scientists to the *vocal tract*, the (nondecaying) cavity between the glottis and the lips as the main site of acoustic articulation. Unfortunately for the ultimate fate of his speaking machine, the clever count conceived and demonstrated a chess-playing machine at precisely the same time that he worked on his talking contraption. But his widely exhibited chess "automaton" was anything but automatic: it concealed a midget chess master in its innards who communicated magnetically with the above-board chessmen. While the shifty machine (actually the hidden midget) is said to have beaten even Napoleon – no slouch at chess – the discovered deception cost von Kempelen his hard won credibility. People simply assumed that his speaking

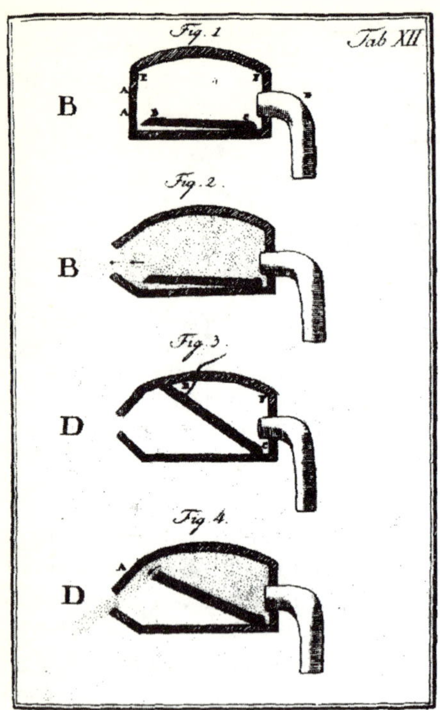

Fig. 2.3. Von Kempelen's model for the production of plosive sounds, such as *b* (as in *bin*) and *d* (as in *din*), characterized by a sudden pressure release at the lips (*b*) or tongue tip (*d*)

machine, too, was just another fraud, merely conveying the speech sounds of a hidden human.

2.3 From Kratzenstein to Helmholtz

But von Kempelen's travail was not for naught and his impact far from nil. His early forays into synthetic speech stimulated much research into the physiology of speech production and experimental phonetics.

In 1779, the Imperial Academy of St. Petersburg (home to Euler for much of his prolific life) proffered its annual prize for explaining the physiological differences between the five long vowels: /a/ (as in p*a*rt), /e/ (as in German R*e*h), /i/ (as in s*ee*), /o/ (as in German r*o*h), and /u/ (as in f*oo*l); and for producing these sounds artificially. The prize was won by the physiologist Christian Gottlieb Kratzenstein, born in Wernigerode, in the Harz mountains (not far from the now defunct iron curtain). These resonators, see Fig. 2.4, were "energized" by vibrating reeds, much as in musical instruments.

Of course, as we now know, the resonator shapes for a given sound are not unique, a fact exploited by the ventriloquist when he keeps his lips fixed while effecting (invisible) articulatory compensations with his tongue. This articu-

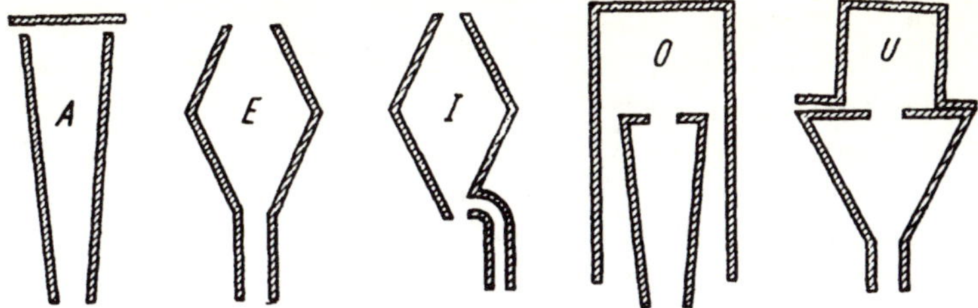

Fig. 2.4. Von Kratzenstein's resonators for the five German vowels that won him the annual prize of the Russian Imperial Academy of Sciences at St. Petersburg in 1779

latory ambiguity – different shapes having identical resonances – was already pointed out by the British scientist W. Willis in the early 19th century.[2]

Willis clinched the connection between a specific vowel sound and the geometry of the vocal *tract*, as opposed to the shape of the articulators. He was able to synthesize different vowels by means of tube resonators ("organ pipes"). In the process, he made the important discovery that vowel quality depended only on the *length* of the tube and not its diameter.

The noted British physicist Sir Charles Wheatstone (1802–1875), inventor of the Wheatstone bridge, elaborated Willis' theory, pointing out that the "cavity tone" of the tube (vocal tract) was excited by one of the partials (Fourier components) of the reed source.

2.4 Helmholtz and Rayleigh

It was on this "Fourier" concept that the great German physicist and physiologist Hermann von Helmholtz (1821–1894) built his vowel theory, included in his monumental oeuvre on auditory perception [2.4]. According to Helmholtz, the vocal tract acts as an *acoustic filter* enhancing those harmonics of the exciting puffs of air emanating from the glottis that lie near one of the filter's resonances – a crucial concept, still current today. The frequency regions around these resonant frequencies were – and still are – called *formants*. Helmholtz, preferring spherical resonators with narrow necks over tube resonators, was able to synthesize the vowels /a/, /o/, and /u/ with a *single* formant. But he needed two formants for /ä/ (as in c*a*t), /e/, and /i/. In his theory, Helmholtz associated different coexisting formant resonances with different parts of his resonators, the different parts acting as coupled oscillators.

---

[2] Amusingly, a method was recently described for synthesizing different diphthongs all having the *same* (flat) power spectrum. This feat was accomplished by exploiting certain properties of monaural phase sensitivity, or waveform dependence, of human auditory perception [2.3].

In parallel with the work of Helmholtz, L. Hermann developed a "puff-theory" of speech production according to which puffs of air excite the vocal tract to oscillations that decay over time. Just as Helmholtz's viewpoint, stressing frequencies and resonances, was stimulated by his experimental tools – frequency-selective resonators – so was Hermann's theory engendered by *his* apparatus: a phonograph with an Edison-cylinder that actually recorded these decaying oscillations and made them visible.

While seemingly at odds, the two viewpoints of Helmholtz and Hermann represent the same physical reality, as emphasized by none other than the great Lord Rayleigh, the connection being mediated by a Fourier transformation [2.5].

This parallelism between two apparently divergent theories is much the same as the equivalence between Heisenberg's matrix formulation of quantum mechanics and Schrödinger's wave equation: one theory is simply the Fourier transform of the other. Heisenberg's uncertainty principle is an immediate consequence of this Fourier relationship.

2.5 The Bells:
Alexander Melville and Alexander Graham Bell

While speaking of Helmholtz and Rayleigh, we should not neglect to mention the work of two other giants: Alexander Graham Bell (1847–1922), and his elocutionist father Alexander Melville Bell [2.6]. During his childhood in Edinburgh, A. G. Bell, the future inventor of the telephone,[3] had an opportunity to see and hear a reconstruction of von Kempelen's machine by Wheatstone. Encouraged by his father, little Alexander proceeded to produce his own speaking machine, a replica of the human speech organs, complete with rubber lips and a wooden tongue [2.8].

Bell was stimulated also by Hermann von Helmholtz and especially by an article Helmholtz wrote around 1863 on the creation of "intelligent" sounds through the use of electrically driven tuning forks [2.9]. Bell's limited grasp of German suggested to him that Helmholtz was talking about a "talking telegraph". But, although Bell was later disabused, his intense interest in electrical transmission of speech did not abate one bit.

In what must have been one of the drollest antecedents of modern telecommunications, Bell even enlisted the help of his pet terrier [2.10]. He taught the

---

[3] As early as 1860 Philipp Reis, a German professor, had constructed a premature telephone, which however was not officially recognized as capable of transmitting intelligible speech because it was basically an on-off switch activated by sound waves. Of course, we now know that one-bit ("infinitely clipped") speech can be quite intelligible, but a hundred years ago Reis did not prevail with his binary speech signal. To complete the irony, Reis' device *did* produce multi-valued ("analog") signals at very low amplitudes because his switch in fact constituted a variable resistance (called *Wackelkontakt* in German) [2.7].

dog to sit up on his hind legs and emit a continuous growl. While the growling was going on, Bell changed the shape of the dog's vocal tract by squeezing it (lightly) from the outside [2.11]. After mastering the vowels /a/ and /u/, the diphthong /ou/, and the syllables /ma/ and /ga/, the manipulated dog rose to new linguistic heights, growling complete sentences such as: "How are you Grandmama?" This feat, according to Bell, may have led to the rumor that he once taught a dog to speak. Needless to say, the *un*attended dog did not utter a single word beyond the usual canine vocabulary.

However, I once did encounter a dog that *sang*. But then synthetic "singing" is simpler than speaking – in the sense that it is easier for some animals to emit a succession of notes of different pitches than to produce different speech-like sounds. This, incidentally, is true also for electronic speaking machines: a singing computer, although perhaps unintelligible, is much more impressive to lay audiences than a speaking computer with its unpleasant electronic accent. In fact, the *New York Times* once reported that a speech research establishment in Dresden (in what was then East Germany) was far ahead of the West because their computer could even sing. Well, John L. Kelly and Carol Lochbaum at Bell Laboratories had a singing computer (intoning "Daisy, Daisy, give me your answer true. . . ") way back in the early 1960s [2.12].

2.6 Modern Times

Helmholtz's theory of vowel production gained further support from the work of C. Stumpf, O. G. Russel and Sir R. Paget [2.13]. Stumpf studied the spectral structure of vowels with an acoustic interferometer of his design – a Rube Goldberg contraption that occupied five rooms! With the same apparatus he was able to synthesize good-sounding vowels from the fundamental tones of 28 flue pipes. In a refinement of Helmholtz's finding, Stumpf showed that *all* vowels have at least two formants [2.14].

Russel's contributions, following the work of E. A. Meyer [2.15], were the excellent x-ray images of the articulators that finally refuted the faulty physiology of earlier investigators and laid the ground work of modern x-ray analysis in speech research [2.16–18].

Sir Paget introduced *whispered* sounds into speech analysis, thereby eliminating the confusing interference between the harmonic frequency components of voiced speech sounds and their formant frequencies [2.19]. (The ultimate solution of this stubborn "pitch" problem did not emerge until the arrival of the cepstrum in 1962 [2.20].) Paget also constructed pliable vocal tracts made of wood, rubber, and deformable plastic.

In the 1930s two Japanese researchers, J. Obata and T. Teshima, and the German musicologist E. Thienhaus discovered the third formant in vowels [2.22, 2.23]. Thienhaus employed a new approach to spectral analysis – a superheterodyne method – spawned by emerging radio receiver technology and invented by M. Grützmacher, known in German as *Suchton-Analyse* [2.23]. Grützmacher's method has become the method of choice for modern non-realtime spectrum analyzers, as embodied in sound spectrographs used in making "voice prints," see Chap. 1.

2.7 The Vocal Tract

Building on previous progress, the human vocal tract soon assumed a central role in speech research. Figure 2.5 shows a simplified cross-section of the vocal tract for the vowel sounds /ee/ and /oo/ and the corresponding (smoothed) frequency spectra of the resulting speech sounds showing the three first resonances of the tract. Following the nomenclature of musicology, these resonances are called *formants* [2.24]. It is these formants and their movements that the ear perceives and the brain combines when we listen to speech.

Note the different tongue position for /ee/ and /oo/. All vowel sounds are nicely distinguished, both in production geometry and resulting spectrum. This is the basis of human vowel production and perception. Of course, the vocal tract has more resonances at higher frequencies, but they are not as important linguistically as the first three.

The main articulatory organs are the tongue (body and tip positions), the soft palate or *velum* that guards the entrance to the nasal tract, and the lips (opening area and degree of rounding). Among the different speech sounds the vocal tract can produce, some pairs are distinguished by the change in a single articulatory parameter. Such pairs of speech sounds are called *minimal pairs*, such as /ee/ (as in bee) and the German umlaut /ü/. The German /ü/

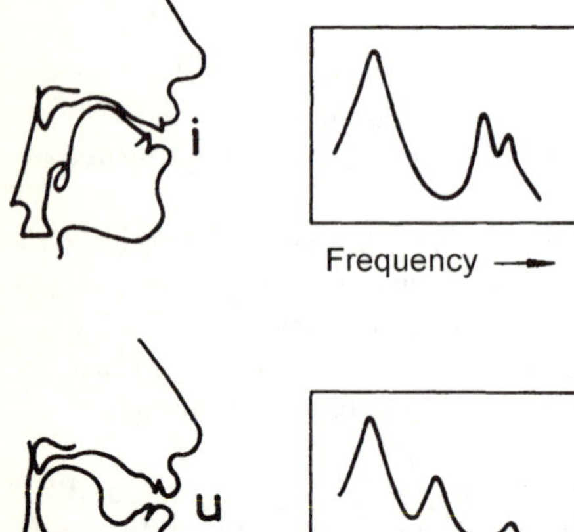

Fig. 2.5. Cross-sections through the human vocal tract for the vowels i (/ee/) and u (/oo/) and the resulting frequency spectra. Note the different tongue positions for these two speech sounds and the corresponding differences in the resonance (formant) patterns

Fig. 2.6. A minimal mechanical model of the vocal tract consisting of a plexiglass tube with square cross-section and a "tongue" mimicked by a plastic cube. A little loudspeaker at one end emitting quasiperiodic pulse trains plays the role of the vocal cords. By moving the plastic cube, different vowel sounds can be approximated. Partial closing of the opening at the end of the plexiglass tube (the "lips") changes an /ee/ sound to the German umlaut /ü/. – A steady, periodic pulse train as excitation signal makes the artificial vowels sound like an electric door buzzer. Only dynamically variable sounds are interpreted as speech. For human perception to "perk up," sufficient *contrast* in a temporal or spatial stimulus is required. [For the eye looking at a steady scene, the required contrast is provided by involuntary rapid ("saccadic") eye movements.]

(equivalent to the Dutch or French pronunciation of "u") can be produced from the articulation of the /ee/ sound by just rounding one's lips while keeping the tongue immobile. This can be nicely demonstrated by a simple plexiglas model of the vocal tract, see Fig. 2.6. The teacher, by holding his hand over the lip opening of the model (and thereby decreasing its opening area), can change the /ee/ sound to a respectable /ü/.[4]

2.8 Articulatory Dynamics

How important the *movements* of the formants are as we speak is evidenced by the fact that a stationary vowel spectrum does not even sound like a

---

[4] Considering that /ee/ and /ü/ are a minimal pair, it may be difficult to understand why many native English speakers have so much trouble with the French pronunciation of "u," as in "déjà-vu," which often comes out as "deja vous." When alerted to their mistake, (in a French study class), the typical answer is "that's what I just said: deja vous." In other words, these English-speaking students of French apparently don't even *hear* the difference between the French vowels *ou* and *u* – much like some Japanese have difficulty in *perceiving*, let alone articulating, the difference between *r* and *l*. Of course it is now well known that linguistic distinctions that are not "absorbed" at an early age lead to dysfunctions later on.

speech sound. After having been held steady for several seconds (easy for a computer, but not for a human speaker), some "vowels" sound more like a buzzer or some other inanimate squawk box. On the other hand, short utterances, like "ba," "da" and "ga" are perceptually distinguished by initial formant movements. In fact, as A. Liberman, F. Cooper and other researchers at Haskins Laboratories have shown, one can clip the initial consonants ("b," "d," or "g") from the speech waveform (in the pre-computer age this could be accomplished by applying scissors to magnetic tape recordings of the utterances) and still perceive the correct consonant if only enough of the formant *movement* was kept [2.25].

Thus, if we want to study speech signals from a linguistic point of view, we need a device that portrays the spectral *dynamics* of the vocal utterance. Such a device, as already mentioned, is the *sound spectrograph*, invented in the Second World War to analyze the voices of enemy radio operators and thus track their movements behind the front (an important clue in predicting imminent military offensives). Unfortunately, although the sound spectrogram contains all the important linguistic information of a speech signal, it has proved impossible to teach people to "read" running speech that way – which would have been a great boon for the deaf [2.26].

Figure 1.1 shows the spectrogram of an utterance lasting about three seconds. Time increases along the abscissa to the right and frequency goes up along the ordinate. Spectral intensity is shown as an increasing degree of blackness. When embellished by contour lines of equal spectral intensities, such sound spectrograms vaguely resemble fingerprints, which earned them the nickname *voiceprints*. However, this is a (deliberately?) misleading designation, because for forensic purposes, the usefulness of voiceprints is limited [2.27].

One focus of modern speech research has been the relationship between articulatory dynamics and the acoustic speech signal. Articulatory motions can be studied by x-rays as has been practiced by Fant [2.18] and Fujimura, who invented an x-ray microbeam method [2.28]. A continuing challenge has been the derivation of vocal-tract area functions from the speech signal itself. Of course, this approach is afflicted by problems of articulatory ambiguity. However, this ambiguity can be defeated by measuring the impedance at the lips. Figure 2.7 shows a lip impedance measuring tube with a loudspeaker on the left and two closely spaced microphones on the right. The microphone outputs are fed to a computer which separates the incident sound wave from the sound wave reflected at the lips and calculates the area function computed from the lip impedance. Figure 2.8 compares the area function computed from a measured impedance function with an actual (test) area function.

The kind of ambiguity encountered here in speech research occurs in many contexts and is characteristic of "inverse problems". Thus, the Swedish mathematician (and later Rector of the Royal Institute of Technology in Stockholm) Borg discovered sometime ago that knowledge of the resonant frequen-

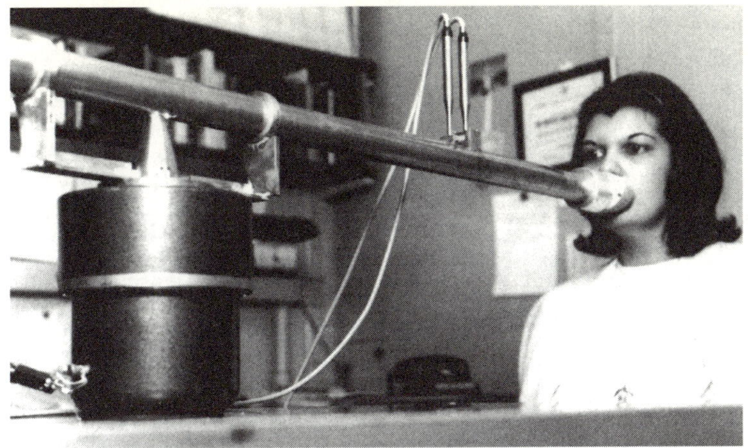

Fig. 2.7. Experimental setup for measuring the input impedance function at the lips. During the measurement the subject articulates (but does not phonate) different speech sounds

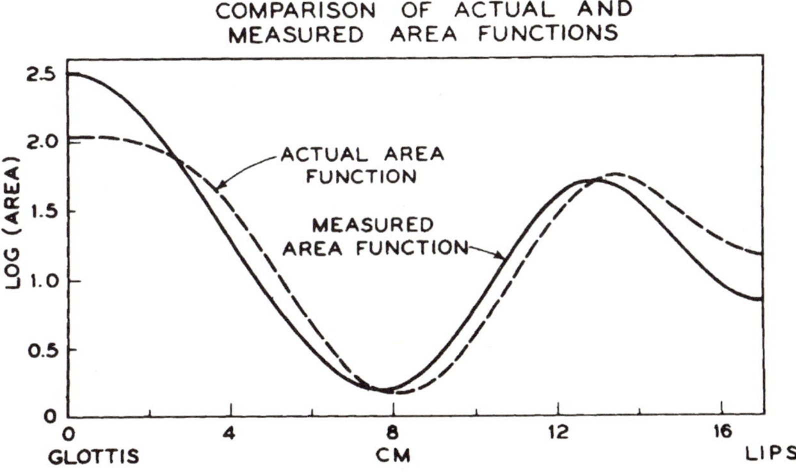

Fig. 2.8. Area function, computed from a measured lip impedance function as shown in Fig. 2.7, compared with the actual (test) area function. The achievable spatial resolution is limited by the shortest measured wavelength (the highest measured frequency) in accordance with the spatial sampling theorem

cies of a violin string is not sufficient to derive its mass density distribution [2.29]. But knowing two independent sets of resonant frequencies (for two different boundary conditions) would suffice (up to a spatial resolution determined by the highest known frequency). When reading Borg's paper, it occurred to me that the frequency locations of the poles and zeros of the input impedance of the vocal tract, as measured at the lips, are equivalent to two such independent sets of resonant frequencies (for the open and closed tract, respectively) [2.30].

Another endeavor of current speech research is to investigate the functioning of the vocal cords and their interaction with the vocal tract [2.31].

So far I have stressed spectral properties of speech. But temporal aspects are just as important not only for prosody but even for vowel perception, as W. Endres has demonstrated. For example, the long vowel $/ee/$ (as in bee) can be changed to a short $/i/$ (as in bit) just by accelerating the rate of reproduction.

The modulation transfer function measures the preservation of temporal features and is an important tool for predicting speech intelligibility [2.32, 2.33].

2.9 The Vocoder and Some of Its Progeny

In 1928, one-hundred-and-fifty years after von Kempelen's wooden speaking machine, *electronic* speech coding was inaugurated by H. Dudley, an electrical engineer at Bell Telephone Laboratories. Dudley proposed to send speech signals over a new transatlantic telegraph cable with the (then) enormous bandwidth of 100 Hz. As mentioned in Chap. 1, he argued that speech was generated by slowly moving articulators and should therefore require only some 100 Hz total bandwidth for transmission. Since extraction of these parameters proved difficult, Dudley suggested, as an alternative, the transmission of the likewise slowly changing spectral information. The result was the *frequency channel vocoder*, which is based on the spectral decomposition of sounds in the inner ear. Early vocoders had 10 to 16 channels. In 1956, the author designed a nearly unintelligible 6-channel vocoder based on hearing-like lateral "inhibition" between adjacent channels.

A somewhat more successful approach to reducing the number of channels in a vocoder (and therefore the amount of information to be transmitted) is based on the fact that adjacent frequency channels carry correlated information. Attempting to exploit these correlations Henry P. Kramer and Max V. Mathews asked themselves how best (in a minimum r.m.s. sense) to represent 16 vocoder channels by, say, 8 signals. The answer is a linear transformation by a 16×8 matrix. Of course such a "contracting" matrix has no inverse. However, there is an optimum 8×16 matrix, called a *pseudoinverse*, that recreates an approximation to the original 16 channels [2.34]. When actually implemented, it appeared that this 2-to-1 compression scheme didn't perform any better (in terms of speech quality and intelligibility) than just suppressing every other channel. So the great invention was not further pursued. (But it did teach the author, and perhaps other bystanders, a bit of linear algebra and pseudo-inverses.) – In retrospect, the Kramer-Mathews scheme might have worked better if, instead of minimizing r.m.s. spectral error, it had been based on a perceptual error criterion.

The "electronic accent" of speech synthesis can be reduced by choosing proper phase angles, thereby lowering the peak factor of the excitation signal [2.35]. Surprisingly, by manipulating the phase angles of a *flat-spectrum* signal intelligible speech can be created [2.3].

As already mentioned, the channel vocoder was first used to scramble speech signals in the secret telephone link between Churchill and Roosevelt. Renewed efforts after the war to develop a vocoder for universal use foundered on the obstinacy of the pitch problem – the difficulty of extracting accurate pitch periods from running telephone speech signals [2.36]. In an ingenious dodge, the pitch problem was circumvented by the voice-excited vocoder (VEV), which allowed the transmission of high-quality (10-kHz bandwidth) speech over ordinary telephone lines; see Chap. 1.

Another attempt at improving the quality of synthetic speech was the *phase vocoder* by J.L. Flanagan and Roger M. Golden [2.37].

2.10 Formant Vocoders

Another method of reducing the number of signals to specify the spectrum of a speech sound focuses on the formant frequencies, the resonances of the vocal tract that show up as peaks in the spectrum. Early work on the difficult task of tracking the formant frequencies of running speech was described in James L. Flanagan's thesis at MIT [2.38].

It so happened that the author's first invention at Bell was a method of tracking formant frequencies by means of spectral moments in four subbands covering non-overlapping formant-frequency ranges. Since such moments can be measured in the time domain, the instrumentation is quite simple. (For example the first spectral moment of a signal is proportional to the average absolute slope of the signal.)

Formant synthesis can be accomplished by a *series synthesizer* with three or more resonance circuits connected in series. Alternatively, the resonators can be connected in parallel. This allows greater flexibility because the amplitudes of the formants can be specified independently. However, as E. Weibel has emphasized, adjacent resonators must be connected with a sign reversal to avoid generating spectral zeros between the formants [2.39].

It is interesting to note that LPC all-pole synthesizers are implicitly also formant synthesizers (without the need to specify the formant frequencies!).

2.11 Correlation Vocoders

According to a well-known theorem by Wiener and Khinchin, the autocorrelation function of a signal is the Fourier transform of its power spectrum (Chap. 10). Thus, the linguistically important spectral information is fully represented by the autocorrelation function. The question is how to resynthesize a speech signal from the autocorrelation function. Converting a section of the autocorrelation function into a time signal by scanning it with the proper periodicity would create a signal whose spectrum would be the *square* of the original spectrum.

To undo this squaring, the author proposed taking square roots in three or four frequency channels [2.40]. The resulting autocorrelation vocoder was a limited success (to put it mildly), but it did produce something vaguely speech-like at its output. (It took the advent of linear predictive coding (LPC) several years later, to teach the proper way of going from autocorrelation sequences to time signals, namely by matrix inversion.)

2.12 The Voice-Excited Vocoder

Frequency-channel vocoders were originally invented to compress the transmission bandwidth required by speech signals. In 1957 John R. Pierce asked me to apply the vocoder principle to improve the quality of speech signals sent over ordinary telephone lines by compressing a wide band ("high-fidelity") speech signal into the 3-kHz telephone band. Given that vocoders had the bad habit of *lowering* speech quality, this seemed a tall order indeed. Even in the unlikely case that a "good" pitch detector could be designed – good enough to produce telephone-quality speech – to attain the intended superior speech quality via a vocoder (or any other speaking machine) seemed utterly beyond the state of the art in the 1950s.

Nevertheless, I thought that the goal of a high-fidelity vocoder, covering frequencies up to 10 kHz, could perhaps be realized by transmitting part of the speech signal, a so-called *baseband*, uncoded. For a baseband covering frequencies up to 2 kHz, the remaining 1 kHz bandwidth of a 3-kHz telephone band could be used to transmit the vocoder channel information for the speech frequencies between 2 kHz and 10 kHz. With six channels of constant relative bandwidth, each channel would correspond to about two critical frequency bands of human hearing. Such partial vocoders are also called *semi-vocoders*.

The pitch accuracy problem for a semi-vocoder is even more stringent than for full-band vocoders due to the requirement that the pitch in the coded part of the spectrum (2 kHz to 10 kHz) should match *exactly* the natural pitch below 2 kHz to avoid talking with two "voices" at the same time. To "solve" this impossible pitch problem, I resolved to circumvent it. Specifically, I decided to use as the excitation signal for the frequency components above 2 kHz a heavily distorted version of the baseband available at the receiver. Center clipping or cubing are well suited as nonlinearities. The spectral flatness of the excitation signal can be enhanced by a multi-channel equalizer.

Vocoders using an excitation function derived from (a subband of) the speech signal without pitch detection were called *voice-excited vocoders* or VEVs [2.41]. Voice excitation guarantees the complete coherence between the original speech (in the baseband) and the coded portion of the spectrum. The first voice-excited vocoder was called by critical listeners "the first vocoder that sounded natural, like a human speaking" without the "electronic accent" of earlier vocoders that relied on pitch detection.[5] (One of the test utterances I used for the VEV was a short dialogue in a Rhenish dialect, replete with fricatives, concerning a child licking the frost figures off the window pane of a street car. Here it is in full:"Daaf dat dat dann? – Dat daaf dat! – Dat dat dat daaf!!")

The success of the voice-excitation principle taught speech researchers an important lesson, namely that there is more to the excitation function than just a fundamental frequency and a dichotomous voiced/unvoiced distinction. The lengths of successive pitch periods do not follow a smooth course over time; there are small "random" fluctuations, and there is a continuous range of excitations between completely unvoiced and short-time periodic – not to mention voiced fricatives, such as /z/ as in bu*zz* in which the turbulent energy *pulsates* in synchrony with the pitch leading to a modulated-noise excitation.

As related before, further progress on the pitch problem was made possible by the cepstrum method, originally invented to distinguish underground nuclear explosions from earthquakes

There are many applications of vocoders besides speech scrambling and bandwidth compression, applications such as noise suppression and the restoration of helium speech. Time domain processing has also been employed, based on pitch-synchronous gating and *frequency division* originally proposed by H. Seki. Frequency compression factors of 2 to 1, while preserving high speech quality, where demonstrated by a method called *analytic rooting* [2.42] and by *harmonic compression* [2.43]. Claims of compression factors as high as 8 and, facetiously, 32 (by A. Solzhenitsyn in his sarcastic *The First Circle of Hell*) were shown to be fallacious; they were based on bandpass filters with insufficient out-of-band frequency rejection.

2.13 Center Clipping for Spectrum Flattening

As we have seen, amplitude compression, even in its extreme form of infinite clipping, does not destroy speech intelligibility. By contrast, *center clipping,*

---

[5] Before voice-excited vocoders, people, jocularly, distinguished between two kinds of vocoders: those that were intelligible but sounded inhuman (like channel vocoders) and those that sounded human but were unintelligible (like early formant vocoders).

defined as setting the central amplitude values of a signal (within a given threshold range) equal to zero while leaving the signal amplitudes outside this range unchanged, renders a speech signal virtually unintelligible for high enough threshold settings, say 90% of a running peak value. Such severe center clipping eliminates most of the oscillatory waveform characterizing the formants. As a result, the spectrum of severely center-clipped speech lacks the typical formant structure and has a roughly flat spectral envelope. Yet the *fine structure* of the spectrum is preserved. Such *spectral flatteners* are useful in *voice-excited vocoders* to generate a flat-spectrum excitation signal coherent with the uncoded speech signal.

Another, "softer" operation for spectrum flattening is *cubing* the speech signal. Since cubing (or distortion by any other *homogeneous* power law) is a *scale free* operation, it does not require the setting of a threshold, which can be tricky.

2.14 Linear Prediction

A new area in speech analysis/synthesis dawned in 1967 with *linear predictive coding* (LPC), based on an all-pole model of speech signals [2.44]. LPC is used in practically all of today's most successful speech analysis/synthesis systems. With LPC, formant-like analysis was made possible without encountering the difficulties of formant frequency measurements inherent in formant vocoders [2.45]. Another great boost was given to LPC by the method of partial correlations pioneered by Itakura [2.46].

2.15 Subjective Error Criteria

Minimizing the *perceived* quantizing noise (rather than the root-mean-square error) by introducing the masking properties of the human ear into the coding process was proposed by the author in the 1970s [2.47]. This permitted bit rates below 1 bit/sample for the prediction residual [2.48]. In combination with code-excited linear prediction (CELP), rates as low as 0.25 bits/sample were achieved while maintaining high speech quality and full intelligibility [2.49].

Based on these achievements, once thought unattainable, LPC has become the preferred method for speech synthesis in innumerable applications from talking toys to spoken message services. It is interesting to note that LPC is closely related to the Maximum Entropy Principle, first used in geophysics (for oil prospecting) and in astronomy (for image enhancement).

2.16 Neural Networks

Neural networks (NN), have been applied successfully in speech recognition and speech synthesis from text [2.50]. In fact, T. Sejnowski succeeded in demonstrating the *learning* process of a NN talker, which went from baby-like babble to more mature speech as it improved its own diction by "backward propagation" of corrective instructions. Their potential for speech coding, however, has not been sufficiently explored.

Neural networks have, however, been used to advantage in automatic speech recognition [2.51] as an alternative to hidden Markov models [2.52].

2.17 Wavelets

Wavelets have a long history. As early as 1909 Alfred Haar, a student of David Hilbert at Göttingen, submitted a Ph.D. thesis in which he proposed binary-valued wavelets, published a year later in the *Mathematische Annalen*, vol. 69 ("Zur Theorie der orthogonalen Funktionssysteme", pp. 331–371). Another binary transformation that has long been used successfully in signal analysis is based on Walsh–Hadamard matrices.

In recent years, wavelets have become very popular in signal processing, including speech analysis/synthesis [2.53].

There are two broad classes of wavelets: those that "live" on a linear frequency scale and those whose frequencies scale logarithmically, called affine wavelets. Linear scale wavelets correspond, roughly, to the impulse responses of the individual filters of a "linear" filter bank, i.e. a bank of filters with contiguous constant-bandwidth filters.

Affine wavelets, by contrast, correspond to an "octave" or "third-octave" filter bank in which each filter has a constant *relative* bandwidth. More precisely, *scaled wavelets*, as they are also called, have waveforms that are derived from a single prototype by repeatedly applying a scale factor ("multiresolution wavelets"). For "octave wavelets" the scale factor is 2, but other scale factors – and indeed variable scale factors – may be preferable for a good representation of speech signals and optimum subjective (hearing related) error criteria. Scaling is one of the fundamental concepts of nature that governs many of its laws and designs from fractals to power laws [2.54].

Affine wavelets are particularly germane to speech signals and synthesis for two important reasons:

1. They mimic the (nearly) constant-Q character of the resonances of the human vocal tract.
2. Above about 800 Hz, the frequency analysis of the human ear is approximately logarithmic, i.e. the analysis is in terms of constant *relative* bandwidth. For normal hearing the relative bandwidth is around 0.15 corresponding to a constant Q of about 7.

Viewed as a logarithmic filter bank, the human auditory "filter bank" has therefore a roughly constant scaling factor of 1.15 which corresponds approximately to the fifth root of 2. A set of wavelets covering the speech bandwidth 250–4000 Hz would therefore have 39 members. Of these, the lower 7 channels can be combined into 3 channels of approximately constant bandwidth of 120–160 Hz. This would be in accordance with the spectral analysis in the inner ear, which is on a nearly linear frequency scale below 800 Hz.

It is not clear at the time of writing whether wavelets will in fact become the wave of the future for speech signals. More research is needed to optimize the various options that wavelets offer (basic waveform, sampling grid in time and frequency, bit allocations, etc.).

2.18 Conclusion

Computer speech can look forward to a promising future, both in terms of challenging research and useful applications, to wit:

- efficient storage and transmission
- mobile communication
- spoken message services
- "real audio" on the World Wide Web
- maneuvering of wheelchair by the voice of the handicapped
- attitude control of space capsules by astronauts
- Internet speech security
- educational tools
- foreign language acquisition
- reading aids for the blind
- reduction of noise and reverberation
- talking cars, cameras, and toys

Additional applications, agreeable or noisome, are surely waiting in the wings.

3. Speech Recognition and Speaker Identification

Civilization advances by extending the number of important operations which we can perform without thinking.

Alfred North Whitehead

If anything can go wrong, it will.

Murphy's Law

In this chapter we discuss, in an informal manner, some of the successes and a few of the outstanding problems of automatic speech recognition (ASR) and speaker identification – for forensic, business and banking purposes. ASR can also help the hard-of-hearing by giving them printed text to read, and the wheelchair-bound by allowing them to control their vehicles by voice. Together with speech synthesis from text, human–machine dialogue systems offer attractive possibilities for all manner of information services.

Speech recognition is basically a pattern matching process. The objective in pattern matching is to compare an unknown test pattern with a set of stored reference patterns ("templates"), established from the training data, and to provide a set of similarity scores between test and reference patterns. The development of statistical pattern matching techniques based on dynamic programming and on hidden Markov models (HMM) represents a major breakthrough in automatic speech recognition. Because of its statistical nature and its simple algorithmic structure for handling the large variability in speech signals, these methods have found widespread use in automatic speech recognition.

Neural networks and Kohonen maps are likewise among the promising techniques employed.

Another important ingredient of automatic speech recognition that has come to the fore recently is the enhancement of the *modulation spectrum*.

It has been known for some time that modulating frequencies (i.e. the frequencies at which the amplitude or *envelope* of a speech signal fluctuates) peaks at about 4 Hz at a normal rate of speaking. Thus a modified speech signal in which the modulation frequencies around 4 Hz are enhanced is more intelligible to a human listener in the presence of noise.[1] And what helps human listeners also helps computers to better understand speech from noisy or reverberant environments.

3.1 Speech Recognition

The automatic recognition of spoken language and its transcription into readable text has been a long-held dream. I wish I could dictate this book into an automatic speech recognizer rather than laboriously tapping it out with my two index fingers. Of course many people would miss the human typist brightening up the office as an intelligent working partner. But still, automatic speech recognition has many practical applications including, ultimately, the voice-typewriter [3.1].

Human communication by voice appears to be so simple that we tend to forget how variable a signal speech is. In fact, spoken utterances even of the same text are characterized by large differences that depend on context, speaking style, the speaker's dialect, the acoustic environment, microphone characteristics, etc. In fact, even identical texts spoken by the *same* speaker can show sizable acoustic differences. Automatic methods of speech recognition must be able to handle this large variability in a fault-free fashion.

In addition to phonological and lexical information, good automatic speech recognizers also rely on the *grammar* of the language to be recognized and – as far as possible – on the semantics of the text, the potential *meaning*. How little grammar without meaning can accomplish is nicely demonstrated by Chomsky's grammatically correct nonsense sentence "Colorless green ideas sleep furiously". (But nonsense, albeit not as obvious, remains a favorite device of the politician – and the professional doubletalker.)

Not surprisingly, the success of automatic speech recognition depends on the language. Just think of the names of the Old Continent in Italian and English. In Italian, the pronunciation of *Europa* is allotted 4 clearly enunciated syllables: E-u-ro-pa. By contrast, the English *Europe* has at best just two syllables (the second of which does not even contain a full vowel).

Automatic speech recognition also depends critically on the specific task. Thus the recognition of a few words from a small vocabulary, spoken in isolation, preferably by a "master's voice," has been within reach for decades:

---

[1] Indeed such modulation enhancement is now routinely practiced in better hearing aids. Interestingly human sensitivity to modulation frequencies (in amplitude-modulated tones, for example) also peaks around 4Hz, suggesting some degree of coevolution of human speech and hearing.

witness the toy dog "Rex" of yore who wagged his tail in recognition (!) when addressed as "Rex." (Actually, the mechanical marvel responded in the same manner to any loud enough sound or noise – so much for early speech recognition.)

Hower stuffed animals – stuffed with electronics – have become much wiser recently and even outright dangerous. Thus Furby, the fluffy phantasy toy, according to a report in the *Washington Post*, has forced the National Security Agency in Fort Meade, Maryland, to issue a "Furby Alert". It appears that NSA employees had "smuggled" the high-tec cyperpets into the supersecret agency and officials are naturally worried that people would take the Furbys home with them and the stuffed pets would start talking and divulge all manner of highly sensitive stuff (*International Herald Tribune*, January 14th, 1999).

Another precocious speech recognition system was Bell Laboratories' Automatic Digit Recognizer, dubbed "Audrey," intended for voice dialing [3.2]. After a brief training session on a new voice, it would dial correctly *most* of the numbers much of the time – but rarely a complete seven-digit number correctly. In the meantime, fairly reliable voice-dialing (in a moving car, for example, see Fig. 3.1) is accomplished by pronouncing pre-selected distinctive words like "home" or "office" or "Anny," instead of digit strings.

Speech sounds can be described in terms of their distinctive features, such as nasality and voicing. In theory, speech recognition could be based on first recognizing distinctive features and then inferring the sounds themselves from an appropriate dictionary. However, distinctive features in running speech are often difficult to pin down. A better way for automatic speech recognition is to consider speech signals as stochastic sequences and treat them by statistical pattern recognition techniques incorporating linguistic constraints. An example is Bayes' rule, which gives *a posteriori* probabilities in terms of *a priori* probabilities:

$$p(W|A) = p(A|W) \cdot p(W)/p(A) \, .$$

Here $p(W|A)$ is the *a posteriori* probability that a given word W was spoken given an acoustic input (sound wave) A. It depends on the conditional probability $p(A|W)$ for an acoustic input A given a word W, which can in principle be measured. The factor $p(W)$ reflects the different *a priori* probabilities of different words. When looking for the most likely word W going with a given acoustic input A, the factor $p(A)$ becomes immaterial.

Speech recognition algorithms can be used in either a "speaker-dependent" or "speaker-independent" mode. As the size of the vocabulary grows and the circle of talkers is widened, reliable speech recognition becomes more difficult. If words are not pronounced in isolation but strung together into fluent, conversational speech – if there are background noises, echoes and reverberation – useful speech recognition soon strains present capabilities. In isolated words, or speech where words are separated by distinct pauses, the beginning and end of words are more clearly marked. In continuous speech, word bound-

Fig. 3.1. Modern mobile communication: the proper priorities of last calls as seen by J.B. Handelsman, *The New Yorker*

aries are blurred and automatic methods of segmenting continuous speech into words must be devised – not a trivial task. Machine recognition of continuous speech with a large vocabulary requires that syntactic and semantic constraints be incorporated in the recognition process.

However, in spite of these difficulties, interest in speech recognition and speaker identification refuses to wither and research continues vigorously. After all, the automobile, originally conceived as an ersatz horse, runs tirelessly – although it still balks at leaping fences. And the airplane, too, inspired by the swift bird, has grown in size and importance without ever having mastered the fine art of alighting on a tree.

3.2 Dialogue Systems

Among the numerous applications for automatic speech recognition perhaps the most (im)pertinent are task-oriented dialogue systems, such as travel information services. These require of course (limited) speech synthesis as well as recognition. One prominent example is the Philips Train Timetable Information System, which has been running in Switzerland and the Netherlands since 1996 [3.3]. Another, earlier, example is the AT&T Bell Laboratories "Conversational Mode Speech Understanding System" by S. E. Levinson and L. R. Rabiner [3.4]. Here is a brief dialogue with the Bell system (not the long-defunct Bell System):

Customer: *I want one first class seat on flight number 31 to Denver on Sunday.*
Machine: *I am sorry the flight is not available on Sunday.*
Customer: *I want to go on Saturday then.*
Machine: *Flight number 31 leaves New York at 09:45 and arrives in Denver at 13:10.* Etc.

The machine can, reportedly, also cope with some non-sequiturs and nonsensical questions by the customer (without losing its temper).

3.3 Speaker Identification

Speech recognition's sibling, automatic speaker identification, too, has many potential applications. I remember, as mentioned, a visit to my Murray Hill office, in 1965, by a delegation from the American Bankers Association who wanted to know the chances of replacing payment by paper check by voice-actuated money transfer. The customer's voice was to take the place of the signature on the check. When I pointed out the unreliability of automatic speaker verification, they were not discouraged: North American banks were losing (I forget how many) millions of dollars every year owing to forged or illegible signatures – or no signatures at all. So a certain "false accept" rate was quite acceptable to the bankers. But 33 years later, in 1998 – in spite of sizable inroads by electronic money transfers – Americans still wrote 70 billion paper checks.

Speaker identification or verification could also be of crucial importance in allowing (or denying) access to restricted data or facilities. Think of confidential medical reports or bank statements. A crazy colonel could conceivably start a war by pretending to be someone much higher up in the chain of command. In World War II, speaker identification (by visual inspection of spectrograms) was used to track the movements of German radio communicators, thereby allowing the Allies to anticipate forthcoming enemy forays. This was the first "field" application of the sound-spectrograph and "visible speech" [3.5].

Beyond verifying a given speaker, identifying his accent or *dialect* is sometimes the goal. Again, I remember a visit, this time by a pair of "spooks" from Virginia. They were eager to learn whether it was possible to build a machine that could identify the dialect of an unknown voice. They brought a secret recording, taped in a bar in Rio de Janeiro, of a Russian-speaking voice and they wanted to know whether a machine could tell if it had an Odessa accent. (I'll spare you my answer, which is "top secret" anyhow.) For another breakthrough, see Fig. 3.2.

Another Breakthrough from A. T. & T.

Fig. 3.2. The latest advance in reliable communication, witnessed by J.B. Handelsman, *The New Yorker*

3.4 Word Spotting

To stay with the Cold War for a while, the Soviets, too, were not sitting on their hands or ears. In fact, they excelled at a speech recognition task called *word spotting.* As is well known, the new Soviet embassy in Washington had been erected in a strategic position, directly in the path of a major U.S. microwave highway, affording the Russian "diplomats" an easy opportunity to snoop on untold toll calls. Of course, you can't listen to thousands of conversations. But you can design a speech recognizer that pricks up its ears at the occurrence of certain key words, such as "wheat" or "wheat price" and only then record the conversation. It is said that in this manner the Soviets were able to strike a very advantageous wheat deal when another food shortage was threatening the motherland.

Stalin, it appears, had no small interest in speech research. As mentioned before, he supported speech recognition and speaker identification originally to be able to trap "traitors" on the telephone. The Generalissimo and his surviving military minions were also interested in speech compression because it facilitated digital speech scrambling. All this is expertly told by one of the prisoner-scientists involved, Alexander Isayevich Solzhenitsyn in his *The First Circle of Hell.*

While visiting the Soviet Union in 1963, as a guest of the Committee for the Coordination of Scientific Research, I was able to get a fair sample of Soviet capabilities in speech research but, curiously, one of their main laboratories (*Lab 26* I think it was callled) was "closed for repairs" during my visit.[2]

3.5 Pinpointing Disasters by Speaker Identification

My first encounter with the usefulness of voice recognition was in 1956, when two airliners collided over the Grand Canyon. There was a last message, just before the crash, from one of the planes ending in the words "We are going in..." After that: Silence. The Federal Aviation Authority surmised that the speaker had just seen the other plane and was crying out his fateful discovery. But who was the speaker? The answer would identify the position of the speaker in the cockpit and therefore the probable direction of the other plane. Careful analysis of the spectrogram of the unknown voice by L. G. Kersta revealed that it matched the characteristics of the flight engineer. This modest piece of information helped the Authority to reconstruct the course of the collision. Subsequently, the FAA issued orders aimed at forestalling future accidents of this type.

Another tragedy that caught the world's attention was the burning up of three U.S. astronauts, Virgil Grissom, Edward White and Roger Chaffee, on the ground during a training session on 27 January 1967. Again I was at the receiving end of a horrible tape recording: the last words of a human being engulfed in flames. The voice screamed, at a pitch exceeding 400 Hz,

---

[2] I was, however, able to meet the speech research people in another location where I was asked to preface my scheduled talk with a brief description of Bell Laboratories. I started out by saying "Bell Labs is the research and development arm of the American Telephone and Telegraph Company. We are 14 000 people" – which was translated as "u nikh 14 chlen" (they have 14 members). Whereupon I cried in desperation (forgetting that I wasn't supposed to understand Russian) "nyet, 14 *tysyacha* (14 *000*) chlen." The audience burst into laughter, but I felt sorry for the interpreter knowing from painful personal experience how difficult translating can be.

Incidentally, after my talk several Soviet colleagues commented that "I was the first American they could readily understand." Well, speaking with a sound German accent – and being very much aware of the difficulties of transcending language barriers – I was not surprised.

"Fire! We're burning up!!" Whoever said those words probably saw the fire first, implying that it had started on his side. But whose voice was it? The screaming had distorted it beyond human, let alone machine identification. But spectral analysis allowed us to identify the screamer and helped NASA to take corrective action. (This included replacing the highly flammable pure-oxygen breathing atmosphere by a safer mixture of oxygen and nitrogen. The Russians had been able to do this much earlier in their space program because their rockets were more powerful and could carry the required greater payload.)

3.6 Speaker Identification for Forensic Purposes

With these successes in voice identification it is not surprising that linguists soon thought of enlisting spectral analysis for forensic purposes. The main interest was in identifying the voice of an extortionist or suspected criminal. Before long, sound spectrograms were christened "voice prints" by those eager to sell the new "art," the implication being that they were as reliable as fingerprints.

To keep the discussion on safe scientific ground, the Acoustical Society of America formed a committee of speech experts to look into these claims [3.6]. The main conclusions of the committee's report emphasized that a suspect's voice could sometimes be *excluded* with certainty on the basis of incompatible spectral data. In other words, the suspect, given his or her vocal apparatus, could have never produced all the features of the given utterance. Furthermore, a voice could sometimes be "identified" with some probability from a limited pool of potential candidates. But all bets were off, the committee concluded, for the identification of a voice from an *open* ensemble of speakers. Voiceprints are just not as uniquely characteristic of a person's identity as the genetic code (DNA) or fingerprints – notwithstanding the entry in the *American Heritage Dictionary of the English Language (Third Edition, 1992):*

> **voiceprint** (vois¹•prînt') noun. An electronically recorded graphic representation of a person's voice, in which the configuration for any given utterance is uniquely characteristic of the individual speaker.

The Random House Dictionary of the English Language (Second Unabridged Edition, 1978) has a more appropriate definition; its entry under voiceprint reads:

> A graphic representation of a person's voice, showing the component frequencies as analyzed by a sound spectrograph.

3.7 Dynamic Programming

Automatic recognition systems contain, in their memories, reference patterns or templates of the words to be recognized. These templates may be a succession of amplitude spectra (on a linear frequency scale or a more ear-like progression) or they may be cepstra or any other set of parameters that characterize speech sounds. These templates usually imply a fixed time scale.

An utterance to be recognized has of course its own time scale that rarely coincides with that of a template. Thus, the problem of proper alignment in time between unknown utterance and template becomes paramount. In discrete time, at every time step, the question arises of whether the unknown utterance is lagging behind the template, just in step, or ahead of the template. Depending on the answer, the template sample is held in place or advanced by one or several steps. This process of "clock comparison" or time registration, called *dynamic time warping* or *dynamic programming*, is a crucial ingredient of most automatic recognizers.

Dynamic programming is also used as search strategy for longer speech segments including entire words [3.7]. In another approach, which avoids the problem of time alignment, the spectrograms of entire words are recognized without cutting them up into shorter segments [3.8].

3.8 Markov Models

The theory of Markov chains has a long history in mathematics and statistics. Markov chains were named after Andrei Andreevich Markov (1856–1922), who, along with Lyapunov, was a student of Pafnutii Chebyshev.[3] Markov chains model statistical time series in which the probability of occurrence of a given event depends only on the near past. Applicatons of Markov chains abound in physics, economics, biology and, more recently, in speech processing.

Many real-world events can be modeled by a first-order Markov process: the probability of an event is given solely by the immediately preceding state of the model. In other words, first-order Markov processes have a very short direct memory. Think of a radioactive atom (as used in radiation therapy for cancer). Its probability of decaying during the next second is independent of the prior history of the (ground-state) atom – as long as it still exists. Of course, once it has decayed, the probability of decaying again in the future is zero.

---

[3] Among electrical engineers, Chebyshev (1821–1894) is known mostly for the equal-ripple filter, also called "Chebyshev filter" because it is based on the Chebyshev polynomials. These polynomials resulted from Chebyshev's work on transforming circular into straight-line motion in the newly-invented steam engine. He is also noted for his work on the distribution of prime numbers and the generalized law of large numbers.

A somewhat more sophisticated Markov model concerns N_0 couples on a dance floor. When the music starts, each dancer is assigned a random dancing mate. If it is his own partner, the couple, after one dance, is ordered to leave the dance floor and go home. As a result there are now only $N_1 \leq N_0$ (newly assigned) couples still dancing. This number is the new state of the dance floor model. The music starts again and the process of selection and expulsion is repeated. After a while the dance floor is empty. The question is, what is the expected number of dances before all the couples are safely home?

To calculate the required transition probabilities, one needs the probability distribution of the number n of fixed points for a random permutation of N different objects:

$$p_N(n) = \frac{1}{n!} \sum_{k=0}^{N-n} (-1)^k \frac{1}{k!} \; .$$

For large N, the above formula gives the well-known $p_N(0) \approx 1/e$, answering the question "if N letters are stuffed randomly into N envelopes, what is the probability that none is properly addressed?"[4]

3.9 Shannon's Outguessing Machine
– A Hidden Markov Model Analyzer

Not all games of chance are as fair and rousing as dancing with a random mate. But some games make no pretensions of fair play; in fact, *un*fairness is their very reason for being – such as Claude Shannon's "outguessing machine", a beautiful application of a hidden Markov model in which the guessing behavior of a human being is modeled as a Markov process [3.10]. On the basis of observing and analyzing the outputs of a human player in a heads-tails guessing game, the outguessing machine constructs a model of an

---

[4] This formula was once guessed by the author – on the basis of the trivial facts that $p_N(n) = 1/n!$ and $p_N(n-1) = 0$ and the further fact that $0! = 1!$ so that an alternating series would give $p_N(n-1) = 0$.

The above distribution, as serendipity taught me, can be generalized by multiplying it by m^n and, inside the sum, by m^k. This yields, for $N \to \infty$, the Poisson distribution with mean m. Curiously, for finite N (and $m \leq 1$) the generalized formula is again a *bona fide* probability distribution with many interesting applications. It shares numerous properties with the Poisson distribution, except that the maximum number of events is bounded. It has the same factorial moments and cumulants as the Poisson distribution (which is not the case for a Poisson distribution that is simply truncated).

This generalized Poisson distribution was already studied in the 1930s by the German mathematician Emil Julius Gumbel (1891–1966). Gumbel was a world authority on the "statistics of extremes" (floods, climate, fatigue failure) [3.9] and an early uncompromising pacifist whom Albert Einstein honored with the title *Apostle of Justice*.

assumed Markov process underlying the human responses. The machine then exploits this model to predict future human behavior.

More specifically, the entrapping contraption, built by Shannon's close collaborator David Hagelbarger, initially makes random heads-tails choices against a human contender. But once the machine has experienced its first wins, it begins analyzing the opponent's "strategy" to a depth of two throws. Does he or she change after losing a throw? Does the player keep on choosing tails if tails has brought two previous wins? Or does the gambler get chary and heads for heads next? For most people such strategies are mostly subconscious, but the machine assumes the human to act like a *second-order Markov process* and uncovers the underlying transition probabilities without fail.

Exploiting these, the machine always wins over the long haul, except against its creator. Shannon, keeping track of his machine's inner states, can beat it 6 times out of 10. Of course, anyone could win 5 out of 10 throws on average by playing random (perhaps by flipping a true coin). But this is precisely what people, deprived of proper props, are incapable of doing, as Shannon's machine has demonstrated again and again by beating a wide variety of human would-be winners. Specifically, the human mind appears to abhor long strings of like outcomes – as occur perfectly naturally in truly random sequences.

Of course, the machine can have bad luck, too, especially in its initial guessing phase. I once wanted to show off the machine's prowess to a foreign friend (the mathematician Fritz Hirzebruch) visiting Bell Laboratories. As luck would have it, Hirzebruch won 13 times in a row before his first loss. But thereafter the machine took off with a vengeance, overtaking the renowned mathematician on throw 31 (i.e. the machine won 16 out of the next 18 throws!) and never fell behind again – in spite of the fact that Hirzebruch had been told (in general terms) how the machine worked.

3.10 Hidden Markov Models in Speech Recognition

First-order Markov processes are characterized by a set of states, a matrix of transition probabilities between these states, and the observable outputs that the process generates for each transition. The process is set in motion by a probability distribution for the initial states.

Hidden Markov Models have been successfully applied in many difficult analysis tasks ranging from the deciphering of cryptograms to speech recognition. Let us therefore look at a hidden Markov model (HMM) in somewhat greater detail. Assume there are N urns filled with a large number of colored balls, say red, yellow or blue. The relative frequencies of the colors for each urn are known.

At the beginning an urn is chosen according to a given probability distribution for the initial states. A ball is picked at random from that urn, its color, c_1, is announced and the ball is replaced into its urn.

At each clock time thereafter one of the urns is chosen according to the given distribution of transition probabilities. Again a ball is picked from that urn, its color, c_2, is announced and it is replaced. One of the problems is to reconstruct the parameters of the model from the sequence of colors $c_1, c_2, c_3, \ldots$. More specifically,

- Given the observations, what sequence of states (urns) is the most likely?
- How do we adjust the model parameters to best conform to a large number of observations?

In the first problem we may recognize the speech recognition problem. The observations are the result of acoustical measurements or a speech signal, say (quantized) spectra or predictor coefficients. The different states represent the different words (or syllables or phonemes) to be recognized. The second problem is the "training problem" in which the parameters of the model are optimized to best describe the observation sequences.

3.11 Neural Networks

Serial or von Neumann computers[5], the type of computer that dominates present markets – from laptop to mainframes – have become faster and faster over the years. Yet, compared to biological computers, they are still frustratingly slow. The human eye, for example, almost immediately recognizes another human face – no small computational feat. The reason of course is that biological computers, such as our brains, process data not in a slow serial mode but in highly parallel fashion. Taking a cue from nature, engineers too have developed parallel computers but none with the breathtaking parallelism that we find in living systems. It is possible that this picture will change once "nonstandard" computers [3.12] based on genetic ingredients (DNA, RNA, etc.) or quantum mechanics are available.[6] In the meantime parallel computation has advanced along a different avenue: neural networks. Neural networks have their origin in the work of Warren McCulloch and his student Walter Pitts in the early 1940s [3.13]. They showed that with a network of simple two-state logical decision elements ("artificial neurons") they could perform

---

[5] The designation of serial computers as von Neumann computers could be misleading because von Neumann was one of the early thinkers about artificial neurons and neural networks for computing [3.11].

[6] One of the quirks of quantum systems is that, like a super juggler, they can keep innumerable "balls" in the air at the same time – until they are observed, when the wave function is said to collapse to a single state. Anticipated applications are factoring of 1000-digit numbers and pattern recognition, including automatic speech recognition.

Boolean algebra. And, according to A. M. Turing, any computable function can be computed by Boolean algebra.

In 1949 D. O. Hebb introduced "Hebb's rules" for changing the strengths of the connections between individual artificial neurons and thereby enabling such networks to adapt and *learn* from past experience. Early applications of neural nets, although not usually identified as such, are adaptive equalizers for telephone lines (important for maximizing the bit rate of your computer's modem) and adaptive echo cancelers (crucial in satellite communication). Tino Gramss simulated a neural network that learned to walk upright – after innumerable tumbles during the learning phase. And Terrence Sejnowski designed a neural net for learning how to speak (given a written text). Apart from such instructive demonstrations as walking, reading or balancing a broom on a fingertip, neural networks have found many useful applications in pattern recognition (handprinted characters, faces, speech), the assessment of risks and credit ratings, the control of automated manufacturing plants, predicting stock and bond prices, optimal resource allocation, the traveling salesman problem, and how to back up a monster trailer truck.

In all, neural networks have become an important ingredient of Artificial Intelligence (AI); see the Glossary. Early pioneers of AI include Herbert Simon, Allan Newell, and Marvin Minsky.

By 1987 the time was ripe for the First International Conference in Neural Networks in San Diego, a mammoth meeting attended by such luminaries as Leon Cooper of superconductivity Cooper-pair fame.

3.11.1 The Perceptron

But already in 1957, F. Rosenblatt designed his famous *perceptron* for clarifying data [3.14]. The perceptron adds weighted inputs from two or more sensors and feeds the sum into a hard limiter with a given threshold. If the sum exceeds the threshold, the perceptron's output is 1; otherwise it is 0. The perceptron is trained by adaptively changing its weights. During the training phase, each weight is updated by adding or subtracting a small increment proportional to the difference between the desired and the actual output. While the perceptron enjoyed its year in the limelight, it soon became apparent that perceptrons could only classify data if the different classes fell on different sides of a straight line (or hyperplane) in the data space. In fact, in 1969, Minsky and Papert gave a formal proof of the perceptron's main deficiency, which, incidentally, implied that one of the most basic logical operations, the "exclusive or" or XOR function, could not be implemented by a perceptron. This was, however, already known to Rosenblatt and he had proposed *multi-layer* perceptrons to overcome this problem. But the impact of the Minsky/Papert paper was so powerful that much of neural network work came to a virtual standstill until its rebirth – with a vengeance – in the 1980s.

3.11.2 Multilayer Networks

Multilayer perceptrons lead to general multilayer neural networks, in which the outputs of the first layer are weighted and summed to form the inputs to the next or "hidden" layer. In this manner an arbitrary number of hidden layers could be interposed between inputs and output, but it was shown that, given enough nodes, just one hidden layer is sufficient to distinguish between arbitrarily complex decision regions in the input space.[7] However, multiple hidden layers are sometimes preferred because they can lead to faster learning.

3.11.3 Backward Error Propagation

One of the main reasons for the resurgence of neural networks was the invention by Paul Werbos in 1974 of the backward error propagation or "backprop" algorithm to train multilayer networks. This backprop algorithm was rediscovered and patented by D. Parker in 1982 and brought to wide attention by the influential group led by Rumelhart on "parallel distributed processing" at the University of California in San Diego [3.15]. In the backprop algorithm the input information is propagated through the network from one layer to the next in a feedforward manner. The outputs of the last (highest) layer are then subtracted from the desired outputs and the differences are used to adjust the weights of all the layers in order to minimize the differences (in a least-squares sense). The weight corrections are computed layer by layer, starting with the highest one and propagating the differences downwards through the network, which is then operating in a reversed manner.

Not infrequently the hidden layer or layers of a fully trained network represent some pivotal aspects of the task. Thus, in Sejnowski's speaking network some of the internal nodes represent, at least vaguely, the vowel sounds of the language.

Backprop networks can also be used for noise reduction of noisy signals. In the learning phase noise-free signals are used as inputs. Furthermore, by progressively reducing the number of internal nodes, such networks can also be used for data compression. But no matter how well multilayer networks perform, it is always advantageous to *pre*process the data, for example by transforming speech spectra to the hearing-related Bark-scale or by replacing spectra by cepstra. (Using only the low quefrency portion of a cepstrum eliminates sensitivity to the possibly irrelevant fine structure ("pitch") of the spectrum.)

---

[7] The formal proof is based on work by Andrei Kolmogorov in connection with David Hilbert's 13th problem concerning the factorizability of polynomials. (Of the total of 23 crucial problems that Hilbert posed at the International Mathematics Congress in Paris in 1900, several remain unsolved to this day.)

3.11.4 Kohonen Self-Organizing Maps

Kohonen's self-organizing feature maps are an example of *unsupervised* learning – as opposed to the supervised learning in which, during the learning phase, the outputs of a neural net are compared with the desired ("correct") outputs [3.16].

Learning in a two-dimensional Kohonen net proceeds as follows. Starting with "random" weights w_{ij}, the squared distances $(x_i - w_{ij})^2$ between the inputs x_i and their weights are summed to yield the total squared distance d_j to the jth node. (Note that the two-dimensional Kohonen net is indexed by a single discrete variable.) Then select the minimum d_j and, for a given neighborhood of the jth node, update all weights by the following rule

$$w_{ij}(t+1) = w_{ij}(t) + \alpha(x_i - w_{ij}(t)) \,,$$

where the factor α and the size of the neighborhood are slowly decreased during the learning phase. Once the learning is completed for a neighborhood, select another neighborhood and repeat the procedure until all nodes in the net have been trained. The result of this procedure for speech spectra as inputs is a two-dimensional "phonemic" map that is traversed from one node to a nearby node as the utterance proceeds. The two dimensions of a trained Kohonen map for speech recognition often resemble the plane of the first two formant frequencies that distinguish the different vowel sounds.

3.11.5 Hopfield Nets and Associative Memory

The work of the physicist John Hopfield at Bell Laboratories and Princeton University was one of the strongest stimuli for the revival of artificial neural networks in the 1980s [3.17]. In contrast to the networks discussed so far, Hopfield nets have *fixed weights*. Furthermore, they are symmetric: $w_{ij} = w_{ji}$. These weights represent a number of "memorized" patterns v_i^m, $m = 1, 2, \ldots, M$, as follows

$$w_{ij} = \sum_m v_i^m v_j^m \,, \quad i \neq j = 1, 2, \ldots, N \,.$$

The diagonal elements w_{ii} are set equal to 0. To associate an unknown input pattern x_i^0 with the different memorized pattern, the following expression is computed

$$x_i(1) = \text{sign}\left[\sum_j w_{ij} x_j(0) \right]$$

and iterated until the $x_i(n)$ do not change much anymore. For symmetric w_{ij}, this procedure is equivalent to a search in an energy landscape. Thermodynamics teaches that this procedure always converges to a, possibly local, minimum in the energy landscape.

Sometimes the convergence gets stuck in a "wrong" local minimum. To allow the convergence to proceed to a new, lower and therefore better, minimum, the energy landscape is moved up and down in a random fashion as if the corresponding physical system was sitting in a heat bath and the heat was turned on. (This is akin to the – illegal – tilting and shaking of pinball machines.) Subsequently, the temperature is slowly lowered until a new, hopefully lower, minimum is reached. In analogy to metallurgy, this powerful procedure is called "simulated annealing."

If the input pattern $x_i(0)$ is near one of the memorized patterns v_i^m, then $x_i(n)$ will converge on that pattern. In addition, even if the input is degraded, convergence to the "correct" pattern will usually occur. Here the degradation can consist of additive or multiplicative noise or partial obliteration. Thus, the Hopfield net acts as an *associative memory*: you show the net part of a human face and it will reconstruct the rest.

Associative memory is one of the preeminent attributes of the human brain: play a certain dance tune and you will suddenly see in your mind your long-lost partner with whom you danced, etc.

The number M of different memorized patterns a Hopfield net can distinguish is limited to about one seventh of the number N of its nodes, provided the patterns are reasonably orthogonal to each other. This must be compared to 2^N patterns for a binary memory. Thus, in terms of pure storage capacity, Hopfield nets are a poor medium indeed. Their strengths lie in their computational abilities. In addition to associative memory tasks, Hopfield nets have been used for waveform reconstruction and numerous other tasks, including the (in)famous traveling salesman problem: what is the shortest route between a large number of cities.

If the weights w_{ij} are not symmetric, convergence will usually not take place, but new applications become possible such as recognizing a sequence of patterns (such as the phonemes in running speech).

3.12 Whole Word Recognition

Most automatic speech recognizers attempt to identify simple phonemes or syllables and then string these together into words. By contrast whole-word recognition is based on the analysis of an entire word or even a sequence of words. In this approach the speech spectrogram of a word, i.e. its energy (on a gray scale) is considered as a *picture* and analyzed by known image processing methods [3.18]. Specifically, the two-dimensional Fourier transform of the speech energy (or an equivalent transform) is calculated.

Only the low-frequency components of the transformed image are retained, thereby making the analysis independent of limited fluctuations in speaking rate and formant frequencies. Typically, a total of 49 Fourier coefficients gains excellent recognition results for both high-quality and telephone-quality speech [3.8].

3.13 Robust Speech Recognition

Robust speech recognition addresses the multifarious adverse conditions encountered in practical applications of ASR such as noise, reverberation, poor frequency response, and speaker variability. These questions have recently been addressed in a special issue of *Speech Communication* [3.19]. Among the important remedies is the emphasis on the modulation transfer function [3.20]. Like human hearing, which is most sensitive to modulation frequencies around 4 Hz, see Fig. 3.3, machines, too, stand much to gain from enhancing those modulation frequencies that are predominant in speech, i.e. 2–8 Hz [3.21], [3.22]. Figures 3.4–3.8 show the effects of modulation-frequency filtering on "clean," moderately noisy, very noisy, moderately reverberant and very reverberant speech.

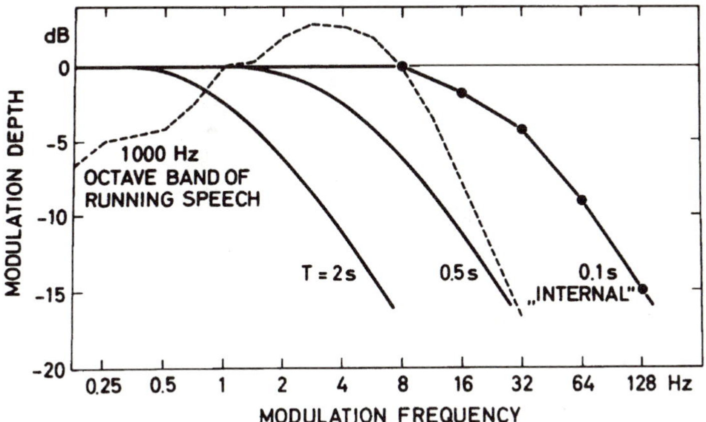

Fig. 3.3. The modulation transfer function of human hearing (labeled "internal") compared to the modulation spectrum of speech at a normal speaking rate. Note that the drop-off of the auditory system beyond 8 Hz allows all speech modulations to pass unhindered. – Also shown is the modulation tranfer function of a lecture hall (reverberation time $T = 0.5\,\text{s}$) and a concert hall ($T = 2\,\text{s}$). The latter especially makes speech very difficult to understand because long reverberation "blurs" the modulation

3.14 The Modulation Transfer Function

The modulation transfer function of a system characterizes the loss (or gain) of the degree of modulation of a modulated signal applied to its input. The fact that the human eye cannot follow rapid fluctuations in light intensity but perceives a steady luminance has allowed the motion picture and television industries to replace a continuously moving image by a discrete sequence

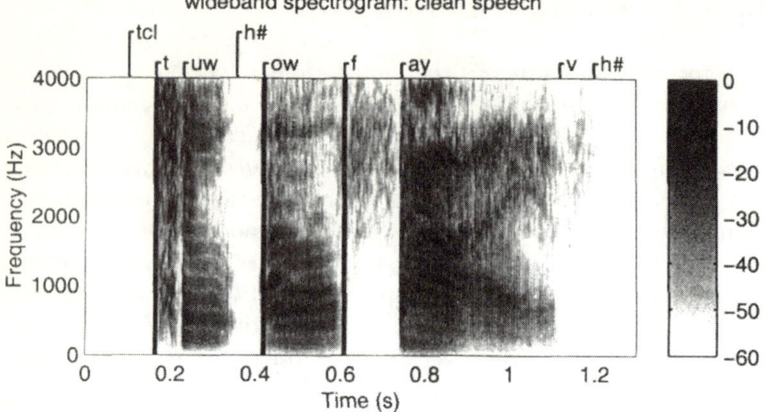

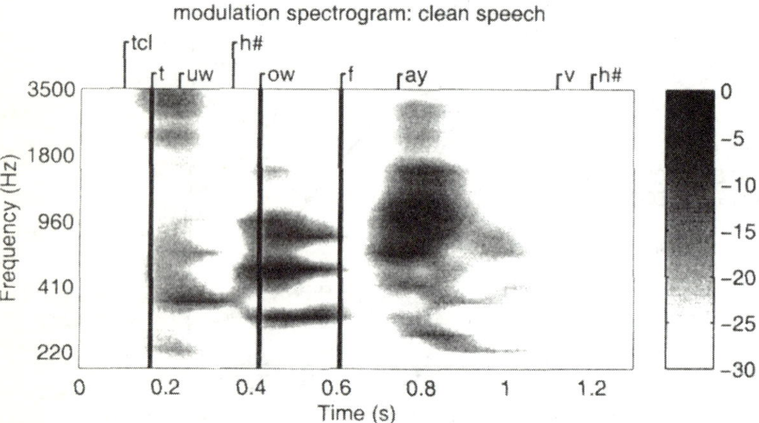

Fig. 3.4. *Top:* spectrogram of the utterance "two oh five" by a female speaker. *Bottom:* spectrogram for the same signal with modulation frequencies between 2 and 8 Hz enhanced. (Figures 3.4–3.8 were kindly supplied by Steven Greenberg and Brian E.D. Kingsbury)

of still images called frames. In television this inertia in visual perception is calles "flicker fusion": above a certain frame rate, say 60 per second, depending on viewing angle and light intensity, continuous motion is perceived.

Similarly, our sense of hearing is characterized by a certain inertia. The human ear perceives best modulation frequencies around 4 Hz. For modulation frequencies above 20 Hz there is a rapid fall-off of our ability to hear the modulation as modulation. [Certain birds, guineafowl (*numida maleagris*) among them, are sensitive to and in fact use much higher modulation frequencies.]

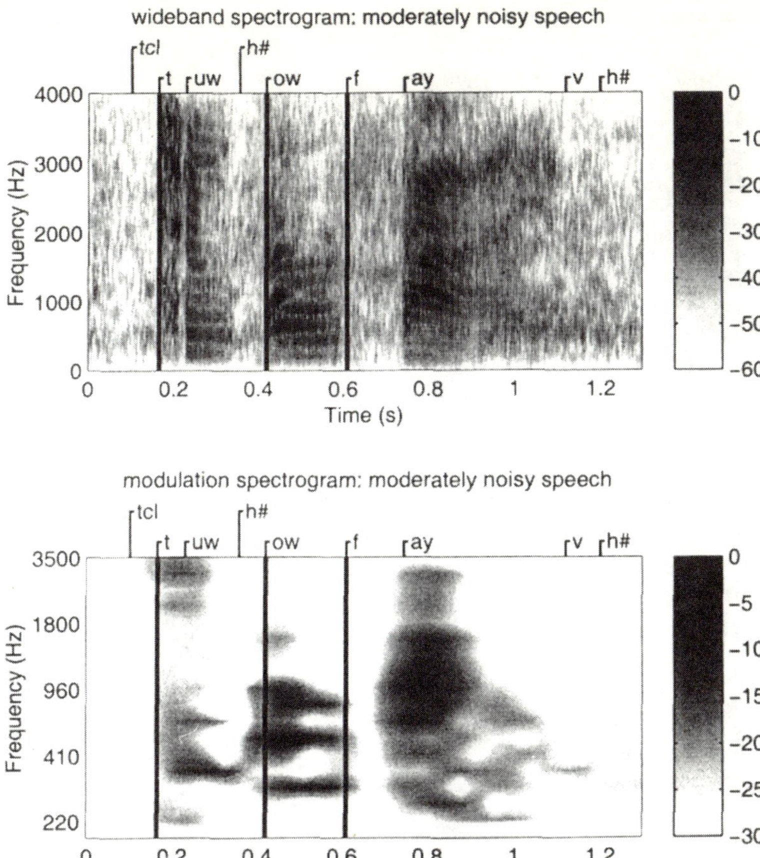

Fig. 3.5. The same as Fig. 3.4 for moderately noisy speech

It is interesting to note that human speech at normal speaking rates has a peak in its modulation-frequency distribution at 4 Hz. Is this a case of co-evolution of human speech and human hearing?

In a reverberant environment (think of a concert hall) the higher modulation frequencies of speech and music are attenuated by the smoothing effect of the reverberation. (This is in fact why music needs sufficient reverberation to sound good.) This attenuation in the degree of modulation is described by the modulation transfer function (MTF). In fact, by measuring the MTF with music, the reverberation time of a hall can be determined during an ongoing concert in the presence of an audience. (Habitually reverberation is measured by means of bangs – pistol or cannon shots – and filtered noise in the empty hall whose acoustics are of course quite different from the response of the occupied hall.)

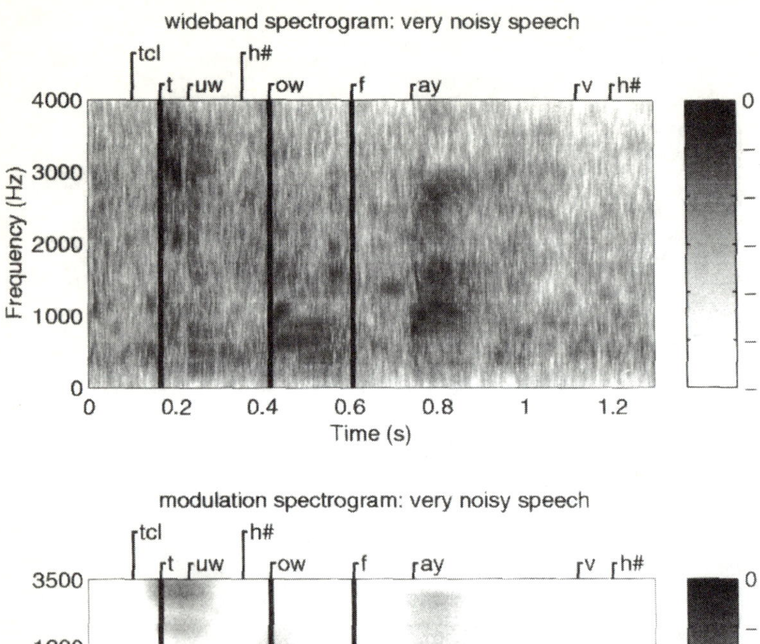

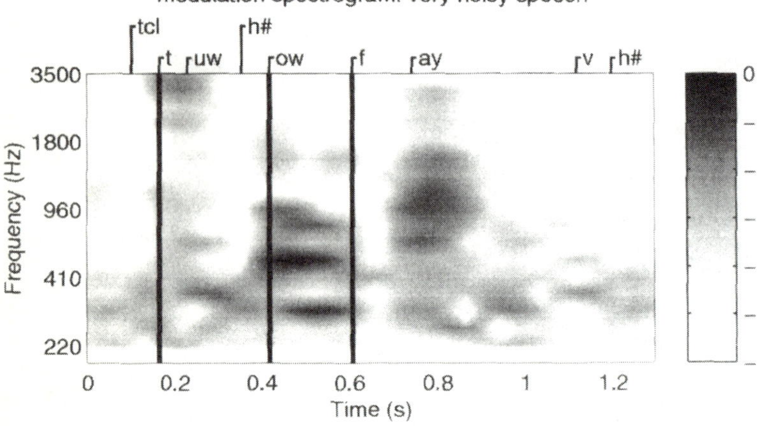

Fig. 3.6. The same as Fig. 3.4 for very noisy speech

Measurement of the MTF, which is also reduced by ambient noise, is now a preferred method of estimating speech intelligibility [3.23]. It is interesting to note that, for linear systems, the inverse Fourier transform of the MTF is the *squared* impulse response of the system [3.24] – just as the inverse Fourier transform of the transfer function itself is the impulse response. Thus, the MTF fits into a nice symmetrical pattern when Fourier transforms are considered: What the transfer function is to the impulse response is the MTF to the *squared* impulse response.

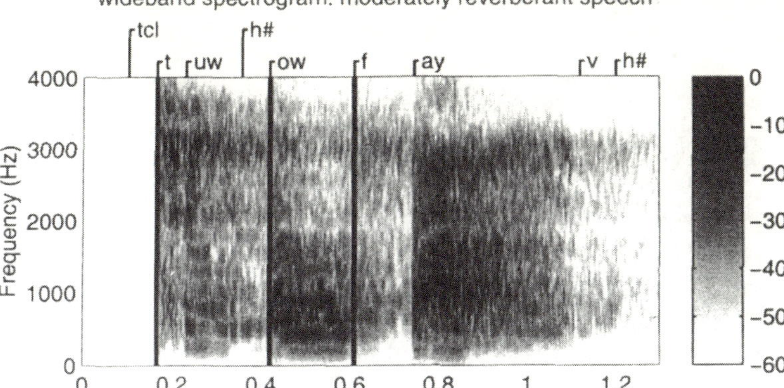

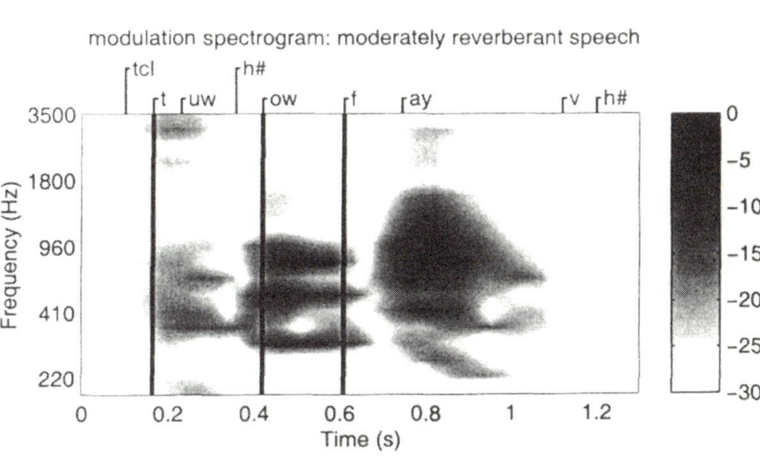

Fig. 3.7. The same as Fig. 3.4 for moderately reverberant speech

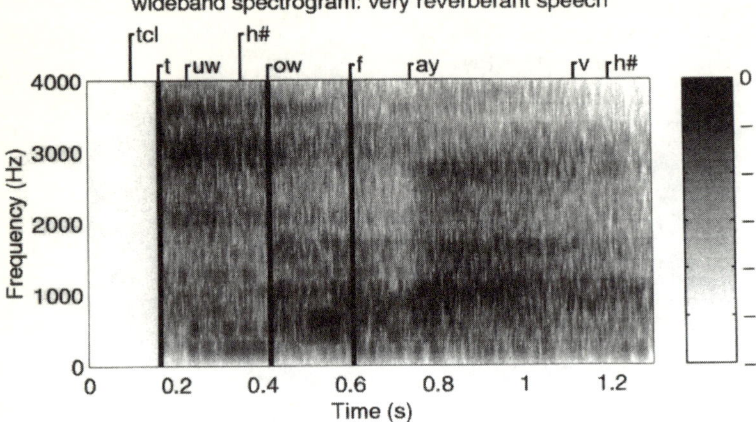

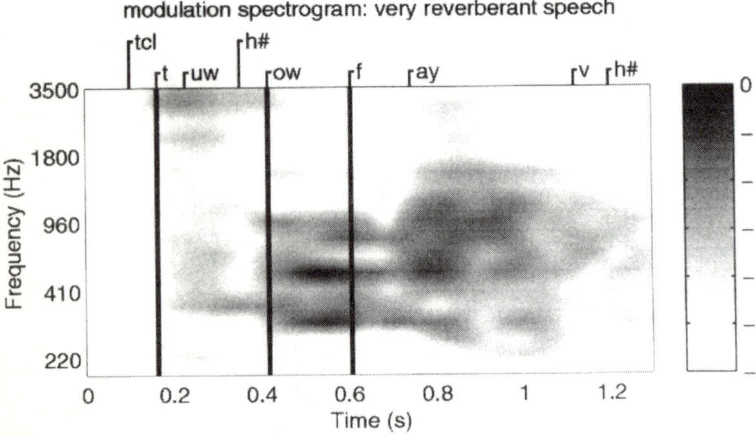

Fig. 3.8. The same as Fig. 3.4 for very reverberant speech. The improvements due to modulation-frequency filtering are evident for all tested impairments

4. Speech Compression

[British Prime Minister Ramsey] MacDonald has the gift of compressing the largest amount of words into the smallest amount of thought.

Winston Churchill (1874–1965)

Speeches in our culture are the vacuum that fill a vacuum.

John Kenneth Galbraith (born 1908)

Speech compression, once an esoteric preoccupation of a few speech enthusiasts, has taken on a practical significance of singular proportion. As mentioned before, it all began in 1928 when Homer Dudley, an engineer at Bell Laboratories, had a brilliant idea for compressing a speech signal with a bandwidth of over 3000 Hz into the 100-Hz bandwidth of a new transatlantic telegraph cable. Instead of sending the speech signal itself, he thought it would suffice to transmit a *description* of the signal to the far end. This basic idea of substituting for the signal a sufficient specification from which it could be recreated is still with us in the latest linear prediction standards and other methods of speech compression for mobile phones, secure digital voice channels, compressed-speech storage for multimedia applications, and, last but not least, Internet telephony and broadcasting via the World Wide Web.

The ultimate speech compression could be achieved by first recognizing speech and then resynthesizing a speech signal from the recognized text. Given that the entropy of written English, according to Shannon, is about 2.3 bits per letter and assuming a speaking rate equivalent to 10 letters per second, speech – without intonation and other personal characteristics – can be compressed into some 23 bits per second. Whether anyone would like to listen to the output from such a scheme is of course doubtful. But there may well be situations where this ultimate compression is the only option for speech transmission.

4.1 Vocoders

Dudley's original idea was to transmit information about the motions of the speaker's articulatory organs, the tongue, the lips, and so forth. When this turned out to be impossible (in fact, it is still difficult to extract these parameters from a running speech signal), Dudley suggested sending a succession of *short-time spectra* instead. This led to the *channel vocoder* in which each speech spectrum is described by its smooth spectral *envelope* and, in the case of voiced sounds, the spectral *fine structure*, that is, the spacing of the harmonics of the fundamental frequency or voice "pitch" [4.1].

As described previously, the first important application of the vocoder occurred in World War II when it was used to encrypt the telephone link between Churchill in London and Roosevelt in Washington. The compression made possible by the vocoder permitted the speech signal to be encoded by as few as 1551 bits per second, a bitrate that fitted into existing transatlantic radio channels [4.2].

The first X-System, as it was called, was operated on 1 April 1943, just seven months after this complex project had been launched. This short time span is all the more astonishing considering that much of the circuitry was completely new. One of the ingredients of this lightning success – always crucial in a national emergency – was the decision to assemble the system, as far as possible, from existing, off-the-shelf Western Electric hardware even if it was not always ideal.

The X-System occupied 30 seven-foot relay racks and consumed 30 kW of electrical power (to produce, as the sarcastic saying went, "one milliwatt of poor-quality speech."). After Washington and London, X-Systems were installed in North Africa, Paris, Hawaii, Australia and the Philippines [4.3]. The design of the X-System gave a considerable impetus to pulse code modulation or PCM [4.4]. It also stimulated renewed thinking about secrecy systems in general, especially on the part of Claude Shannon, who had returned to Bell Labs in 1941 from MIT and Princeton and who served on several committees dealing with cryptanalysis [4.5]. In particular Shannon was asked to take a close look at the modular arithmetic (then called "reentry process") used in the encryption to make sure that nothing had been overlooked in the assumption that the key was unbreakable.

It is interesting to note that Shannon's subsequent paper on "information theory" (as it has been misleadingly called) was closely tied to his work on secrecy systems [4.6].

The vocoder work for civilian applications was resumed after the war, but it had to start almost from scratch because the progress made during the war, along with numerous patents, were classified "top secret" and kept under wraps for decades [4.7]. For general telephony, the principal difficulty was the "pitch problem," the need to track the exact fundamental frequency in real time. To make matters worse, the fundamental frequency of most telephone speech is actually missing in telephone lines that do not transmit frequencies below 200 or 300 Hz.

When the author joined these efforts at Bell Telephone Laboratories in 1954, the most promising approach to the pitch problem was autocorrelation analysis. Of course, for a steady, noise-free voiced speech sound, the first maximum of the autocorrelation function (at nonzero delay) occurs at a delay corresponding to an integral pitch period. But, unfortunately, speech signals are not stationary and the highest maximum in the delay region of interest often corresponds to a delay of one pitch period plus or minus one *formant* period. A vocoder driven from such a pitch signal sounds rather queer – drunk or "tipsy," to be more precise. To overcome these difficulties dozens of schemes were floated and tried – and found wanting for various reasons [4.8]. The pitch problem was finally laid to rest with the invention of cepstrum pitch detectors [4.9]. The cepstrum is defined as the Fourier transform of the *logarithm* of the power spectrum, see Chap. 10.

However, even the cepstrum had problems with tracking the pitch of two different voices on the same line. For such cases, a better solution than the cepstrum turned out to be the Fourier transform of the *magnitude* of the Fourier transform, in other words, replacing the logarithm of the power spectrum (as in the cepstrum) by the square root of the power spectrum [4.10].

Another method that sometimes outperformed the cepstrum is the "harmonic product spectrum," in which each observed harmonic frequency is considered, in a probabilistic manner, an integer multiple of the fundamental frequency [4.11].

The frequency-channel vocoder was soon joined by numerous other parametric compression schemes such as formant vocoders [4.12], harmonic compressors [4.13], correlation vocoders [4.14], and phase vocoders [4.15]; see [4.16] for a review of speech analysis and synthesis by vocoders, see J. L. Flanagan's comprehensive survey [4.17].

4.2 Digital Simulation

Before the advent of digital simulation in the late 1950s, new ideas for speech processing had to be tried out by building analog devices. More often than not, failure was attributed not to the idea per se but to a flawed implementation. All this was changed drastically by digital simulation [4.18], facilitated by the BLODI (for BLOck DIagram) compiler of J. L. Kelly, V. A. Vyssotsky and Carol Lochbaum [4.19].

One of the first applications of digital simulation was made by M. V. Mathews, namely a method for audio *waveform* compression called *extremal coding* [4.20]. In extremal coding only the positions and amplitudes of the maxima and minima of the waveform are maintained, while intermediate values are approximated by a cubic "spline function."

This was one of the first successful digital simulations of a signal processor on a general purpose computer at Bell Labs. Digital simulation had been transplanted from MIT to Bell Labs by Mathews in 1955, when he joined Bell's acoustics research. Extremal coding was tailor-made for digital simulation because computer-running times were quite reasonable. (The author later took digital simulation to "unreasonable" lengths by simulating signal processors containing hundreds of sharp bandpass filters [4.13] and simulating sound transmission and reverberation in full-size concert halls [4.21].)

Some of the processing was done on the largest extant IBM computer at their New York City headquarters at Madison Avenue and 57th Street. A few seconds of speech typically filled a large car trunk with punched cards. At that moment in the history of signal processing, digital simulation involved risking parking tickets.

4.3 Linear Prediction

Linear prediction, especially in the form of *code-excited linear prediction* (CELP) has become the method of choice for speech- and even audio compression.

The mathematics of linear prediction goes back to Carl Friedrich Gauss (1777–1855) and Norbert Wiener (1894–1964). Gauss correctly predicted the reappearance of the asteroid Ceres after it had been lost in the glare of the sun and he gained world-wide fame for this feat. Wiener was instrumental in marshaling prediction for anti-aircraft fire-control during World War II.

Linear prediction came to the fore in speech research in 1966. After 12 years of work on vocoders, the author had become somewhat impatient with their unsatisfactory speech quality. The idea was to encode speech signals not in a rigid vocoder-like fashion but to leave room for 'error' in the coding process. Specifically each new speech sample was "predicted" by a weighted linear combination of, typically, 8 to 12 immediately preceding samples. The weights were determined to minimize the r.m.s. error of the prediction.

Thus was born linear predictive coding (LPC) for speech signals with a prediction residual or "error" signal to take up the slack from the prediction. Since speech is a highly variable signal, B. S. Atal and the author opted for an *adaptive* predictor [4.22].

There are in fact two kinds of major redundancies in a voiced speech signal: from the formant structure (decaying resonances of the vocal tract) and the quasiperiodicity ("pitch") of the vocal tract oscillations. Thus, our adaptive predictor consisted of two parts: a short-time (ca. 1 ms) predictor for the formant structure or spectral envelope and a long-time (3 to 20 ms) predictor for the pitch of voiced speech. We chose 8 predictor coefficients for the short-time predictor: two each for the three formants in the telephone band and two more to take care of the glottal pulse and the frequency dependence of the radiation from the lips. With only one bit per sample allotted to the prediction residual (but no coding of the slowly-varying predictor coefficients) a speech quality indistinguishable from the input was achieved [4.23].

Having taken up research in hearing in the 1950s (with the aim of designing better-sounding speech coders), the author proposed replacing the r.m.s. error criterion in linear prediction by a *subjective* measure, namely the perceived *loudness of the quantizing noise*. Given a proper spectral shape, the quantizing noise becomes less audible or is even completely *masked* by the speech signal itself. Beginning in 1972, J. L. Hall, Jr., and the author measured the *masking of noise by signals* (as opposed to the customary masking of signals by noise) [4.24]. The result was linear prediction with a perceptual error criterion [4.25].

Methods of perceptual audio coding (PAC) have now found wide application in speech, music, and general audio coding. Together with an excitation signal derived from a code book (code-excited linear predictor or CELP), bit rates for the prediction residual of 1/4 bit per sample for high-quality speech were realized by Atal and the author in the early 1980s [4.26]. For audio compression, rates as low as 16 kilobits per sample were demonstrated by D. Sinha, J. D. Johnston, S. Dorward and S. R. Quackenbush. Near compact-disc (CD) quality was achieved at 64 kbps [4.27]!

4.3.1 Linear Prediction and Resonances

The fact that a single resonance is characterized by just two parameters manifests itself in another way – in a manner that is much easier to exploit. If we turn our attention from the frequency domain, we can see that for a single, unperturbed, freely decaying resonance (after excitation has ceased) just three successive samples determine the entire future of the waveform. More generally, if we consider speech below 4 kHz to be equivalent to four resonances, then $4 \cdot 2 + 1 = 9$ speech waveform samples suffice for a complete specification of the *free* decay. Any additional samples are useful for the specification of the vocal cord excitation function, the effect (if any) of the nasal cavity, and the radiation characteristics of the lips.

Now, if we insist on extracting the resonance frequencies and bandwidths from these waveform samples, we would be back where we started: the "intractable" formant-tracking problem. Instead, let us ask whether we cannot generate the speech spectrum from these waveform samples *directly*, without the detour via the formant frequencies. The answer is a resounding "yes". The proper prescription is the aforementioned *linear prediction*, which, together with the development of potent chips, has led to the great growth of speech processing that we have witnessed during the past decade.

Historically, the introduction of linear prediction to speech was triggered by a train of thought different from the one sketched above. The problem that the author and his collaborator B.S. Atal turned their attention to in

1966 was the following: for television pictures, the encoding of each picture element ("pixel") as if it was completely unpredictable is of course rather wasteful, because adjacent pixels are correlated. Similarly, for voiced speech, each sample is known to be highly correlated with the corresponding sample that occurred one pitch period earlier. In addition, each sample is correlated with the *immediately* preceding samples, because the resonances of the vocal tract "ring" for a finite time that equals their reciprocal bandwidth (roughly 10 ms). Therefore, at a sampling rate of 8 kHz, blocks of 80 samples show an appreciable correlation. However, since the number of "independent" parameters in a speech signal is approximately 12 (two parameters for each resonance and a few extra parameters for the excitation function, nasal coupling and lip radiation) it suffices to consider the first 12 or so correlation coefficients and use only these in the prediction process.

Pursuing this predictive philosophy then, and focusing on the short-time correlations first, we want to approximate a current sample s_n by a linear combination of immediately preceding samples s_{n-k}:

$$s_n = -a_1 s_{n-1} - a_2 s_{n-2} - \ldots - a_p s_{n-p} + e_n \, , \tag{4.1}$$

where p is the "order" of the predictor and e_n is the "prediction residual," that is, that part of s_n that cannot be represented by the weighted sum of p previous samples. The weights in (4.1) are called the predictor coefficients [4.28].

How should the weights a_k be chosen? The analytically simplest method is to minimize the squared prediction residual averaged over N samples:

$$E := \sum_{n=1}^{N} e_n^2 = \sum_{n=1}^{N} \left(\sum_{k=0}^{p} a_k s_{n-k} \right)^2 \, , \quad a_0 = 1 \, . \tag{4.2}$$

A typical value for N is 80, corresponding to a "time window" of 10 ms. Larger values of N, implying summation over longer time intervals, would interfere with the proper analysis of the perceptually important rapid transitions between successive speech sounds. Much smaller values of N would make the analysis unnecessarily prone to noise and other disturbing influences.

Minimization of E with respect to the a_k means setting the partial derivatives $\partial E / \partial a_m$ equal to zero:

$$\frac{\partial E}{\partial a_m} = \sum_{n=1}^{N} 2 s_{n-m} \sum_{k=0}^{p} a_k s_{n-k} = 0 \, . \tag{4.3}$$

Inverting the order of the two summations in equation 4.3 yields:

$$\sum_{k=0}^{p} r_{mk} a_k = 0 \, , \tag{4.4}$$

where we have introduced the correlation coefficients:

$$r_{mk} = \sum_{n=1}^{N} s_{n-m} s_{n-k} \; . \tag{4.5}$$

Having determined the correlation coefficients r_{km} from the speech signal, we can use (4.4) to calculate the predictor coefficients a_k. Remembering that $a_0 = 1$, we have:

$$\sum_{k=1}^{p} r_{mk} a_k = -r_{m0} \; , \tag{4.6}$$

or in matrix notation:

$$Ra = -r_0 \; , \tag{4.7}$$

where R is the $p \times p$ matrix with entries r_{mk}, and a and r_0 are the column vectors corresponding to a_k and r_{m0} in equation (4.6), respectively. Equation (4.7) is solved by matrix inversion, giving the desired predictor coefficients:

$$a = -R^{-1} r_0 \; . \tag{4.8}$$

Of course, for R^{-1} to exist, the rank of R must be p.

Numerous algorithms have been proposed to speed up the calculation of R^{-1}. Some are based on the fact that R becomes a *Toeplitz* matrix if we set

$$r_{mk} = r_{|m-k|} \; . \tag{4.9}$$

This is a justified simplification because the correlation r_{mk} depends mostly on the *relative* delay $|m - k|$ between s_{n-m} and s_{n-k}. Other algorithms exploit the fact that the partial correlation coefficients [4.29] can be computed by simple recursion, which reduces the total number of multiply-and-add operations. These are very important savings when it comes to the design of coders working in real-time.

The partial correlations are also directly related to the reflection coefficients of a lossless acoustic tube consisting of cylindrical sections of equal length [4.30]. Thus, there is a one-to-one relationship between partial correlations and cross-sectional areas, i.e. the geometry, of such a tube.

Figure 4.1 shows a speech signal (upper trace) and the prediction residuals after formant prediction (center trace, amplified by 10 dB). As expected, the short-time correlation is almost completely removed. But the long-time correlation, from pitch period to pitch period, still persists – as evidenced by the large spikes at pitch-period intervals.

To remove this correlation, we have to find out for which delay in the pitch range (for example, 3–20 ms) the autocorrelation function of the prediction residual has a maximum and how high it is. Then we subtract the properly delayed and amplitude scaled prediction residual from itself. The result is the lower trace in Fig. 4.1, amplified by another 10 dB for better visibility. The resulting residual, after both short-time ("formant") and long-time ("pitch") prediction is a highly unpredictable waveform of relatively small power. The signal power divided by the power of the prediction residual is

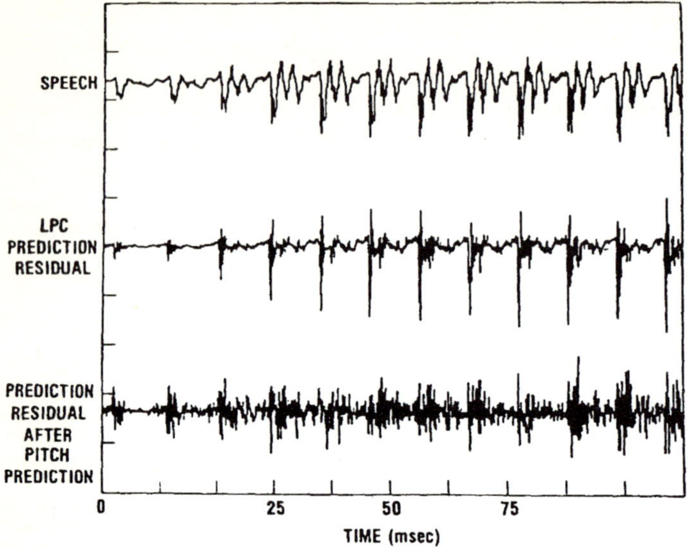

Fig. 4.1. From the speech signal to the prediction residual. The top trace shows a 100-ms excerpt from a male speech signal, the onset of a vowel. Note the increasing intensity and periodicity with a period of about 8.3 ms (120 Hz). – The center trace, amplified by 10 dB to show more detail, illustrates the effect of predicting the formant structure, which manifests itself in "bumpy" spectral envelope and short-delay correlations. The "LPC" residual resulting from linear prediction has a (nearly) flat spectral envelope, but a pronounced harmonic line structure. This spectrally flattened signal is ideal for pitch detection purposes, because the periodicity due to the voice pitch stands out clearly, unencumbered by the formant structure (which has given classical pitch detection so much trouble). – The bottom trace, amplified by 20 dB relative to the top trace, shows the prediction residual after both short-delay (formant) and long-delay (pitch) prediction. This residual signal, although still showing traces of pitch and formant structure, has an essentially flat spectrum. Encoding it under a minimum mean-square-error criterion leads to more *audible* quantizing noise than would a spectrally weighted error-criterion. An appropriately chosen *subjective* error criterion exploits the fact that the spectral regions of the quantizing noise that coincide with a formant are reduced in loudness or are even inaudible as a result of auditory masking (see Figs. 4.4 and 4.5)

called the *prediction gain.* In Fig. 4.1 the prediction gain is about 20 dB. Again, note that this removal of redundancy from the original speech signal has been achieved by exploiting the formant and pitch structures of speech signals *without explicitly measuring formant frequencies and pitch-periods.* For example, if the delay for which the long-time correlation was a maximum was *not* equal to the pitch period, it would not matter at all. In fact, we do not *want* to measure the pitch period (a difficult task, just like precise formant tracking); we want to remove as much *correlation* as possible by the prediction process. This robustness to measurement "error" is just one more reason for the success of linear prediction!

There is an interesting frequency-domain interpretation of minimizing the prediction error: minimizing the prediction error in the time domain is equivalent to minimizing the average ratio of the speech energy spectrum to the estimated energy spectrum based on the all-pole model. The minimization is also equivalent to maximizing the *spectral flatness* of the prediction error, defined as the ratio of the geometric mean of the error energy spectrum to its algebraic mean. For a flat spectrum this ratio is 1; for highly nonflat spectra the ratio tends to 0 [4.31].

4.3.2 The Innovation Sequence

From (4.1), it is obvious that we could synthesize the speech samples s_n by feeding he prediction residual or "innovation sequence" e_n (if it were available) into a synthesis filter. Defining a prediction filter with the (discrete and finite) impulse response $1, a_1, a_2, \ldots, a_p$ and adopting the z-transform notation $s(z)$ for s_n, $e(z)$ for e_n and

$$A(z) = 1 + a_1 z^{-1} + \cdots + a_p z^{-p} \tag{4.10}$$

for the prediction filter, (4.1) can be written as:

$$s(z) \cdot A(z) = e(z) \tag{4.1a}$$

that is, the speech signal could be obtained from the innovation sequence $e(z)$ by filtering it with $1/A(z)$:

$$s(z) = e(z)\frac{1}{A(z)} \ . \tag{4.11}$$

According to the fundamental theorem of algebra, the polynomial $A(z)$ has precisely p zeros and no poles. The filter $1/A(z)$ therefore has only poles and is called an "all-pole filter".

Now the circle is complete; we wanted to exploit the fact that speech signals can be efficiently represented by poles – without actually having to specify them. Equation (4.11) is the desired answer – the prediction filter $A(z)$ represents these poles, a fact which is brought into evidence by writing $A(z)$ as a product, according to the fundamental theorem of algebra

$$A(z) = (1 - z_1/z)(1 - z_2/z)\cdots \ , \tag{4.12}$$

where $z_1, z_2, \cdots$ are the zeros of $A(z)$ or the poles of $1/A(z)$. The relationship between the complex poles z_k and the formant frequencies ω_k and bandwidths $\Delta\omega_k$, in units of the sampling angular frequency, is the following:

$$\omega_k = \mathrm{Im}\{\ln z_k\} \tag{4.13}$$

$$\Delta\omega_k = -2\ln|z_k| \ , \tag{4.14}$$

where ln is the natural logarithm. Figure 4.2 shows a voiced speech waveform segment (upper right) and the corresponding spectrum together with spectral

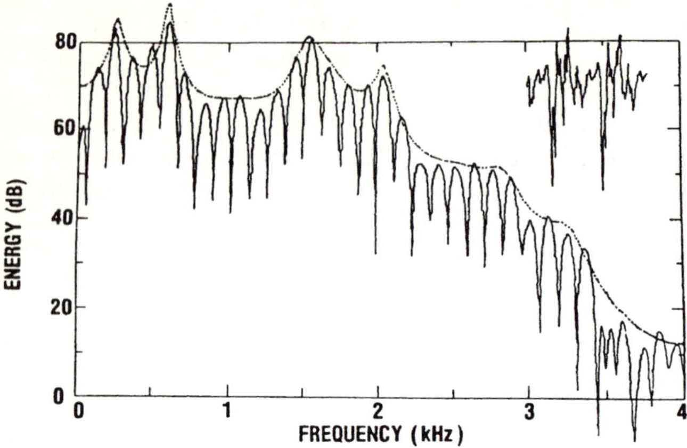

Fig. 4.2. A short segment of a voiced speech signal (upper right inset) is Fourier transformed to yield this logarithmic power spectrum. Note the regular harmonic structure of the spectrum at multiples of the fundamental frequency (ca. 120 Hz). The dotted line is the spectral envelope computed from the frequency response of the prediction filter. – Short-time spectra, such as those shown in Figure 4.2 and 4.3, have a high frequency resolution in spite of the shortness of the time window. This feat is accomplished by performing the Fourier transform on the *spectrally flattened* speech signal, thereby minimizing the frequency uncertainties ("splatter") resulting from short time windows

envelope defined by the filter $1/A(z)$. Note the harmonics of the fundamental frequency, characteristic of quasi-periodic voiced speech sounds and the good approximation of the spectral envelope $1/A(z)$ (the continuous line "riding" on the spectrum).

Figure 4.3 shows corresponding results for an unvoiced (fricative) speech sound. There is no periodicity in the time waveform (upper right) and no harmonic line structure in the spectrum. Although the spectral envelope may not have been produced by poles alone (there is evidence of spectral zeros), the approximation of the spectral envelope by $1/A(z)$ is still more than adequate.

4.3.3 Single Pulse Excitation

In a linear predictive coder (LPC), the excitation is exactly as in the classical frequency-channel vocoder. An excitation source, emitting either pitch pulses or random noise, is controlled by voiced–unvoiced decisions and pitch detection at the transmitter. However, the excitation signal does not drive a set of parallel frequency channels but rather the synthesis filter $1/A(z)$ whose parameters are set by the predictive analysis at the receiver.

Linear prediction represented a great leap forward in the analysis and synthesis of speech, but the quality of the LPC speech, although noticeably improved over that of the channel vocoder, still had a buzzy twang to it (possibly because the sharp ("zero-phase") pulses used in the excitation

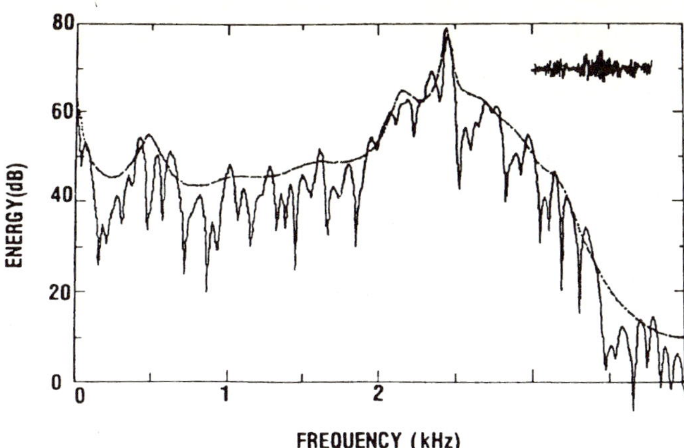

Fig. 4.3. A short segment of an unvoiced speech signal (upper right inset) and its Fourier transform, obtained by the method described in the caption to Fig. 4.2. Note the absence of harmonic frequencies and the broad spectral peak, characteristic of unvoiced sounds. Noise-free coding of such hiss-like sounds is not critical, because "noise plus noise equals noise" and the ear is somewhat more tolerant to spectral distortions of fricative speech sounds

have too much phase coherence between their harmonic frequency components). To alleviate this problem two rather different approaches have been pursued: *multipulse excitation* and *stochastic coding* of the prediction residual. While single-pulse excitation requires pitch detection, multipulse and stochastic coding proceed *without pitch detection*, thereby bypassing one of the most difficult problems of speech analysis.

The measurement of the voice fundamental frequency [4.32] must be very accurate because the human ear is highly sensitive to pitch errors. One reason why precise pitch detection has been so difficult is due to the formant structure of speech signals. For example, a low first-formant frequency will sometimes be confused with the fundamental frequency (especially for female voices, which generally have a higher pitch).

Two methods have been very successful in eliminating the bothersome formant structure: *cepstrum* pitch detection [4.9] and *spectrum flattening*, first practiced in the voice-excited vocoders (VEV) [4.33] and proposed for pitch detection by M.M. Sondhi [4.34]. In the context of linear predictive coding, spectrum flattening is particularly germane, because the prediction filter $A(z)$ is in fact a very effective spectrum flattener. How prominent the fundamental frequency becomes after filtering with $A(z)$ is illustrated by the center trace of Fig. 4.1, which shows prominent pitch pulses that should certainly ease the task of almost any pitch detector. Interestingly, there is a close connection between predictor coefficients and the *cepstrum* (see Sect. 10.14) which allows the computation of one from the other, either recursively or directly, see Appendix B.

4.3.4 Multipulse Excitation

Careful listening – and subsequent spectral analysis – has shown that replacing the excitation signal by a single pulse per pitch period, no matter how well positioned the pulse may be, produces audible distortion (the already noted twang). B.S. Atal [4.35] therefore suggested using more than one pulse, typically eight, per period and adjusting the individual pulse positions and amplitudes sequentially to minimize a "perceptual error," that is, a spectrally weighted mean-square error. This technique results in a better speech quality, not only because the prediction residual is better approximated by several pulses per pitch period (instead of a single one), but also because the multipulse algorithm does not require pitch detection. In fact, a predetermined number of excitation pulses are assigned to each time window regardless of the pitch.

However, herein lies also the weakness of multipulse excitation: the fixed rectangular time window associated with multipulse synthesis causes some roughness in the output speech because of rapid non-pitch-synchronous variations of the predictor and multipulse parameters. Thus, while multipulse excitation has led to further progress in speech coding, problems of speech quality persist. These shortcomings can be avoided by our next approach.

4.3.5 Adaptive Predictive Coding

Adaptive predictive coding (APC) of speech signals was in fact the original route taken when predictive analysis was first applied to speech in 1967 [4.22]. The idea was to avoid the pitch problem and associated difficulties of excitation altogether by transmitting a quantized version of the prediction residual itself to the receiver to drive the synthesis filter $1/A(z)$. Because of the *prediction gain* [4.23] of APC, typically 20 dB or more for stationary voiced speech sounds, a very rough quantization of the prediction residual could be expected to suffice. In fact, in the earliest implementations of APC, a *one-bit* quantizer gave respectable quality, corresponding in subjective quality to 5- or 6-bit PCM!

To this day, it is not entirely clear why the perceived quality of one-bit APC was *that* high. The author speculated then (and still believes) that the ear is more sensitive to spectral errors during stationary speech sounds – precisely when the prediction gain is high and the quantizing error correspondingly low. By contrast, during rapid transitions between different speech sounds, when the prediction gain is *a fortiori* small, the ear's sensitivity to spectral error is small, so that it does not notice the greater quantizing error during transitions.

This seductive hypothesis would explain the success of APC, but is has never been formally tested. It could be that the ear has available, in parallel, spectral analysis channels with different amounts of frequency resolution and that it uses wider channels (which would "gloss over" much spectral detail) when analyzing fast transients, because narrow channels – according to the Uncertainty Principle – lack the necessary time resolution to decode the important temporal cues in speech sound transients.

The fact that the ear uses wider frequency channels when listening to speech (as opposed to slowly varying tones, for example) is nicely illustrated in reverberant rooms: the frequency response of such rooms fluctuates by 40 dB or more [4.36], yet we are not aware of these fluctuations. As E.C. Wente, inventor of the condensor microphone, remarked when he first saw such a response "how can we hear at all in rooms?" – considering that we strive to keep frequency response irregularities in our transducers (microphones and loudspeakers) down to a few decibels. The answer in this case has been unambiguous: the frequency analysis of the ear, when listening to fast-changing signals, is so wideband that it does not resolve the peaks and valleys of the room response that are very narrowly spaced. (The average spacing is $4/T$, or about 4 Hz for a reverberation time T of 1 s [4.36].)

4.3.6 Masking of Quantizing Noise

We have just encountered one of the important subjective viewpoints, namely the ear's frequency resolution, that hold the key to efficient high-quality speech coding. Another important observation is that the quantizing noise in APC (or any quantizing scheme) is "masked," that is, made inaudible, or at least reduced in loudness, by the simultaneous presence of the speech signal itself. Auditory masking is a pervasive phenomenon of hearing. One of the latest manifestations is the walkman-cum-earphones equipped jogger (cyclist or mere pedestrian) who is completely oblivious to the acoustic traffic surrounding him – including such potentially life-saving sounds as that of an approaching truck or a simple honk of a car horn.

A basic psychoacoustic observation is that any spectral prominence (such as a speech formant) will mask less intense sounds in its immediate frequency neighborhood. These neighborhoods are called "critical bands" (about 100 Hz below 600 Hz and one sixth of the center frequency above 600 Hz). In addition, there is considerable masking or loudness reduction at frequencies *higher* than that of the masker. This frequency asymmetry of masking has a simple physiological explanation: sounds are propagated in the inner ear by traveling waves that go from the places where high frequencies are detected to those for the lower frequencies. Thus, the detectors ("hair cells") for high frequencies "see" both high and low frequencies, while the low-frequency detectors see only low frequencies. Hence, low frequency components can interfere with (mask) higher frequencies, but not the other way around.

While much data pertaining to the masking of tones and speech by noise has accumulated in the literature, there is relatively little known about the reverse masking situation: the masking of noise, such as quantizing noise, by tones or speech. To fill this void, J.L. Hall and the author have performed numerous masking experiments of noise by tones [4.24]. While some aspects of masking, such as the shapes and widths of the critical bands were found to be similar in the two masking situations, astounding differences were also discovered. While a tone masked by noise becomes inaudible when its level falls more than 4–6 dB below the noise level in the tone's critical band, a *noise*, to become inaudible in the presence of a masking tone, must fall from 20 to 30 dB below the tone level.

Why this asymmetry? The reason becomes clear through introspection when listening to a noise just above its masked threshold, that is, when the noise is barely audible. At levels that far below the tone level, the noise does not even sound like an additive noise. Rather the tone, which sounds clean and pure without the noise, sounds a little rough or distorted – and this roughness is just the kind of distortion caused by quantizing noise that we want to avoid in APC and other digital representations of speech signals. Luckily, multitone signals and speech are not quite as sensitive to distortion by noise. However, the spectral shapes associated with the masking phenomena are in all cases similar and these spectral shapes should enter the design of speech coders in the form of *weighting functions* for the quantizing noise [4.25]. More specifically, in optimizing the subjective quality of synthetic speech, one should minimize the spectrally weighted quantizing noise power that appears in the output signal, as illustrated in Figs. 4.4 and 4.5.

4.3.7 Instantaneous Quantizing Versus Block Coding

Instantaneous quantizers have two grave disadvantages: the achievable signal-to-noise ratio (SNR) is below optimum and the quantizing noise spectrum is difficult to control at the desired low bit-rates. An optimum one-bit instantaneous quantizer for a memory-less Gaussian source, for example, gives an SNR of 4.4 dB, while rate-distortion theory tells us that 6 dB can be approached when coding long blocks of samples together [4.31].

This is true even though the samples are independent! This is, in fact, one of the main lessons of Shannon's information theory: Its promises (of error-free transmission at rates below the channel capacity, for example) come true only in the limit of large sample numbers. (Shannon's famous discovery is related to what mathematicians now call *ultrametricity*. In an ultrametric space, such as formed by long blocks of signal samples, the usual triangular inequality $a \leq b + c$, where a, b, and c are the sides of a triangle, is replaced by the *ultrametric inequality* $a \leq \mathrm{Max}\{b, c\}$, which permits only an isosceles triangle whose base does not exceed its sides in length. Specifically, the three Euclidean distances between three normalized Gaussian vectors of N dimensions, $N \gg 1$, are all approximately equal, giving rise to an equilateral triangle in multidimensional space.)

Thus, we are forced to give up, for two compelling reasons, the convenience of quantizing the prediction residual sample by sample. Instead, we must consider many samples together – blocks of samples – and to select one

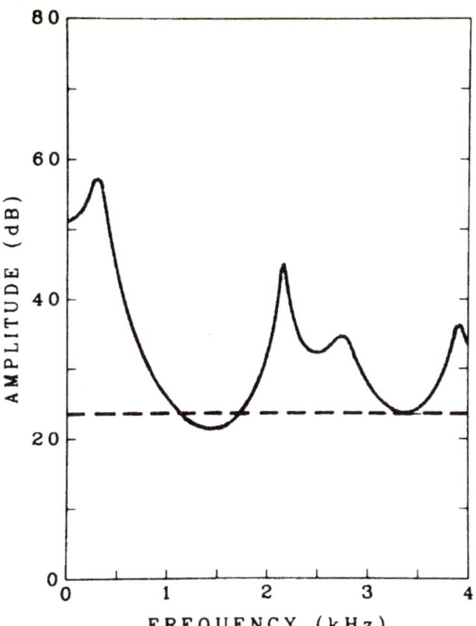

Fig. 4.4. The spectral envelope of a vowel sound and that of the (idealized) flat quantizing noise resulting from minimizing the mean-square error. The noise would be audible where its level exceeds a level about 3 dB below the spectral envelope

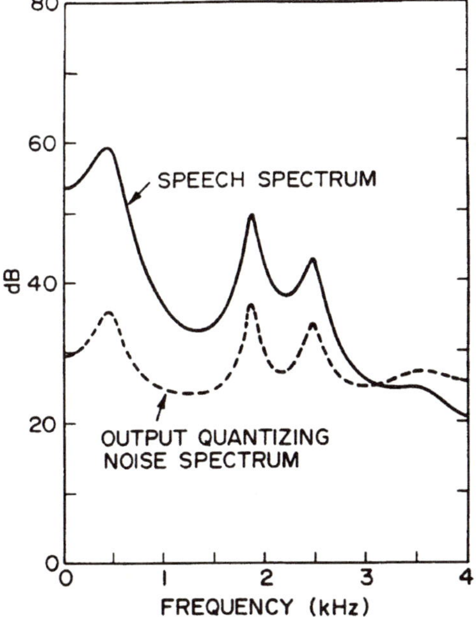

Fig. 4.5. The optimum noise shape (dashed line) for the vowel envelope spectrum shown (solid line). This shaped noise spectrum results from minimizing the subjective *loudness* – not the physical power – of the quantizing noise. This strategy, based on human auditory perception, is equivalent to a spectral weighting criterion. In the example shown here, the quantizing noise, although only a few decibels below the speech spectral envelope at most frequencies, is nearly inaudible

code word from a given codebook to represent each block of samples. This "codebook" coding replaces the inappropriate instantaneous quantizing by vector quantization.

The difficulty of this approach lies in the searching of voluminous codebooks. For example, the coding of blocks of 80 samples at just 1 bit/sample requires a codebook containing $2^{80} \approx 10^{24}$ different codewords! Obviously, such astronomical codebooks can never be searched completely – in fact, they cannot even be written down.

One is therefore forced to adopt incomplete search methods, hoping that the best codeword found in this manner will not be too bad. One promising approach is *tree coding*, in which never more than a given manageable number of alternatives is kept open during a sequential search procedure through the tree (see [4.37]). In this manner, searching trees of height 80 while keeping up to 64 different paths open at any one time during the search, it has been possible to represent the prediction residual by one or even as little as one-half bit per sample (40 bits for a block of length 80) with excellent quality – thanks, no doubt, also to the proper error weighting) [4.26].

4.3.8 Delays

Another problem with the coding of long blocks of data is the extra delay it engenders. While such delays are quite tolerable in one-way transmissions, they may play havoc in real-time two-way communications such as telephone conversations. Geostationary communication satellites, for example, introduce a roundtrip delay of 600 ms which is quite annoying to the talkers and even disruptive, especially when the parties involved are "in a hurry" or impatient. (Both speakers may start speaking at the same time, then – when they hear the other side speaking – stop, then start speaking again etc.) Whereas the telephone *equipment* may not break down, tempers sometimes do.[1]

In the early days of digital simulations and digital signal processing people were also afraid of extra delays due to finite processing speeds (stemming, for example, from the complex algorithms to incorporate subjective error criteria in the coder). But, the author, not knowing much about hardware, always thought that problems due to high processing complexity would simply go away sooner or later – which they did, sooner rather than later.

---

[1] There is an easy way to check whether one is connected by a high-altitude, long-delay satellite or a fast transoceanic cable: the first party saying "one" and the other side responding with "two" as soon as it hears the "one," then the first party responding with "three" etc. If the result is "one (pause) two (pause) three" etc., there surely is a long delay lurking in the link. – The author once suggested establishing a research department at Bell to work on increasing the speed of light but nobody in higher management took him up on this "impossible" idea. (Actually it *might* be done – in a sufficiently intense anti-gravitational field and the ensuing high space-time curvature.)

4.3.9 Code Excited Linear Prediction (CELP)

One of the results of the block coding by trees was a demonstration of how good speech can sound even at 0.5 bits/sample for the prediction residual. Might not 0.25 bits/sample, when used with a spectrally weighted error-criterion, still give high quality? At such a low bit rate, there is even a chance for an exhaustive codebook search. Suppose we make the processing time window as short as 5 ms. At a sampling rate of 8 kHz, this corresponds to a block length of 40 samples for the prediction residual. If we want to transmit this residual information at a rate of 0.25 bits/sample (corresponding to 2000 b/s), then 10 bits are available for each frame. In other words, we could represent each block of 40 samples by one out of $2^{10} = 1024$ equally likely codewords.

The simplest way to do this is to work with a random codebook whose individual samples are independently Gaussian distributed (because the prediction residual is closely approximated by a white Gaussian process). Such a system has been successfully simulated on a large computer [4.38]. Speech quality even at this low bit rate was so high that still lower bit rates might be possible – always observing proper subjective error criteria!

4.3.10 Algebraic Codes

The only stumbling block to large-scale hardware realization of stochastic coding systems is the time it takes to search huge codebook entries for the best fit. What we need are codes for which fast search algorithms, amenable to complex error criteria, exist. This is one area where present efforts toward high-quality speech coding at very low bit rates are focused.

Fast search algorithms imply of course that useful codebooks are not random but possess sufficient internal structure of a geometric or algebraic nature. This structure can then be exploited to "factorize" the N-dimensional search space into smaller, more easily digestible, chunks. The attendant increase in computational speed is of order $N/\log_b N$, where the base b reflects the degree of factorization. Ideally, $b = 2$, as in the Fast Fourier and Hadamard Transforms (FFT and FHT, respectively). One effort in this direction is a new code based on the FHT and permutation codes [4.39].

4.3.11 Efficient Coding of Parameters

For the first 15 years of adaptive predictive coding the parameter efficiency did not matter because the innovation sequence "ate up" 10 kb/s or more. But now, with transmission rates as low as 2 kb/s for the prediction residual even for very high quality, the efficient encoding of the "slowly varying" parameters – predictor coefficients, gain, and pitch-loop gains and delays – becomes important.

As is well known, the different parameters have different energies and differ in their subjective importance. Thus, transformations in parameter space, such as Karhunen-Loeve and singular-value decomposition, are called for. Together with "dynamic bit allocation," which allots more bits per frame to those components in transformed parameter space that have larger eigenvalues, considerable reductions in bit-rate have been achieved [4.40]. However, as in other instances of dynamic bit allocation (transform coding, for example), the results fell short of expectations because constantly varying bit assignments (including the "zero-bits" case) can introduce noticeable spectral and temporal discontinuity into the speech signal.

4.4 Waveform Coding

For continuous analog signals (such as speech, music, or video) to be transmitted digitally, the signal has to be made discrete in both time and amplitude. If the signal contains frequencies only below some cut-off frequency f_c, then – as Harry Nyquist has taught us – $2f_c$ samples per second suffice for a complete reconstruction of the signal. The basic method of converting a stream of analog signal samples into digital form is by pulse code modulation (PCM). In PCM each signal amplitude is converted into a digital, often binary code. In principle, PCM signals can be transmitted over arbitrary distances without cumulative degradation by noise if they are "regenerated" at appropriate intervals [4.4]. For telephone speech signals sampled at 8 kHz, 8 bits per sample suffice (especially if amplitude compression and non-uniform quantizing levels are used). The resulting "benchmark" bit rate is therefore 64 kbits per second.

The optimum design of the quantizer to minimize a given error criterion depends on the signal statistics. Rules for such quantizers were given by J. Max and S.P. Lloyd [4.41]. The total signal range is sectioned into a preselected number of contiguous signal ranges ("bins"), each represented by one quantizing level. The borders between two adjacent bins lie halfway between the respective quantizing levels. The quantizing levels themselves (for minimizing r.m.s. error) are the weighted mean of the signal distribution for each bin. If the *absolute* error is to be minimized, the means are replaced by bin medians.

For multi-dimensional quantizers the borders between quantizing regions are called *Voronoi* cells, defined such that each point inside a given cell is closer to its quantized value than any other quantized value. For minimizing the r.m.s. quantizing error, the quantizing values are again the centers of gravity of the individual cells.

Pulse code modulators used to be quite complex. In the search for simpler coders, de Jager and Geefkes hit upon the idea of delta-modulation (ΔMod), in which only a positive or negative pulse of fixed size is transmitted at each sample time [4.42]. Integration at the receiver restores an approximation to the original waveform. While ΔMod is much simpler to implement than PCM, it is not particularly conservative of bandwidth or bitrate because of the high sampling rate ("oversampling") required.

In 1950 C. C. Cutler, in connection with predictive picture coding, invented Differential Pulse Code Modulation (DPCM), a kind of multi-bit delta modulation [4.43]. In 1970 N. S. Jayant demonstrated the now widely used adaptive delta modulation (ADM) in which the quantizing steps were adapted to accommodate time-varying properties of speech signals [4.44]. Later D. J. Goodman and J. L. Flanagan demonstrated direct conversion between PCM, delta modulation and adaptive delta modulation [4.45]. In a further advance, Flanagan, in 1973, suggested adaptively quantized differential PCM (ADPCM) and, with Jayant and P. Cummiskey, demonstrated the excellent speech performance at bit rates as low as 24 kb/s [4.46].

Subband coding and wavelets have further enhanced the possibilities of waveform coding [4.47].

Although requiring higher bit rates than parametric compressors, waveform coding, combined with proper *subjective* error criteria, is still much in the running for high-quality audio coding for high-definition television (HDTV), and for motion-picture industry standards (MPEG). But for the highest compression factors, parametric compressors, especially vocoders based on linear prediction, reign supreme.

4.5 Transform Coding

In transform coding, the signal is segmented into finite-length chunks that are then subjected to a, usually linear, transformation, such as the Fourier or Hadamard transformations. Of particular interest is the so-called *discrete cosine transform* (DCT) which is much like the real part of a Fourier transform [4.48]. But because the sine-terms are missing, the DCT implies a symmetric input. As an example, the DCT of the (symmetric!) energy spectrum of a real signal is identical to the autocorrelation of that signal.

One of the main advantages of the DCT in speech compression is that the transform coefficients are not all of equal perceptual importance. Sizable compression factors can therefore often be realized by dynamic bit-allocation in which the less important channels receive relatively few (or no) quantizing bits. The same principle of dynamic bit-allocation is also exploited in wavelet and subband coding, of which the DCT can be considered a special case.

The DCT has recently found extensive application in image quantizing. It has become part of the JPEG (Joint Photographic Expert Group) standard for the Internet, in which each 8×8 block of pixels of an image is subjected to a DCT.

One of the most advanced methods of transform coding is based on the Prometheus orthonormal set, which, like the Hadamard and Walsh transforms, uses multiplication by $+1$ or -1 only [4.49]. In addition, the

Prometheus orthonormal set, which is derived from the Rudin–Shapiro polynomials [4.50], has ideal energy spreading properties [4.51].

4.6 Audio Compression

Much of speech compression is based on *source coding*. This means that the compression strategy is based on the characteristics of the human vocal apparatus and the constraints it imposes on possible speech signals. A prime example is linear predictive coding (LPC) which is based on the fact that the spectra of many speech sounds are governed by poles (resonances of the vocal tract).

However, even some dark-age speech coders, like the channel vocoder, incorporate properties of human *hearing*: the channel vocoder preserves only the amplitude spectrum of speech sounds and discards the phases – which, perceptually, are not as significant as the amplitudes. While the human ear is certainly not "phase deaf," monaural phase sensitivity is limited. Coders that exploit such limitations of human perception are called *perceptual coders*.

Another limitation of human hearing that looms large in modern audio coders is auditory masking, i.e., the inability to perceive those frequency components that are close to stronger frequency components. The latter are then said to mask the weaker ones. Thus, information pertaining to certain weak frequency components are irrelevant. In efficient perceptual audio coders (PAC) this information is suppressed [4.26]. See also the overview by A. Gersho [4.52].

But no matter how much progress in speech compression the future will bring, books on paper, it seems, are here to stay, see Fig. 4.6.

Fig. 4.6. Fad or fiction? – books on *paper*, spotted by Mike Twohy, *The New Yorker*

5. Speech Synthesis

The word 'meaningful' when used today is nearly always meaningless.

Paul Johnson (1982)

It depends on what the meaning of the word 'is' is.

William Jefferson Clinton (1998)

Our task now is not to fix the blame for the past,
but to fix the course for the future.

John Fitzgerald Kennedy (1917–1963)

Speech synthesis from written text has been a long-standing goal of engineers and linguists alike. One of the early incentives for "talking machines" came from the desire to permit the blind to "read" books and newspapers. True, tape-recorded texts give the blind access to some books, magazines and other written information, but tape recordings are often not available. Here a reading machine might come in handy, a machine that could transform letters on the printed page into intelligible speech. Scanning a page and optically recognizing the printed characters is no longer a big problem – witness the plethora of optical scanners available in computer stores today. The real problem is the conversion of strings of letters, the *graphemes*, to phonetic symbols and finally the properly concatenated sequence of speech sounds [5.1].

In speech synthesis from written material, one of the first steps is usually the identification of whole words in the text and their pronunciation, as given by a string of phonetic symbols. But this string is only a "guide" to pronouncing the word in isolation and not as embedded in a meaningful grammatical sentence. Speech is decidedly not, as had long been innocently assumed, a succession of separate speech sounds strung together like a string of pearls on a necklace. Rather, the ultimate pronunciation is determined by the syntactical function of the word within its sentence and the *meaning* of the text. This meaning can often be inferred only by inspecting several sentences. Thus, proper speech synthesis from general texts requires lexicographical, syntactical, and semantic analyses. These prerequisites are the same as for automatic translation from one language to another, and they are one reason why translation by machines remains difficult. (Another reason of course is that some utterances in one language are literally untranslatable into certain other languages.) Not surprisingly, good, natural-sounding automatic speech synthesis from unrestricted texts is anything but easy!

Beyond reading machines for the blind, there is an ever-increasing need to convert text, be it on the printed page or in computer memory, into audible form as speech. With the spreading Internet, a huge store of information is only a mouse click away for ever more people. While much of this information is best absorbed by looking at a printed document, in many cases an oral readout would be preferable: think of a driver in a moving car, the surgeon bent over the operating table or any other operator of machinery who has his hands and eyes already fully occupied by other tasks. Or think of receiving text information over cable or over the air (by mobile phone, say). In such cases a voice output of text would be a good option to have. This is particularly true for people on the go who could receive their text email by listening to the output of a text-to-speech synthesizer. Such *voice email* would obviate the need of lugging a portable printer around the country (or the world). – Finally, many people on our globe cannot read; they *have* to rely on pictorial information or the spoken word.

Still other applications of speech synthesis from text result from the great bit compression it permits. Waveform and parameter coding of speech signals allow compression down to a few thousand bits per second. By contrast, the corresponding written text, albeit lacking intonation, requires only a hundred bits per second at normal read-out rates and even less with proper entropy coding. In fact, Shannon, in an ingenious experiment, estimated that the entropy of printed English is but 2.3 bits per letter – one half of the entropy (4.7 bits/letter) if all 26 letters and the space between letters were equiprobable and independent of each other [5.2]. Thus text-to-speech synthesis (in connection with automatic speech recognition) would allow the ultimate in bit compression.

Synthesis of natural speech from unrestricted text also requires proper *prosody:* word and sentence intonation, segment durations and stress pattern. All three aspects of prosody have inherent ("default") values, which govern the word when spoken in isolation. But necessary modifications from these standards depend on the structure of the sentence and, again, the intended meaning and mode of speaking: Is the utterance a question, an order, a neutral statement or what? [5.3].

A related aspect of human speech is its "style": Is the speaker shouting or preaching? Is he reading from a newspaper or a detective novel? How fast is he or she speaking? Does the speaker feel anxiety? How confident is he?

A person can produce and recognize the intonation and type of voice employed in coaxing, in pleading, in browbeating, and in threatening, in pleasure, and in anger, as well as those appropriate for matter-of-fact statements. This is one of the areas of speech about which little is currently known.

All these different styles affect not only the prosody but reach into the articulatory domain and influence the course of the formant frequencies. (For example, for fast speech, vowels tend to be "neutralized," i.e. the formant frequencies migrate to those of the uniform-area vocal tract.) There are also many interesting interactions. The pause structure, for instance, influences the intonation. The beginning of a talk sounds subtly different from its ending. (This writer, apparently on the basis of such subtle linguistic cues, is almost always aware – he may even wake up in time to applaud – when the end of a lecture is near.)

A person's speech, supplemented by facial expression and gesture, indicates a great deal more than factual information. Some of these other functions performed by language are usually mastered later by foreigners and give rise to misinterpretation, sometimes making foreign speakers appear insensitive when they are simply deploying fewer resources in the language.

5.1 Model-Based Speech Synthesis

Most synthetic speech is "manufactured" by speech synthesizers such as linear predictive coders (LPC), formant vocoders or "terminal analogs" of the vocal tract. These synthesizers may exist either as hardware or, more commonly, as software. The low-level parameters (predictor coefficients, formant frequencies, samples of the area functions) that control these synthesizers are computed from a few high-level parameters (such as tongue position, lip rounding, etc.). These parameters are obtained from articulatory models that incorporate the physical and linguistic constraints of human speech production.

Needless to say, the algorithms necessary for these conversions are not exactly simple. A vast body of research has been devoted to the study of the human speaking process, including high-speed motion pictures of the human vocal cords, x-ray movies of the articulators, electrical contacts on the palate, hot-wire flow meters in front of the lips or nose, magnetic field probes to track the motions of various articulators (adorned with minuscule magnets), and myographic recordings from the muscles that activate the articulators. In addition, neural networks have been trained to speak in an attempt to learn more about human speaking [5.4].

One of the several areas in which still more research is required is the functioning of the vocal chords [5.5]. Future high-quality speech synthesizers may also have to forego the fiction that   vocal cords and vocal tract are completely decoupled mechanical systems. There is no dearth of research topics in speech synthesis! In fact, the quality of synthetic speech (or the lack thereof) is one of the severest tests of our linguistic knowledge.

5.2 Synthesis by Concatenation

One of the most seductive methods of synthesizing speech from text is by stringing together, or *concatenating*, prerecorded words, syllables, or other speech segments [5.6]. This avoids many of problems encountered in phoneme-by-phoneme synthesis, such as the coarticulatory effects between neighboring speech sounds [5.7]. Still, even words do not usually occur in isolation: the words immediately preceding or following a given word influence its articulation, its pitch, its duration and stress – often depending on the *meaning* of the utterance. Thus, a (single) lighthouse keeper may advertise for a light housekeeper. And it is icecream I scream for. – You just can't get away from meaning in speech, be it synthesis, recognition, and, perforce, translation.

Another problem of word concatenation is the large dictionary required for general-purpose texts.[1]

The size-of-the dictionary problem is of course alleviated if one concatenates *syllables* rather than whole words. But then coarticulation effects become more complex again. To minimize the more difficult coarticulation effects, it is best to base the dictionary on consonant-vowel-consonant (CVC) strings and to cut these strings in the center of the steady-state vowel, yielding *demisyllables* [5.8]. Another approach to divide and conquer syllables are *diphones* (vowel to postvocalic consonant transitions).

For many languages, demisyllables minimize the coarticulation effects at syllable boundaries because the demisyllables are obtained from natural utterances by "cutting" in the middle of a steady-state vowel. Thus only relatively simple concatenation rules might be required – in the best of all worlds. But the reality of human speech is more complex and a successful concatenation system may have to rely on a combination of demisyllables, diphones, and suffixes (postvocalic consonant clusters).

---

[1] I once gave a talk in Philadelphia and had the computer deliver the introduction by text-to-speech synthesis using word concatenation. I wanted the machine to say "I just arrived from New Jersey," but, alas, the word *Jersey* wasn't in the dictionary. What to do? Well, Philadelphia isn't Brooklyn, but, as I had hoped, *Joy-See* was readily understood.

5.3 Prosody

I don't want to talk grammar, I want to talk like a lady.

(*Lisa Doolittle in Shaw's* Pygmalion)

For some time now, text-to-speech (TTS) systems have produced intelligible, if unpleasant sounding, speech. Much synthetic speech still has an unnatural ("electronic") accent and the fault lies largely at the door of prosody: voice pitch, segment durations, loudness fluctuations and other aspects of speech that go beyond the sequence of phonemes of the utterance. It has been shown that proper prosody is also crucial to ease of understanding. For example, subjects who have to perform a "competing" task do so more reliably while listening to high-quality speech and they tire later compared to subjects listening to speech with improper prosody [5.9]. And as is well known, improper prosody can render a foreign speaker difficult – sometimes impossible – to understand.

Prosody is also heavily dependent on the gender of the speaker. And there is more to the gender difference than pitch height. As mentioned before B.S. Atal and the writer once tried to change a male into a female voice by just raising the fundamental frequency. The resulting "hermaphrodite" was a linguistic calamity. Even changing the formant frequencies and bandwidths in accordance with female vocal tract physiology did not help much: the voice of the gynandroid never sounded very attractive.

But there is considerable commercial interest in changing voices and accents, not only from male to female (and vice versa), but from, say, "Deep South" to Oxford English (and vice versa?).

In spite of persisting difficulties, considerable progress toward more human sounding, intelligible speech has been made during the last several decades. In his inaugural lecture at the University of Göttingen in 1970, the writer demonstrated the then current standard of TTS by playing a German poem by Heinrich Heine[2], synthesized on an American computer (slightly modified for the occasion by Noriko Umeda and Cecil Coker). No one in the select audience seemed to understand more than a few words. Then the wily lecturer played the same tape once more, this time around with a simultaneous (but unannounced) slide projection of the text. Suddenly everybody understood. But most listeners were not aware why they understood the second playing, namely by reading the text. Thus (30 years ago anyhow) providing visual cues (preferably the complete text) was a great help in rendering TTS intelligible.

The importance of prosody is nicely illustrated by the following observation. Like most people I do not recognize my own voice when listening to

---

[2] Mit Deinen blauen Augen
 siehst Du mich lieblich an.
 Da wird mir so träumend zu Sinne,
 daß ich nicht *sprechen* kann.

it over a tape recorder. However, even when speaking English (my second language), I notice the German accent and can tell that the speaker grew up in the *Münsterland* (don't drop the *Umlaut!*) where I lived a long, long time ago and where I *haven't* lived since I was 10. In other words, in speaking English, my accent is not a generic German accent but that of a specific region near the Dutch border. And accent means primarily prosody. It's the native prosody that is so hard to disguise in speaking a foreign language. (I have little trouble with the English speech sounds. In fact, some Münsterland words are closer to English than to high German – like water which is *Water* in Münsterland and not the high-German *Wasser.*)

6. Speech Production

Speech is of Time, Silence is of Eternity.

Thomas Carlyle (1795–1881)

The right word may be effective, but no word was ever as effective as a rightly timed pause.

Mark Twain (1835–1910)

Compared to something sound and simple, such as getting a playground swing to oscillate, speech production is a mess. Not just the subtle thought that should precede the speech act, even the purely physical and physiological processes of speech production are difficult to comprehend. Everything, but the teeth, that is involved in forming the sounds of speech – the glottis, the tongue, the soft palate, the lips – is soft, both in biological consistency and algorithmic determinacy of articulatory features. The production of a human utterance, from mental intent to emitted sound wave, is utterly complex – a truly elaborate production.

One of the greatest marvels of evolution and human life is how children ever learn such a complicated task as speaking, seemingly without great effort. But then, how do they learn sucking and, a bit later, walking? The answer is: by an innate "preprogrammed" ability that we call instinct, in our case the *language instinct*, enticingly analyzed by Steven Pinker [6.1].

In spite of these complexities, linguists and engineers, following well established scientific precedent, have succeeded in developing models of speech production that, though often grossly simplified, have made the process comprehensible and amenable to mathematical analysis. Rational analysis in turn has led to sustained progress in such practical endeavors as speech recognition, speech synthesis and speech compression (for more efficient storage and transmission and for enhanced digital scrambling).

6.1 Sources and Filters

The first step in order to inject rational sense into an irrational situation is to "divide and conquer". And this is exactly what speech scientists have done in trying to better understand the speech production process. They have divided the sources of acoustic energy (quasiperiodic puffs of air or turbulent air flow) from the acoustic resonators (the vocal and nasal tracts) that shape the power spectrum of the source [6.2]. Modern study of the motions of the vocal cords have shown how much they are influenced by the geometry of articulators downstream: the tongue, the soft palate, and, last but not least, the lips [6.3]. It is therefore not a little surprising that the production of vowel sounds can be described, quite adequately for many purposes, by a simple two-part model that comprises an energy source, representing the vocal cords, for generating quasiperiodic pulses and a filter with multiple resonances emulating the action of the vocal tract.

6.2 The Vocal Source

Figure 6.1 shows a typical *glottal waveform*, i.e. the volume velocity, measured in milliliters[1] per second, of air discharged from the vocal cords into the vocal tract. The waveform is characterized by a relatively slow rise during the opening phase of the vocal cords and a more sudden descent during the cord's closing [6.4]. This basic "wavelet" is repeated, with some fluctuation in its shape, more or less periodically with period lengths ranging from 6 to 20 milliseconds (ms) for most male voices, from 4 to 7 ms for female speech and even shorter periods for high-pitched children and screaming adults. The corresponding fundamental frequency ranges are 50–167 Hz for males with typical values clustering around 110 Hz, and 140–250 Hz for females with a peak near 200 Hz.

The pitch of singing voices covers of course a wider range: for a bass singer the range extends from below 65 Hz (C2 in musical notation) up to 330 Hz (E4); for a tenor from 120 to 500 Hz; for an alto between 170 and 700 Hz; and for a soprano from 250 to 1300 Hz [6.5].

Basically, the oscillations of the vocal cords are produced by the air pressure from the lungs, which forces the cords to open to let the air escape, and the negative Bernoulli pressure, which pulls the cords together again once the air starts flowing at high speed. This mechanism is similar to the one employed in the Bronx cheer and the (nonwhispered) flatus.

The short-time Fourier spectrum of the glottal wave, owing to the quasiperiodicity of the waveform, consists of harmonically related lines at

---

[1] One milliliter, i.e. one thousandth of a liter, has the same volume as one cubic centimeter (cm^3). Throughout this book, following international usage, I will use modern units with integer powers of one thousand (10^3), expressed as milli-, micro-, kilo etc.)

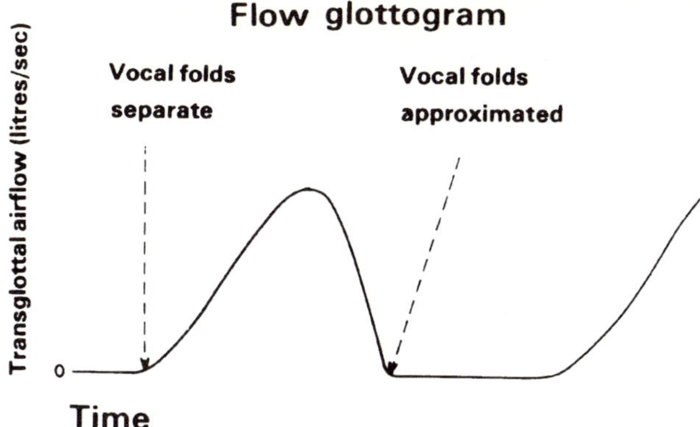

Fig. 6.1. Schematic representation of airflow through the vocal cords for normal vowel phonation. The vocal cords ("folds") typically open relatively slowly, in a manner that can be modeled by half a cosine-wave. After the maximum airflow is reached, they close quite rapidly with the airflow decreasing like a quarter sine-wave

multiples of the fundamental frequency $f_0 = 1/T_0$, where T_0 is the length of the fundamental period. The spectral amplitudes show an overall drop-off with frequency, reflecting the fact that the glottal pulses are not sharp spikes but rounded waveforms. For normal speech effort the drop-off rate is about 12 decibels per octave (dB/octave). (A difference of 12 dB corresponds to a factor of 4 in sound pressure amplitude and a factor of 16 in sound energy density.) This sharp decline of high-frequency content is partly offset by a better radiation of high frequencies from the human lips. The lips, being more like high-frequency tweeters in size than low-frequency woofers, produce a high-frequency *emphasis* of about 6 dB/octave.

By increasing the air pressure in the lungs from 0.5 kilopascal (kPa) for normal speech to 1 or 1.5 kPa, the amplitude of the glottal waveform and consequently the speech loudness can be substantially increased[2]. At the same time the glottal waveform becomes "sharper" (less rounded) thereby further increasing the high-frequency content of the speech signal that bears much of its linguistic information.

Singers singing fortissimo can push their lung pressure to 5 or even 10 kPa while, it is hoped, maintaining perfect pitch control [6.6]. But even such high-pressure singing does not always fill a voluminous concert hall with sufficient voice volume – something that pop singers have discovered long ago when they lunged for the first microphones.

The glottal waveform can be measured directly by an air-flow meter consisting of a small length of an electrically heated wire cooled by the air flow around it. The resulting drop in electrical resistance is a measure of the flow

---

[2] The modern unit of pressure, one *Pascal*, is defined as one *Newton per square meter*; it equals ten times the old dyne per square centimeter (dyn/cm^2).

velocity. Multiplication of the flow velocity by the open cross-section area of the vocal cords (assuming uniform flow) gives the *volume velocity*.

The shape of the glottal waveform can also be obtained indirectly by a method called *inverse filtering* [6.7]. In inverse filtering, a microphone is placed near the lips of the speaker and the recorded acoustic signal is subjected to an electrical filtering process whose transfer function is the reciprocal of the transfer function between the vocal cords and the microphone. This transfer function is adjusted interactively, while a tape loop of the recorded speech signal is played back, until a reasonable looking, smooth waveform is obtained. This suspiciously circular sounding "bootstrap" method is actually quite useful in speech research.[3]

The motion of the vocal cords have been studied by high-speed films and modeled as spring-coupled masses. Dynamical systems with two or more degrees of freedom are subject to period doubling and chaotic motion [6.8]. Such irregular motions of the vocal cords have indeed been observed and are now tackled by modern chaos theory [6.9].

Puffs of air provide the energy for the quasi-periodic voiced speech sounds, such as the vowels and the voiced consonants. The aperiodic *un*voiced speech sounds, especially the sibilants like /s/, /sh/ and /f/ but also the whispered vowels and whispered speech in general, receive the energy from turbulent air flow in the vocal tract. Such turbulence is generated particularly near narrow constrictions of the tract, say between the tip of the tongue and the front teeth, as for the /th/-sound in "teeth". Since the energy source for these sounds is located somewhere *between* the glottis and the lips (and not at the glottal end of the tract), the vocal tract transmission function is not that of a minimum-phase all-pole filter (see Chap. 8 for more detail on these concepts). Instead, the transmission function has spectral *zeros* ("antiresonances" or spectral minima) in addition to poles (resonances). However, these antiresonances are not very important perceptually, because they are often inaudible due to auditory masking by the surrounding resonances (see Chap. 7). (For obvious reasons evolution has seen to it that we respond well to *concentrations* of energy in the spectrum because *they*, and not the *absence* of spectral energy, signal approaching danger or sources of live food.) Turbulent airflow also plays a role, albeit a less important one, in the production of vowels and other voiced speech sounds.

---

[3] This bootstrap situation is not uncommon in scientific endeavors. As the great Danish physicist Niels Bohr once remarked to Werner Heisenberg of *Uncertainty* fame while washing dishes in a mountain hut during a skiing vacation: "The dish water is dirty, the rags we use are dirty but in the end, after enough rubbing, we get sparkling clean glasses. It's not much different with our scientific theories: we start with dirty data, apply wrong reasoning but (with a little bit of luck) end up with reasonable theories."

Bohr is also famous for his quip when asked whether he was superstitious when a visitor saw a horseshoe nailed to his door. "No," Bohr answered, "but I understand that it helps even if you don't believe in it."

6.3 The Vocal Tract

For the speech scientist the vocal tract, originally designed by evolution for breathing, eating, and drinking before it was coopted for speaking, is an acoustic resonator with variable geometry under control of the (sober) speaker [6.10]. The geometrical configuration of the vocal tract determines its resonances which in turn imprint their spectral pattern on the spectrum of the glottal pulses. For nasalized sounds (/m/ and /n/ and some vowels, in French and other languages) the spectrum is further modified by the coupling of the vocal tract to the nasal cavity [6.11]. The resulting spectrum is then radiated from the lip and nose openings to impinge on the listeners' ears and, ultimately, their minds.

From a perceptual point of view, the first two formants are the most important constituents of a speech signal. In fact, for most speech sounds, the third formant has a relatively constant frequency, usually above 2 kHz. (However, in English, for the retroflex /r/ sound, as in "bird," the third formant does dip below 2 kHz for adult speakers.) It therefore makes eminent sense to characterize the vowels by the frequencies, f_1 and f_2, of their first two formants, usually portrayed in the f_1/f_2 plane, see Fig. 6.2 and the pivotal paper by Peterson and Barney [6.12].

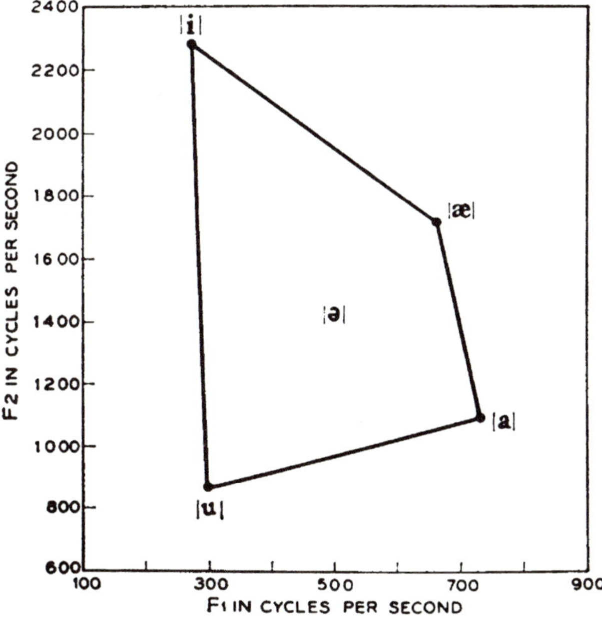

Fig. 6.2. Frequency of the second formant (F_2) versus that of the first formant (F_1) for five different vowels spoken by adult male speakers. The solid points are averages of the Peterson and Barney data. The central point represents the neutral vowel /ə/ or "schwa" sound

During continuous speech, the steady-state vowel frequencies are seldom reached, especially in unstressed syllables. In English, Russian and many other languages, there is a general tendency to "neutralize" the vowels, meaning that the formant frequencies will migrate to the frequencies of the "schwa" sound /schwa/, also called the neutral vowel, whose formant frequencies are those of the uniform-area vocal tract (about 500 Hz, 1500 Hz, 2500 Hz etc. for the adult male). In other words, the "vowel" triangle has a tendency to shrink. This phenomenon is also called *vowel reduction* [6.13]. In Russian, for example, the unstressed /oh/ sound turns into a short /ah/ sound. The tendencies for neutralization increase with increasing speed of speaking. It is as if the tongue was too lazy to follow its prescribed contortions and preferred to stay closer to a "middle" position. But of course, this vowel reduction is mostly a matter of physical constraints and economy in the speaking process.

The same "least-effort" principle also leads to the ubiquitous phenomenon of "coarticulation" in running speech. This means that the vocal tract shape of a given vowel blends into the shapes of the preceding and following speech sound [6.14].

Coarticulation is also very important for speech synthesis [6.15, 16]. The author, for his inaugural lecture at the University of Göttingen, once demonstrated the importance of proper coarticulation in speech synthesis by synthesizing the Latin name of the university (*Georgia Augusta*, after its founder George II of England and Elector of Hanover) by splicing together magnetic tape snippets with the sounds G-E-O-R-G-I-A A-U-G-U-S-T-A and, predictably, nobody in the audience understood. This little demonstration also shows how important it is to pay proper attention to coarticulation, and other articulatory constraints, in speech synthesis. These constraints reflect the geometry and the masses of the articulators and the finite muscular forces acting on them. For speech recognition, too, building the proper constraints into the speech production model can improve correct recognition rates substantially.

Another peculiarity of many languages, not least English and American English, is a tendency to eschew some pure vowels and turn them into diphthongs [6.13]. This tendency persists when native-English speakers speak a foreign language, such as Italian or Hungarian (perish the thought), languages that abhor English-style diphthongs. (Conversely, native Hungarians often betray their linguistic home by pronouncing English diphthongs as pure vowels, such as crying "rehp" instead of "rape" when the need arises – as happened to a friend who found his house "devastated" after returning from a long absence).

6.3.1 Radiation from the Lips

The acoustic radiation from the lips acts much like what engineers call a first-order highpass filter. In a rough approximation, the radiation from the lips with opening area A can be likened to that of a little loudspeaker ("tweeter") or, more formally, to an oscillating piston with area A in an infinitely large baffle. Such an oscillating piston in turn can be well approximated by an oscillating sphere with a surface area equal to A, see Appendix A. The sound field of a spherical wave of angular frequency ω emitted by such a sphere is given by the *velocity potential*

$$\phi \sim \frac{1}{r} e^{i(\omega t - kr)} , \qquad (6.1)$$

where r is the distance from the center of the sphere, t is time, and k is the magnitude of the wavevector; $k = \omega/c = 2\pi/\lambda$ where c is the velocity of sound and λ is the wavelength [6.17].

Differentiation of ϕ with respect to time and multiplying by the specific gravity of air ρ yields the sound pressure and differentiation with respect to the position coordinate and multiplying by –1 gives the *particle velocity* of the air. The ratio of the pressure to the particle velocity is called the *characteristic impedance*; for a spherical wave it is given by

$$Z(r) = \rho c \frac{ikr}{1 + ikr} . \qquad (6.2)$$

The radiation efficiency η is defined as the ratio of the real part of $Z(r)$ at the surface of the sphere $(r = R)$ divided by the characteristic impedance, ρc, of the surrounding medium:

$$\eta = \frac{k^2 R^2}{1 + k^2 R^2} . \qquad (6.3)$$

The sound radiation of a sphere can be represented by a first-order highpass filter. Its cutoff angular frequency ω_c corresponds to $kR = 1$ and thus equals c/R. Introducing the surface area $A = 4\pi R^2$ of the sphere, we obtain for $f_c := \omega_c/2\pi$

$$f_c = c(\pi A)^{-1/2} . \qquad (6.4)$$

In terms of the corresponding cutoff wavelength $\lambda_c = c/f_c$, equation (6.4) takes on the simple form $\lambda_c = 1.8\, A^{1/2}$ which is independent of c and valid for arbitrary units. (If the mouth area A is given in square feet (foot in mouth?), then the calculated cutoff wavelength is also in feet.) Thus, the larger the sphere or piston, the lower the cutoff frequency – a well-known result that has governed loudspeaker design for decades. For a lip opening with an area of, say, $5 \cdot 10^{-4}$ m^2 (formerly 5 square centimeters) the cutoff frequency is 8600 Hz. Hence, sound radiation from the lips is essentially a highpass affair with a slope of +6dB/octave over most of the speech spectrum.

The total radiated power P is proportional to η times the mouth opening area A. Thus, with (6.3), for frequencies below the cutoff,

$$P \sim A k^2 R^2 \sim f^2 A^2 . \qquad (6.5)$$

Hence, for equal vocal effort, the "big mouths" have it. [Whoever said "keep your mouth *shut*"? Did they know about the factor A^2 in (6.5)?]

It is interesting to note that the lower frequency components of a speech signal are also radiated, albeit attenuated, through the speaker's cheeks, especially if these are not too thick. More precisely, the cheeks act somewhat like a sound-leaking single-layer wall between two apartments, i.e. like a first-order *low*pass filter with a cutoff angular frequency ω_c equal to $2\rho c/md$. Here ρ is the specific gravity of air, c the sound velocity in air and m the specific gravity of the cheeks and d their thickness. With $\rho c = 414$ kg m^{-2}s^{-1}, $m = 10^3$ kg m^{-3} (like water) and $d = 0.005$ m, the cutoff frequency $f_c = \omega_c/2\pi$ equals 26 Hz. Thus, the cheek impedance is a significant factor in the first-formant frequency range (150–900 Hz for adult speakers). In fact it is the controlling factor for the first formant when the lips are closed, as in the closed-lip epoch of the voiced plosive sound /b/. While for heavy metal cheeks the first formant frequency would drop to near zero, the finite acoustic impedance of cheeks made of flesh limits the drop of the first-formant to a finite frequency. This is a significant effect in the production and the perception of plosive sounds.

6.4 The Acoustic Tube Model of the Vocal Tract

The shape of the vocal tract is anything but straight and simple. But fortunately for lower frequencies it is its cross-sectional *area* that matters most, not its actual shape and curvature. The vocal tract can therefore be modeled by a straight acoustic tube of variable cross-section $A(x)$, where $x = 0$ corresponds to the input, i.e. the glottis end of the tract, and $x = L$ (typically 0.17 m in an adult) corresponds to the output, i.e. the lip end of the tract, see Appendix A. For an optimum straightening strategy, the intermediate values of x are obtained from the flow lines of a laminar flow through the tract [6.18].

The sound transmission of a tube of variable cross-section $A(x)$ can be described by *Webster's Horn Equation* for the sound pressure $p(x,t)$ along its length:

$$\frac{\partial^2 p}{\partial x^2} + \frac{1}{A}\frac{dA}{dx}\frac{\partial p}{\partial x} = \frac{1}{c^2}\frac{\partial^2 p}{\partial t^2} \tag{6.6}$$

which for constant area $(dA/dx = 0)$ reverts to the customary wave equation in a one-dimensional lossless medium [6.19].

One important requirement for (6.6) to be valid is that the tract support no cross-modes. This means, roughly, that the largest cross dimension of the tract be smaller than half the shortest wavelength to be considered. As a consequence, sound transmission in a tract as wide as 40 millimeters (mm) is not properly described by (6.6) for wavelengths smaller than 80 mm or frequencies above about 5 kHz.

Several methods exist for solving the Horn equation [6.20]. For smoothly varying cross-section $A(x)$, a perturbation method borrowed from quantum mechanics, the Wentzel-Kramers-Brillouin (WKB) method, is particularly simple to use. The smoothness condition is that the relative change of area within one wavelength be smaller than 1:

$$\frac{1}{A}\frac{dA}{dx}\lambda < 1. \tag{6.7}$$

For an exponentially flaring horn, $A(x) \sim \exp(\epsilon x)$, where ϵ is the flare constant, solution of the horn equation (6.6) shows that the horn acts like a highpass filter with a cutoff frequency f_c equal to $c\epsilon/4\pi$. Thus, horns with a large flare have a high cutoff frequency which makes them ineffective in woofer design. For a good woofer with $f_c = 30\,\mathrm{Hz}$, we have $\epsilon \approx 1.1\,\mathrm{m}^{-1}$. This means that the area $A(x)$ can only increase by a factor $\exp(1.1) \approx 3$ over the length of one meter. For a tenfold increase in area, typical for large woofers, the length of the horn must therefore exceed $2\,\mathrm{m}$. To fit such a long horn into a box of reasonable size, the horn must be folded, as in fact they are in most modern woofers.

The connection between geometry and resonance frequencies is particularly simple for small deviations from a tract with uniform area functions. For a uniform tube with an effective length of $172\,\mathrm{mm}$ closed at one end and open at the other, the resonances are odd multiples of $500\,\mathrm{Hz}$, namely $500\,\mathrm{Hz}$, $1500\,\mathrm{Hz}$, $2500\,\mathrm{Hz}$ etc. For small sinusoidal perturbations of the logarithmic area function, symmetric about the tract's midpoint, all formant frequencies will stay fixed to first order. This is another case of articulatory ambiguity. A small perturbation corresponding to a half-period cosine will affect only the

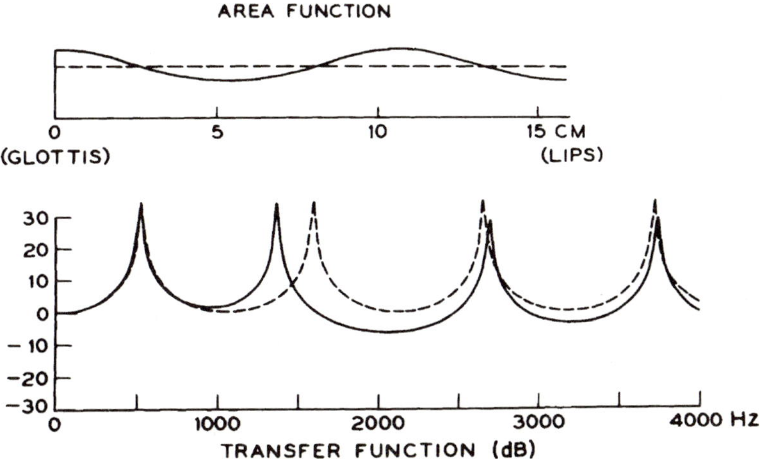

Fig. 6.3. A cosinusoidal deformation of the vocal-tract area function that changes only the second formant frequency appreciably

first formant frequency. Similarly, a 3 half-period cosine perturbation will affect only the second formant frequency, see Fig. 6.3; and a 5 half-period cosine will change only the third formant frequency [6.21]. By contrast, pertubations corresponding to full-period cosines do not change the formant frequencies to first-order. More generally, changes in the area function that are symmetric about the midpoint of the vocal tract (open at the lips) have no effect on the formant frequencies. This is a case of articulatory ambiguity – widely exploited by ventriloquists, who can produce understandable speech without moving their lips. Thus, calculating area functions from acoustic information (formant frequencies) is difficult, see Fig. 6.4, unless other constraints are marshalled to resolve the ambiguity.

As mentioned before, one method to overcome the articulatory ambiguity is to measure the impedance at the lips, see Fig. 2.7. The vocal tract area function for the utterance /iba/ determined by lip impedance measurements are shown in Fig. 6.5.

The exact change in formant frequency δf can be calculated from the work δW done against the acoustic *radiation pressure* as the tract area function is deformed by $\delta A(x)$:

$$\frac{\delta f}{f} = \frac{\delta W}{W} , \tag{6.8}$$

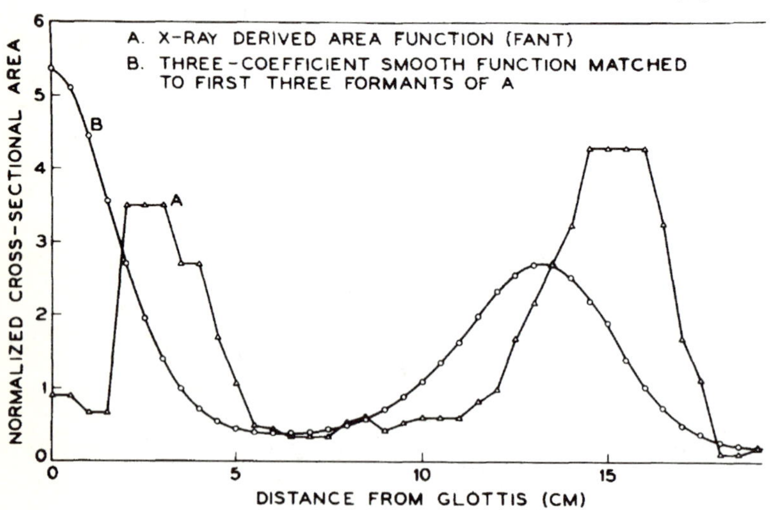

Fig. 6.4. A: area functions derived from x-ray data for the vowel /u/ (G. Fant). **B:** Smooth area function calculated from the first three formants of the vowel. Note the large differences especially near the glottis. However, the linguistically important constrictions of the vocal tract around 7 cm from the glottis and at the lips are well represented by the formant data

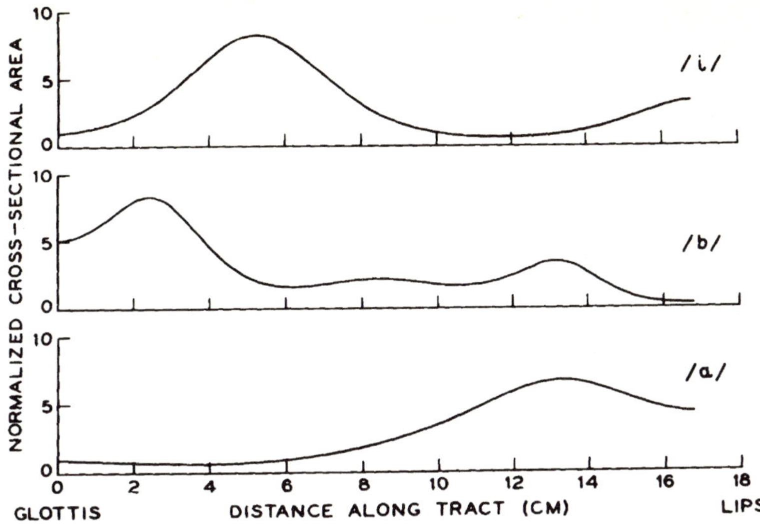

Fig. 6.5. Vocal tract area functions for the utterance /iba/ calculated from measurements of the lip impedance. Note the movements of the "tongue" in the transition from /i/ to /a/ and the properly found closure at the lips during the labial plosive /b/

where W is the total energy in the normal mode considered. Equation (6.8) embodies the *adiabatic principle*, so called because it is valid for "adiabatic" changes, i.e. changes (of the area function) slow compared to the resonance frequency.[4]

For large deviations from a uniform area function, its computation from the tract transfer function has been tackled by the mathematical concept of fiber bundles [6.22].

A detailed mathematical treatment of vocal tract acoustics and modeling of the tract is given in Appendix A by H. W. Strube.

In the following section we shall introduce the reader to the concept of convolution, in both its analog and digital form, in connection with the source-filter model of speech production.

---

[4] The *adiabatic principle* is one of the most elegant and widely valid principles in all of physics. It was developed in 1913–16 by the Austrian-Dutch physicist Paul Ehrenfest (1880–1933) who proved that, in every periodic system under slow ("adiabatic") changes in its parameters, the ratio of the energy to the resonant frequency was invariant.

Ehrenfest, well known for his statistical urn models, received his Ph.D. in statistical mechanics under Ludwig Boltzman in Vienna and later became one of Einstein's closest friends – in physics, music (violin), and political sympathies.

6.5 Discrete Time Description

For the source-filter model of speech production, the sound pressure wave $\dot{p}(t)$ emanating from the lips can be described by

$$p(t) = s(t) \star h(t) \tag{6.9}$$

where $s(t)$ is the source signal, $h(t)$ is the impulse response of the vocal tract filter, including lip radiation, and $\star$ stands for a *convolution* integral:

$$p(t) = \int_0^\infty s(t - t')h(t')dt'.$$

Fourier transforming (6.9) results in

$$\hat{p}(\omega) = \hat{s}(\omega) \cdot \hat{h}(\omega), \tag{6.10}$$

which shows that the Fourier transform of the speech signal, $\hat{p}(\omega)$, is obtained by multiplying the source transform, $\hat{s}(\omega)$, by the vocal-tract transfer function, $\hat{h}(\omega)$.

For discrete-time ("sampled") signals, the proper analytic tool is the *z-transform* [6.23]. Instead of an impulse response as a function of time, $h(t)$, we consider only discrete samples $h[n] := h(nT)$, where T is the sampling interval.[5] The impulse response is then represented by its z-transform

$$H(z) := \sum_n h[n]z^{-n}. \tag{6.11}$$

Mathematically speaking, the z-transform is a generating function in which the customary variable x has been replaced by z^{-1}. Thus, to know the nth sample, $h[n]$ of the impulse response, we have to look at the factor of z^{-n}. For causal impulse responses, $h[n] = 0$ for $n < 0$.

By setting $z = \exp(i\omega T)$, one obtains the transfer function of the sampled impulse response

$$H[\omega] = \sum_n h[n]e^{-in\omega T} . \tag{6.12}$$

Note that the transfer function of a sampled response is periodic in the frequency variable ω with a period length of $2\pi/T$. $H[\omega]$ is therefore only considered in a finite frequency interval, usually

$$-\frac{\pi}{T} < \omega \le \frac{\pi}{T} . \tag{6.13}$$

In terms of z-transforms, equation (6.10) appears as follows

$$P(z) = S(z) \cdot H(z) , \tag{6.14}$$

---

[5] In this book a change in variable is signalled by going from parentheses ( ) to brackets [ ]. Fourier transforms are indicated by a circumflex ˆ or a capital letter.

which can be interpreted both in the frequency domain

$$P[\omega] = S[\omega] \cdot H[\omega] \tag{6.15}$$

and in the discrete time domain, as can be seen when we sample both the source signal $s(t)$ and the speech signal $p(t)$ and introduce their z-transforms

$$S(z) := \sum_n s[n] z^{-n} \,,$$

$$P(z) := \sum_p p[n] z^{-n} \,. \tag{6.16}$$

Plugging these definitions into (6.14) and looking at the coefficients of z^{-n}, we see that $p[n]$ is given by a *discrete* convolution:

$$p[n] = \sum_k s[n] \cdot h[n-k] \,. \tag{6.17}$$

Equation (6.17) replaces the continuous-time convolution (6.9). Thus, the z-transform gives both frequency or spectral information and time-domain information; it is *the* proper tool for discrete-time systems.

7. The Speech Signal

Take care of the sense and the sounds will take care of themselves.

Lewis Carroll (1832–1898)

The speech signal, as it emerges from a speaker's mouth, nose and cheeks, is a one-dimensional function (air pressure) of time. Microphones convert the fluctuating air pressure into electrical signals, voltages or currents, in which form we usually deal with speech signals in speech processing. Digital-to-analog converters change the analog voltages into binary (or n-ary) digital signals. Bandlimited speech signals (bandlimited by a telephone system, for example) of less than 4000 Hz bandwidth can be represented, according to the sampling theorem, by 8000 samples per second. Each sample can be quantized to 256 levels (8 bits) with little audible degradation if the levels properly cover the voltage range of the signal. (One or two bits per sample can be saved by a judicious, non-uniform choice of levels at the cost of only minor audible distortion.) Thus the total information rate required for a high-quality representation of a speech signal bandlimited to 4 kHz is 8 bits/sample times 8000 samples/second or 64 kbits per second. (For comparison, the bit rate on a stereo compact disc (CD) exceeds 1.4 Mbits/second.) The aim of speech compression is to reduce this bit rate as much as possible for more efficient storage and transmission.

Although the speech signal is a one-dimensional function (air pressure) of a one-dimensional variable (time), it is generated by a plethora of parallel nerve commands from the brain, controlling the muscles of the various organs participating in the articulatory process – vocal cords, tongue body, tongue tip, lips, soft palate (velum), etc. These nerve commands do not only occur in parallel, they are noticeably desynchronized to compensate for different delays on different nerve fibers and to promote the numerous "coarticulatory" effects observed in speech in which the articulation of one speech sound is substantially influenced by its neighbors. These phenomena are documented in great detail for one widely understood language in the book *Acoustics of*

American English Speech: A Dynamic Approach by J. P. Olive, A. Greenwood, and [7.1].

In spite of the great complexity of the speech production process – from thought and intent in the brain to the acoustic signal – a more simplistic view of speech signals, disregarding most of these complexities, suffices for simple speech signal compression. But some of these complexities cannot be safely ignored in speech recognition and particularly in speech synthesis from written material. Not paying proper attention to the human production process is precisely the reason why machine speech, to this day, has a flavor of, well, machine speech. Exorcising the "electronic accent" from synthetic speech is a continuing challenge.

7.1 Spectral Envelope and Fine Structure

Of the many distinctive features of speech that even speech compression cannot ignore is the dichotomy between *voiced* and *unvoiced* sounds. For voiced sounds, like the vowels and voiced consonants in non-whispered speech, the vocal cords vibrate more or less periodically, chopping up the air stream from the lungs into individual puffs of air at a fundamental frequency f_0 ranging from roughly 50 Hz (low male) to 300 Hz (high female). The resulting "quasiperiodicity" of the speech signal is manifest both in the waveform and the short-time spectrum: the waveform shows a repetitive pattern at the rate f_0 and the spectrum has equidistant peaks ("lines") at integer multiples of the fundamental frequency f_0 ("harmonics"), see Fig. 4.2.

7.2 Unvoiced Sounds

During unvoiced sounds, the vocal cords do not vibrate and they do not undulate the air flow from the lungs. (But they may be nearly closed causing audible friction as for the /h/ sound.) The acoustic energy is produced by turbulence at one or several narrow air passages in the mouth (tongue tip against or between the teeth, tongue against the palate etc.). This turbulent energy has a "smooth" spectrum like that of noise, without a line structure, see Fig. 4.3.

7.3 The Voiced–Unvoiced Classification

But not all speech sounds are either purely voiced or turbulent. The voiced fricatives /v/ as in *veal*, /z/ as in *zeal*, and /ʒ/ as in *pleasure* are voiced, because the vocal cords vibrate, and they are turbulent because of noise generated at narrow constrictions in the vocal tract. The speech signal therefore contains a *periodically modulated* noise, a fact ignored by speech synthesizers that distinguish only between voiced and unvoiced sounds.

The spectral envelope is defined as the smooth outline drawn over the relative maxima of the short-time spectrum. It is clear that this is not a precise definition. A more quantitative definition can be based on the low quefrencies of the cepstrum, see Chap. 10. In other words, considering the logarithmic spectrum as a signal and smoothing it with an ideal lowpass filter would give the spectral envelope, as shown in Figs. 4.2,3.

The distinction between spectral envelope and fine structure is not the same as that between the transfer ("filter") function of the vocal tract and the vocal source signal. The latter has its own spectral envelope that is included in the overall spectral envelope of the speech signal. Most speech compression systems separate the spectrum into an overall spectral envelope and the remaining time structure (if any) with a *flat* spectral envelope. Thus, vocoder channel signals and linear prediction coefficients, for example, usually include aspects of the excitation function – another fact that is easily overlooked in uni(n)formed analyses of such systems.

7.4 The Formant Frequencies

The most prominent spectral feature of vowel spectra are the peaks in the spectral envelope caused by the resonances of the vocal tract. Following musicology, these vowel resonances are called formants because they shape ("form") the spectrum. The spectrum determines the sound quality or *timbre* that we hear. The positioning and even more so the *dynamics* of the formant frequencies define the syllables and words that we perceive as speech. The first three formant frequencies fall below 3000 Hz for adult speakers. The third formant frequency falls near 2600 Hz for most vowels, except the retroflex /r/ sound. Thus, vowels can be largely distinguished on the basis of their first two formant frequencies.

The formant frequencies in turn are determined by the geometry of the vocal tract as illustrated in Fig. 2.5. Depending on the height of the tongue body, phoneticians distinguish between high, mid, and low vowels. Similarly, the different positions of the tongue body in the forward/backward direction lead to the distinction between front, central, and back vowels. For example, /iː/ as in b*ee* is a high front vowel, while /aː/ as in f*a*ther is a low back vowel.

Vowels with extreme front/back positions are also called *tense*. Thus /iː/ as in b*ee* is tense, but /ɪ/ as in bid is lax (not tense). The laxest of all vowels is the so-called *schwa* sound or neutral vowel /ə/ as in *a*bout, a sound that abounds in English. The vocal tract for the /a/ sound has a nearly constant cross-sectional area along its length. It is the vowel that requires the least muscular effort to produce – the laziest vowel, so to speak. It is interesting to ask whether this makes English harder to understand, by machines and even humans, than some other languages, like Italian, that have a smaller tendency to neutralize their vowels in unstressed positions. (Russian is another great neutralizer.)

English vowel phonemes are often described in terms of binary (+ or −) *distinctive features* which includes the feature round for the degree of lip rounding [7.2,3]. Thus, /i/ has the distinctive features + high, − low, − back, − round, and + tense. The feature vector for /ɪ/ is + − − − − and that for /a/ is − + + − +.

English, including American English, is also rich in *diphthongs*, boasting a total of five such combinations of vowels with the *glides* /ɹ/ and /ʊ/: /aɹ/ as in b*i*te, /eɹ/ as in b*ai*t, /ɔɹ/ as in b*oy*, /aʊ/ as in b*ou*t, and /oʊ/ as in b*oa*t. Diphthongs occur more frequently in English than in, say, French. In fact, one of the difficulties of proper English pronunciation for a French speaker is to know how to *mis*pronounce certain French words. Thus, in English, the French *valet* invariably comes out as /valej/ with a diphthong at the end. Conversely, native speakers of French (and Hungarian) have a tendency to substitute pure vowels for English diphthongs.

In Italian of course all vowels (and consonants, including double consonants) are pronounced separately. Thus, *Europe*, which in English is barely two syllables, comes out in Italian as Eh-oo-roh-pa. Would that all languages were pronounced like that − it would make speech recognition a lot simpler!

8. Hearing[1]

Language is the dress of thought.

Samuel Johnson (1709–1784)

One of the best hearing aids a man can have is an attentive wife.

Groucho Marx (1895–1977)

Hearing is one of the senses that evolution has bestowed on us to better survive in a complex and not always friendly environment. In the process, "natural selection" has wrought some real marvels. At the threshold of hearing people can hear sounds just above the thermal limit of molecular Brownian motion in the inner ear. At the other end of the loudness scale, our ears can cope with intensities a *thousand* billion times greater than the threshold value.

The protective function of our ears is enhanced by the fact that sound travels around corners – not just in straight lines as light rays do. Thus we are warned even of invisible dangers. And wisely, nature did not supply us with "ear-lids" to shut ourselves off from the sounds of approaching disaster. In contrast to our eyes, our ears are always on guard. Our hearing analyzes sounds with respect to two important dimensions: frequency and direction [8.1]. The frequency analysis in the inner ear, a marvel of selectivity and sensitivity, allows us to detect weak spectral prominences in the presence of strong broadband noises. As a special bonus, so to speak, spectral analysis enables us to perceive spectrally coded signals, such as music, song, and above all speech. One of the foremost features of human hearing is *masking* [8.2]. Auditory masking means that one (loud) sound makes another (soft) sound inaudible. Masking is most effective at frequencies near the frequencies contained in the masker. In addition, there is *upward spread of masking*, meaning

---

[1] Adapted in part from *Proc. IEEE* **63**, 1332–1350 (1975).

that frequencies *above* the masker frequencies are also rendered inaudible or reduced in loudness.

This upward spread of masking results directly from the anatomy of the inner ear and the traveling waves on the basilar membrane: the low fre-.quencies in a signal traverse the places along the basilar membrane in the inner ear where higher frequencies are detected. Thus, strong low frequencies can "swamp" high frequencies. By contrast, high frequencies are strongly attenuated beyond their place of detection and have therefore relatively little masking effect on the lower frequencies. The basilar membrane is in effect a nonuniform transmission line with progressively lower cut-off frequency.

Upward spread of masking is the principal cause for the loss of speech intelligibility for most older people. The fact that their threshold of hearing at 2000 Hz, compared to 500 Hz, is elevated by perhaps as much as 60 dB (a million-fold drop in sensitivity to sound intensity) is an affliction that they could live with in many situations, for example when listening to music.[1] But in the presence of interfering sounds, especially those containing low frequency components, below 500 Hz say, masking and especially upward spread of masking will drown out many intelligible speech sounds that have their most important spectral components between 500 Hz and 2500 Hz.

This predicament is further aggravated by the fact that in many locations, a crowded restaurant for example, the interfering noises are other people's voices whose *low*-frequency components are little absorbed by draperies, rugs and even "acoustic ceilings." (As mentioned before, the most effective countermeasures to copious clamor include small tables with large distances between tables – and, by the way, guzzling less disinhibiting liquids by the clientele.)

By contrast, for the speech-synthesizing scientist, masking is a good thing. It means that he can "hide" the inevitable quantizing noise under the speech spectrum by tailoring it so as to maximally exploit auditory masking [8.3]. High-quality speech signals have thus been synthesized from bit streams of less than 1 bit per sample [8.4].

People have thought about their ears (and those of many animals) for a long time. Intelligent speculation, supplemented by experiment (and vice versa), has brought us a long way toward understanding how the ear works – from subtle monaural phase effects (*verboten* by Ohm's law of acoustics) to expansive binaural stereophony (welcomed by almost everyone). Much of this newfound knowledge, some of it acquired only very recently, has found its formal expression – as it has in other fields – in *models*: mathematical models or physical models (or both) of how the ear "does it" – or *might* do it if it had been designed by fanciful model builders instead of by pragmatic evolution.

---

[1] Auditory researchers are at a loss to explain why such a sharp loss in high-frequency hearing does not play havoc with musical enjoyment – perhaps older people get used to the spectral distortion as it builds up gradually over the years.

This chapter gives a brief introduction to the human ear – not with claims of exhaustiveness, but with the intent to give a *flavor* of what is going on in a very active field concerning a fascinating, and ultimately still mysterious, subject: Homo sapiens' sense of hearing.

8.1 Historical Antecedents

An understanding of our sense of hearing has been a goal of human science and speculation since the very beginning of civilization. As early as the first century BC, the Roman poet and philosopher Lucretius postulated little grains of sand in the inner ear responding to different tones. Lucretius' theory constituted what we would call today a "particle theory" of sound, anticipating in a most amusing manner the *phonons* of modern quantum acoustics. In his book [8.5] he held forth on speech and hearing as follows.

"In the first place, all forms of sound and vocal utterance become audible when they have slipped into the ear and provoked sensation by the impact of their own bodies. The fact that voices and other sounds can impinge on the senses is itself a proof of their corporeal nature. Besides, the voice often scrapes the throat and a shout roughens the windpipe on its outward path. What happens is that, when atoms of voice in greater numbers than usual have begun to squeeze out through the narrow outlet, the doorway of the overcrowded mouth gets scraped...

"Again, you must have noticed how much it takes out of a man, and what wear and tear it causes to his thews and sinews, to keep on talking from the first glow of dawn till the evening shadows darken, especially if his words are uttered at the pitch of his voice. Since much talking actually takes something out of the body, it follows that voice is composed of bodily stuff.

"When we force out these utterances from the depths of our body and launch them through the direct outlet of the mouth, they are cut up into lengths by the flexible tongue, the craftsman of words, and moulded in turn by the configuration of the lips.

"It often happens that a single word, uttered from the mouth of a crier, penetrates the ears of a whole crowd. Evidently, a single utterance must split up immediately into a multitude of utterances, since it is parcelled out amongst a number of separate ears, imprinting upon each the shape of a word and its distinctive sound. Some of these utterances as do not strike upon the ears float by and are scattered to the winds and lost without effect. Some of them, however, bump against solid objects and bounce back, so as to carry back a sound and sometimes mislead with the replica of a word...

> "I have observed places tossing back six or seven utterances when you have launched a single one: with their tendency to rebound, the words were reverberated and reiterated from hill to hill. According to local legend, these places are haunted by goat-footed Satyrs and by Nymphs. Tales are told of Fauns, whose noisy revels and merry pranks shatter the mute hush of night for miles around...
>
> "There remains the problem, not a very puzzling one, of how sounds can penetrate and strike on the ear through media through which objects cannot be clearly perceived by the eye. The obvious reason why we often hear a conversation going on through closed doors is that an utterance can make its way intact through circuitous fissures in objects impervious to visual films. For these are broken up, unless they are passing through straight fissures such as those in glass, which is penetrable by any sort of image. Again, sounds are disseminated in all directions because each one, after its initial splintering into great many parts, gives birth to others, just as a spark of fire often propagates itself by starting fires of its own. So places out of the direct path are often filled with voices, which surge round every obstacle, one sound being provoked by another."

As fantastic as some of Lucretius' ideas may sound to the modern ear, we can recognize in his writings concepts which today, 2000 years later, form the very basis of our understanding of sound: *energy, reverberation, diffraction,* and even *Huyghens' Principle* (here likened to the spread of fire).

Nevertheless, many centuries were to pass before more *quantitative* observations about sound and hearing emerged. In the 18th century, Tartini [8.6], the noted Italian violinist, described his "terzi suoni" – "third tones" that the ear itself manufactures from two tones played simultaneously. These tones occupy a very important place in our attempts to understand the workings of the inner ear and particularly its *nonlinear* behavior. Contrary to long held views, the ear is not a highly linear receiver, even at very low sound intensities. Rather, "combination tones", such as those observed by Tartini, become in fact audible near the very threshold of hearing where the mechanical motions in the inner ear are fractions of Angstroms (10^{-7}mm) or the diameter of the hydrogen atom! The origin of these nonlinearities is still not completely clear, but the fact that they occur at atomic dimensions strongly implicates molecular processes – molecular processes, moreover, that appear to be intimately connected with the metabolism in the inner ear because the nonlinear phenomena observed in animals change when the blood supply to the ear is interrupted.

Besides Tartini, numerous other composers and performers of music contributed observations (or speculations) on our sense of hearing. But sustained research on the ear did not begin until the middle of the 19th century.

8.2 Thomas Seebeck and Georg Simon Ohm

Contemporary research into hearing had its inception with the work of Thomas Seebeck (1770–1831), Georg Simon Ohm (1789–1854), and Hermann von Helmholtz (1821–1894).

Seebeck discovered what is now known as "periodicity pitch," i.e. the sensation of a pitch-like sound quality without the presence of a physical component in the acoustic stimulus at the perceived frequency [8.7]. Seebeck's observation and subsequent work by Jan Schouten [8.8, 9] and his Dutch school on "residue pitch" (so named because a sensation of pitch remains even after the removal of the corresponding frequency component in the signal) was one of the great discoveries in hearing.

Ohm postulated his acoustic "phase law" which said that the perceived quality of a sound depended solely on its *power* spectrum and was independent of the phase angles of its frequency components. This phase law, although shown by modern research to admit exceptions, is one of the fundamental facts of "psychoacoustics" as the study of hearing by listening tests has come to be called. Together with physiological studies and mathematical modeling (now called "computational hearing"), psychoacoustic experiments, using elaborate acoustic signals, play a central role in modern hearing research. Well-designed psychoacoustic experiments allow us to penetrate, as it were, through the ear to the very centers of consciousness in our brains. And although Ohm and his contemporaries did not have the sophisticated equipment modern researchers enjoy (particularly digital computers and signal processors) for the generation of precisely tailored sounds, Ohm is clearly the father (or perhaps grandfather) of the psychoacoustic approach to the ear.

8.3 More on Monaural Phase Sensitivity

One of the most fascinating problems in hearing – one that has puzzled psychoacousticians, hi-fi fans and laypersons alike – is the ability, or "inability," of the human ear to perceive "phase." As already mentioned, as long ago as the middle of the last century, Ohm formulated his famous Acoustic Law which states that aural perception depends only on the amplitude spectrum of a sound and is independent of the phase angles of the various frequency components contained in its spectrum.

In order to avoid obvious violations of Ohm's Acoustic Law, we are forced to make its language more precise in several respects. Thus we have to add the modifier "short-time" before "amplitude spectrum" in the above formulation. Otherwise, a counterexample to the phase law could easily be constructed as follows:

1. Take a 100-second long segment of a speech signal;
2. calculate its discrete Fourier transform (assuming 100-s periodic repetition). This yields a frequency component every 1/100 Hz;
3. randomize the phase angles, i.e. choose each phase angle independently from a uniform distribution between 0 and 2π ($0°$ and $360°$);
4. calculate the inverse Fourier transform.

The result is a signal which, for all practical purposes, during intervals shorter than 100 s, looks and sounds like a Gaussian noise (with an energy spectrum equal to that of the speech signal). Thus, manipulating the phase angles in this case has not only altered the acoustical quality but completely changed the signal from intelligible speech to random noise.

If instead of taking the Fourier transform over 100 s, we had performed the phase operation on a Fourier transform over time intervals corresponding to the speech-analysis time of the ear, say 50 ms, the acoustical quality would have remained intact – at least on informal listening.

Thus in speaking of the "phase deafness" of the ear, we must remember that we are talking about *short-time* spectra.

8.4 Hermann von Helmholtz and Georg von Békésy

Helmholtz was interested not only in the sensations of tone; he also did considerable *physiological* work on the anatomy of the ear. Based on his observations, Helmholtz propounded a *resonance* theory of the inner ear which, although no longer acceptable in a literal sense, caught the essence of the inner ear mechanics: *frequency selectivity* [8.10].

In our own century, Georg von Békésy (1899–1972) [8.11] discovered the all-important *traveling waves* on the basilar membrane (BM) and, as a former telephone engineer, correctly recognized the medium of these traveling waves as a *nonuniform* transmission line: high frequencies travel only a short distance on the BM and are then rapidly attenuated, while low frequencies travel farther along the BM – the lower the farther – before being stopped. This low-pass behavior, together with a local resonance, leads to the observed frequency selectivity of the BM motion, seen first by Békésy himself and more recently by Johnstone, Rhode [8.12], Kohllöffel, Wilson, and Helfenstein using the most advanced tools that physics has to offer such as the ultrasensitive Mössbauer–Doppler effect, laser interferometry, and capacitative microphone probing.

8.4.1 Thresholds of Hearing

Békésy, who was awarded the 1961 Nobel Prize for his work on hearing, is also remembered for his audiometer, now widely used in auditory research and clinical audiometry. In Békésy audiometry, thresholds of hearing are measured by an "up–down" tracking method: the subject keeps a button pressed as long as he or she hears the signal whose amplitude is progressively reduced in small steps. Once the signal becomes inaudible, the subject releases the button whereupon the signal amplitude is increased in small steps – until the subject hears the signal again and starts pressing the button anew. H. Levitt has considerably extended Békésy's up-down methods to yield more accurate results [8.13].

In addition to measuring absolute thresholds of hearing as a function of frequency (for selecting the proper hearing aid, for example), the Békésy method is also used for determining *masked* thresholds, for instance of a tone "buried" in noise.

8.4.2 Pulsation Threshold and Continuity Effect

In addition to absolute and masked thresholds, another kind of threshold has gained prominence since the 1970s: the *pulsation threshold* introduced by T. Houtgast to study lateral inhibition in hearing (in analogy to "Mach bands" in vision) and to find a psychophysical equivalent of neurophysiological "tuning curves."

In the pulsation threshold paradigm, short (ca. 100 ms) test-tone presentations alternate with short bursts of noise. For low tone levels, the tone is of course completely masked and inaudible. For high enough tone levels, the tone is heard to alternate with the noise, as physically presented. By lowering the tone level progressively in small decrements, a situation is eventually reached when the short tone bursts are heard as a *continuous tone*. This is the pulsation threshold: above it the tone percept pulsates, as presented whereas just below it the tonal percept is continuous.

The reason for this remarkable phenomenon is thought to be the *continuity effect*, observed in all sensory modalities, not least vision. The continuity effect leads to a stimulus being perceived as still present even after it has been turned off if the turning off leaves no perceptual trace. (Apparently evolution has found it wise to "rig" perception to suggest that a danger that has not perceptically gone away is still present.)

One of the more impressive demonstrations of a pulsation threshold, due to G.A. Miller and J.C.R. Licklider, uses a speech signal alternatingly turned on and off: 100 ms of speech, 100 ms silence, 100 ms speech etc. Such a chopped-up speech signal is of course unintelligible. Naturally, adding a lot of noise to the chopped speech does not improve its intelligibility. However, at a certain noise level (the pulsation threshold), the speech sounds continuous. This continuity effect is so convincing that listeners are sure to be hearing uninterrupted speech and would actually understand it "with a little extra effort." Needless to say, they don't understand a thing.

For a binaural example of the continuity effect, see Fig. 9.3.

8.5 Anatomy and Basic Capabilities of the Ear

Figure 8.1 shows a sketch of the outer, middle, and inner ear based on the anatomical studies of Helmholtz. Sound waves striking the outer ear are conducted through the *external* ear canal to the eardrum at the entrance to the *middle* ear.

The middle ear contains three small bones (ossicles) which transmit the sound vibrations to the *oval window* at the entrance to the inner ear.

The inner ear or cochlea (named after its snail-like appearance) is filled with fluid and separated by membranes into several ducts.

8.6 The Pinnae and the Outer Ear Canal

In spite of their relatively simple construction, compared to the complex structure and innervations of the inner ear, the pinnae ("auricles") and outer ear canal perform important functions in sound localization.

It had long been a mystery how people were able to localize sound in the "median plane" (an imaginary vertical plane, through the head normal to the connecting line between the ear drums and equidistant from them). In the horizontal plane, the ability to distinguish different directions of arrival of sound waves at his ears has been explained by the intensity and phase differences of the sound waves at the two ears [8.14]. For sound sources in the *median* plane (and symmetric head shapes), however, the sound waves impinging on the left-ear and right-ear are *identical* functions of time for all angles of elevation of the sound source. Yet for a large variety of signals, people can easily distinguish between the forward direction (elevation angle $0°$), the overhead direction ($90°$), the rearward direction ($180°$), and even several intermediate directions [8.15].

8.7 The Middle Ear

The middle ear is perhaps best known to suffering humanity through the vicious infections it can contract. The middle ear, however, is also the site of more agreeable happenings. Our ears have evolved to a state of perfection that seems to leave little room for redundancy. Thus it is not surprising to find some important auditory functions being implemented in the space between eardrum and oval window (the entrance to the inner ear, see Fig. 8.1).

By far the most important of these is the *impedance matching* between the airborne sound in the outer ear and the fluidborne sound in the inner ear. The characteristic impedance of air is $414\,\mathrm{kg \cdot m^{-2} \cdot s^{-1}}$ and that of water $1\,480\,000\,\mathrm{kg \cdot m^{-2} \cdot s^{-1}}$ or almost 3600 times greater. However, the input impedance of the inner ear, although filled with a water-like liquid, is considerably smaller because the liquid can bulge out the membrane over the

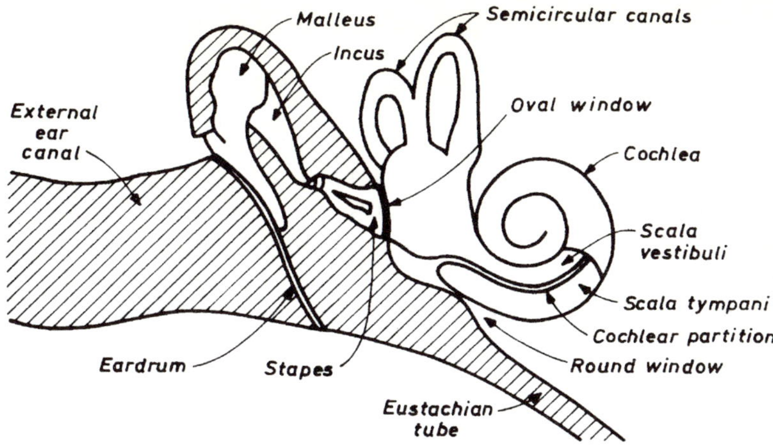

Fig. 8.1. Schematic drawing of the middle ear and inner ear. Sound "caught" by the outer ear is transmitted via the middle ear to the ear drum, where it causes the ossicles to vibrate and excite the inner ear. In the inner ear (the snail-like "cochlea") the sound, now fluid-borne, travels along the basilar membrane where it is converted by the hair cells to electrical pulses in the acoustic nerve, see Fig. 8.2

round window. Nevertheless, a considerable amount of impedance transformation has to be accomplished in going from outer to inner ear. Most of this transformation is effected by the ratio of the eardrum area to the area of the stapes footplate. The lever ratio of the ossicle motion also plays a role, and the combined effect is an impedance transformation of about 1 to 20, improving power transmission through the middle ear more than fivefold.

The other important middle-ear function is a "gain control," mediated by what is known as the *acoustic reflex* [8.16], which protects the delicate inner ear from overloading and possible destruction.

At very high sound levels, the middle-ear transmission becomes nonlinear with a predominant quadratic term in its input–output amplitude characteristic. This nonlinearity produces *combination tones* if two or more primary tones are applied simultaneously to the outer ear. Thus if two large amplitude tones with frequencies f_1 and f_2 are presented to one ear, a "difference tone" of frequency $f_2 - f_1$ can be heard. Its amplitude increases proportional to the product of the two primary amplitudes – as would be expected for a quadratic nonlinearity.[2]

The sum tone with frequency $f_1 + f_2$ can also sometimes be heard but it is usually much fainter due to masking and the low-pass character of the

---

[2] The difference tone $f_2 - f_1$ can best be demonstrated by slightly varying f_1 or f_2 in frequency so that the diffference also changes in frequency. More generally, in a multitone complex, a tone varied in frequency becomes more easily identifiable; it perceptually "pops out" from a stationary background. This phenomenon is an instance of a pervasive psychophysical fact: Our attention is drawn to *changes* in a stimulus.

middle-ear frequency transfer function which attenuates frequencies above about 1 kHz.

A particularly impressive demonstration of middle-ear distortion can be obtained with two broadband noises obtained by randomly frequency-modulating two carriers with a fixed frequency difference Δf. These noises are applied to the ear via two separate transducers (to circumvent possible distortion in the transducer). At low sound pressure levels, the linear sum of the noises is heard. This is just another broadband noise with no audible periodicities. However, at sufficiently high levels, a tone of frequency Δf is heard. Since this tone is not present in the stimulus, the tone must have been "manufactured" by the ear itself. Furthermore, this tone is not just "subjective" (meaning that it is created in higher nervous centers) but is physically present in the middle and inner ears. In fact, it can be cancelled by a tone of frequency Δf and proper amplitude and phase applied to the outer ear.

8.8 The Inner Ear

The "cochlea" (from the Greek word for a snail with a spiral shell) in the inner ear is the frequency-selective part of our hearing organ. A cross section through the cochlea can be seen in Fig. 8.2 showing the cochlear duct with its three fluid-filled channels separated by membranes.

One of these membranes, the basilar membrane (BM), supports the organ of Corti, the sense organ of hearing. The organ of Corti contains the *hair cells* which convert the relative motion between BM and tectorial membrane into nerve impulses. There are two kinds of hair cells: inner and outer hair cells; and although much was known about the organization of the cochlea receptor the *raison d'être* for these two kinds of cells was long a mystery. It is now believed that the inner hair cells are the primary receptors converting mechanical motion of the BM into electrical impulses and that the outer hair cells feed energy *into* the BM to compensate for its mechanical losses thereby increasing its sensitivity and frequency selectivity.

The first to ascribe frequency-selective properties to the BM was Helmholtz who visualized it as a succession of tuned strings (as in a piano) resonant at different frequencies. However, when Békésy actually looked through his microscope to observe the vibrations of the BM under acoustic stimulation, he saw traveling waves, traveling (with decreasing velocity) from the stapes at the base of cochlea to the helicotrema at the apex about 25 mm from the stapes. Figure 8.3 illustrates such a traveling wave, with a frequency of 200 Hz, at two instants in time separated by 1.25 ms or one-quarter period. At the first instant, the deflection of the BM (grossly magnified) is shown by the solid line. A quarter-period later, the deflection corresponds to the short-dashed line. During this time, the minimum (the negative peak) of the wave has traveled from about 27 mm to 28.5 mm – corresponding to a phase

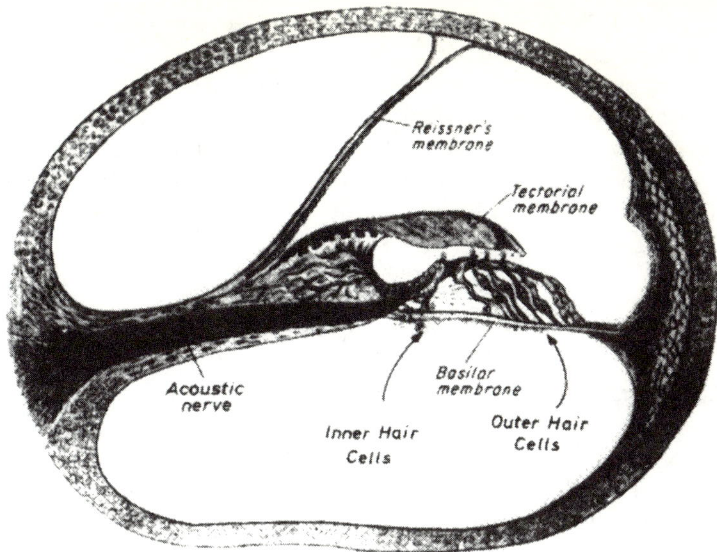

Fig. 8.2. Cross-section through the inner ear showing the basilar membrane, along which sound waves travel, and the hair cells which transduce mechanical vibrations into electrical pulses (and vice versa)

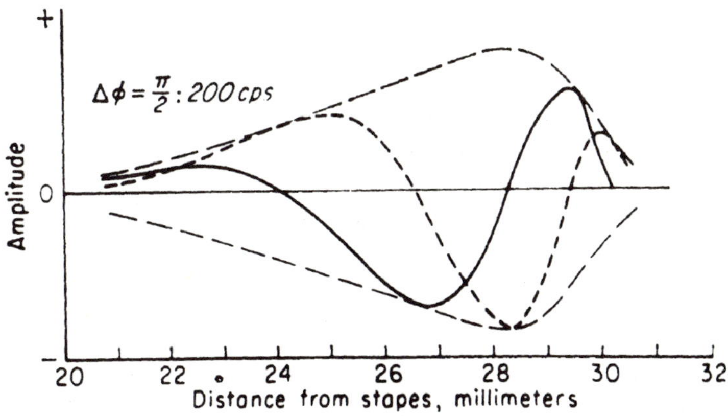

Fig. 8.3. Wave traveling along the basilar membrane. Its amplitude first increases slowly and then, beyond its place of resonance, drops rapidly. The phase velocity decreases along the entire length of the membrane, as evidenced by the decreasing wavelength

velocity of 1.2 m/s, or 1/300 of the velocity of sound in air (and an even smaller fraction of the sound velocity in water).

Simple inspection of Fig. 8.3 shows that, at larger distances, the phase velocity is even lower, whereas nearer to the stapes it is considerably higher. But phase (and group) velocities on the BM are not only a function of space but depend also on frequency. In the language of the electrical engineer, the BM is a nonuniform (dispersive) transmission line.

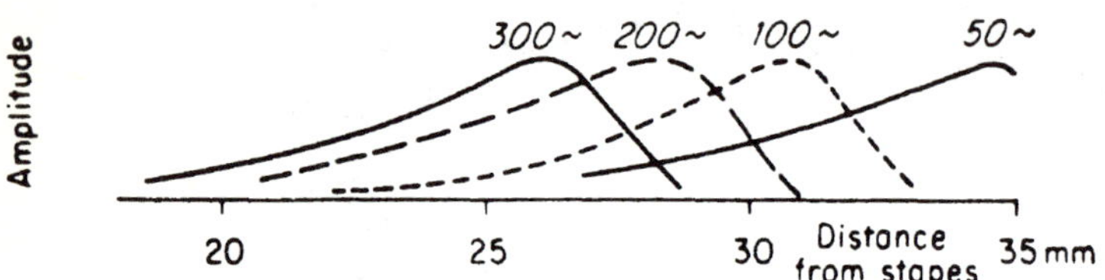

Fig. 8.4. Envelope of the waves traveling along the basilar membrane. The lower the frequency, the farther from the stapes a wave will peak

The two long-dashed lines in Fig. 8.3 trace the positions of the wave's positive and negative peaks, respectively, as they travel along the BM. This wave "envelope" reaches a highest value near 28 mm for a frequency of 200 Hz. The lower the frequency of the wave, the farther along the BM it travels before it is attenuated, as can be seen in Fig. 8.4 which shows wave envelopes for 4 different frequencies. Thus, while a wave of 300 Hz travels about 25 mm before it is attenuated, a wave of 100 Hz reaches its maximum at about 30 mm.

Figure 8.5 shows the propagation of short pulses of alternating sign along the basilar membrane. At its input end, the waveform is fully preserved. But for places on the basilar membrane with increasing distance from the input, an increasing degree of lowpass filtering becomes evident until, beyond 28 mm, only two and finally just one Fourier component (the fundamental frequency) "survives."

A simple electrical model of the BM is shown in Fig. 8.6. The inductances represent inertia of longitudinal and lateral fluid motions and the mass of the BM. The capacitances stand for the elasticity of the BM and the resistances represent the losses. The transverse branches of this ladder network are series resonance circuits with decreasing resonant fequency from left (input) to right. For a single frequency, the impedances of the transverse branches can be approximated by capacitances to the left of the resonance, a resistance at the place of resonance, and inductances beyond. Thus, in the language of electrical engineering, the BM acts like a low-loss LC-delay line to the left of the resonance place and an inductive attenuator to its right. The energy absorbed by the resistance goes to stimulating the hair cells attached to the place of resonance for the frequency considered. Although highly simplified, this model captures the salient features of BM mechanics.

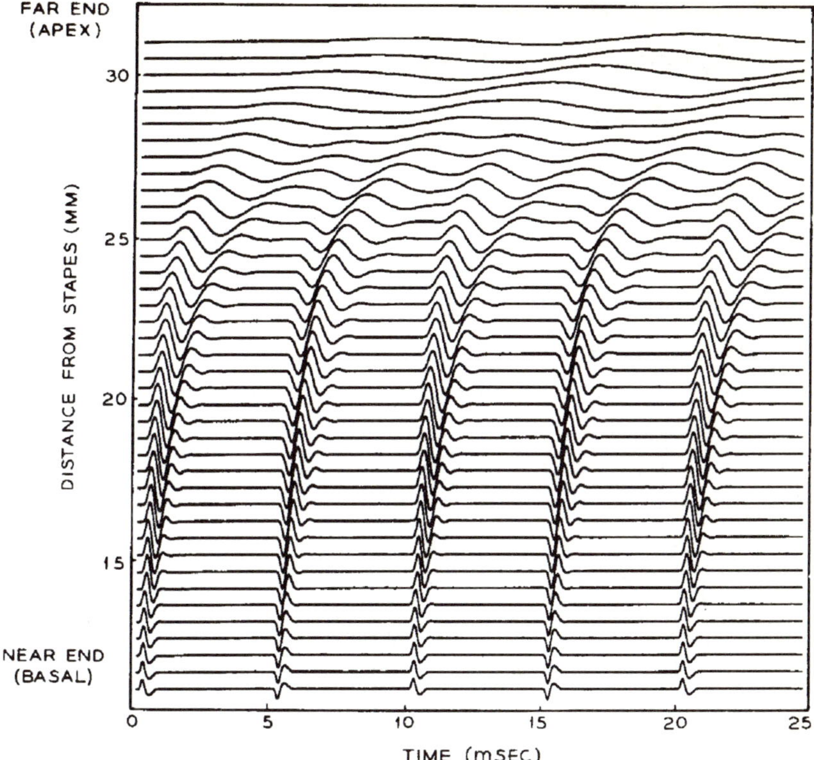

Fig. 8.5. Propagation of short pulses of alternating sign along the basilar membrane, from its input at the stapes ("basal end," shown at the bottom) to the far end ("apex"). As these pulses travel along the basilar membrane, nonlinearly growing time delay and an increasing degree of lowpass filtering (smoothing) can be observed. At the far end, only one sinusoidal component of the pulse train, its fundamental frequency, remains. (Computer simulation by J.L. Flanagan)

One of the mysteries of the inner ear is its ability to convert the energy of incoming sound waves to nerve stimulation with minimum loss and reflection along the BM. This is all the more astonishing if one considers that the BM has to cope with frequencies from 20 Hz to 20 000 Hz – a range of one to one thousand! For this to happen the logarithmic rate of change per wavelength of the parameters determining the resonance behavior of the BM must be small compared to 1 – otherwise some or most of the incident sound energy will be reflected before it reaches its proper place to stimulate the nerves. The fact that evolution has "fine-tuned" the basilar membrane to accomplish this feat is called the *cochlear compromise*: large frequency range and little squandered energy – and all this in a small "box" that fits inside the human head and leaves enough room for seeing, feeling, speaking and the rest.

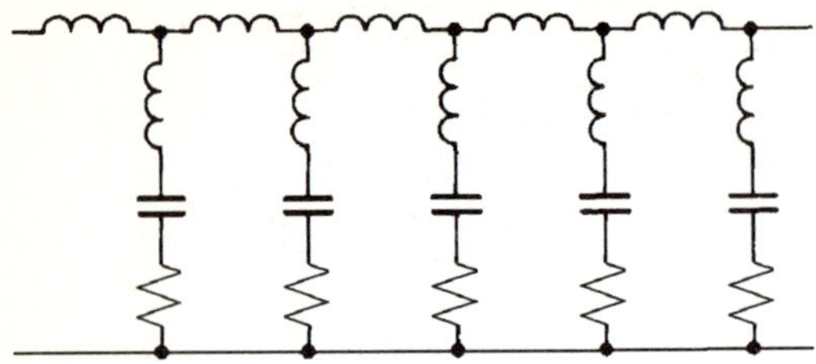

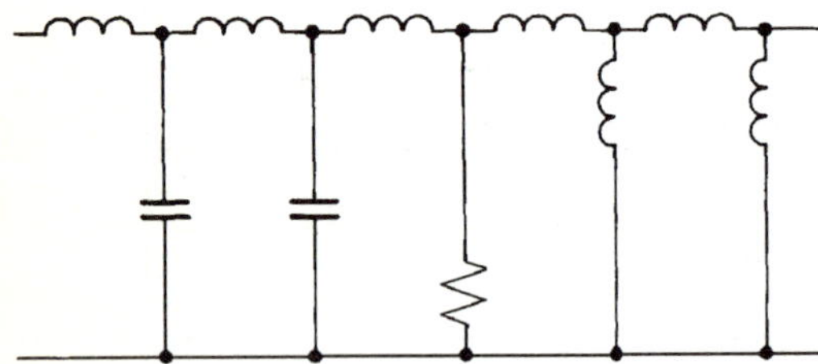

Fig. 8.6. Simplified electrical model of the basilar membrane: inductances represent fluid and membrane inertias, capacitances stand for membrane elasticities, and resistances represent mechanical losses. For a single frequency, the model can be further simplified as shown at the bottom: to the left of the resonance place, the basilar membrane acts as a delay line and beyond the resonance as an attenuator

In this manner, each frequency in the audio frequency range has its own "place" on the BM where it will cause maximum vibration. This observation has led to the so-called "place theories" of pitch perception, according to which the position of maximum vibration of the BM determines the pitch of a pure tone.

The inner ear, or *cochlea*, acts essentially like a bank of overlapping band-pass filters. The mechanical filtering action is provided by the basilar membrane in the inner ear. The bandwidths of these filters are called *critical bands* of hearing. Below 500 Hz, the critical bandwidth is a constant 100 Hz. For higher frequencies the bandwidths are roughly one fifth of the center frequencies [8.17].

The size of these critical bands is based on the anatomy of the basilar membrane, each critical band corresponding to about 1.5 mm in length along the membrane, which has a total length of about 36 mm. Thus there are a total of 24 critical bands, covering the auditory range of the healthy human ear between 20 Hz and 20 000 Hz. The critical bands are usually numbered from $z = 1$ Bark (50–150 Hz) to $z = 24$ Bark (12 000–15 500 Hz).[3] Since the relation between frequency f and Bark is linear for small frequencies and exponential for large frequencies, the author once commandeered the hyperbolic sine-function for an analytic conversion formula between f and Bark [8.19]. But H. Traunmüller had a better idea; a simple rational function will do:

$$z = \frac{26.81 f}{1960 Hz + f} - 0.53 \, ,$$

where the frequency is in Hertz [8.20]. For $f = 1000$ Hz, this formula yields $z = 8.53$, in close agreement with Zwicker's value ($z = 8.50$).

The inner ear is uniformly innervated by about 30 000 ascending nerve fibers connecting the cochlea with the auditory centers in the brain. The mechanical motion of each critical band is therefore "sensed" by some 1200 nerve fibers. As one might expect, signals whose frequency content falls within one critical band are simply added together. This means that, for incoherent signals (such as independent noises), the total power is the sum of the individual powers or intensities.

By contrast, signals whose frequency components do not fall into the same critical band are combined at a higher level in the auditory pathway to the brain. It is as if the *third* or *fourth roots* of the powers are added together (and the sum taken to the third or fourth power). As a result, two noises of the same power, but falling into different critical bands, have a loudness corresponding to an increase in power by a factor of between 8 and 16, rather than just a factor of 2 for two noises with overlapping frequency content.

The observation that there are two different laws for adding the effects of different sounds (to calculate their combined loudness, for example) has in fact led to the discovery of the critical bands in the first place. Apart from loudness, many other subjective phenomena of hearing are governed by the critical bands, including masking. A narrow band noise masks a pure tone within the same critical band much more effectively than outside its critical band.

A serious obstacle in these place theories was the relatively low frequency resolution (the low "Q") of the BM as observed by Békésy. *Psycho*acoustically, the just-noticeable frequency difference between two tones presented in succession to a human listener is less than 3 Hz at 1000 Hz! Nevertheless, undaunted model builders were hardly at a loss to "explain" this impressive frequency discrimination. They explained it by assuming sophisticated neural processing following the crude mechanical filtering action of the

---

[3] The designation of the critical bands by "Bark" is unrelated to dogs. It was coined by Zwicker [8.18] after the German engineer Heinrich Georg Barkhausen (1881–1956) who invented an early cm-wave oscillator and, in 1911, was appointed to the first professorship in communications engineering (*Schwachstromtechnik*). He proposed subjective measurements of loudness and introduced the loudness unit *phon*.

BM. We will not trace their intricate (and probably erroneous) reasoning and simply remark that in more recent work the mechanical filtering of the BM was shown to be much more frequency-selective than found by Békésy. The reason why Békésy did not observe this high frequency resolution is that he worked with cadavers and had to use large sound amplitudes in order to be able to see the BM motions under his microscope. It is now known, through the work of Rhode and others [8.21], that frequency selectivity, is substantially lowered at high amplitudes and within minutes after metabolism ceases.

The great sensitivity and frequency selectivity of our hearing is now believed to be the result of *active* amplification mechanisms in the inner ear. Convincing evidence that such mechanisms are at work come from "Kemp echoes" and other oto-acoustic emissions [8.22]. In the Kemp echo, named after its discoverer D.T. Kemp, a short acoustic impulse or tone burst is reflected in the inner ear and emerges from the ear canal to the outside air with a delay that exceeds the roundtrip delay expected for purely mechanical processes including the traveling wave transmission on the BM. Even more surprising, the *energy* of the echo exceeds the energy expected for a purely passive reflection in the inner ear. Rather the relatively long delay and the gain in energy point to an active amplification mechanism at or near the point of mechanical-to-neural transduction.

Besides the Kemp echo, even *spontaneous* oto-acoustic emission, i.e. sounds coming out of the ear without any acoustic "provocation," have been observed [8.23]. These probably reflect feedback instabilities of the amplifiers responsible for the Kemp echo. The nonlinearities of the inner ear, as evidenced in Tartini's *terzi suoni* and other combination tones are now thought to result from an *overloading* of these amplifiers rather than purely mechanical nonlinearities (violations of Hooke's law of elasticity), which were always unbelievable because, as mentioned before, these nonlinearities are observable near the threshold of hearing when mechanical motion is comparable to the diameter of the hydrogen atom! Further evidence that the nonlinear distortions stem from overloading amplifiers is furnished by the fact that these low-level nonlinearities disappear when inner-ear metabolism ceases as a result of cutting the oxygen supply or administering ototoxic drugs – or death.

On the basis of these observations, the amplifiers involved in sharpening the BM response are believed to be of a biochemical nature. The hypothesized chain of events is as follows

- mechanical motion of the BM is sensed by the *inner* hair cells which stimulate the release of biochemical energy sources, i.e. energy-laden molecules like those found in muscle tissue.
- the energy is converted into mechanical strains which are transmitted by the *outer* hair cells back to BM to amplify its motion.

Of course, such a feedback arrangement can lead to instabilities: a screeching or otherwise unpleasant sound perceived by the sufferer and that occasionally can even be heard by bystanders (external tinnitus).

8.9 Mechanical to Neural Transduction

If an acoustic sinewave impinges on the outer ear, the BM is set into a motion which is (approximately) a sinusoidal function of time. This motion is transmitted to the outer hair cells, "riding on top" of the BM, via "cilia," the little tufts of hair growing on each hair cell. These hairs are believed to be attached to the tectorial membrane. The relative motion between the BM and the tectorial membrane will bend (or otherwise deform or displace) these little hairs which thus play a role not unlike that of a phonograph pickup needle in converting mechanical vibrations into electrical signals. The motion of the cilia alters the electrical conductance of a biological membrane at the surface of the hair cell thereby modulating an electrical current flowing through the hair cell [8.24]. The sources of this current are well-documented potential differences between the different channels (*scalae*) of the inner ear.

The alternating current in turn is believed to influence the release of synaptic "vesicles" in the hair cell. These vesicles, little packets containing a chemical "transmitter" substance, migrate to the inner surface of the hair cell opposite the terminal of an "afferent" nerve fiber which they cause to "fire". These nerve firings can be recorded by means of a microelectrode whose tiny tip (less than a thousandth of millimeter in diameter!) has been inserted into the inside of the nerve fiber.

Electrical pulses ("spikes") in the acoustic nerve are about 0.5 ms in duration and can occur at an average rate exceeding 100 pulses per second even without acoustic stimulation, i.e. "spontaneously". A typical figure for the spontaneous firing rate is about 50 pulses per second. During strong steady-state acoustic stimulation, the firing rate can go to 150 or more pulses per second.

During the *onset* of strong stimulation, the firing rate can, for a short time, go up as high as 1000 pulses per second. Much higher rates are not possible because of the *refractory period* ("dead time") of the nerve after each firing. This dead time, during which the nerve fiber restores its membrane characteristics is about 1 ms in the acoustic nerve.

For continued stimulation, the high-onset firing rate decays quickly to the so-called *adapted* firing rate. This "adaptation" is a property the acoustic nerves share with other neural structures.

Adaptation appears to be one of the pervading facts of neural life which any serious model must take into account. In a typical model, adaptation is brought about by a "depletion" mechanism, i.e. a mechanism by which quanta (vesicles) of a chemical agent in the hair cell are used up in firing the attached nerve [8.25].

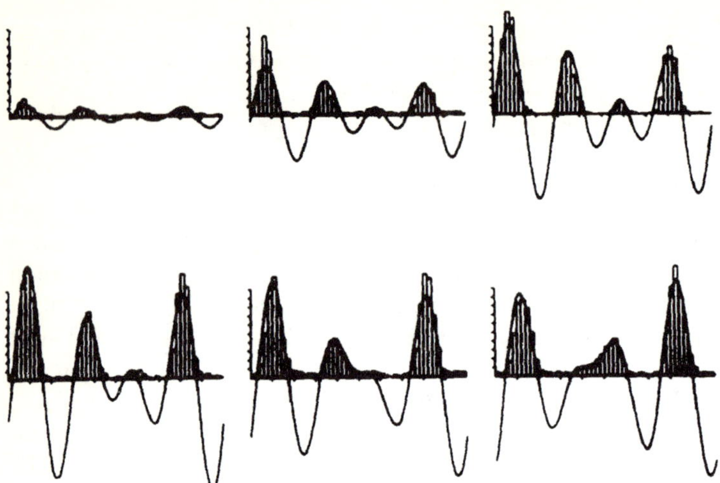

Fig. 8.7. Firing rates of nerve spikes as a function of time for different waveforms. The individual nerve acts as a nearly linear half-wave rectifier

Besides adaptation and refractoriness, *the* outstanding features of acoustic nerve activity are a kind of (one-sided) *linearity* and an *automatic gain control*. Linearity means that the firing probability of the acoustic nerve, as determined during many cycles of a periodic stimulus, is a close (almost linear) replica of the "positive" portions of the stimulating waveform, see Fig. 8.7. During negative portions of the stimulus waveforms, the firing probability is suppressed below the spontaneous rate. Thus the transduction process, at least for a finite range of amplitudes, acts as an approximate *linear half-wave rectifier*.

The automatic gain control inherent in the transduction process means that, within a certain range of amplitudes, the firing probability is almost independent of the signal amplitude. It is particularly noteworthy that the gain control mechanism leaves the wave*form* largely intact. Thus the gain control seen in the acoustic neuron does *not* act like an instantaneous compressor – let alone like an amplitude clipper. Its action resembles the adjustment of a volume control with a response time of some 20 ms.

One of the striking features of the auditory cortex is its tonotopic organisation for both "carrier" frequencies and modulation frequencies. It has been known for some time that two pure tones of similar frequency stimulate adjacent neurons in the cortex. More recently it was discovered that the all-important *modulation* frequencies, too, are represented tonotopically in the brain: similar modulation frequencies stimulate adjacent columns of neural tissue. This type of neural organization is reminiscent of the discoveries of Hubel and Wiesel for the visual system.

8.10 Some Astounding Monaural Phase Effects

In order to explain this remarkable insensitivity of the ear to phase and thus to the signal *waveform*, Ohm and Helmholtz proposed the following model:

- the ear has a set of tuned "bandpass filters" covering the audio frequency range, and
- the ear measures the *amplitude* at the output of each filter and transmits *only* this information to the brain.

The bandpass filters were thought to be realized by "tuned strings" in the BM. The hair cells were the obvious candidates for the amplitude measuring device.

Controversy has raged throughout the latter part of the last century and the first half of our century as to the validity of Ohm's Acoustic Law. Most published counterexamples were eventually traced to faulty equipment which generated distortion products whose *interference* (with the signal and with each other) *did* depend on relative phase angles. (Note that much of the early work on phase perception was done before electronic filters and amplifiers had become available!)

Nevertheless, a hard core of genuine phase effects remained – the elegant "AM–FM" experiment by Mathes and Miller being perhaps the best known. The stimulus in the AM–FM experiment consists of an AM carrier at, say, 2000 Hz, the modulation frequency being, for example, 100 Hz. The signal thus consists of three frequency components at 1900, 2000, and 2100 Hz.

If the phase of one of the sidebands at 1900 or 2100 Hz is changed by 180°, the AM signal changes into a "quasi-FM" (QFM) signal ("quasi," because the frequency modulation is accompanied by a small amplitude modulation at twice the modulation frequency).

On listening alternately to the AM and QFM signals, a pronounced acoustic quality difference is perceived. (If Ohm or Helmholtz had been able to listen to these signals, they might have been reluctant to formulate their phase law. They would have had to discard their simple ideas – to the detriment of their followers whose work was based on the tuned-filter model of hearing. Primitive equipment, such as Helmholtz had to work with, sometimes helps to formulate powerful ideas – even if, in the end, these ideas emerge as mere approximations. (Would Newton have dared to formulate his laws of motion and gravitation if Kepler's observations had been beset by relativistic side effects such as the perihelion motion of Mercury?)

The outcome of the AM–FM experiment revived interest in the ear's capability to decode *waveforms* (as opposed to amplitude spectra). As early as 1954, upon joining Bell Laboratories, I became intrigued by the possible effects of waveform on the quality of synthetic speech. To what extent was the poor quality of vocoder speech [8.26] caused by *waveform* effects? Vocoders, in conformity with Helmholtz' thinking, reproduced the short-time

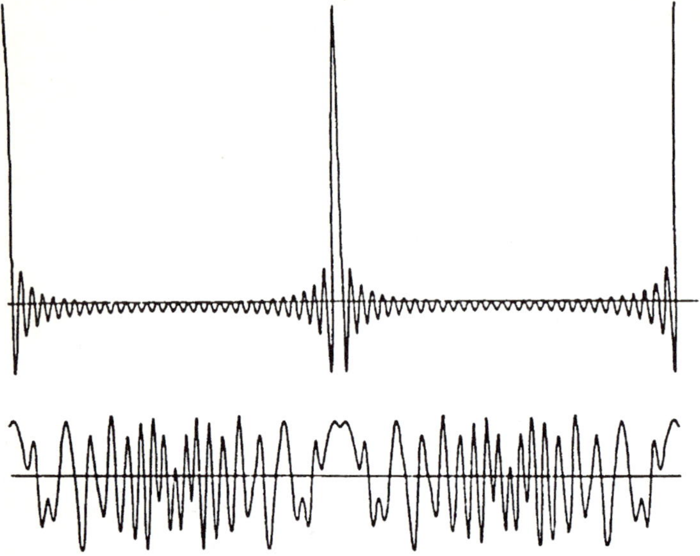

Fig. 8.8. *Top:* one period of a periodic pulse train consisting of 31 harmonics (1 through 31) in cosine phase (0°). *Bottom:* the same 31 harmonics but with "random" phase angles (0° or 180°). The range from maximum-to-minimum signal amplitude (the "peak factor") is reduced by a factor 2.64 compared to the signal shown at the top. In this illustration, the phase angles were computed from a theoretical formula based on frequency-modulated signals [8.27]

amplitude spectrum of speech signals with no regard to the phase angles of the analyzed speech signal. Specifically, voiced speech sounds are synthesized from quasiperiodic pulse trains whose harmonics all have equal (zero) phase angles. If one randomized these phase angles, a signal with a much smaller "peak factor" (defined as maximum-to-minimum amplitude range divided by the rms amplitude) would result. Figure 8.8 shows the result of such a phase angle "randomization".

In listening to the two waveforms depicted in Fig. 8.8 an astonishingly large quality difference is perceived – in spite of the identity of their amplitude spectra (31 harmonics of equal amplitude from 100 Hz to 3100 Hz). Synthetic speech signals obtained from these two "excitation" signals likewise sounded quite different (less "buzzy" for the low-peak-factor waveform).

The first explanation attributed this quality difference to the large difference in peak factor. But subsequent experiments with waveforms of similarly low peak-factors showed that every one of them sounded different – except when their phase angles were related by a "linear" transformation [8.28], i.e. if the two sets of phase angles ϕ_k and ψ_k were related to each other as

$$\psi_k = \phi_k + \alpha + \beta k \, , \tag{8.1}$$

where α and β are arbitrary constants and k is the harmonic number.

The term βk in (8.1) is trivial since it causes a simple delay of $(\beta/2\pi f_1)$, where f_1 is the fundamental frequency.

The α term in (8.1), however, is significant because it does lead to a change in the *waveform* – yet, as already stated, it leaves the acoustic quality unchanged.

Which aspect of the *signal* $s(t)$ remains invariant when the phase of each harmonic is changed by the same amount? The answer: the signal *envelope* $e(t)$ defined by (see also Chap. 10)

$$e^2(t) = s^2(t) + \tilde{s}^2(t) \, , \tag{8.2}$$

where $\tilde{s}(t)$ is the *Hilbert* transform of $s(t)$:

$$\tilde{s}(t) = \frac{1}{\pi} \int_{-\infty}^{\infty} \frac{s(\tau)}{\tau - t} d\tau. \tag{8.3}$$

With the aid of the Hilbert transform, an *analytic signal* $\sigma(t)$ can be defined

$$\sigma(t) = s(t) - i\tilde{s}(t) \, , \tag{8.4}$$

whose Fourier transform vanishes for all negative frequencies.

An alternate way of writing the analytic signal uses the previously defined envelope $e(t)$ and a phase function $\gamma(t)$:

$$\sigma(t) = e(t) \exp[i\gamma(t)] \, , \tag{8.5}$$

where

$$\gamma(t) = \arctan\left[\frac{-s(t)}{\tilde{s}(t)}\right] . \tag{8.6}$$

Since $\sigma(t)$ has no negative frequencies, a phase shift by α is equivalent to a multiplication of $\sigma(t)$ by $\exp(i\alpha)$:

$$\sigma_\alpha(t) = e(t) \exp[i\gamma(t) + i\alpha]. \tag{8.7}$$

The corresponding phase-shifted real signal is

$$s_\alpha(t) = e(t) \cos[\gamma(t) + \alpha] \, , \tag{8.8}$$

whose envelope $e(t)$ is thus seen to be independent of a phase shift.

In other words, phase transformations of the form $\psi_k = \phi_k + \alpha + \beta k$ which do not change the acoustical quality of a signal also leave the *envelope* invariant (except for a delay undetectable in monaural listening).

What would thus be more natural than to assume that the ear acts as an envelope detector on the BM waveforms it "sees". This is, in fact, the view originally suggested and widely accepted among acousticians.

Nevertheless, a strict envelope hearing hypothesis and the linear-phase transformation rule are contradicted by several listening experiments with signals containing only *two* frequency components. For such signals, *any* phase transformation is a *linear*-phase transformation of the form (8.1) and the envelope is given solely by the amplitude spectrum. Thus phase manipulations on such signals should be undetectable. However, Craig and Jeffress [8.29] have shown that this is not so, although the phase effects they found were rather subtle.

8.11 Masking

Masking is one of the most pervasive facts of human hearing. Masking means that one sound makes another, weaker sound, inaudible. A pedestrian wearing a walkman playing loud music may not hear the oncoming truck. Reverberation makes the following weaker speech sounds inaudible and therefore unintelligible.

But even if a sound is not rendered completely inaudible, its perceived loudness may be reduced by a stronger sound. This is called loudness reduction or *partial masking*. The masking effect is typically limited to the frequencies near that of the masker which could be a tone, a tone complex (chord), or a noise – narrow or wide.

Except at very low sound levels, the frequency dependence of masking is asymmetric: there is more upward than downward spread of masking. In other words, a noise around 1000 Hz masks a tone at 1200 Hz more effectively than a tone at 800 Hz. For masking within a critical band, the tone can have a sound level as low as 3 to 6 dB below the noise level before it is completely masked.

For the quantization of speech signals the masking – not of a tone by noise, but of noise (quantizing noise) by tones (speech) – is the interesting question. Psychoacoustic experiments by J. L. Hall, Jr., and the author have revealed that the presence of a weak noise, as weak as 24 dB below a pure tone, can still be detected. How is this possible? Listening to such stimuli shows that, at such low levels, the presence of a noise is not perceived as a noise per se but as a slight "quaver" in the tone. Hence masking of noise by tones is quite different from masking of tones by noise.

8.12 Loudness

The loudness of a pure tone depends not only on its physical intensity or level but also on its frequency. The loudness level of a test tone (or any acoustic signal) is determined by adjusting the level of a 1-kHz tone until it sounds equally loud as the test stimulus. The level in decibel above threshold of the 1-kHz tone is then called the *loudness level* of the test stimulus. The unit of loudness level is the *phon*.

Loudness is the perceptual attribute of the physical intensity of a sound. The unit of loudness, the *sone*, is defined as the loudness of a binaural 1-kHz tone at 40 dB sound pressure level (SPL) above the threshold of hearing. A sound that is perceived as twice as loud is given the loudness value $L = 2$. In this manner, by subjective loudness judgments, an entire loudness scale can be established ranging from zero sones at the threshold of hearing to 256 sones at a sound intensity $I = 120\,\mathrm{dB}$ SPL. Over a large range of hearing (above about 20 dB SPL) a simple power law exists between loudness L and intensity I:

$$L \propto I^{0.3} \ . \tag{8.9}$$

This law means that merely to double the loudness of a rock group of five musicians, say, we have to increase their number *tenfold*, to 50 players of equal power output. (This minor calculation explains the resounding enamoration of popular music makers with electronic amplifiers.)

By the same token, if we want to halve the loudness of a continuous "rumble" emanating from a busy highway, we have to reduce the acoustic noise output by a factor of ten! This may sound difficult, but it is not, at least not from a purely physical point of view: tire noise – the main culprit at steady highway speeds – decreases drastically with decreasing vehicle speed. In fact, the noise intensity is approximately proportional to the *fourth* power of speed.

On the other hand, a tenfold increase in the average intensity of traffic noise caused by a tenfold increase in traffic *density* can raise the rate of complaints by irate residents perhaps a *hundred* fold: one loud truck every 5 minutes may be tolerable, but one every 30 seconds could be a nightmare and would certainly make outdoor conversation nearly impossible. And what is true for trucks is just as true for low-flying aircraft.

8.13 Scaling in Psychology

Whereas measurement in classical physics is a well-understood process, relating an observed quantity to a well-defined unit, the situation in psychology was not so clear-cut until the physiologist E. H. Weber (1795–1878) – brother of the physicist Wilhelm Weber (1804–1891) – made careful studies of the sensations of sound and touch, thereby laying the foundations of a new science, the science of sensations. According to Weber's law, an increase in stimulus necessary to elicit a just noticeable increase in sensation is not a fixed quantity, but depends on the ratio of increase to the original stimulus. Later, the physicist and philosopher G. T. Fechner (1801–1887) restated Weber's law (now called the Weber–Fechner law) and specified its domain of validity.[4] Modern psychologists, and particularly S. S. Stevens, have suc-

---

[4] Fechner also fathomed experimental aesthetics by measuring which shapes and dimensions are most pleasing. He may have been the first to conduct a public opinion poll (to discover which of two Holbein paintings was preferred by viewers).

ceeded in introducing measurement methods into psychology that are nearly as unambiguous as objective measurements in physics [8.30]. The new discipline has therefore rightly earned the designation *psychophysics*, of which psychoacoustics is a special branch, as is psychovisual research.

One of Steven's great contributions was the introduction of *ratio scales* for subjective variables (like loudness and brightness) and the discovery of simple power-law relations between these subjective variables and corresponding physical quantities (like energy flux or intensity) [8.31].

As already mentioned, for a sound to double in loudness L, its intensity I has to be multiplied by a factor or 10. Thus, because $\log_{10} 2 \approx 0.3$, we have the following power law for loudness as a function of acoustic intensity: $L \propto I^{0.3}$.

Someone who has not participated in a psychoacoustic scaling test might object that "loudness doubling" is not a well-defined concept. But surprisingly, the random scatter encountered in such tests is remarkably small even between different listeners.

The exponents found in psychophysical power laws, such as the value 0.3 in the above equation, are not universal but are specific to the sense modality studied (subjective brightness, perceived weight, or apparent length, for example) and have been analyzed in great detail by psychophysicists. One important research question concerns the *transitivity* of these exponents when comparing loudness with weight and weight with brightness, for example, and what it might reveal about brain functions.

If we replace the sound intensity I in (8.9) by the sound pressure p, then, because intensity is proportional to pressure *squared*, we have

$$L \propto p^{0.6} \ .$$

Interestingly, the exponent 0.6 can be derived from an exponent of 0.5 found at a more fundamental level, the Fourier-like "critical" frequency-band decomposition of sounds in the inner ear. The exponent 0.5, in turn, turns our attention in the direction of statistical analysis and uncertainty resulting from the firing rate of nerve pulses traveling along the acoustic nerve up to higher auditory centers in the brain. If these pulses were a modulated Poisson process whose mean rate was proportional to the sound pressure p, then the uncertainty of the number of pulses in a given time interval (100 ms, say) would be proportional to $p^{0.5}$. Since many ratio scales in psychophysics are found to be directly related to perceptual uncertainties ("just noticeable differences"), the observed power law for subjective loudness *versus* physical intensity would then indeed be predicted by such a statistical model of neural firing rates.

In reality, loudness perception is more complicated, but the observed power laws and their exponents have yielded important clues and steered researchers in the right direction.

8.14 Pitch Perception and Uncertainty

The just noticeable frequency difference between two tones around 1000 Hz is less than 1% for normal listeners. Trained listeners can achieve a frequency discrimination of at least 3 Hz (0.3%) at 1000 Hz. According to the Heisenberg uncertainty principle, this high frequency resolution implies a time window longer than about 0.3 s. On the other hand, in listening to speech humans are known to discriminate temporal detail of 0.01 s or less. In other words, the time-bandwidth uncertainty product of the human ear appears to equal 0.03 instead of 1, making human hearing 30 times better than the laws of physics allows. How is this possible?

The only answer seems to be that, depending on the task, the human auditory system can use one of several spectral analyzers with different time resolutions and frequency discriminations. Thus, in listening to speech, the hearer uses an analyzer with a high time resolution (0.01 s). When listening to (slow) music, he or she switches to an analyzer with high frequency discrimination.

9. Binaural Hearing –
Listening with Both Ears[1]

Hear the other side.

St. Augustine (354–430)

Although, at present, telephone speech is mostly monaural, the future promises much binaural business. Think of tele-conferences and virtual acoustic spaces. The following informal overview of binaural hearing covers directional hearing (in the horizontal and vertical planes), the precedence and Haas effects (and their applications in public-address and "assisted-resonance" systems), artificial reverberation, pseudo-stereophony, binaural release from masking, the cocktail-party effect, central-pitch phenomena, Deutsch's octave illusion, the creation of virtual sound images, and the faithful reproduction of concert hall recordings in an anechoic environment for acoustical quality studies. The chapter concludes with a brief review of sound-diffusing surfaces based on number theory that have become standard equipment in sound recording studios, including those for speech signals.

9.1 Directional Hearing

Our directional sense of hearing is astounding. Differences of arrival times at the two ears of a few tens of *micro*seconds can be clearly perceived as a change in direction. Thus the time resolution, Δt, of our ears in binaural hearing exceeds by a factor of 10 or more that of monaural hearing which lies in the millisecond range.

This exquisite time resolution translates to an angular discrimination $\Delta\alpha$ of just a few degrees in the horizontal plane – and the horizontal plane is, of course, the place where the sound sources of greatest interest to us cavort and where much of the danger lurks. The approximate relationship is

---

[1] Adapted in part from *Music Perception* **10**, 225–280 (1993).

Fig. 9.1. A Swiss naval pilot, on board a lake steamer, wearing a listening device with an extended binaural base to better locate a fog horn

$$\Delta\alpha = 180°\frac{c}{d}\Delta t \ , \tag{9.1}$$

where c is the velocity of sound in air and d is the "baseline," i.e. the effective distance between the two ears [9.1].

Of course, with a longer baseline between our ears, our directional hearing would be even more acute, as furniture designers and the military have discovered early on. Figure 9.1 shows a Swiss ship's pilot and Fig. 9.2 depicts an armchair with "ear-trumpets," an early binaural preprocessor.

How do we localize in the *vertical* plane? Admittedly, this is not as important to humans as localization in the horizontal plane. But, as already mentioned, people do have considerable vertical directional discrimination. This is a bit puzzling because there are no arrival time or intensity differences between the ears for sounds arriving in the symmetry plane through the human head. Could slight head motions be responsible? This possibility has been eliminated by having subjects bite into bite-boards to immobilize their heads. Finally, Jens Blauert came along and showed that the *frequency content* of a signal was responsible for elevation judgments [9.2].

Differences in spectral content are mediated by sound diffraction at the listener's head, causing different filtering actions for sound waves arriving from different directions in the symmetry plane. Thus, for example, certain high frequencies coming from behind the listener are attenuated by the shadowing effect of his outer ears (pinnae). Distance judgments, too, are facilitated by spectral content [9.3].

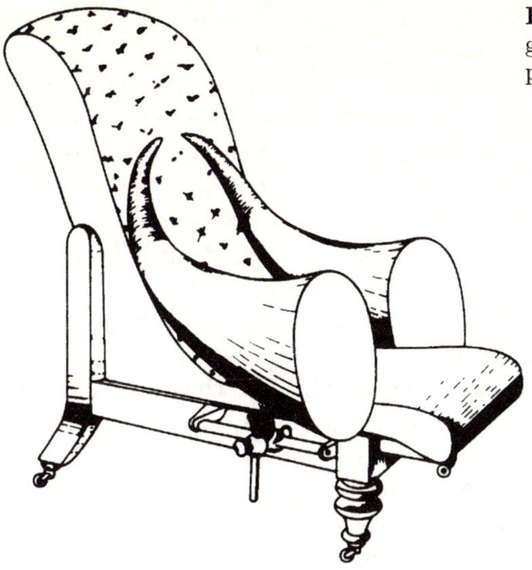

Fig. 9.2. Early model of an integrated binaural hearing aid. (Patent pending?)

9.2 Precedence and Haas Effects

One of the more astonishing attributes of binaural hearing is the precedence effect, or "law of the first wavefront." This effect was first described over 100 years ago by the Princeton physicist Joseph Henry (1797–1878), whose name is enshrined in the unit for magnetic inductance. Henry observed that when two (or more) similar transient sounds reach a listener from different directions in rapid succession, the listener hears a single sound from the direction of the first-arriving sound.

It has been hypothesized that the precedence effect has evolved because, in a reverberant environment (think of a dense forest or an echoic cave), it is the direction of the first wavefront that betrays the direction of a predator on the prowl or a potential mate – or a source of live food.

In 1950, Helmut Haas, in his Göttingen thesis, showed that the later sounds can exceed the first sound in intensity by some 10 dB without causing the perceived direction to change much [9.4].

This so-called Haas effect (so named by R. H. Bolt) allows the enhancement of sound levels in a public-address system by means of loudspeakers radiating an amplified but delayed signal without becoming audible and distracting the listener's attention from the original, albeit weaker, sound source. A "smart" public-address system exploiting the Haas effect was first installed in 1953 by Parkin in St. Paul's Cathedral in London. The "assisted resonance" system in Royal Festival Hall (to improve its low-frequency response) is a further exploitation of the first-wavefront principle. And the Palace of Congresses in the Moscow Kremlin is an example of a hall where artificial reverberation completely dominates the natural sound. (The reverberation is "manufactured" in the subterranean chambers of the Palace and piped into the main hall by a plethora of loudspeakers.)

The precedence effect can be nicely demonstrated in an amusing experiment conceived by the late Nico Franssen of the Phillips research laboratories in Eindhoven, the Netherlands. A tone signal is fed to two loudspeakers, the left speaker radiating only a short transient and then falling silent, see Fig. 9.3. The right speaker radiates a slightly delayed and softly turned-on steady tone. Because of the precedence effect, the sound is located at the left speaker.

In a reverberant environment, listeners invariably perceive the tone as continuing to come from the silent speaker and are amazed when the demonstrator "pulls the plug" on the left loudspeaker and the thus disconnected loudspeaker still seems to be the active source. Interestingly, this paradoxical percept only works in a reverberant environment with lateral reflections in which the binaural cues for a steady tone (amplitude and phase differences) are ambiguous as a result of multipass transmission. In this kind of situation the ear appears to cling to the only unambiguous clue, the initial transient. This is another instance of the "continuity effect" which is also manifest in other sensory modalities, including monaural perception, see Sect. 8.4.2.

Equally surprising is the famous "cocktail-party effect" which allows a binaural listener to suppress unwanted sounds when their directions do not coincide with that of the wanted signal. I think it is fair to say that without this remarkable ability of human hearing the cocktail-party as a social institution would have become extinct long ago (assuming, of course, that people actually want to listen to what other people have to say, see Fig. 9.4).

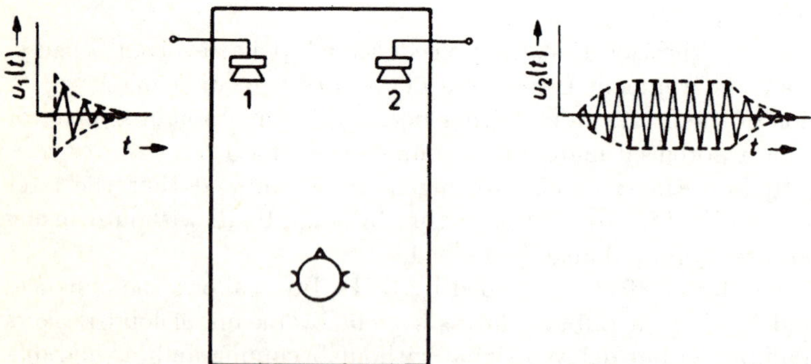

Fig. 9.3. Binaural localization completely gone astray. In a reverberant room, the tone is heard as emanating from the left loudspeaker even after it has long been turned off there and, in fact, is radiated only from the right loudspeaker. This is another instance of the "continuity effect" that pervades all sensory modalities. – By contrast, in an anechoic environment, on an open lawn, for example, the auditory percept switches immediately from left to right after the left loudspeaker ceases to emit sound because there is no binaural amplitude and phase ambiguity as in a reverberant space

**"Although humans make sounds with their mouths and occasionally
look at each other, there is no solid evidence that they
actually communicate among themselves."**

Fig. 9.4. A duo of dolphins belittling human communication – caught in the act
by Sidney Harris

The electronic simulation of the cocktail-party effect and other schemes
for suppressing unwanted noises are among the more ambitious aims of future
binaural hearing aids and conference telephone systems.

9.3 Vertical Localization

How is vertical localization possible? One older theory attributed this ability
to small (involuntary) head motions. But the ability to localize in the median
plane persists even when the listener's head is rigidly fixed (e.g. by a "bite-
board").

The answer is that for different directions of incidence, the sound is differ-
ently diffracted at the head and the pinnae. Thus the sound waves entering
the external ear canal are, in fact, "filtered" by diffraction. For each direction,
characteristic peaks and *valleys* are superimposed on the spectrum of the incident sound. If the sound has a sufficiently broad spectrum (as is true for
speech, music, and most noises), these peaks and valleys in the spectrum of
the acoustic signal that strikes the ear drums can be recognized and utilized
to determine the direction of incidence [9.5]. People have apparently learned,
over many listening experiences, to associate different spectral characteristics
with different vertical directions!

If this hypothesis is correct, then a broadband noise, whose spectrum has
been shaped in accordance with the diffraction process for a given direction
of incidence, should elicit the corresponding subjective direction *irrespective
of the actual direction*. Subjective tests employing such filtered signals have
confirmed this hypothesis to an astounding degree [9.2], see Fig. 9.5.

In fact, another puzzle that has defied solution for many decades, has
finally been explained by considering *spectral* characteristics. The puzzle is

Fig. 9.5. Sound localization in the vertical plane – long a mystery because of the absence of binaural difference cues – is apparently determined by spectral shape and frequency content. Strong frequency components around 300 Hz and 3 kHz elicit a frontal perception, frequency bands around 1 kHz and 10 kHz favor the perception of sound arriving from the back; emphasis of spectral components around 8 kHz elicit a "from above" percept

the following. Why, when listening over earphones, do we hear the sound as originating *inside* our head? Why is it so difficult, or even impossible, to "externalize" the sound source as we habitually do when listening to primary sound sources or to loudspeakers?

One answer, that evoked some credence for a time, was that, with earphone listening, sound sources followed head motions and that such seemingly nonstationary sound sources evoked sound images inside the listener's head. Another "theory" held the mechanical pressure of the headset's ear cushion on the head responsible for "internalization". Benjamin Bauer of CBS Laboratories, in an ingenious experiment, disproved both theories by "pressureless" earphones whose signals were automatically modified when the listener's head moved, to correspond to the modifications experienced when listening in a free sound field. Again, many listeners (including the author) failed to externalize the sound images.

The failure to externalize with earphone listening is now attributed to the following set of circumstances. When wearing earphones, standing waves are set up in the external ear canal between the ear drum and the membrane of the earphone. These standing waves have a filtering action which is rather different from the spectral peaks and valleys caused by diffraction at the listener's head in a free-field listening situation [9.6]. Thus the listener can associate *no* external location with earphone listening and consequently associates the sound sources with the only remaining location: inside the listener's head.

If this theory is correct, then *inverse* filtering (to remove the effect of standing waves in the ear canal) combined with a filter response corresponding to free-field listening should give externalized sound sources. This has, in fact, been demonstrated by Laws [9.7] and others.

The late R. L. Wallace, Jr., of Bell Laboratories has constructed earphones which minimize standing waves between the earphone membrane and the eardrum by placing absorbing materials at the entrance to the ear canal. With these earphones people are able to externalize sound sources although not as consistently as with electrical filters, which not only eliminate the effect of the standing waves but substitute the proper filtering action of head diffraction.

9.4 Virtual Sound Sources and Quasi-Stereophony

An important application of filtering sound signals to evoke proper localization was demonstrated as early as 1962 [9.8]. In ordinary two-channel stereophonic systems, perceived sound sources are usually restricted to the space between the two reproducing loudspeakers. Physical sound sources to the rear, overhead, and to the sides (outside the line connecting the two loudspeakers) are not properly reproduced in their apparent positions. Yet, because we have only *two* ears, *two* loudspeakers should suffice to evoke all the proper perceptions of acoustic space – *provided* the sound waves radiated from the two loudspeakers are "tailored" in such a way as to produce, at the listener's eardrums, pressure waves indistinguishable from those that the ears would have received in a free sound field set up by the desired sources (including sources to the rear, overhead, and to the extreme sides).

Implementation of this idea requires the prior measurement of the complex transmission functions (i.e. amplitude and phase as functions of frequency) between a loudspeaker in an anechoic chamber and the right and left eardrums of a human listener.

Suppose two loudspeakers are placed in front of a listener, one, say, $30°$ to the right and the other $30°$ to the left. Call the transmission function from a loudspeaker to the eardrum on the same side $S(f)$ and that to the eardrum on the other side $A(f)$.

If $A(f)$ were zero, i.e. if there was no "crosstalk" from the loudspeakers to the "far" ears, the task of providing each eardrum with a specified sound signal would be simple. The loudspeaker signals must be filtered by the *inverse* of the "same-side" transmission function $S^{-1}(f)$. However, regrettably for our purposes, there *is* crosstalk to the "other-side" ear due to sound diffraction around the human head. This crosstalk must be cancelled.

This can be accomplished by the other loudspeaker radiating an appropriately filtered crosstalk compensation signal. Of course this crosstalk compensation signal also "talks across" to the ear for which it is not intended and must, therefore, be compensated by a compensation signal supplied to the first loudspeaker – and so on *ad infinitum*.

The all-inclusive solution to this multiple filtering and cancellation problem is illustrated in Fig. 9.6, where $C(f) = -A(f)S^{-1}(f)$ is the transfer function of the crosstalk compensation filter. The overall transmission function from the right input (R) to the right ear (r) is then

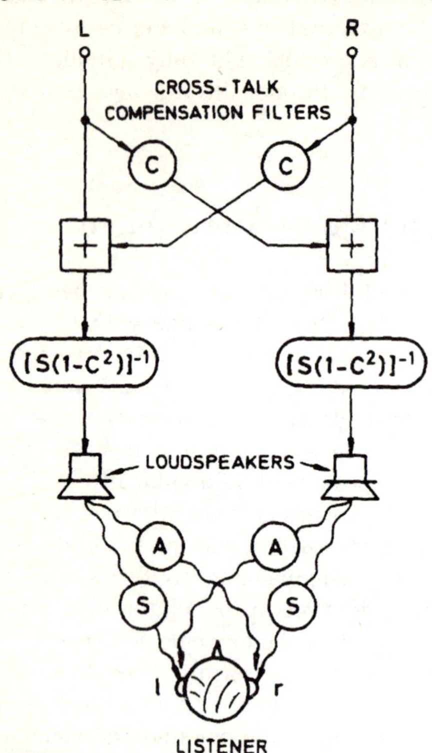

Fig. 9.6. How can one transfer a pair of binaural signals, recorded, say, from a dummy head (see Fig. 9.7), to the ears of a human listener by means of loudspeakers (instead of earphones)? This schematic drawing shows how to compensate, by means of electronic filters, the cross-talk from the left loudspeaker to right ear and the right speaker to the left ear. This arrangement allows free-field listening and has been used for concert-hall simulations. With earphone listening, by contrast, the simulated ("virtual") acoustic space would follow head motions instead of remaining stationary. The depicted presentation also avoids the "in-head" localizations that bedevil earphone listening

$$R_r(f) = (1 - C^2)^{-1}S^{-1}S + C(1 - C^2)^{-1}S^{-1}A \,,$$

with $C = -AS^{-1}$, $R_r = 1$ as required. The overall response from the right input to the *left* ear (ℓ) can also easily be read off Fig. 9.6:

$$R_\ell(f) = (1 - C^2)^{-1}S^{-1}A + C(1 - C^2)^{-1}S^{-1}S = 0 \,,$$

as required.

The practical experience with the filtering scheme illustrated in Fig. 9.6 has been nothing less than amazing. Although the two loudspeakers are the only sound sources, virtual sound images can be created far off to the sides and even *behind* the listener. In fact, even the *elevation* angle of a sound source is properly perceived (best by people with proper head shapes!). Since the entire system is linear, many sound sources and their echoes can be reproduced simultaneously, without mutual interference, provided the listener is sitting in the proper position between the loudspeakers and does not turn his head away from the front direction by more than about $\pm 10°$. The spatial illusion is, in fact, so convincing that the listener is tempted to "look around" for any invisible sound sources. However, the moment he gives in to this temptation the realistic illusion disappears, frequently changing into an "inside-the-head" sensation.

The sound reproduction method illustrated in Fig. 9.6 has opened up completely new possibilities in the study of concert hall acoustics [9.9]. Before, in comparing two halls, one had to base one's judgment on listening to pieces of music, played at different times, perhaps by different orchestras under different conductors. Even if all other factors were equal, the fact that two musical experiences are separated by days, weeks, or even months make any subtle quality assessments exceedingly unreliable if not impossible.

Fig. 9.7. Dummy head, equipped with condenser microphones for eardrums, accompanied by K.F. Siebrasse and D. Gottlob who earned their Ph.D. degrees on concert hall evaluation using dummy-head sound field recording

Now, tape recordings of orchestral music are made with a Kunstkopf (artificial head), see Fig 9.7, in several "strategic" locations of the hall to be evaluated. These recordings are then played back over the system illustrated in Fig. 9.6.

With the new reproduction method, *instantaneous* comparisons of identical program material has become possible. The author will never forget the moment he first "switched" himself from a seat in the Berlin Philharmonie to one in the Vienna Musikvereinssaal listening to a British Orchestra playing Mozart's Jupiter Symphony. All he *believed* about the differences between these two halls based on previous visits (but was none too sure about) suddenly became a matter of easy distinction.

9.5 Binaural Release from Masking

The cocktail-party effect is closely related to binaural masking level differences, BMLD for short. For example, the audibility of a binaural tone buried in noise is improved by as much as 18 dB when the polarity of the tone in one ear is reversed. In fact, and paradoxically, the audibility goes up even when the tone in one ear is completely absent, see Fig. 9.8.

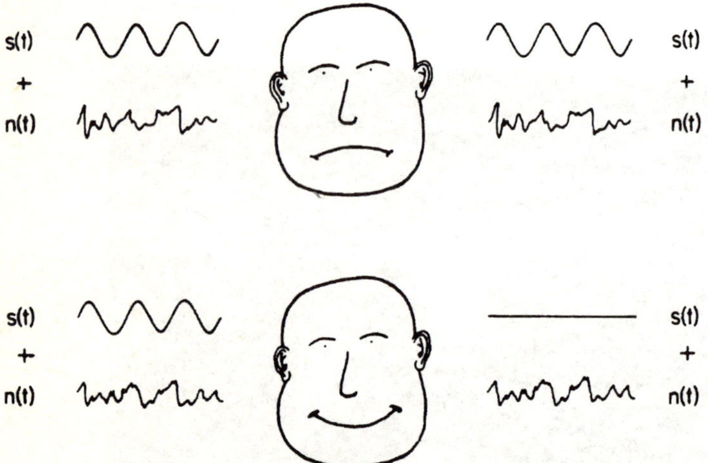

Fig. 9.8. Binaural release from masking. *Top:* presenting the same tone and the same sufficiently strong noise to both ears leaves the tone inaudible; the tone is masked by the noise. *Bottom:* paradoxically, *removing* the tone from one ear makes it audible. Numerous other experiments on binaural masking and unmasking (!) suggest that the human binaural system can, if it is advantageous in a signal detection task, form the difference of the two ear signals (with an error of about 10 %). This ability results in a binaural improvement of detecting signals in noise of up to 20 dB. Such binaural masking level differences are also responsible for the "cocktail-party effect," the ability to suppress unwanted sounds (such as the speech babble during a noisy cocktail party) and concentrate on the desired voice

Theories of BMLDs postulate, among other processes, a binaural subtraction mechanism, mediated perhaps by contralateral neural inhibition. Such a subtraction circuit in our brains would, of course, act as a noise suppressor when identical noises are fed to the two ears [9.10].

Figure 9.9 illustrates a similarly paradoxical paradigm in vision. Whereas the clutter of grey pieces on the left make no sense, *adding* the masker (black) provides enough context to make the grey pattern intelligible. A.S. Bregman: Auditory Scene Analysis: the Perceptual Organization of Sound (The MIT Press, Cambridge, Massachussetts, 1990)

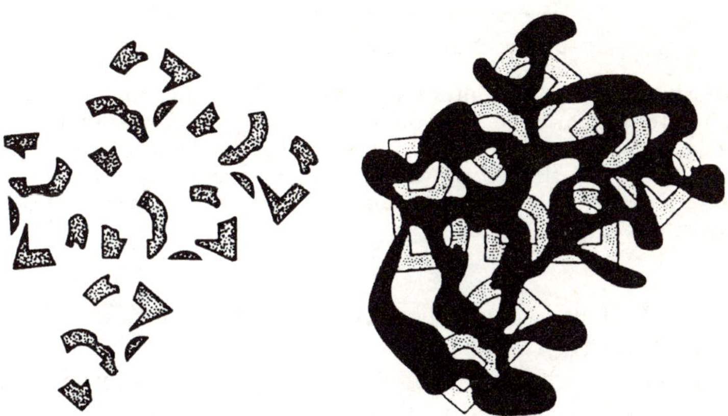

Fig. 9.9. A visual paradox. Adding the masker (black) to the jumble of grey pieces on the left can make them intelligible

9.6 Binaural Beats and Pitch

The same interaural mechanism seems to be active also in the creation of binaural beats when tones of slightly different frequencies are applied to the two ears. Binaural subtraction would also explain a curious binaural pitch phenomenon, called Huggins pitch, in which two white noises with a relative phase shift create a sensation of a whistle-like pitch. The white or broadband noise is applied directly to one ear and through an allpass filter to the other ear, see Fig. 9.10. The allpass filter produces a phase shift of 360° in a narrow frequency region, say 30 Hz centered on 800 Hz. Subtracting the two earphone signals produces a narrow band of noise around 800 Hz. Such a noise sounds like a noisy whistle with an 800 Hz pitch, much like the binaural percept engendered by the arrangement of Fig. 9.10.

In the 1960s, while exploring binaural pitch phenomena, I asked myself whether an intelligible speech signal could be created from two flat-spectrum (unintelligible) signals whose difference is the running short-time spectrum of a given speech signal. The required trick is to convert all spectral amplitude information of the speech signal into phase information and to do it in such a way that the amplitude information can be recovered by subtracting two

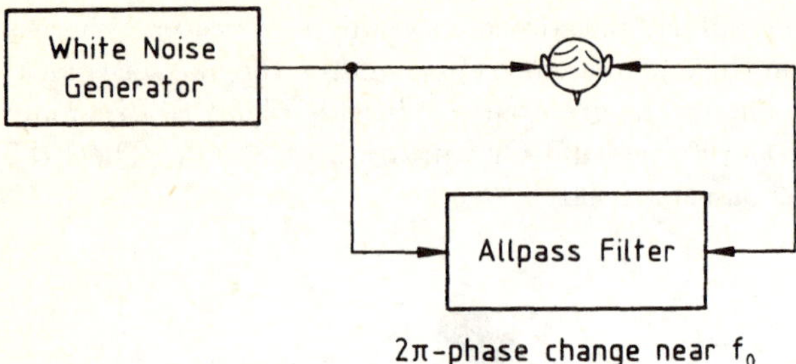

Fig. 9.10. The Huggins pitch, named after its discoverer W.H. Huggins. A broadband noise is applied to one ear. The same noise, filtered by an allpass filter that changes the phase by 360° at a frequency f_0, is also applied to the other ear. This creates the sensation of a whistling noise with a pitch corresponding to the frequency f_0. The effect can be explained by assuming that the auditory system can form the difference of the two ear signals

such phase-only signals. This is indeed possible and it makes for an impressive demonstration. When the two phase-only signals are fed to stereophonic earphones, each signal by itself is an unintelligible buzz, but listening to the earphones simultaneously, one hears intelligible speech. This idea, incidentally, can be turned into an amusing speech "secrecy" system involving two separate transmitting channels in which either channel is completely unintelligible and only the combination of the two unintelligible channels renders the result intelligible [9.11].

9.7 Direction and Pitch Confused

The Huggins pitch is an example of a binaural interaction – a sense that is supposed to tell us something about direction – but that instead produces a pitch sensation. This "misuse" of human binaural processing is even more evident in the so-called Fourcin pitch [9.12], another example of a pitch sensation produced centrally (inside the head). In its simplest form a broadband noise is applied directly to one ear and with a delay τ of, say, 5 ms to the other ear, see Fig. 9.11. This setup creates two sensations, one being, as expected, a lateral noise heard on the side of the undelayed input and the other, surprisingly, a noisy pitch sensation with a pitch corresponding to a frequency of $1/\tau$, i.e. 200 Hz for $\tau = 5$ ms. Again the pitch percept can be explained by binaural subtraction: the difference between the two ear inputs in Fig. 9.11 is a combfiltered noise with spectral peaks at $1/2\tau$, $3/2\tau$, $5/2\tau$, ... The spacing between adjacent peaks is $1/\tau$. By a well-studied extension of the pitch-residue phenomenon to noise-like inputs, the resulting residue pitch should be $1/\tau$ within appropriate frequency and delay ranges. And this is indeed what is heard.

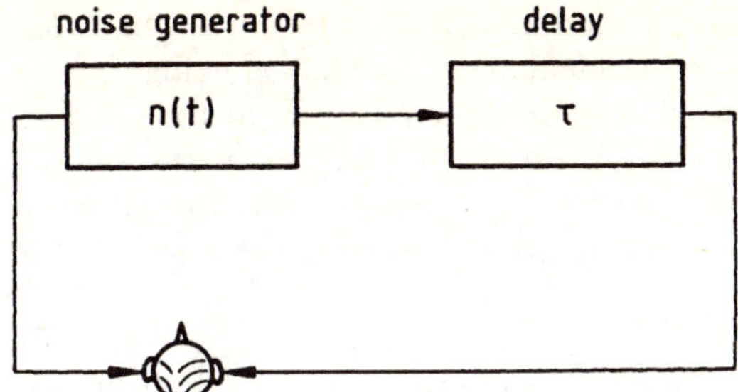

Fig. 9.11. The Fourcin pitch, named after its discoverer A.J. Fourcin. Applying a broadband noise to the left ear and the same through a delay to the right ear creates, in addition to an apparent displacement of the noise source to the left ear, a pitch sensation corresponding to the reciprocal delay. Again the effect can be explained by assuming that the auditory system can form the difference between the two ear signals which creates a "combfilter" with periodic peaks spaced $1/\tau$ apart

Even more impressive is the central pitch created by the circuit sketched in Fig. 9.12. Here two independent noise generators and two different delays are involved. Again, both ears receive broadband noises that separately have no pitch attributes. But there is a subjective binaural pitch that corresponds to a frequency of $1/|\tau_2 - \tau_1|$.

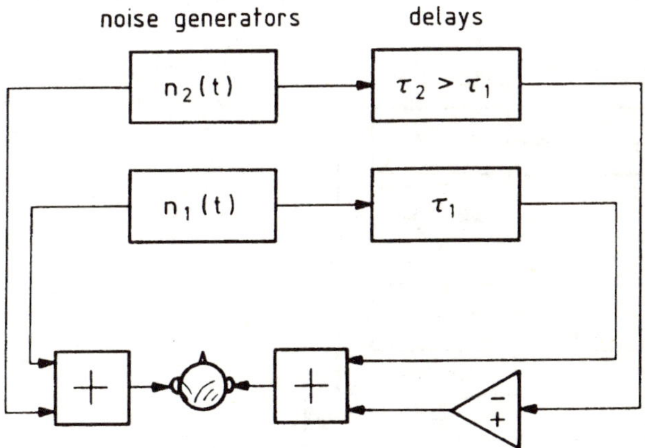

Fig. 9.12. Two independent broadband noises, feeding the two ears of a listener via two different delays, create a subjective binaural pitch with a frequency that corresponds to the reciprocal delay difference $1/|\tau_2 - \tau_1|$. This surprising effect can be explained as shown in Fig. 9.13

How can we explain this? Does the human auditory processor extract both delays separately, form the absolute difference, calculate the reciprocal, and then decide to perceive the corresponding pitch? Our brains can wring many miracles, but they are no pocket calculators. So what *is* going on?

Figure 9.13 shows a setup that is completely equivalent to that of Fig. 9.12, using two new noises: $n_1'(t) = n_1(t) + n_2(t)$ and $n_2'(t) = n_1(t) - n_2(t)$. The redrawing is based on only one, purely mathematical assumption: when independent noises are added, the resulting power spectrum is the sum of the individual power spectra.

As the redrawing, Fig. 9.13, shows, one noise, $n_2'(t)$, is applied to only one ear and is therefore irrelevant for the perceived binaural pitch height. The other noise, $n_1'(t)$, is applied to both ears: unfiltered to the left ear and combfiltered to the right ear. The combfilter has a peak spacing of $1/|\tau_2 - \tau_1|$ Hz, corresponding to the perceived pitch. The explanation of this pitch phenomenon therefore involves something other than mere binaural subtraction: our auditory processor can apparently detect binaurally correlated signals and extract them from an uncorrelated background. (If either noise source in Fig. 9.13 is left out, a monoaural combfiltered noise is created at the right ear with the corresponding monoaural pitch perception.)

These paradoxical pitch perceptions are nicely accounted for by Licklider's duplex and triplex theories of hearing in which binaural signals are analyzed according to three dimensions: frequency, delay difference, and periodicity, of which the latter two are occasionally confused [9.14].

The ultimate confusion between localization and pitch is observed in Diana Deutsch's octave illusion in which alternating high and low notes are applied to the two ears, and "the wrong note is perceived at the wrong time

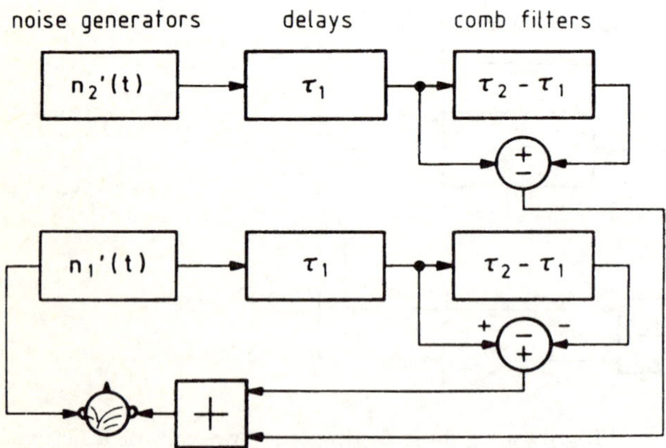

Fig. 9.13. If the two noises in Fig. 9.12 are independent, then Fig. 9.12 can be redrawn as shown here, where $n_1'(t)$ and $n_2'(t)$ are the sum and the difference, respectively, of the two noises $n_1(t)$ and $n_2(t)$ in Fig. 9.12. It is now clear that the delay τ_1 is immaterial and only the delay difference $\tau_2 - \tau_1$ enters the paradigm, producing combfiltered noises that are known to elicit a pitch sensation corresponding to a frequency $1/|\tau_2 - \tau_1|$

at the wrong ear," see Fig. 9.14. The two notes, applied in binaurally alternating fashion, are in an octave relationship, 400 and 800 Hz, say. For most (especially right-handed) listeners the perceived sounds differ from the physically present signals in the following respects: the high notes applied to the left ear are inaudible; they are only heard at the right ear. The low notes are only perceived at the left ear and – paradoxically – at a time when they are actually present at the other ear! Switching the two earphones does not change the illusion: the earphone that seemed to have been emitting the low note is now emitting the high note and vice versa [9.13]!

The explanation of this stunning illusion is not simple. We have to postulate two separate brain mechanisms for pitch and location. Further, we have to assume that the perceived *pitch* is determined by the pitch at the right ear (for right-handed listeners) while the tone at the left ear is ignored. And finally, we have to suppose that the *location* of the perceived tone is given by the location of the higher tone, regardless of whether the higher or lower note is in fact perceived. These assumptions are consistent with the neurological evidence that most right-handers process speech in the left hemisphere, assuming that these tone pulses are processed by the listeners

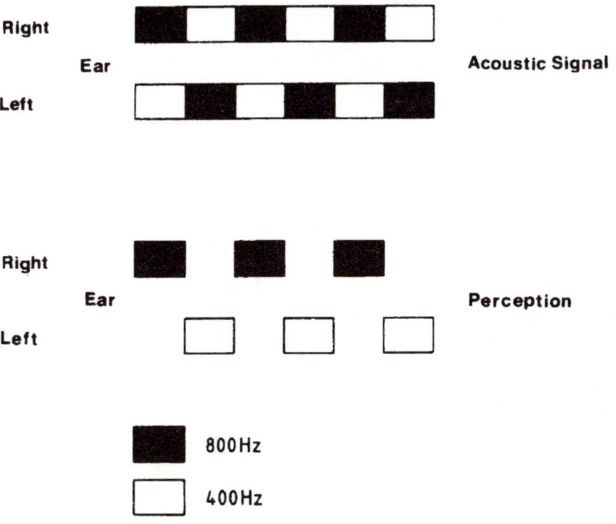

Fig. 9.14. Diana Deutsch's octave illusion. Two tones, one an octave higher than the other, are fed via earphones to the two ears of a listener, as shown at the top. What listeners typically hear is shown below it. Paradoxically, they never hear the low note when it is actually present at the left ear; they hear the low note only when it is present at the right ear – but they hear it at the "wrong" ear. Similarly, the high note is never heard when it is actually present at the left ear; instead the low note (present at the other ear) is heard in its place. This confusion of location and pitch apparently involves higher brain centers, as it depends on handedness of the listeners

as speech-like signals and not as complex musical compositions (for which a left-ear advantage is usually found).

9.8 Pseudo-Stereophony

Having two ears, we naturally prefer stereophonic sounds over monophonic sounds – a fact amply exploited by the high-fidelity industry. Curiously, stereophonic perceptions can be produced from single-channel audio signals by appropriate manipulations. An early example of such "pseudo-stereophony" is the Lauridsen effect [9.15].

In Lauridsen's original setup a single (monophonic) sound signal is radiated from a loudspeaker facing the listener, see Fig. 9.15. In addition, the same signal is radiated from a second loudspeaker, more distant from the listener, facing sideways and open at the back. Thus, the phase of the signal from this second loudspeaker differs by 180° at the listener's two ears. Together with the (in-phase) signal from the closer loudspeaker and, after

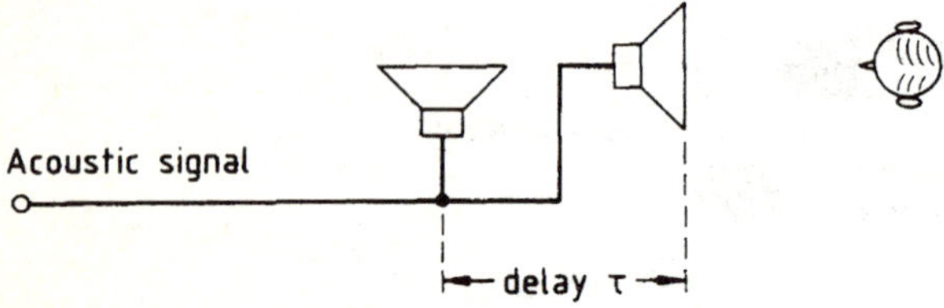

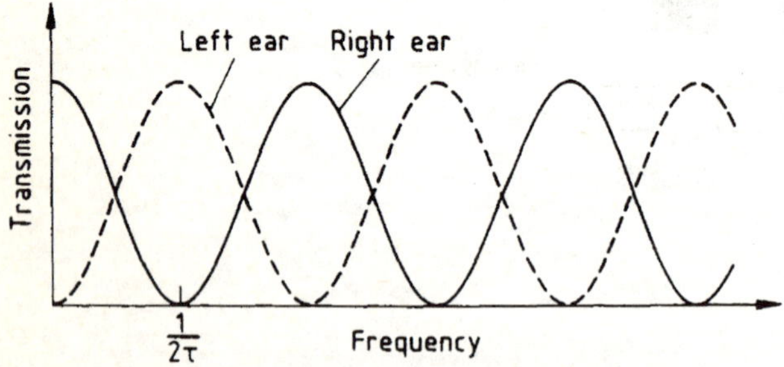

Fig. 9.15. Lauridsen's stereophonic effect obtained from a single (monophonic) signal. The two loudspeakers, if properly equalized, produce interleaving comb-like frequency responses at the two ears of a listener facing the loudspeakers. Thus roughly half the frequency components of a music signal are perceived at the right ear and the other half at the left ear. Our auditory system, not knowing what to make of such a confusing situation, apparently gives up on ordinary localization and seems to be telling the brain "everything comes from everywhere" – an overwhelming, albeit artificial, stereophonic effect

appropriate equalization, two complementary comb-like frequency responses
are generated at the two ears. In other words, half the spectrum of the monophonic signal goes to one ear while the other half goes to the other ear. The
subjective result is a strong "stereophonic" feeling of being totally immersed
in the sound. The relative delay between the two loudspeakers should exceed
10 ms for best results.

If this interpretation of the Lauridsen effect is correct, then a bank of
contiguous bandpass filters, alternate filter outputs applied to the two ears,
should also give a pseudo-stereophonic effect. This is indeed the case as
demonstrated in the late 1950s with an available vocoder filterbank [9.16],
see Fig. 9.16.

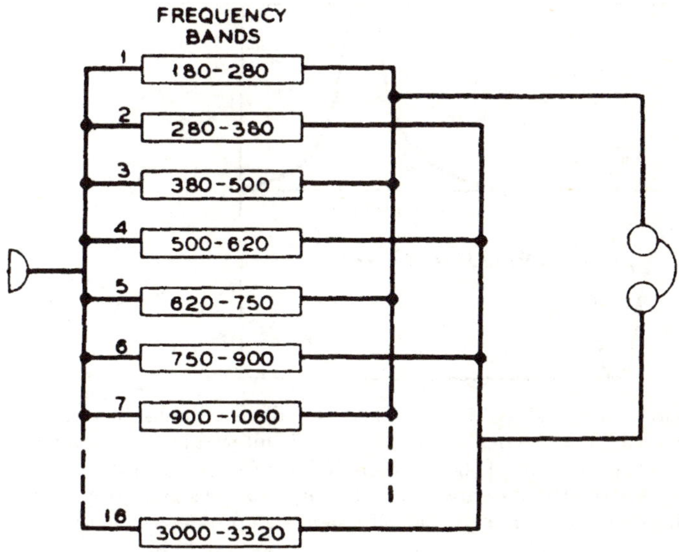

Fig. 9.16. A (successful) attempt to duplicate Lauridsen's stereophonic effect, see
Fig. 9.15, with a vocoder filterbank. With a monophonic input (*left*) a strong spatial
sensation is created for a listener wearing the earphones (*right*)

Pseudo-stereophony can even be attained without spectral distortion,
namely by means of allpass filters [9.17]. Figure 9.17 shows the impulse response of an allpass filter originally suggested for artificial reverberation. By
inverting the signal of every other impulse, another allpass filter with a different phase response is created. The group delay difference between the two
allpass filters is shown in Fig. 9.18. In certain frequency ranges the group
delay of one filter exceeds that of the other filter. For the remaining, interleaved, frequency ranges the delays are reversed. Thus, if a monophonic signal
is fed to the two filters and their outputs connected to binaural earphones

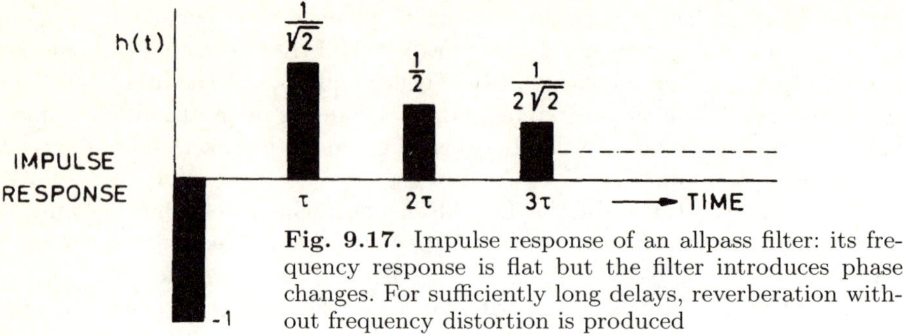

Fig. 9.17. Impulse response of an allpass filter: its frequency response is flat but the filter introduces phase changes. For sufficiently long delays, reverberation without frequency distortion is produced

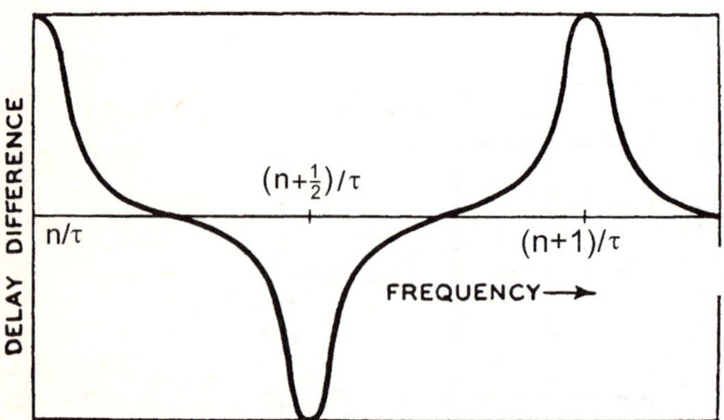

Fig. 9.18. A monophonic audio signal is filtered by the allpass filter shown in Fig. 9.17 and applied to one ear. For the other ear the signal is filtered by a complementary allpass filter (in which the signs of the pulses in its impulse response alternate). The resulting percept is strongly stereophonic. This figure shows the group delay difference between the two ear channels: some frequencies are delayed at one ear, others are delayed at the other ear, thereby creating the observed effect

or stereophonic loudspeakers, the listener perceives spatially dispersed sound without the spectral distortion inherent in Lauridsen's setup or combfilter [9.17].

9.9 Virtual Sound Images

In the mid-1960s, B.S. Atal and the author had the idea that sound could be made to appear as arriving from *any* desired direction by appropriately filtering a single-channel audio signal before radiating it from just *two* loudspeakers positioned in front of the listener [9.18]. And this is indeed possible,

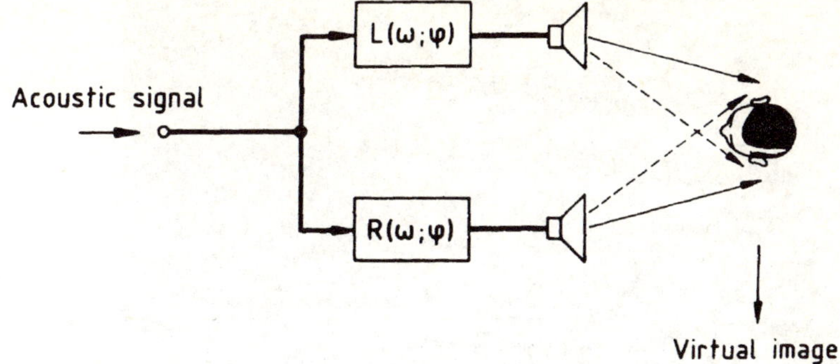

Fig. 9.19. The creation of virtual sound images by linear filtering of a monophonic signal. The filter characteristics depend on sound diffraction around the listener's head

see Fig. 9.19. The effect of a lateral echo was so convincing that many listeners turned their heads to look for the (absent) lateral sound source. Of course, when they did so, the effect disappeared because the two filters are designed for a given head orientation. (In fact, even the head *shape* has some influence. For once, it's not what's inside the human head that determines the outcome of the experiment but its external geometry.)

By means of such and similar filters John Chowning and others have created sounds that seem to swirl around in three-dimensional space, thus giving music a third, controlled dimension: pitch, rhythm, and *space* [9.19]. It is even possible to simulate digitally sound transmission in a full-blown concert hall – either existing or in the planning stage, thereby reducing the risk of expensive design errors.

Good acoustic quality of a concert hall requires strong laterally traveling soundwaves. This was pointed out by Michael Barron, Harold Marshall [9.20] and others. And it was also the main result of an investigation of numerous (mostly European) concert halls carried out at Göttingen by P. Damaske, V. Mellert, D. Gottlob, S. Mehrgardt, U. Eysholdt, and K.F. Siebrasse [9.21].

9.10 Philharmonic Hall, New York

One of the parameters thought to be important for good acoustical quality of a concert hall is the initial time gap, i.e. the delay between the arrival times at a listener's ears between the direct sound and the first reflection from the ceiling or side walls. To keep the value of this time gap below its upper limit for good quality (about 25 ms), acoustic reflection panels were installed over the audience area in Philharmonic Hall at Lincoln Center for the Performing Arts in New York City, see Fig. 9.20.

However, in spite of this precaution (or, more likely, *because* of the acoustic panels) the acoustics of Philharmonic Hall seemed to suffer. One of the

Fig. 9.20. Philharmonic Hall (now Avery Fisher Hall) at the Lincoln Center for the Performing Arts in New York City (before any acoustic alterations). The overhead reflecting panels were found too small to properly reflect low frequencies (especially from the celli and double basses) leading to a lack of "warmth." They also emphasized the overhead ("monophonic") component of the sound arriving at a listeners ear as opposed to the lateral ("stereophonic") sound. This led to a feeling of detachment for the listeners, a lack of being enveloped by music

persistent complaints was a sense of detachment from the music and a feeling of not being enveloped by the sound. The culprit, it turned out, were indeed the reflecting panels, which increased the sound energy arriving in the symmetry plane of the listeners' heads thus emphasizing the "monophonic" effect of the hall.

9.11 The Proper Reproduction of Spatial Sound Fields

To get at the source of the acoustic quality problems, a group of physicists at the University of Göttingen, with the support by the German Science Foundation (DFG), investigated 22 halls in Europe and beyond. To ensure identical music signals for the subjective comparisons, reverberation-free music (recorded for this purpose by the London Chamber Orchestra in an anechoic environment) was radiated from the stages of the halls under investigation and recorded by means of a specially designed "Kunstkopf," see Fig. 9.7 center.

The recorded signals were radiated from two loudspeakers fed through a "crosstalk compensation" filter system which transfers the left(right)-ear signal exclusively to the left(right)-ear with negligible crosstalk for listen-

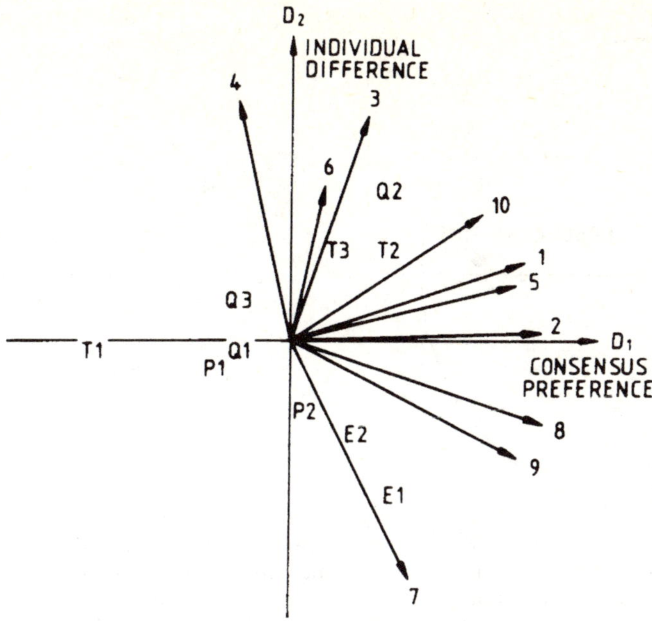

Fig. 9.21. Acoustic preference space for four different concert halls (designated by the letters E, P, Q, T) and a total of 10 different listening locations in these halls (E_1 through T_3). A recording of classical music, (Mozart's Jupiter Symphony) was played from the stages of these halls and recorded with a dummy head. The recordings were reproduced by a special sound system in an anechoic space and evaluated by experienced listeners in paired comparison preference tests. A three-dimensional "preference space" was constructed from the subjective judgements by multi-dimensional scaling. The first two dimensions are shown in this figure. The 10 different listeners are represented here by 10 vectors pointing in different directions. The different halls and seats (E_1 through T_3) are arranged in this space in such a manner that their normal projections on the different listeners' vectors reproduce the preference scores with minimum error. (The two dimensions shown here account for more than 80 % of the total variance.) Because all listeners' vectors (except listener 4) point into the right half plane, the abscissa can be labelled "consensus preference." The ordinate reflects "individual differences" in musical tastes of these listeners

ers whose head shapes are within a certain range of the standard used for calibrating the crosstalk filters, see Fig. 9.6.

The results of thousands of paired comparisons were analyzed by multi-dimensional-scaling. The two main dimensions of the resulting three-dimensional "preference space" are shown in Fig. 9.21.

The ten arrows are unit vectors representing ten different listeners. Each letter/number pair refers to a specific hall/seat location. Projecting the hall/seat points normally (at right angles) onto a listener's vector reproduces that listener's preference scores (within the 85% of the total variance accounted for by the first two dimensions of the solution).

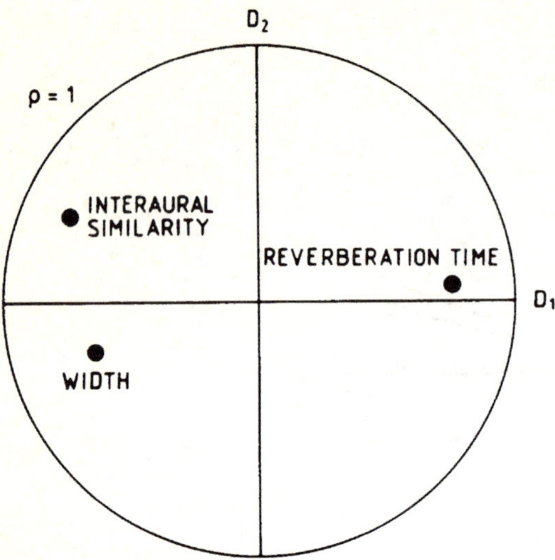

Fig. 9.22. Correlation of the subjective preference dimensions, D_1 and D_2, with two acoustical parameters (reverberation time and interaural similarity) and one architectural measure (width). Whereas reverberation time is, as expected, positively correlated with the consensus preference dimension (D_1), interaural similarity shows a strong negative correlation. This means that people prefer stereophonic sound over monophonic sound. The negative correlation of the halls' widths can be explained by the weakness of lateral sounds that such hall shapes engender leading to a more monophonic sound

Except for listener 4, all listeners' vectors point into the right half-place. Thus, the horizontal axis can be called "consensus preference" because if (by some architectural modification, for example) a hall/seat point is moved to the right, all listeners (except listener 4) would prefer the new condition. The fact that some listener vectors point up, while others point down, reflects their individual differences in musical taste. The vertical dimension has therefore been called "individual difference".

To extract further useful information from this data, the two main subjective preference coordinates, D_1 and D_2, have been correlated with various objective (acoustic and architectural) parameters such as reverberation time measured at the corresponding hall/seat, interaural similarity measured at the "dummy's" ears, and the (average) width of the hall, see Fig. 9.22. As expected, reverberation time showed a strong positive correlation with consensus preference, independent of musical taste.

9.12 The Importance of Lateral Sound

Another strong, albeit negative, correlation is found between interaural similarity and consensus preference. This means that ear signals that are too similar ("monophonic") are bad for good acoustics. The negative correlation for the widths of the hall is a result of this "stereophonic" preference because wide halls produce weak lateral sound. These findings may in fact explain why so many modern halls are acoustically disliked: larger audiences and "wider" people force the construction of wider halls. In order to lower building costs, modern ceilings are much lower than in the old-style "shoe-box" halls such as the Vienna Musikvereinssaal. (The air for breathing in a modern hall is typically supplied by an air-conditioning system.) These two trends – wide halls and low ceilings – conspire to diminish the energy of laterally traveling sounds relative to the sound energy arriving in the symmetry plane through the listeners' heads, leading to the deleterious "monophonic" sound in many a modern hall [9.22].

The importance of lateral sound for good acoustic quality may be further confirmed by a method called *digital modification*. Instead of tearing a hall

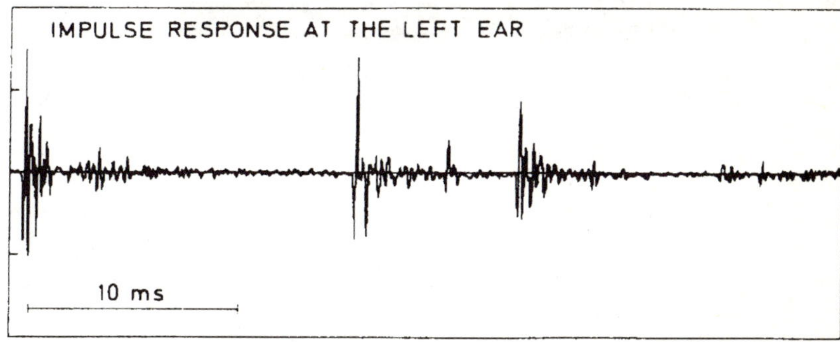

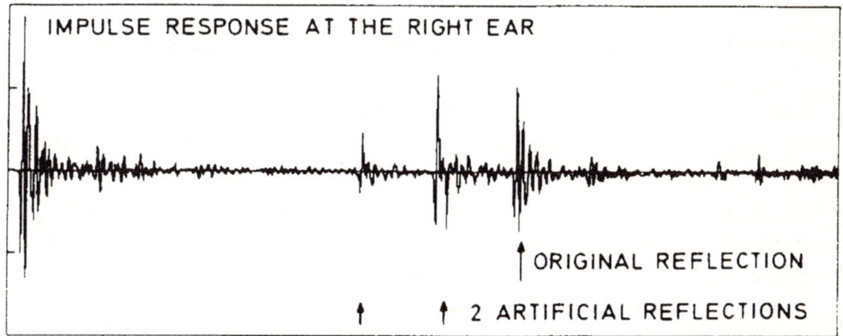

Fig. 9.23. A pair of binaural impulse responses showing sound directly transmitted from the stage to the listener's ears (*left*) and an original reflection from the ceiling arriving simultaneously at the two ears. Also shown are two artificial reflections added by computer, one from the left (arriving at the left ear first) and one from the right (arriving at the right ear first). Listening tests with such digitally modified impulse responses, when convolved with music signals, demonstrated the possible improvements in acoustic quality of concert halls (without tearing down any walls and rebuilding)

Fig. 9.24. The author evaluating virtual, digitally created sound fields in the anechoic chamber ("free-space room") of Bell Laboratories at Murray Hill, New Jersey

down and building a new one, lateral echoes can be added to the recorded impulse response of a hall/seat on the computer, see Figs. 9.23 and 9.24. In subjective tests of halls with such digitally enhanced lateral sounds the preference always increased.

9.13 How to Increase Lateral Sounds in Real Halls

Given that building costs and audience size (in both senses of the word "size") forbids reverting to the old style narrow-and-high halls, what can one do to enhance laterally traveling sounds? One possible answer is the introduction of "corrugated" surfaces (on the ceiling and elsewhere) that scatter an incoming wave into a broad pattern of reflected wavelets, see Fig. 9.25. Sound-diffusing surfaces are also important for recording studios, including those for speech signals, to diminish standing waves between opposite walls that interfere with musical sound quality and make accurate speech signal analysis more difficult.

For the scattering of a single wavelength, λ, the optimal depth of the corrugations is $\lambda/4$ corresponding to a phase shift of the reflected wave by $180°$ or half a wavelength. The spatial sampling theorem dictates that the lateral spacing ("grating constant") should not exceed $\lambda/2$ for effective scattering by $\pm 90°$. But where should the surface be up and where down? The answer comes from a branch of number theory called finite fields or *Galois fields*, abbreviated $GF(p^m)$, where p is a prime number and m is a natural number

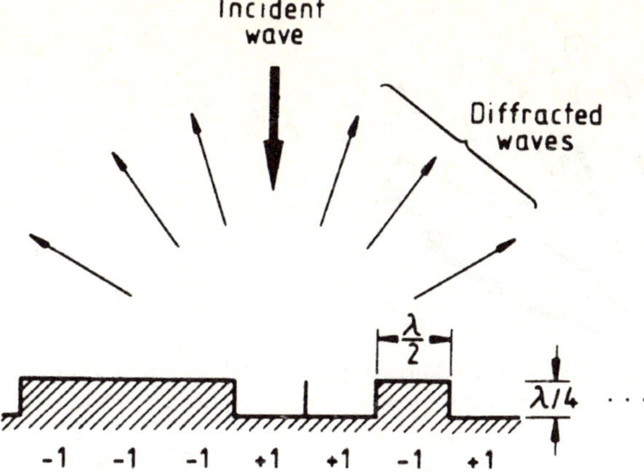

Fig. 9.25. Sound-diffusing surface for a single wavelength, based on a number-theoretic formula (primitive polynomials in finite fields over the prime number 2)

[9.23]. For $p = 2$ and $m = 3$, for example, resulting in a periodic scattering surface with a period length of $p^m - 1 = 2^3 - 1 = 7$, one has to factor the polynomial $x^7 + 1$ into irreducible factors over $GF(2^3)$:

$$x^7 + 1 = (x + 1)(x^3 + x^2 + 1)(x^3 + x + 1) \ .$$

(The reader who intends to check the factorization should bear in mind that $1 + 1 = 0$ for $p = 2$.) From these factors one has to select one that does not occur as a factor in $x^n + 1$ for $n < 7$. Such a factor, $x^3 + x^2 + 1$ or $x^3 + x + 1$, is called a primitive polynomial. By setting one of these, say $x^3 + x + 1$, equal to zero, one obtains the equation

$$x^3 = x + 1 \ ,$$

which is then considered as a generating function for a recursion relation yielding

$$a_{n+3} = a_{n+1} + a_n \ .$$

With the initial values $a_1 = a_2 = a_3 = 1$, for example, a periodic sequence with period length 7 is generated:

$$a_n = 1, 1, 1, 0, 0, 1, 0; \ \ 1, 1, 1, \ldots \ .$$

The a_n are converted to reflection coefficients by the formula

$$r_n = \exp(i2\pi a_n/p)$$

yielding, with the above a_n and $p = 2$,

$$r_n = -1, -1, -1, 1, 1, -1, 1; \ \ -1, -1, -1, \ldots \ .$$

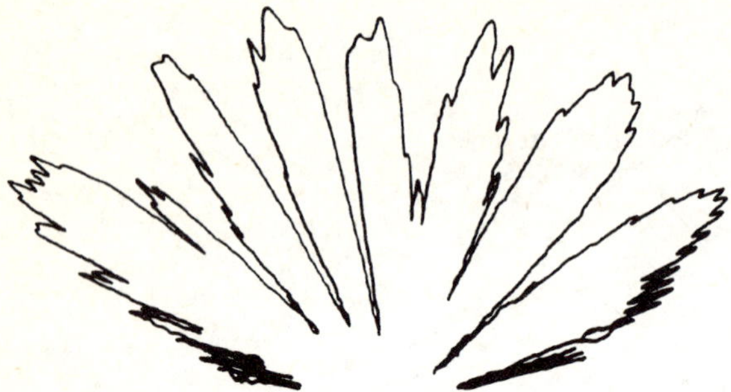

Fig. 9.26. Reflection pattern from the surface shown in Fig. 9.25. A single incident plane wave is scattered into 7 different directions with nearly equal amplitudes

The two different reflection coefficients (1 and -1) are realized by troughs of depth $\lambda/4$, as shown in Fig. 9.25. Figure 9.26 shows the angular scatter from such a surface, made out of sheet metal, irradiated by a 3-cm microwave. (There is no essential difference of the scattering from such surfaces of properly polarized microwaves and sound waves.) As expected, the incident wave is scattered into many different directions covering the entire space.

However, the "one-step" corrugation shown in Fig. 9.25 works only for "one" frequency (actually about one octave). To cover more octaves, as needed for speech and music applications, one has to use more than one step-size in the diffusor. There are two solutions, one is based again on primitive polynomials over $GF(p^m)$ with p a prime larger than 2. For example, for $p = 11$ and $m = 1$ one (of the four) primitive polynomials over $GF(11^1)$ is $x + 9$. Setting $x + 9$ equal to 0 gives $x = -9$ or, modulo 11, $x = 2$, called a *primitive root*. Thus the recursion is $a_{n+1} = 2a_n$. Starting with $a_1 = 2$, the periodic Galois sequence is

$$a_n = 2, 4, 8, 5, 10, 9, 7, 3, 6, 1; \; 2, \ldots .$$

It has the proper period-length $p^m - 1 = 11^1 - 1 = 10$. It also has 10 different values (from 1 to 10) and a frequency range of about 1 to 21 ($10.5/0.5 = 21$), i.e. more than four octaves, are covered.

Another solution to the scattering problem for broad frequency ranges is based on *quadratic residues*, another number-theoretic concept [9.23]. The quadratic residues modulo the prime $p = 7$, for example, are given by the periodic sequence with period length 7,

$$a_n = 0, 1, 4, 9 \equiv 2, 16 \equiv 2, 25 \equiv 4, 36 \equiv 1; \; 0, 1, 4, \ldots .$$

Here $\equiv$ stands for "congruent to," i.e. the remainder after dividing by 7. To convert these numbers to local reflection coefficients, r_n, one uses again the equation $r_n = \exp(i2\pi a_n/p)$. The required phase shifts are once more realized by corrugations or troughs of different depths. Figure 9.27 shows a surface

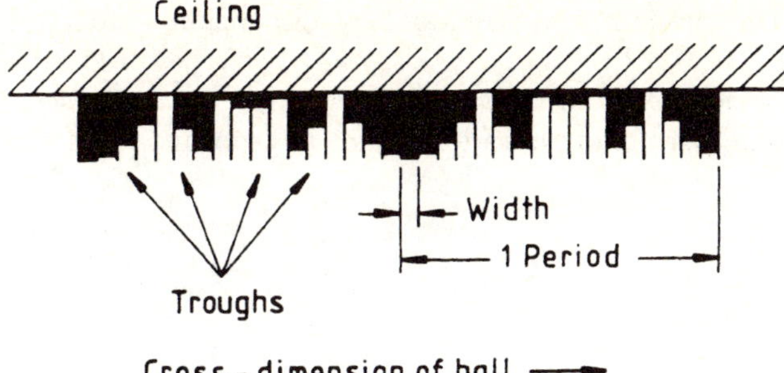

Fig. 9.27. Reflection phase grating for scattering sound waves containing many musical octaves, based on quadratic residues modulo the prime number 17

based on the prime number $p = 17$, effective for a frequency range of 0.5 to 16.5 exceeding five musical octaves.

Figure 9.28 shows the scattering of an incident plane wave from this surface. Again, the reflected energy is distributed over the entire space. There is no single strong reflection, only many weak ones. No wonder these *quadratic-residue diffusors* "make a wall disappear" as one apt description has it.

For even more effective scattering, two-dimensional reflection phase gratings and even fractal structures have been successfully employed [9.24, 9.25].

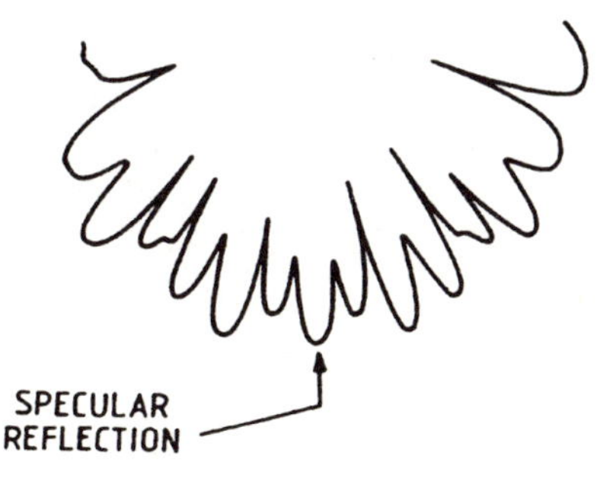

Fig. 9.28. Angular reflection diagram showing the broad sound scattering of a single incident plane wave

9.14 Summary

The spatial attributes of acoustic fields are an important factor for good sound reproduction, including good acoustics for lecture halls, rooms for tele-conferences and concert halls. Beyond this, the three-dimensional aspects of sound perception offer the modern composer a new dimension to exploit creatively.

Binaural listening is a delightful subject with many surprises and useful applications as well as some perplexing paradoxes that instruct us about the workings of our brains.

10. Basic Signal Concepts

In this chapter we introduce the basic concepts that govern signal analysis for both continuous and discrete signals, including *Fourier* and *Hilbert transforms, correlation functions*, and the *cepstrum*.

The sampling theorems for lowpass and bandpass signals play a central role, allowing the description of bandlimited signals in terms of discrete samples. Since most of our discussions are in terms of discrete signals, we pay special attention to the *z-transform*, its properties and applications.

Many methods of signal analysis transform the input from one domain into another, typically from the time domain to the frequency domain or vice versa. These transformations are accomplished by one form or another of Fourier's famous transformation: real (sine and cosine) transforms, complex transforms, and the fast Fourier transform (FFT). For finite blocks of samples, the *discrete Fourier transform* (DFT) replaces the customary Fourier integral and Fourier sum. The importance of the DFT is further highlighted by the fact that digital computers and digital signal processors inevitably deal with finite sets of discrete data.

A considerable broadening of our view of signals is brought about by the introduction of the *Hilbert transform* of a signal and the closely related *analytic signal*. These useful concepts lead in turn to the definition of the *Hilbert envelope* and *phase*, and the *instantaneous frequency*.

10.1 The Sampling Theorem and Some Notational Conventions

In speech signal analysis we are dealing with functions of time that represent, typically, sound pressure in air or a voltage on an electric conductor. Generic symbols for representing such functions are lower case letters like s and x. Continuous time is represented by the letter t. Thus $s(t)$ is our generic speech signal.

Before we can feed a signal into a digital computer or a digital signal processor (DSP), which accept only discrete, finite-precision numbers, we have to bandlimit the signal so that it can be represented by a discrete sequence, which we write $s[n]$. Here n represents discrete time, $t_n = t_0 + nT$, where

T is the sampling interval. Nyquist's *sampling theorem* [10.1] tells us that T should be *smaller* than $1/2B$, where B is the (one-sided) frequency bandwidth of the signal:

$$T < 1/2B \, . \tag{10.1}$$

Note that a sampling interval $T = 1/2B$ is already in violation of the sampling theorem. The reason behind the inequality (10.1) of the sampling theorem is that sampling a signal corresponds to multiplying by a periodic spike train. This multiplication superimposes multiple replicas of its Fourier transform on itself with a frequency spacing Δf equal to $1/T$. To avoid overlap between two adjacent replicas, Δf has to be *larger* than the total (two-sided) bandwidth $2B$ of the signal (including both positive and negative frequencies); thus $\Delta f > 2B$. Because $T = 1/\Delta f$, the sampling theorem for signals (10.1) follows immediately.

To go from the samples $s[n]$ to the continuous function $s(t)$, we need an *interpolation formula* [10.2]:

$$s(t) = \sum s[kT] \, \mathrm{sinc}\left(\frac{\pi}{T}(t - kT)\right)$$

here the function $\mathrm{sinc}(x)$ is the so-called *sinc function*:

$$\mathrm{sinc}(x) := \frac{\sin(x)}{x} \, .$$

It is the Fourier transform of a sharply bandlimited pulse. The sinc function was first introduced in wave optics to describe the diffraction of coherent light at a sharp slit in an opaque screen. (Hence its German name *Spaltfunktion*, from *Spalt* meaning slit.)

Note that in going from the continuous signal $s(t)$ to the sampled version $s[n]$, we have kept the same letter, s, for the *function* but indicated a change of *variable* by switching from parentheses ( ) to brackets [ ]. This seems a good notational convention.

10.2 Fourier Transforms

No mathematical transformation is as basic to linear signal analysis as the Fourier transform. For a continuous, square-integrable[1] signal $s(t)$, we define the Fourier transform $\hat{s}(\omega)$ as follows:

$$\hat{s}(\omega) := \int_{-\infty}^{\infty} s(t) \exp(-\mathrm{i}\omega t)\mathrm{d}t \, . \tag{10.2}$$

---

[1] A function is called square-integrable if it has "finite energy," that is the integral from $-\infty$ to $+\infty$ over its absolute square exists. A sine wave of infinite duration or a constant-power noise are not square-integrable unless properly "windowed."

The Fourier variable ω is called *angular frequency* or *radian frequency*; it equals 2π times the frequency, which is usually measured in Hertz, abbreviated Hz.

In (10.2) we have again kept the same letter, s, embellished by a "hat," or circumflex, $\hat{s}$, to emphasize the close connection and the one-to-one relation between a signal s and its Fourier transform $\hat{s}$.

The absolute square of $\hat{s}(\omega)$ is called the *energy spectrum* of $s(t)$ because it tells us how the energy of $s(t)$ is distributed over the different angular frequencies. Note that the energy spectrum is *shift-invariant*, that is, it does not change with phase or time shifts – an important "symmetry" of the Fourier transform [10.3].

Another reason for the importance of the Fourier transform is that it converts differential and integral equations into *algebraic equations*, which are usually easier to solve. In fact, differentiation simply corresponds to multiplying the Fourier transform by $i\omega$, and integration (if legitimate) corresponds to a multiplication by $(i\omega)^{-1}$.

Jean Baptiste Joseph Fourier (1768–1830), who solved the differential equation for heat conduction with the mathematical transformation named after him encountered stubborn opposition from many of his fellow mathematicians who wouldn't believe his claim that *any* function could be represented by a Fourier series. This debate has not entirely abated. While *sufficient* conditions for the existence of the Fourier transform are known, the *jury* on necessary conditions is still out (200 years after the original "hearing"). However, the (occasionally acrimonious) altercation has spawned much good mathematics and led to a considerable broadening of the function concept. Just think of such "insane" creations as the *continuous but nowhere differentiable* functions concocted by Karl Weierstrass (1815–1897), an early example of what is now called a *fractal* [10.5].

As a result of this work on the foundations of analysis, we now have theories of integration free of contradictions. And various sufficient conditions for Fourier integrals to exist are known. For example, the signal may have discontinuities (even infinitely many discontinuities if they have no accumulation points). In such cases, the inverse Fourier transform will give a value that is the *average* of the two values just to the left and the right of the discontinuity.

If desired, the Fourier transform can be decomposed into its real and imaginary parts. For real signals, we have

$$\mathrm{Re}\{\hat{s}(\omega)\} = \int_{-\infty}^{\infty} s(t)\cos(\omega t)\, \mathrm{d}t \tag{10.3}$$

and

$$\mathrm{Im}\{\hat{s}(\omega)\} = -\int_{-\infty}^{\infty} s(t)\sin(\omega t)\, \mathrm{d}t \ . \tag{10.4}$$

Note that for symmetric real signals, $s(t) = s(-t)$, the imaginary part of the Fourier transform vanishes (because $\sin(\omega t)$ is antisymmetric).

The *inverse* Fourier transform gives $s(t)$ in terms of $\hat{s}(\omega)$:

$$s(t) = \frac{1}{2\pi} \int_{-\infty}^{\infty} \hat{s} \exp(i\omega t)\, d\omega \ . \tag{10.5}$$

Note the factor $1/2\pi$ and the "missing" minus sign in (10.5) compared to (10.2). For *periodic* signals $s(t) = s(t + kT)$ with fundamental angular frequency $\omega_0 = 2\pi/T$, the integral is extended over a single period $T = 2\pi/\omega_0$ of the signal, resulting in a Fourier transform with *discrete* Fourier components (spectral "lines").

$$\hat{s}[m] = \frac{1}{T} \int_{t_0}^{t_0 + 2\pi/\omega_0} s(t) \exp(-im\omega_0 t)\, dt \ , \tag{10.6}$$

where the integer m is called *harmonic number*. Here again, we have expressed the change of variable (from continuous angular frequency ω to discrete harmonic number m) by switching from parentheses to brackets while keeping the same symbol, $\hat{s}$, for the function.

The absolute square of $\hat{s}[m]$ is called a *line spectrum*, as opposed to a continuous spectrum. The line spectrum, a term borrowed from optical spectroscopy, shows how the signal power is distributed over the different harmonics.

The corresponding *inverse* Fourier transform is given by a sum over complex exponentials:

$$s(t) = \frac{\omega_0}{2\pi} \sum_{m=-\infty}^{\infty} \hat{s}[m] \exp(im\omega_0 t) \ . \tag{10.7}$$

This is the famous *Fourier series* which describes a periodic signal (think of a note played on a violin) in terms of its fundamental frequency component and its harmonics. (Here the Fourier series is given in the complex notation where each physical frequency component is represented by *two* terms, one positive, $m > 0$, and one negative, $m < 0$.)

Note that even if $s(t)$ was not periodic, the inversion formula (10.7) will produce a signal that is periodic with a period $2\pi/\omega_0$. In other words, the original $s(t)$ is continued periodically outside the analysis interval $[t_0, t_0 + 2\pi/\omega_0]$. (This simple fact has occasionally been ignored with rather peculiar consequences; for example, in signal detection theory "ideal observers" were created that can detect signals in noise at arbitrarily low signal-to-noise ratios, which is of course hocus-pocus.)

Another discipline in which the Fourier transform has found important applications is probability theory. The *characteristic* function of a probability distribution $p(x)$ is in fact its Fourier transform (except that the minus sign in the exponent is usually omitted). When two independent random variables are added, their probability distributions are given by a convolution integral (or sum). But convolution means simple multiplication in the Fourier domain (see Sect.10.4). Thus characteristic functions are multiplied (and their logarithms are added) when independent random variables are added, a highly satisfactory state of affairs. Proofs of the Central Limit Theorem of probability theory ("everything" tends to a Gaussian distribution) make judicious use of this connection.

One precondition for the validity of the theorem is that the probability distributions involved have finite variances. But the Fourier transform can even make a contribution when variances don't exist, as in the case of the infamous Cauchy distribution

$$p(x) = \frac{1}{\pi(1 + x^2)} \, ,$$

whose second moment is infinite. Incredibly, when averaging Cauchy-distributed variables, estimates of the mean of the distributions do not improve. In fact, the average of two (or more) identically distributed Cauchy variables has the *same* (and not a narrower) Cauchy distribution. This follows from the fact that the Fourier transform of $p(x)$ equals

$$\hat{p}(\xi) = \mathrm{e}^{-|\xi|}$$

and averaging leads to exactly the same expression.

Probability distributions that preserve their functional form when random variables are added play a prominent role in statistics and are called invariant or *infinitely divisible* distributions [10.5]. The best known example is the Gaussian distribution: the sum of two Gaussian variables is again Gaussian. For independent variables, the variance of the sum is the sum of the individual variances. In other words, the squared width of the distribution of the sum is the sum of the individual squared widths.

But the Gaussian distribution is far from alone in the lofty realm of invariant distributions. The Cauchy distribution, too, is preserved when random variables are added, but the *scaling law* is different: the *widths* themselves add, not their squares. For other invariant distributions some other power D of the widths, $0 < D \le 2$, are added with some rather counterintuitive consequences. For example, for $D = 0.5$, averaging two random variables *increases* the width by a factor 2 [10.4]. Benoît Mandelbrot, in his recent *Fractals and Scaling in Finance*, parades a whole panoply of scaling paradoxes before the unsuspecting reader [10.6].

10.3 The Autocorrelation Function

Autocorrelation is one of the most potent concepts in signal analysis. The *autocorrelation function* $a(\tau)$ of a square-integrable signal $s(t)$ is defined by

$$a(\tau) := \int_{-\infty}^{\infty} s(t)s^*(t - \tau)\,\mathrm{d}t \, , \tag{10.8}$$

where s^* is the complex conjugate of s. For real signals, $s^* = s$ and the star superscript can be omitted. As can be seen from (10.8), $a(\tau)$ is *shift-invariant*, i.e. it is not affected by a time shift (delay) of the signal $s(t)$.

The autocorrelation function of a signal measures its correlation at two instants of time separated by a time interval τ. From the definition (10.8) it follows immediately that $a(-\tau) = a^*(\tau)$. For real signals, the autocorrelation function is itself real and therefore symmetric: $a(-\tau) = a(\tau)$.

The autocorrelation function $a(t)$ of a signal $s(t)$ is related to its Fourier transform $\hat{s}(\omega)$ by the famous *Wiener–Khinchin* relation [10.7]:

$$a(\tau) \longleftrightarrow |\hat{s}(\omega)|^2 \ .$$

Here the two-sided arrow means that $a(\tau)$ and the absolute square of the Fourier transform, $|\hat{s}(\omega)|^2$, the *energy spectrum*, are related by a Fourier transformation and its inverse; in other words, they form a *Fourier pair*:

$$|\hat{s}(\omega)|^2 = \int_{-\infty}^{\infty} a(\tau) \exp(-i\omega\tau)\, d\tau \tag{10.9}$$

and

$$a(\tau) = \frac{1}{2\pi} \int_{-\infty}^{\infty} |\hat{s}(\omega)|^2 \exp(i\omega\tau)\, d\omega \ . \tag{10.10}$$

The energy spectrum of a signal measures its "frequency content". For orchestral music the frequency content may exceed the range of the healthy human ear (20 Hz to 20 000 Hz). Old-fashioned (and some not so old-fashioned) telephone speech signals are limited to frequencies between about 300 Hz and 3000 Hz.

The value of the autocorrelation function for $\tau = 0$, according to (10.8), is equal to its total energy, that is the integral of $|s(t)|^2$ over all times:

$$a(0) = \int_{-\infty}^{\infty} |s(t)|^2\, dt \ . \tag{10.11}$$

On the other hand, according to (10.10):

$$a(0) = \frac{1}{2\pi} \int_{-\infty}^{\infty} |\hat{s}(\omega)|^2\, d\omega \ . \tag{10.12}$$

If we interpret $(1/2\pi)|\hat{s}(\omega)|^2$ as the *energy density* at angular frequency ω, then a comparison of (10.11) and (10.12) tells us that we can measure the energy of a signal in either the time domain or in the frequency domain and get the same result. The equality

$$\int_{-\infty}^{\infty} |s(t)|^2\, dt = \frac{1}{2\pi} \int_{-\infty}^{\infty} |\hat{s}(\omega)|^2\, d\omega \tag{10.13}$$

is a special case of *Parseval's theorem*:

$$\int_{-\infty}^{\infty} s_1(t)s_2^*(t)\, dt = \frac{1}{2\pi} \int_{-\infty}^{\infty} \hat{s}_1(\omega)\hat{s}_2^*(\omega)\, d\omega \ , \tag{10.14}$$

named after Marc-Antoine Parseval des Chênes (1755–1836) who derived it as early as 1799 (and then had to flee France to escape Napoleon's wrath over some of his poems, considered too critical of Bonaparte's régime). Equation (10.14) shows that the Fourier transform is a mathematical *mapping* that preserves *inner products* as defined in (10.14) [10.8]. Parseval's theorem is a consequence of the *completeness* of the Fourier transform; it would not be true if some frequencies present in the signal were not represented in its Fourier transform.

For sampled (time-discrete) signals $s[n]$, we speak of an autocorrelation *sequence*, defined by

$$a[k] := \sum_{n=-\infty}^{\infty} s[n] \cdot s^*[n-k] \,. \tag{10.15}$$

Among the innumerable applications of autocorrelation analysis we mention the detection of periodicities in signals, such as the fundamental frequency ("pitch") in speech signals [10.9]. Autocorrelation analysis is also basic to linear prediction.

The second derivative of the autocorrelation function at $\tau = 0$ is proportional to the second moment of the energy spectrum. Thus, an important spectral parameter can be measured without Fourier analysis. More generally, the $2m$th derivative is proportional to the $2m$th spectral moment.

According to a famous formula by S. O. Rice [10.10] for a Gaussian process, the second derivative (of the properly defined) autocorrelation function is also related to average rate of zero crossings. Thus, for example, the zero-crossing rate of such a process, sharply lowpass filtered at 3 kHz, is 3464 zeros per second. In general, the zero-crossing rate of a bandlimited signal does not exceed twice the upper cut-off frequency. (But B. F. Logan has shown that, incredibly, there exist signals whose number of zeros in a given finite time interval can be arbitrarily high, no matter how low the upper cutoff frequency! However, these are highly pathological signals that blow up exponentially outside the time interval considered.)

10.4 The Convolution Integral and the Delta Function

One of the most frequent operations that "ties" two functions, $s_1(t)$ and $s_2(t)$, together is the convolution integral:

$$b(\tau) := \int_{-\infty}^{\infty} s_1(t)s_2(\tau - t)\mathrm{d}t \,. \tag{10.16}$$

Because of its frequent occurrence, the convolution integral is often abbreviated by a "convolution star":

$$s_1 \star s_2 := \int_{-\infty}^{\infty} s_1(t)s_2(\tau - t)\mathrm{d}t \,. \tag{10.17}$$

Thus, instead of (10.16), we may write

$$b(\tau) = s_1 \star s_2 \ . \tag{10.18}$$

Often, one of the functions, say $s_2(t)$, is the *impulse response* of a passive linear system such as an electrical or mechanical filter. The impulse response $s_2(t)$ is defined as the response at the output of the system at time t when a *delta function* impulse, $\delta(t)$, is applied at its input at time $t = 0$. The delta function $\delta(t)$, also called *Dirac function* after the British physicist Paul Adrien Maurice Dirac (1902–1984), who introduced it to facilitate computations in quantum mechanics, is defined as a function that equals 0 everywhere except at $t = 0$, where it is infinite, and whose integral equals 1:

$$\delta(t) = 0 \ \text{ for } t \neq 0 \tag{10.19}$$

$$\int_{-\infty}^{\infty} \delta(t) = 1 \ .$$

The Dirac function, the mathematical idealization of a short pulse, is a useful tool in many areas of engineering and physics, including thermodynamics. It often emerges naturally as the result of a limiting process. For example, it can be obtained from the normal distribution $(2\pi\sigma^2)^{-1/2} \exp(-t^2/2\sigma^2)$ by letting its width (standard deviation) σ, go to zero while its value at $t = 0$ grows without bound.

If instead of a Dirac pulse $\delta(t)$ another function, $s_1(t)$, is applied to the input of the system, then linear superposition results in an output at time τ given by a convolution integral (10.16). Thus, a linear system is said to *convolve* (please don't say "convolute") an input function with its impulse response.

One of the properties of the delta function is that it can "select" the value of any other function $s(t)$ for any given time, say t':

$$s(t') = \int_{-\infty}^{\infty} s(t)\delta(t - t')\mathrm{d}t \ . \tag{10.20}$$

From this property and (10.2) we see that the Fourier transform of $\delta(t)$ is a constant:

$$\hat{\delta}(\omega) = 1 \ . \tag{10.21}$$

Thus, the Dirac function contains all frequencies between $-\infty$ and $+\infty$ with equal amplitude and zero phase; it is the ideal(ized) test function in linear system analysis.

It is interesting to note that the autocorrelation function of a white noise, $n(t)$, is the Dirac delta function. Writing correlation as a time-reversed convolution, we have:

$$n(t) \star n(-t) = \delta(t) \ , \tag{10.22}$$

which, as we just saw, contains all frequencies with equal strength.

Fourier transforming the right side of (10.16) with respect to the variable τ yields one of the more interesting results of system analysis:

$$\hat{b}(\omega) = \hat{s}_1(\omega) \cdot \hat{s}_2(\omega) \,. \tag{10.23}$$

This means that, for linear systems, the Fourier transform of the output function equals the *product* of the Fourier transforms of the input function and of the impulse response. Fourier transformation has turned the often difficult operation of integration into a simple product! Or, in a manner of speaking, it has transformed the convolution star of (10.18) into the simple multiplication dot of (10.23). This feat is yet another reason for the power and prevalence of the Fourier transform. Conversely, the Fourier transform $\hat{s}(\omega)$ of the product of two signals, $s(t) = s_1(t) \cdot s_2(t)$, is given by a convolution of their Fourier transforms:

$$\hat{s}(\omega) = \frac{1}{2\pi} \int_{-\infty}^{\infty} \hat{s}_1(\Omega) \cdot \hat{s}_2(\omega - \Omega) \mathrm{d}\Omega = \frac{1}{2\pi} \hat{s}_1 \star \hat{s}_2(\omega) \,, \tag{10.24}$$

a relation that is quickly confirmed by an inverse Fourier transformation (10.5).

For time-discrete signals the convolution integral is replaced by a *convolution sum*:

$$b[n] := \sum_{m=-\infty}^{\infty} s_1[m] \cdot s_2[n - m] \,. \tag{10.25}$$

10.5 The Cross-Correlation Function and the Cross-Spectrum

The cross-correlation function $c(\tau)$ is a generalization of the autocorrelation function. It measures the linear dependence between two different functions of time, $s_1(t)$ and $s_2(t)$, at two instants of time, separated by a time interval τ, for example the size of the harvest in the fall and the rainfall during the preceding summer. The cross-correlation function is defined by

$$c(\tau) := \int_{-\infty}^{\infty} s_1(t) \cdot s_2^*(t - \tau) \, \mathrm{d}t \,. \tag{10.26}$$

For $s_1 = s_2$, the cross-correlation function turns into the autocorrelation function.

It is interesting to note that the cross-correlation at $\tau = 0$ between a random ergodic signal $s(t)$ with a symmetrical distribution around $s = 0$ and its square, $s^2(t)$, is zero because the integral over $s \cdot s^2 = s^3(t)$ vanishes. However, the correlation coefficient between a random variable and its *cube* (third power) can be substantial. (The correlation coefficient c between *two random* variables, a and b, is defined as $c = (a - \bar{a})(b - \bar{b})/\sigma_a \sigma_b$, where the horizontal bars signify expectations (averages) and σ_a and σ_b are the standard deviations of a and b, respectively.) For a uniformly distributed random variable, the correlation coefficient between it and its cube is 92%. For a Gaussian signal it is 77% and for a sinewave a whopping 95%! (So much for the idea that correlations near 100% are indicative of strong linear dependence.)

Comparing (10.26) with (10.16), we discover a formal similarity between cross-correlation and convolution: replacing $s_2(t)$ in (10.16) by $s_2^*(-t)$, we see that $c(\tau)$ becomes $b(\tau)$. Thus, for real signals, cross-correlation and convolution differ by a time inversion in one of the two signals.

Fourier transforming (10.26) yields the so-called *cross-spectrum*:

$$\hat{c}(\omega) = \hat{s}_1(\omega) \cdot \hat{s}_2^*(\omega) \ . \tag{10.27}$$

Measurement of the cross-correlation function is often the most convenient way to determine the impulse response $h(t)$ of a linear system. A white noise signal $n(t)$ is applied to the input of the system and its output $a(t)$ (the convolution of the input with the impulse response) is cross-correlated with the input white noise. Since cross-correlating and convolving are interchangeable operations, the result is the correlation of the white noise with itself [a Dirac delta pulse, see (10.22)] convolved with the impulse response, i.e. the impulse response itself. Writing correlations as convolutions with an inverted time direction, we have

$$a(t) = n(t) \star h(t)$$
$$a(t) \star n(-t) = n(t) \star n(-t) \star h(t) = \delta(t) \star h(t) = h(t) \ .$$

Instead of white noise with a Gaussian amplitude distribution from a thermal source (e.g. a resistor at room temperature), a preferred noise source these days is the binary white noise from a shift-register with feedback [10.11]. With proper feedback, the shift-register will produce a periodic sequence of binary (0 or 1) pulses with a period length of $2^m - 1$, where m is the number of register stages. A single period will contain all possible combinations of m 0s or 1s except the all-zero m-tuple. The circular autocorrelation function of such a sequence in the ± 1 alphabet (where 0 is replaced by 1 and 1 by -1) equals $2^m - 1$ for zero shift and a constant -1 for all other shifts that do not equal an integer number of period lengths. The off-values (-1) of the autocorrelation function are therefore as small as possible in absolute terms. (They cannot equal 0 because the sequence length is odd.) Such sequences are also called *low-autocorrelation sequences*, with applications in many fields (radar, sound diffusors, error correcting codes, system analysis, and antenna design) [10.12].

The Fourier transform of such a sequence has constant magnitude for all nonzero frequencies. The power spectrum equals 2^m for all frequencies except zero frequency ("dc") [10.12]. Such sequences therefore have an *exact* flat spectrum, as opposed to thermal noise, which has only an expected flat spectrum (approximately flat only with sufficient averaging). Such sequences are of course deterministic rather than truly random and therefore also called *pseudo-random* or *reproducible* noise. These noises have important applications in psychoacoustics (hearing research) because auditory tests often depend on the exact shape of the short-time spectra of signal and noise.

10.5.1 A Bit of Number Theory

The proper feedback connections are obtained from so-called *primitive polynomials* in finite number (Galois) fields $GF(p^m)$. Here p is a prime number ($p = 2$ for binary noise) and m is an integer that determines the period length. For example, for $m = 50$ and a sampling rate of $10\,\mathrm{kHz}$, the period length exceeds 3567 years, i.e. the noise is aperiodic for all practical (nonbiblical) purposes. For system analysis, the period can be much shorter, but it must be longer than the significant memory of the system. For concert halls with a reverberation time of 2 s, a sufficient value of m is 16, giving a period length exceeding 3 s at a sampling rate of 20 kHz.

A primitive polynomial in a Galois field $GF(p^m)$ is defined as an irreducible (nonfactorizable) polynomial which divides without remainder $x^n - 1$ with $n = p^m - 1$ but for no smaller value of n [10.13]. For example, for $p = 2$ and $m = 4$ the polynomial $1 + x^3 + x^4$ is primitive because it cannot be factored, divides $x^{15} - 1$ but does not divide $x^n - 1$ for $n < 2^4 - 1 = 15$. By contrast, the irreducible polynomial $1 + x + x^2 + x^3 + x^4$ divides $x^5 - 1$ and is therefore not primitive. If used in a shift-register with feedback it would result in a sequence of pulses with period length 5 rather than 15. As a consequence not all fifteen possible 4-tuples would appear and the power spectrum would not be flat. (And used as a noise source for synthetic speech – as has been done – the fricatives will sound awfully discolored.)

The primitive polynomial determines the feedback connection applied to the shift-register. For $1 + x^3 + x^4$, for example, the outputs of the third and fourth register are fed to an "exclusive or" (XOR) gate (the logic equivalent of binary additions without carry). The output of the XOR-gate is fed back to the input of the first register.

Number theory guarantees the existence of irreducible and primitive polynomials for all primes p and integers m. In fact, there are

$$\frac{1}{m} \sum \mu \left(\frac{m}{d} \right) p^d$$

irreducible polynomials, where the sum is extended over all divisors d of m and $\mu(\ )$ is the Möbius function. For $p = 2$ and $m = 4$, there are three irreducible polynomials.

The number of primitive polynomials is

$$\frac{1}{m} \phi(p^m - 1) \, ,$$

where $\phi(\ )$ is *Euler's totient function*, which counts the number of integers relative prime to and smaller than its argument. With $\phi(15) = 8$, there are exactly two primitive polynomials in $GF(2^4)$, namely the trinomials $1 + x^3 + x^4$ and $1 + x + x^4$. For $p = 2$ and $m = 16$, there are 2048 primitive polynomials, many of which have more than three terms. Maximum-length sequences generated with polynomials having many terms are advantageous for testing nonlinear systems (e.g. loudspeakers) because they have better high-order correlation properties.

Interestingly, if the white noise is Gaussian, one of the signals in the cross-correlation may be distorted nonlinearly and even be infinitely clipped, i.e. replaced by its algebraic sign (± 1) – a considerable convenience for some types of measurements, especially in underwater sound. In another example, measuring the impulse response of an animal inner ear, it suffices to cross-correlate the acoustic input noise with the nerve *spikes* on the acoustic nerve running from the inner ear to the brain. However, when using non-Gaussian noises, such as binary maximum-length sequences, for such measurements, nonlinearities do give rise to false results.

The reason that in cross-correlating *Gaussian* processes one of the processes may be distorted, for example by clipping, is that, in the frequency domain, distortion products at different frequencies are uncorrelated with the undistorted process.

However, nonlinear distortion does change the scale factor of the correlation. As a result, the ratio

$$0 \leq \gamma_{1,2}^2(\omega) := \frac{\hat{c}(\omega)}{\hat{s}_1(\omega) \cdot \hat{s}_2^*(\omega)} \leq 1 \, ,$$

called the *coherence function*, is no longer equal to unity, in accordance with (10.27). Thus, the cross-spectrum can be used as a test for nonlinearity and noise generated inside the system.

10.6 The Hilbert Transform and the Analytic Signal

Real signals have two-sided Fourier transforms and power spectra with positive and negative frequencies. In fact, for real signals, $s(t) = s^*(t)$, equation (10.2) tells us that

$$\hat{s}(-\omega) = \hat{s}^*(\omega) \, . \tag{10.28}$$

Moreover, the energy spectrum is a symmetric function of frequency:

$$|\hat{s}(-\omega)|^2 = |\hat{s}(\omega)|^2 \, . \tag{10.29}$$

Thus, each positive (physical) frequency is represented twice in the spectrum, a fact that results in unwieldiness for certain signal operations such as frequency and phase shifts. There is also an inelegant lack of symmetry: speech and many other signals are real, but Fourier transforms are in general complex. Let us therefore replace real signals $s(t)$ by complex signals $\sigma(t)$ whose real part equals $s(t)$. This idea leads to the eminently useful definition of the *analytic signal*

$$\sigma(t) := s(t) + i\check{s}(t) \ . \tag{10.30}$$

Here $\check{s}(t)$ is called the *Hilbert transform* of $s(t)$ defined as the principle value of the following integral:

$$\check{s}(t) := \frac{1}{\pi} \int_{-\infty}^{\infty} \frac{s(\tau)}{t - \tau} \, d\tau \ . \tag{10.31}$$

(Principal value means that a small interval $-\epsilon < \tau < \epsilon$ is excluded from the integration. Then the limit $\epsilon \to 0$ is taken.)

The Hilbert transform converts cosine waves into sine waves and sine waves into negative cosine waves. The Hilbert transform therefore effects a 90° phase shift. Two Hilbert transforms in tandem correspond to a 180° phase shift, that is, a reversal of the algebraic sign of the signal. The definition (10.31) is in the form of a convolution integral, to wit:

$$\check{s}(t) = s(t) \star \frac{1}{\pi t} \ . \tag{10.32}$$

Fourier transformation thus yields

$$\tilde{s}(\omega) = \hat{s}(\omega) \left(\widehat{\frac{1}{\pi t}} \right) \ , \tag{10.33}$$

where $\tilde{s}(\omega)$ is the Fourier transform of the Hilbert transform $\check{s}(t)$ and the second factor on the right is the Fourier transform of the function $1/\pi t$:

$$\int_{-\infty}^{\infty} \frac{1}{\pi t} \exp(-i\omega t) dt = -2i \int_{0}^{\infty} \frac{\sin(\omega t)}{t} \, dt \ . \tag{10.34}$$

The integral on the right has a well-known value, namely 0 for $\omega = 0$, $\pi/2$ for $\omega > 0$ and $-\pi/2$ for $\omega < 0$. That the magnitudes of the integrals appearing in (10.34) are independent of ω for $\omega \neq 0$ also follows from a simple scaling argument. (Replace t by a new variable $u = \omega t$ and nothing is changed.) Defining the *sign-function*:

$$\operatorname{sgn}(\omega) := \begin{cases} 1 & \text{for } \omega > 0 \\ 0 & \text{for } \omega = 0 \\ -1 & \text{for } \omega < 0 \end{cases} \tag{10.35}$$

we can write

$$\tilde{s}(\omega) = -i \operatorname{sgn}(\omega) \cdot \hat{s}(\omega) \ . \tag{10.36}$$

In the frequency domain, the Hilbert transform therefore corresponds to a multiplication by $\pm i$, which is equivalent to a 90° phase shift. With (10.36), the Fourier transform of the analytic signal $\sigma(t)$, equation (10.30) becomes

$$\hat{\sigma}(\omega) = \begin{cases} 2\hat{\sigma}(\omega) & \text{for } \omega > 0 \\ \hat{\sigma}(\omega) & \text{for } \omega = 0 \\ 0 & \text{for } \omega < 0 \, . \end{cases} \tag{10.37}$$

The analytic signal therefore contains no negative frequencies, an important and desirable property, which also has interesting applications in the time domain, see Sect. 10.8.

10.7 Hilbert Envelope and Instantaneous Frequency

The magnitude of the analytic signal $|\sigma(t)|$ is called the *Hilbert envelope*. Writing

$$\sigma(t) = |\sigma(t)| \exp(i\varphi(t)) \, , \tag{10.38}$$

$\varphi(t)$ is called the *instantaneous phase*. Its time derivative $d\varphi/dt = \dot{\varphi}$ is called *instantaneous angular frequency*.

For a sine wave $s(t) = A\cos(\omega t + \alpha)$, the analytic signal equals $\sigma(t) = A\exp(i\omega t + \alpha))$. The envelope $|\sigma(t)|$ is a constant and equals A. The instantaneous phase, $\omega t + \alpha$, is a linear function of time, and the instantaneous angular frequency is ω; the angle α is a *phase constant*.

For most amplitude-modulated signals (for example, AM radio signals), $|\sigma(t)|$ is the information-bearing signal and varies slowly as a function of time (slowly compared to the "carrier" frequency ω, which means that $|\dot{\sigma}|/|\sigma| \ll \omega$). For phase or frequency-modulated (FM) signals, $\varphi(t)$ is the information-bearing signal and usually varies slowly with time ($\dot{\varphi} \ll \omega$).

For *narrow-band signals* $|\sigma(t)|\cos(\omega t + \beta(t))$ (narrow compared to the carrier frequency ω), the envelope has an immediate intuitive meaning: it is the envelope curve one would draw over the tops of the waveform just touching each cycle of the carrier near its maximum. But the expression "envelope" for $|\sigma(t)|$ is also justified on more formal grounds: starting with a single signal

$$s(t) = |\sigma(t)| \cos(\varphi(t)) \, , \tag{10.39}$$

one can generate an infinite family of signals by phase shifting:

$$s_\alpha(t) = |\sigma(t)| \cos(\varphi(t) + \alpha) \quad 0 \leq \alpha < 2\pi \, . \tag{10.40}$$

The mathematical definition of the *envelope* of such a family of functions is the (non-negative) function that is as small as possible for each value of t without intersecting any member of the family. It is not too difficult to see that the so-defined envelope is indeed equal to Hilbert envelope $|\sigma(t)|$.

Again for narrow-band signals, the instantaneous angular frequency has an immediate intuitive meaning: it equals (approximately) $2\pi/\Delta t$, where Δt is the time interval between two successive upward (or downward) zero-crossings. In a sine wave Δt is of course constant and equals $2\pi/\omega$.

Shifting the phase of a signal by a constant angle α, as in (10.40), results in simple multiplication of the analytical signal and its Fourier transform by a phase factor

$$\sigma_\alpha(t) = \sigma(t) \exp(i\alpha) \tag{10.41}$$

and

$$\hat{\sigma}_\alpha(\omega) = \hat{\sigma}(\omega) \exp(i\alpha) \ . \tag{10.42}$$

Frequency shifting is obtained by letting the phase α increase linearly with time. If the frequency shift is larger than the one-sided (lower side) bandwidth of the signal, a *single-sideband* (SSB) signal results. Single-sideband modulation is a widely used method of transmitting audio and other signals because it requires only half the transmitter bandwidth compared to double-sideband amplitude modulation. But SSB transmitters are not per se compatible with AM-receivers; they require special receivers – unless a method called *compatible* SSB is employed at the transmitter [10.14].

There are two basic methods of realizing frequency-shifting or SSB-modulation. For large frequency shifts (larger than the bandwidth of the signal), one can first perform a simple amplitude modulation using a carrier frequency equal to the desired shift and then remove the lower sideband and the carrier by a sufficiently selective highpass filter.

In another method, which works even for small frequency shifts, one first generates the Hilbert transform $\check{s}(t) = |\sigma(t)|\sin(\varphi(t))$ of the signal $s(t) = |\sigma(t)|\cos(\varphi(t))$ and combines these two signals as follows to yield the shifted signal

$$s_{\Delta\omega}(t) = s(t)\cos(\Delta\omega t) - \check{s}(t)\sin(\Delta\omega t) = |\sigma(t)|\cos(\varphi(t) + \Delta\omega t), \tag{10.43}$$

whose instantaneous frequency is increased by $\Delta\omega$ compared to $s(t)$. For analog circuits, rather than generating the Hilbert transform of a given signal (which is impossible anyhow because of the delay implicit in Hilbert transforming), *allpass phase filters* are employed that generate, from a given signal, a *pair* of signals one of which is the Hilbert transform of the other.

Frequency shifting is also used to lower the necessary sampling rate for narrow-band signals. Instead of a sampling rate exceeding twice the upper cutoff frequency, the maximally down-shifted signal requires only a sampling rate exceeding twice its bandwidth B. Interestingly, this saving in sampling rate can also be realized without frequency shifting. The trick is to sample both the signal *and* its Hilbert transform at a sampling rate a little above B, for a total rate close to $2B$. Interested readers may wish to discover by themselves how this works.

Besides single-sideband modulation, frequency shifting has been found useful for preventing instabilities ("howling") resulting from acoustic feedback in *public address* (microphone-loudspeaker) systems [10.15]. A frequency shift of about 5 Hz is nearly inaudible for most speech signals and results in a useful extra stability margin of about 6 dB because the excess acoustic energy generated around the response peaks of the room is "dumped" into the nearby troughs of the room's frequency response. Deep troughs are located typically $4/T$ Hz next to a high peak. Here T is the *reverberation time*, which is about 1 s in many lecture halls [10.16].

While the envelope $|\sigma(t)|$ of a finite-bandwidth signal $s(t)$ is usually not itself bandlimited, the *squared* envelope is. In fact, the Fourier transform of $\sigma^2(t)$ is given by the convolution of $\hat{\sigma}(\omega)$ with itself. If the signal $s(t)$ has no frequencies above an upper cut-off angular frequency ω_u, the corresponding analytic signal $\sigma(t)$ has a Fourier transform $\hat{\sigma}(\omega)$ with the same cut-off and the convolution of $\hat{\sigma}(\omega)$ with itself has an upper cutoff angular frequency of $2\omega_\mathrm{u}$.

An even more forceful statement can be made about the Fourier transform of the *absolute* squared envelope $|\sigma(t)|^2$ of a signal with (one-sided) bandwidth B: its Fourier transform is limited to frequencies between $-B$ and B, no matter what the upper cut-off frequency ω_u. This follows from the Wiener–Khinchin theorem which says that taking the absolute square of a function in one Fourier domain corresponds to taking the autocorrelation function in the other domain (see (10.9) with the variable ω replaced by t, and τ replaced by ω). And the autocorrelation of the $\hat{\sigma}(\omega)$, $\hat{\sigma}(\omega)$ being limited to the range $0 \leq \omega < B$, is itself limited to $-B < \omega < B$. Referring to the Fourier transform $\hat{s}(\omega)$ of the signal $s(t)$ itself, we may say that the Fourier transform of the squared envelope of $s(t)$ equals the autocorrelation function of $2\hat{s}(\omega)$ for $\omega > 0$. (For $\omega = 0$, the factor 2 must be omitted, see (10.37).)

The fact that the Fourier transform of the squared envelope of a signal is proportional to the autocorrelation function of the Fourier transform for positive frequencies of the signal itself has several interesting applications. For example, suppose we want to lower the *peak factor* of a periodic signal (defined as its range, i.e. maximum minus minimum value, divided by its root-mean-square value), it would of course help if the envelope were a constant or at least have as little ac (alternating current) power as possible. Thus, the squared values of the autocorrelation sequence $a_1, a_2, a_3, \cdots$ of the positive branch of the Fourier transform of the signal should be as small as possible for a given signal power (a_0). In other words, the Fourier transform should be a *low-autocorrelation sequence* which, as mentioned before, is a kind of sequence that has many applications in signal design for radar and sonar, in filter and antenna design, and in other fields.

Consider a periodic signal consisting of 31 cosine harmonics of equal, unit amplitudes. The Fourier transform of the signal is a sequence of 31 terms of the form $\pm 1, \pm 1, \pm 1, \cdots, \pm 1$. Call the corresponding autocorrelation sequence a_k, $k = 0, 1, 2, \ldots, 30$. Which sign combination has the lowest value of $A = \sum_{k=1}^{30} a_k^2$? This is a problem of combinatorial complexity, a nasty class of "intractable" problems. Obviously, the solution is not all $+1$'s (or all -1's), for which choice A would equal 9455. Nor is a random choice optimal:

the expected value of A would be 465. Better results for this problem, as for other problems of combinatorial complexity (such as the traveling salesperson problem), are obtained with *genetic algorithms* or with *simulated annealing*, a numerical algorithm inspired by the thermodynamics of slowly cooled ("annealed") metals [10.17].

Good results have also been achieved by adjusting the phase angles of a periodic waveform to mimic those of an FM signal (which by definition has a low peak factor) [10.18].

The best results so far come from number theory, specifically the theory of finite number fields, also known as Galois fields. As mentioned in Sect. 10.5.1, Galois sequences, also called maximum-length sequences, are periodic pseudorandom sequences whose squared autocorrelation coefficients, a_k^2 for $k > 0$, are as small as possible, namely equal to 1. The resulting waveform has been used by the author as an excitation signal in vocoders, giving a noticeably smoother sound compared to excitation by high-peak-factor (impulsive) waveforms.

In addition to the squared envelope, another important bandlimited function derivable from the analytic signal $\sigma(t) = |\sigma(t)| \exp(i\varphi(t))$ is the *weighted* instantaneous angular frequency

$$\nu(t) := \dot{\varphi}(t)|\sigma(t)|^2 \,, \tag{10.44}$$

which equals the imaginary part of $\dot{\sigma}\sigma^*$. The time integral of $\nu(t)$ equals the frequency integral of ω weighted with the energy spectrum:

$$\int_{-\infty}^{\infty} \dot{\varphi}(t)|\sigma(t)|^2 \mathrm{d}t = \int_0^{\infty} \omega|\hat{\sigma}(\omega)|^2 \mathrm{d}\omega \,. \tag{10.45}$$

This intriguing relation between two average frequencies, one averaged in the time domain and the other in the frequency domain follows directly from Parseval's theorem (10.14) by setting $s_1(t) = \dot{\sigma}(t)$, and $s_2(t) = \sigma(t)$, and equating imaginary parts. Here we have made use of the fact that the Fourier transform of $\dot{\sigma}(t)$ equals $i\omega\hat{\sigma}(\omega)$. Similar relationships exist for higher-order odd moments of the energy spectrum.

It is interesting to note that the weighted instantaneous frequency $\nu(t) = |\sigma(t)|^2\dot{\varphi}(t)$ has a well-known meaning in astronomy. If we consider the orbit of a planet around the sun as an analytic signal $\sigma(t)$ with the sun at the origin of the complex plane (the orbital plane), then Kepler's Second Law of Planetary Motion, published in 1609, says that $\nu(t)$ is a constant. Planetary motion, i.e. the distances of the planets from the sun, considered as analytic signals, could not be simpler. While the ancient Greeks and even Nicholas Copernicus (1473–1543) and, initially, indeed Johannes Kepler (1571–1630) himself held fast to the dogma of constant *speeds* of the planets, observation taught him otherwise. The constancy of $\nu(t)$ was later explained by Isaac Newton (1642–1727) as the preservation of angular momentum of a (heavenly) body subjected only to central forces, as is the case for a planet attracted by the sun.

For Gaussian processes, the squared envelope and the instantaneous frequency are independent in the sense that, for $T \to \infty$,

$$\frac{1}{2T} \int_{-T}^{T} |\sigma(t)|^2 \dot{\varphi}(t) \mathrm{d}t = \frac{1}{2T} \int_{-T}^{T} |\sigma(t)|^2 \mathrm{d}t \cdot \frac{1}{2T} \int_{-T}^{T} \dot{\sigma}(t) \mathrm{d}t . \tag{10.46}$$

This means that the center of gravity (or first moment) of the spectrum of a Gaussian noise can be determined by merely averaging its instantaneous frequency $\dot{\varphi}(t)$ without regard to its amplitude. (The same is of course trivially true for a single sine wave.) By contrast, as already mentioned in relation to autocorrelation functions, the rate of zero crossings of a Gaussian noise measures the *second* moment of the power spectrum.

There is an interesting application of this result to Gaussian processes in the frequency domain, such as the real (or imaginary) part of the transfer function of a large room or any other linear system with randomly overlapping normal modes [10.20]. To determine the reverberation time τ_e of the system, if defined as the center of gravity of its squared impulse response, it suffices to measure the average rate of phase change with frequency. In fact,

$$\tau_\mathrm{e} = \frac{\varphi(\omega_1) - \varphi(\omega_2)}{\omega_2 - \omega_1} . \tag{10.47}$$

For exponential decays, τ_e is also the time in which the reverberation energy decays by a factor $\mathrm{e} = 2.718\cdots$. The phase difference $\varphi(\omega_1) - \varphi(\omega_2)$ must include the appropriate multiple of 2π accumulated over the frequency interval (ω_1, ω_2) being considered [10.21].

Curiously, the relation (10.47) is also true for a *single* echo with a delay τ_e rather than full-blown reverberation. (In fact, (10.47) is trivially true in the case of a single echo.)

10.8 Causality and the Kramers–Kronig Relations

One of the most important applications of the Hilbert transform is the establishment of the relationship between real and imaginary parts of the Fourier transform of a causal system. A causal system is defined as a passive system whose impulse response $h(t)$ is zero for negative times (no output before an input has been applied):

$$h(t) = 0 \text{ for } t < 0 .$$

This *causality condition* is reminiscent of the Fourier transform $\hat{\sigma}(\omega)$ of an analytic signal, which vanishes for negative frequencies: $\hat{\sigma}(\omega) = 0$ for $\omega < 0$, see (10.36). Since real and imaginary parts of an analytic signal are related by a Hilbert transform, the same Hilbert transform relationship may be expected between the real and imaginary parts of the Fourier transform of a causal signal. Indeed, for a causal system with impulse response $h(t)$,

$$\text{Im}\{\hat{h}(\omega)\} = \int_{-\infty}^{\infty} \frac{\text{Re}\{\hat{h}(\Omega)\}}{\pi(\omega - \Omega)}\,\mathrm{d}\Omega \qquad (10.48\text{a})$$

and

$$\text{Re}\{\hat{h}(\omega)\} = -\int_{-\infty}^{\infty} \frac{\text{Im}\{\hat{h}(\Omega)\}}{\pi(\omega - \Omega)}\,\mathrm{d}\Omega \;, \qquad (10.48\text{b})$$

which, exploiting the symmetry $\hat{h}(-\omega) = \hat{h}^*(\omega)$, can also be written

$$\text{Im}\{\hat{h}(\omega)\} = -\frac{2}{\pi}\int_{0}^{\infty} \frac{\omega\text{Re}\{\hat{h}(\Omega)\}}{\Omega^2 - \omega^2}\,\mathrm{d}\Omega \qquad (10.49\text{a})$$

and

$$\text{Re}\{\hat{h}(\omega)\} = \frac{2}{\pi}\int_{0}^{\infty} \frac{\Omega\text{Im}\{\hat{h}(\Omega)\}}{\Omega^2 - \omega^2}\,\mathrm{d}\Omega \;. \qquad (10.49\text{b})$$

These equations are called *Kramers–Kronig relations* after the physicists Hendrik A. Kramers and Ralph de Laer Kronig who established them in the 1920s in connection with the dispersion of light waves by atoms and molecules. Light dispersion was an important piece of experimental evidence in the budding theory of atomic structure. In fact, Werner Heisenberg (1901–1975) was inspired by these very concepts to emphasize the crucial role of observable physical quantities, called *observables*, in his formulation of quantum mechanics in 1925. The new theory banished unobservable quantities, insinuated into atomic physics by such misleading macroscopic images as electronic orbits around an atomic nucleus (as depicted in the logos of some nuclear enterprises and the Getty oil company before they replaced it by a yellow dot – presumably the sun). Instead of ill-defined electronic orbits, physicists substituted wave amplitudes and relative phases and other actually measurable quantities to describe submicroscopic events.

10.8.1 Anticausal Functions

Occasionally the need arises to consider *anticausal* functions, defined by $g(t) = 0$ for $t > 0$. The simplest example of an anticausal system is a *negative* delay whose impulse response is given by

$$g(t) = \delta(t - t_0), \;\; t_0 < 0. \qquad (10.50)$$

The Fourier transform is $\hat{g}(\omega) = \exp(-\mathrm{i}\omega t_0) = \cos(\omega t_0) + \mathrm{i}\sin(-\omega t_0)$, in which the real part is the Hilbert transform of the imaginary part rather than vice versa.

Anticausal functions occur in the physics of elementary particles and in tape-recorded audio signals in which the tape is run backward in time. If time-reversed speech is heavily reverberated and time-reversed once more (so that the speech signal is running forward again) it becomes completely unintelligible. Human auditory perception suppresses normal reverberation by the acoustic *precedence effect*. According to the precedence effect (also known as, but actually distinct from, the "Haas effect"), the direction of the first-arriving sound determines the perceived direction, even in the presence of strong echoes. The precedence effect has probably evolved in our animal ancestors to signal the proper direction of a predator or prey in the presence of strong reverberation from trees or inside caves. On the other hand, and not surprisingly, the human ear is unable to cope with time-*reversed* reverberation, an anticausal process that does not occur in airborne sound.[2]

10.8.2 Minimum-Phase Systems and Complex Frequencies

Another important application of the Hilbert transform is the relation between the amplitude response $|\hat{h}(\omega)|$ and the phase response $\varphi(\omega)$ of *minimum-phase* systems. A minimum-phase system is defined as a causal linear passive system with transfer function $\hat{h}(\omega)$ whose *inverse* transfer function $1/\hat{h}(\omega)$ is also causal.

Minimum-phase systems are best discussed in the *complex frequency plane*, in terms of the complex frequency variable

$$s := \rho + \mathrm{i}\omega . \tag{10.51}$$

Causal systems that are square-integrable are analytic in the upper halfplane of the complex frequency plane. Thus, neither $\hat{h}(\omega)$ nor $1/\hat{h}(\omega)$ can have poles in the upper halfplane. Since the poles of $1/\hat{h}(\omega)$ are the zeros of $\hat{h}(\omega)$, we can characterize a minimum-phase system by a transfer function $\hat{h}(\omega)$ that has neither poles nor zeros in the upper half of the complex frequency plane.

For such a transfer function $\hat{h}(\omega)$, its *logarithm* $\log[\hat{h}(\omega)]$ is also an analytic function in the upper halfplane. (Note that for this to be true, it is essential that $\hat{h}(\omega)$ have neither poles nor zeros in the upper halfplane because the logarithm diverges for both poles *and* zeros.) From this property of $\log[\hat{h}(\omega)]$ it follows that its imaginary part is the Hilbert transform of its real part. With

$$\hat{h}(\omega) = |\hat{h}(\omega)| \exp(\mathrm{i}\varphi(\omega))$$

or

$$\log[\hat{h}(\omega)] = \log[|\hat{h}(\omega)|] + \mathrm{i}\varphi(\omega) , \tag{10.52}$$

we therefore have

$$\varphi(\omega) = \frac{2}{\pi} \int_0^\infty \frac{\log[|\hat{h}(\Omega)|]}{\omega - \Omega} \mathrm{d}\Omega . \tag{10.53}$$

---

[2] However, time-reversed reverberation does occur in the deep ocean over very long distances. In this so-called *SOFAR* underwater sound channel, say between South Africa and Greenland, the strongest sound, which travels in a straight line, arrives last because the center of the channel has the smallest sound velocity.

Conversely, the logarithmic amplitude response $\log[|\hat{h}(\omega)|]$ is the negative Hilbert transform of the phase response $\varphi(\omega)$. Thus, for minimum-phase systems, amplitude and phase response are closely bound to each other. For every amplitude response there is a unique minimum-phase response and vice versa.

A simple example of a minimum-phase system is a capacitor, charged up at time $t = 0$, whose charge is decaying exponentially for $t > 0$ with time constant τ. Its impulse response is

$$h(t) = \begin{cases} 0 & \text{for } t < 0 \\ \exp(-t/\tau) & \text{for } t \geq 0 \end{cases} \tag{10.54}$$

with Fourier transform

$$\hat{h}(\omega) = \frac{\tau}{1 + i\omega\tau} \ . \tag{10.55}$$

Its phase response

$$\varphi(\omega) = -\arctan(\omega\tau) \tag{10.56}$$

is indeed the Hilbert transform of

$$\log[|\hat{h}(\omega)|] = \frac{1}{2} \log \left(\frac{\tau^2}{1 + \omega^2\tau^2} \right) \ . \tag{10.57}$$

A broad class of minimum-phase systems are so-called *all-pole* systems which are defined as systems having only poles (in the lower half of the frequency plane to be stable) and no zeros. Such systems, as noted above, have causal inverses $1/\hat{h}(\omega)$.

10.8.3 Allpass Systems

Another important class of linear passive systems are *allpass* systems, defined as systems whose transfer function $\hat{h}(\omega)$ has a constant magnitude $|\hat{h}(\omega)|$ equal to 1, that is

$$\hat{h}(\omega) = e^{i\varphi(\omega)} \tag{10.58}$$

or

$$\hat{h}(\omega)\hat{h}^*(\omega) = 1 \ .$$

For an allpass system, we therefore have

$$\hat{h}^{-1}(\omega) = \hat{h}^*(\omega) \ . \tag{10.59}$$

Allpass systems, too, are best discussed in terms of the complex frequency variable $s = \rho + i\omega$. Thus, the frequency (ω) axis becomes the imaginary axis in the complex s plane and we write $\hat{h}[s]$ instead of $\hat{h}(\omega)$, using brackets to indicate the change of variable. Introducing the poles p_k and zeros z_k of $\hat{h}[s]$, we write

$$\hat{h}[s] = \prod_k \frac{s - z_k}{s - p_k} \ . \tag{10.60}$$

Applying (10.59), we obtain for $s = i\omega$ (i.e. on the frequency axis, where $s^* = -s$):

$$\hat{h}^{-1}[s] = \prod_k \frac{s + z_k^*}{s + p_k^*} \tag{10.61}$$

or

$$\hat{h}[s] = \prod_k \frac{s + p_k^*}{s + z_k^*} \ . \tag{10.62}$$

Comparing (10.62) with (10.60), we see that for an allpass system the zeros are given by the poles (and vice versa), namely:

$$z_k = -p_k^* \ . \tag{10.63}$$

Writing $p_k = \rho_k + i\omega_k$, we have

$$z_k = -\rho_k + i\omega_k \ , \tag{10.64}$$

that is, the zeros are the mirror images of poles, mirrored in the ω-axis. Thus each pole ("resonance") is compensated in its amplitude effect by a mirror-image zero, but the phase shift engendered by each pole is doubled by its mirror-image zero.

With (10.60) and (10.63) we may write the transfer function of an allpass system as

$$\hat{h}[s] = \prod_k \frac{s + p_k^*}{s - p_k} \ . \tag{10.65}$$

The impulse response of the inverse of a causal allpass system is *anticausal*. That is, the inverse of an allpass system has an impulse response that is the original impulse response $h(t)$ mirrored in time. This follows from the fact that $\hat{h}^{-1}(\omega) = \hat{h}^*(\omega)$, see (10.59), and that $\hat{h}^*(\omega)$ is the Fourier transform of $h(-t)$. Thus, a causal allpass system has no causal inverse; in fact, the inverse is *anti*causal.

10.8.4 Dereverberation

Anticausality can be circumvented by the method of tape recording the signal (or putting it into computer storage) and running the tape backward or reading out the memory in reverse. (Of course, these operations take time so no causality laws are actually violated.)

To realize the inverse $\hat{h}^{-1}(\omega)$ of a *general* linear passive system $\hat{h}(\omega)$, it must first be factored into a minimum-phase system $m(\omega)$ and an allpass system:

$$\hat{h}(\omega) = m(\omega)\, a(\omega) \ , \tag{10.66}$$

whose inverse is

$$\hat{h}^{-1}(\omega) = m^{-1}(\omega)\,a^{-1}(\omega)\;.\tag{10.67}$$

Here, $m^{-1}(\omega)$ exists and $a^{-1}(\omega)$ has to be realized (or approximated) in nonreal time by a technique that flips the time axis. In this manner, even the exceedingly complex response of a large lecture hall or concert hall can in principle be inverted with a delay of about $2\,$s. Such an inverse filter, used on the acoustic output of a reverberant enclosure, can eliminate the reverberation and restore the original unreverberated sound. This process is an example of *dereverberation.* Dereverberation improves speech quality and intelligibility, for example in "hands-free" speakerphones. Such applications require real-time dereverberation, which can be *realized* (apt word!) by self-steering microphone arrays [10.22] and *volume focussing* arrays that "focus" on a given sound source in three-dimensional space [10.23].

10.9 Matched Filtering

Inverting the time axis of the impulse response $h(t)$ of an arbitrary system or filter results in the so-called *matched filter* whose Fourier transform is given by $\hat{h}^*(\omega)$. (Again, an extra delay is required to make the matched filter realizable.) Matched filters are often used in signal detection to extract useful signals from a contaminating noise. If the Fourier transform of the signal is $\hat{h}(\omega)$, then the output of the matched filter is

$$\hat{h}^*(\omega)\cdot\hat{h}(\omega) = |\hat{h}(\omega)|^2\;,\tag{10.68}$$

which is the energy spectrum of the signal. The corresponding inverse Fourier transform is the *autocorrelation* of the signal. In a manner of speaking, matched filtering turns back to zero all the phase angles $\varphi(\omega)$ in the signal's Fourier transform $\hat{h}(\omega) = |\hat{h}(\omega)|\exp(i\varphi(\omega))$ to result in a large response peak at $t = 0$. At the same time, matched filtering squares the magnitude $|\hat{h}(\omega)|$, see (10.68), thereby emphasizing those frequency components that are relatively strong compared to the noise spectrum (which is considered flat in the simplest case).

The concept of matched filtering was first formalized by Dwight O. North in a 1943 classified report. The name "matched filter" was coined by D. Middleton and J.H. Van Vleck a year later in another classified report.

Two-dimensional matched filtering has found wide application in optical recognition systems. For optical applications, the matched filtering is often carried out by two-dimensional signal processing using coherent (laser) light, profiting from the fact that a focussing lens performs a good approximation to a Fourier transform between its two foci [10.24]. For the properly recognized object, the result of the matched filtering is an easily detected bright spot at the origin of the correlation plane, while no such spot occurs for the incorrect objects.

Matched filtering applied to the outputs of an array of microphones, hydrophones, or other sensors in a multipath medium (such as the oceans) causes a three-dimensionally bounded space to be selected, resulting in "volume-focussing" rather than mere beamforming.

Matched filtering is closely related to the so-called *factorization problem*: given a square-integrable nonnegative function $\hat{a}(\omega)$, find a causal function of time $h(t)$ such that $\hat{a}(\omega)$ is the Fourier transform of its autocorrelation function

$$h(t) \star h^*(-t) = a(t) \tag{10.69}$$

or

$$\hat{h}(\omega)\hat{h}^*(\omega) = \hat{a}(\omega) \, . \tag{10.70}$$

To make the solution unique, we require that $h(t)$ be the impulse response of a minimum-phase system.

The factorization problem as expressed in (10.69) has a solution if and only if $a(\omega)$ satisfies the *Paley–Wiener* condition [10.25]:

$$\int_{-\infty}^{\infty} \frac{|\log a(\omega)|}{1 + \omega^2} \mathrm{d}\omega < \infty \, . \tag{10.71}$$

Thus, $a(\omega)$ cannot vanish on any interval or measurable set.

10.10 Phase and Group Delay

Consider a signal $s(t)$ consisting of two cosine waves with different angular frequencies:

$$s(t) = \cos(\omega_1 t) + \cos(\omega_2 t), \quad \omega_2 > \omega_1 \, . \tag{10.72}$$

How are envelope and phase of $s(t)$ affected if the signal travels through a filter or medium with a frequency-dependent phase $\varphi(\omega)$?

Using a Taylor expansion around $\omega = \omega_1$ and truncating after one term, we have

$$\varphi(\omega) = \varphi(\omega_1) - (\omega - \omega_1)\varphi'(\omega_1) \, , \tag{10.73}$$

where $\varphi'(\omega_1)$ is the *negative* derivative of the phase with respect to angular frequency $\omega = \omega_1$.

The squared envelope of $s(t)$

$$|\sigma(t)|^2 = 2 + 2\cos(\omega_2 - \omega_1)t \tag{10.74}$$

fluctuates or "beats" with a frequency $\omega_2 - \omega_1$ equal to the difference of the two frequencies contained in the signal. If $s(t)$ is subjected to a *phase distortion* $\varphi(\omega)$, (10.73), the squared envelope becomes

$$|\sigma_\varphi(t)|^2 = 2 + 2\cos((\omega_2 - \omega_1)(t - \varphi')) \, . \tag{10.75}$$

For "normal" phase distortion, also called *normal dispersion* by physicists, the phase decreases with increasing frequency. The derivative φ', as defined in (10.73), is therefore positive. Thus, (10.75) tells us that the envelope is *delayed* by an amount

$$\Delta t_{\mathrm{g}} = \varphi' \, . \tag{10.76}$$

This delay is called *envelope delay* or *group delay* (because it affects a "group" of frequencies, not a single frequency). Group delay, which generally depends on frequency, is an important concept, especially in two-way communication links. For example, the smooth flow of a telephone conversation is severely degraded if the round-trip group delay exceeds half a second, as it does in connections that use geo-stationary satellites. Such delays are particularly bothersome in the presence of delayed echoes of one's own voice from a distant location.

Distance traveled divided by group delay is called *group velocity*. According to special relativity, the velocity of light in free space, about 300 000 km/s, is the upper limit for the group velocity of any physically realizable system.[3] Thus, energy or information (which, for AM signals, resides in the envelope variations) cannot travel faster than light. (Yet in quantum mechanics there are situations, the Einstein–Podolski–Rosen paradox being the most celebrated one, in which instantaneous actions at a distance do take place: Einstein's "spooky actions at a distance". But they cannot be exploited for transmitting energy, let alone transporting people ("teleportation") at the speed of light [10.26].)

The *phase delay* Δt_φ, introduced by a phase-distorting medium, is defined as

$$\Delta t_\varphi := \frac{-\varphi(\omega_1)}{\omega_1} \, . \tag{10.77}$$

The phase delay determines the phase shift in the instantaneous (also called "carrier") phase of the signal. Thus, a signal with envelope $|\sigma(t)|$ and instantaneous phase $\varphi(t)$:

$$s(t) = |\sigma(t)| \cos(\varphi(t)) \tag{10.78}$$

emerges from the phase-distorting medium as

$$s_\varphi(t) = |\sigma(t - \Delta t_{\mathrm{g}})| \cos(\varphi(t) - \omega_1 \Delta t_\varphi) \, . \tag{10.79}$$

Equation (10.79) implies that the envelope of the signal emerges from the phase-distorting medium unscathed except for a delay. That is strictly true only for frequency intervals for which the truncated Taylor expansion (10.73) is a perfect approximation. If the second derivative $\varphi''(\omega_1)$ is too large in magnitude, the shape of the envelope will be distorted; for example, a sharp

---

[3] In 1983 the General Conference on Weights and Measures redefined the meter to make the speed of light c come out an exact integer (containing a surprisingly large prime factor) in meters per second: $c = 299792458$ m/s.

pulse will become broader because the different frequencies it contains will suffer different group delays. The condition for envelope shape preservation is

$$|\varphi''(\omega_1)| \ll \left|\frac{2\varphi'(\omega_1)}{\omega_2 - \omega_1}\right| . \tag{10.80}$$

In other words, the relative change in the group delay $|(\omega_2 - \omega_1)\varphi''/\varphi'|$ in the frequency interval $\omega_2 - \omega_1$ must be small. This is an important consideration in the design of optical fiber links.

Distance traveled divided by the phase delay is called phase velocity. Phase velocities can exceed the speed of light because they engender no "extraluminous" causation. A simple example of an arbitrarily high phase velocity is the bright spot projected on a high cloud cover by an earthbound search light. When the search light is whipped to a different direction, that bright spot can travel along the cloud cover faster than light. Another instance of a phase velocity exceeding the speed of light c is the phase velocity v_φ in a metallic wave guide. In fact, for electromagnetic wave guides, group and phase velocity are reciprocally related: $v_\varphi = c^2/v_g$. Since v_g can not exceed c $(v_g < c)$, it follows immediately that $v_\varphi \geq c$.

What is true of guided waves is also true for freely propagating waves: if a plane wave traveling at speed c hits a plane surface at an angle of incidence α from the plane's normal, then wave crests travel along the surface with a speed equal to $c/\sin\alpha$ which, except for grating incidence $(\alpha = \frac{\pi}{2})$, exceeds c.

10.11 Heisenberg Uncertainty and the Fourier Transform

The Fourier transform has an interesting *scaling* property. As is evidenced from its definition (10.2), a compression of the time axis by a factor k causes a dilation of the frequency axis by the reciprocal factor, $1/k$. Indeed, if

$$\hat{s}(\omega) = \int_{-\infty}^{\infty} s(t)\exp(-\mathrm{i}\omega t)\,\mathrm{d}t \tag{10.81}$$

then, for $s_k(t) := s(kt)$, the Fourier transform is

$$\hat{s}_k(\omega) = \frac{1}{k}\hat{s}\left(\frac{\omega}{k}\right) . \tag{10.82}$$

This reciprocal scaling relationship between time and frequency is the reason why *time–bandwidth products* are often a more fundamental quantity than duration or bandwidth of a signal by itself (for example, in signal detection tasks detection probabilities do not depend on scaling).

Another implication of reciprocal scaling is that the smaller the time uncertainty the larger the frequency uncertainty will be (and vice versa).

For example, a rectangularly gated sine wave of duration T has an angular bandwidth between the first two spectral zeros around the spectral peak equal to $4\pi/T$. In other words, the time–bandwidth product equals 4π. Are there pulse shapes which have smaller time–bandwidth products? And what *are* these shapes, called *time windows* by electrical engineers? The answer depends on the *definition* of duration and bandwidth. If we use the standard deviation σ (familiar from statistical analysis) as a measure of width, then we may ask for the pulse shape for which the product $\sigma_t \cdot \sigma_\omega$ is a minimum (provided σ_t and σ_ω exist). For a pulse in the shape of a Gaussian distribution

$$s(t) = \exp(-t^2/2\sigma^2) , \tag{10.83}$$

the Fourier transform is also Gaussian:

$$\hat{s}(\omega) = 2\pi\sigma \exp(-\omega^2\sigma^2/2) . \tag{10.84}$$

By squaring (10.83) we obtain the power of the Gaussian pulse whose standard deviation σ_t is seen to equal $\sigma/\sqrt{2}$. Similarly, by squaring (10.84), we obtain the power in the frequency domain whose standard deviation σ_ω equals $1/\sqrt{2}\sigma$. Thus, the time–bandwidth product of the power distributions in the time and angular frequency domains, as measured by their standard deviations, equals $\sigma_t \cdot \sigma_\omega = 0.5$.[4]

In 1927 the German physicist Werner Heisenberg showed that the Gaussian shape has the smallest uncertainty, that is

$$\sigma_t \cdot \sigma_\omega \geq 0.5 . \tag{10.85}$$

This is the justly famous *uncertainty relation*, except that physicists associate with the frequency ω an energy $E = \hbar\omega$, where $2\pi\hbar = 6.6260755 \times 10^{-34}$ watt $\cdot$ second^2 is called *Planck's constant*. (In quantum mechanics, $\hbar\omega$ is the energy of a photon that "accompanies" an electromagnetic wave of angular frequency ω. Its angular momentum, called *spin*, equals $\pm\hbar$.) More generally, physicists discovered in the mid-1920s that, in quantum mechanics, any two conjugate variables, such as position x and linear momentum p, are (except for a factor $\hbar$) conjugate Fourier variables, just like time and frequency for speech signals. Consequently, the uncertainty relation (10.85) applies to any such pair of variables. For example, for x and p we have

$$\sigma_x \cdot \sigma_p \geq \frac{\hbar}{2} . \tag{10.86}$$

Because linear momentum p equals mass m times velocity v, equation (10.86) also implies a velocity uncertainty $\sigma_v = \sigma_p/m$. For $\sigma_x = 10^{-10}$m (the diameter of the hydrogen atom), the velocity uncertainty of an electron (rest mass

---

[4] In quantum mechanics the squaring of the amplitude distributions (10.83) and (10.84) corresponds to going from the Schrödinger wavefunction ψ to its absolute square, $|\psi|^2$, which (ever since Max Born's proposal) is interpreted as a probability distribution. It is for these probability distributions that the Heisenberg uncertainties are defined.

$m \approx 9.1 \times 10^{-31}\,\mathrm{kg}$) equals roughly $10^6\,\mathrm{m/s}$. (No wonder we can no longer speak meaningfully of orbits on atomic size scales.)

Another pair of conjugate variables is energy E and time t for which the uncertainty relation is

$$\sigma_E \cdot \sigma_t \geq \frac{\hbar}{2}\,. \tag{10.87}$$

People usually think of a vacuum as being totally devoid of matter and energy. But such slipshod thinking is *forbidden* by the uncertainty relation: if the energy is precisely zero, then so is its fluctuation, but $\sigma_E = 0$ would violate (10.87). Thus, even the vacuum has energy – with numerous testable consequences. In fact, our entire universe may have started from a vacuum fluctuation run amok. As Thomas Cranmer, archbishop of Canterbury, put it so aptly in 1520, "Natural reason abhorreth vacuum." (And as John Pierce, who gave the *transistor* its name, remarked 428 years later "Nature abhors vacuum *tubes*.")

One of the most accurate phenomena in all of physics is the Mössbauer effect in which electromagnetic radiation in the form of gamma quanta is emitted with a relative energy uncertainty smaller than 10^{-14}. (This corresponds to a Q-factor, familiar to electrical engineers, exceeding 10^{14}.) This small energy uncertainty leads to a very large time uncertainty and therefore to a very large duration of the associated Schrödinger wave, namely more than 10^{14} periods! Of course, if this wave is chopped into shorter pieces by a kind of camera shutter in the course of a Mössbauer experiment, the energy uncertainty will increase according to (10.87). This is an inescapable conclusion which, however, even some Mössbauer experts refused to believe because, they argued, "a laterally moving shutter cannot possibly change the energy of the quanta passing through it". Well, as Richard Feynman once said, *nobody understands quantum mechanics* (including, it seems, quantum physicists).

10.11.1 Prolate Spheroidal Wave Functions and Uncertainty

Instead of expressing uncertainties in terms of standard deviations, as Heisenberg did, other circumstances require different criteria. For example, an engineer may want to design a pulse shape or time window in such a way that for a given total duration of the window, a maximum amount of the total energy should fall within a given bandwidth. In other words, the spectral energy "splatter" should be kept at a minimum. What shape is the optimum window? The answer, given by David Slepian, Henry Landau and Henry Pollak, is *prolate spheroidal wave functions* [10.27]. These functions have the remarkable property that they are orthogonal to each other both over an infinite and a finite range of the independent variable. And, like the Gaussian distribution, each prolate spheroidal wave function $\varphi_n(t)$ is proportional to its own Fourier transform, except that the proportionality extends only to a finite interval. Thus,

$$\hat{\varphi}_n(\omega) \approx \varphi_n\left(t = \frac{T}{B}\omega\right) \text{ for } |\omega| < \frac{B}{2} \, . \tag{10.88}$$

Here T is half the total duration and B is a bandwidth.

Prolate spheroidal wave functions, as the name implies, are solutions of the wave equation in prolate spheroidal coordinates. A prolate spheroid results from an ellipse rotated about is long axis. An airborne blimp is an approximate prolate spheroid. (When an ellipse is rotated about is *short* axis, an *oblate* spheroid results. The surface of the earth is an approximate oblate spheroid, that is a sphere flattened at the poles and bulging at the equator due to centrifugal forces.)

The basic properties of the prolate spheroidal wave functions $\varphi(x)$ follow from the fact that they are solutions of the integral equation

$$\int_{-T}^{T} \varphi(x)\frac{\sin B(t-x)}{\pi(t-x)}\mathrm{d}x = \lambda\varphi(t) \, , \tag{10.89}$$

for certain values of $\lambda = \lambda_n$, called *eigenvalues*. There are infinitely many eigenvalues, all real, positive and smaller than 1:

$$1 > \lambda_0 > \lambda_1 > \cdots > \lambda_n > \cdots > 0 \, . \tag{10.90}$$

The corresponding *eigenfunctions* $\varphi_n(x)$ form a complete orthonormal set on the interval $(-\infty, \infty)$:

$$\int_{-\infty}^{\infty} \varphi_n(t)\varphi_m(t)\mathrm{d}t = \delta_{nm} \, , \tag{10.91}$$

where δ_{nm} is Kronecker's delta symbol defined as 1 for $n = m$ and 0 otherwise. By changing the time scale, the limits of integration $\pm T$ in (10.89) can be made equal to ± 1, the limits used in the standard definition. The parameter B in (10.89) then changes to BT. Thus, the prolate spheroidals depend only on *one* parameter, the time–bandwidth product BT.

Equation (10.89) has the form of a convolution integral. The convolution kernel $\sin(Bt)/\pi t$ represents a sharp lowpass filtering process in the frequency domain. Thus, $\varphi(t)$ in (10.89) is a lowpass function with no energy at angular frequencies outside the interval $(-B, B)$. Because the $\varphi_n(t)$ form a complete set of orthonormal functions, bandlimited functions $s(t)$ with the same bandwidth can be expanded in terms of the $\varphi_n(t)$:

$$s(t) = \sum_{n=0}^{\infty} a_n\varphi_n(t) \, , \tag{10.92}$$

where

$$a_n = \int_{-\infty}^{\infty} f(t)\varphi_n(t)\mathrm{d}t \, . \tag{10.93}$$

The integral equation (10.89) has an interesting interpretation. It says that gating $\varphi_n(t)$ at $\pm T$ with a rectangular window will reproduce $\varphi_n(t)$ (except for a factor λ_n) when the spectral "splatter" resulting from the gating is removed (by lowpass filtering).

Considering the φ_n as functions of frequency $\varphi_n(\omega)$, their inverse Fourier transforms are *time-limited*. Any bandlimiting of a $\varphi_n(\omega)$ will of course cause "time splatter," but within the original time interval the inverse Fourier transform will be reproduced, except for an attenuation by a factor λ_n.

The most important property of the $\varphi_n(t)$ is that they are not only orthogonal in the infinite interval $(-\infty, \infty)$ but also in the finite interval $(-T, T)$. In fact,

$$\int_{-T}^{T} \varphi_n(t)\varphi_m(t)\mathrm{d}t = \lambda_n \delta_{nm} . \tag{10.94}$$

This orthogonality can be deduced from (10.89) by setting $\varphi(t) = \varphi_n(t)$ and $\lambda = \lambda_n$, multiplying by $\varphi_m(t)$ and integrating over all t. Changing the order of integration gives, with (10.91),

$$\int_{-T}^{T} \varphi_n(x) \int_{-\infty}^{\infty} \varphi_m(t)\frac{\sin B(t - x)}{\pi(t - x)}\mathrm{d}t\mathrm{d}x = \lambda_n \delta_{nm} . \tag{10.95}$$

Here the integral over t equals $\varphi_m(x)$ (because bandlimiting the bandlimited function $\varphi_m(t)$ simply reproduces it) and (10.95) is thus seen to be identical with (10.94).

The main application of the prolate spheroidal wave functions is the design of bandlimited signals with a maximum energy fraction in a given time interval. Given a bandlimited signal $s(t)$, we can expand it into the properly scaled $\varphi_n(t)$, see (10.92). The total energy E of the signal equals

$$E := \int_{-\infty}^{\infty} s^2(t)\mathrm{d}t = \sum_{n=0}^{\infty} a_n^2 .$$

The fraction E_T falling into the time interval $(-T, T)$ follows from (10.94) as

$$E_T := \int_{-T}^{T} s^2(t)\mathrm{d}t = \sum_{n=0}^{\infty} \lambda_n a_n^2 .$$

Thus, the energy fraction $\alpha := E_T/E$ is given by

$$\alpha = \frac{\sum_{n=0}^{\infty} \lambda_n a_n^2}{\sum_{n=0}^{\infty} a_n^2} .$$

Since λ_0 is larger than any other λ_n, α is maximized by setting all a_n except a_0 equal to 0. Thus,

$$\alpha_{\max} = \lambda_0 ,$$

where λ_0 depends on the time–bandwidth product TB. For example, for $TB = 1$, $\alpha \approx 0.6$. If α is required to be as high as 0.95, then TB must be about 3 [10.28].

Similarly, if we wish to maximize the energy fraction of a *time*-limited signal $s(t)$ in the frequency range $(-B, B)$, we expand $s(t)$ in terms of the Fourier transforms $\hat{\varphi}_n$ of the φ_n, which, properly scaled, vanish for $-T < t < T$:

$$s(t) = \sum_{n=0}^{\infty} b_n \hat{\varphi}_n \left(\frac{B}{T} t \right) \ .$$

The energy E_B inside a given frequency interval $(-B, B)$ is given by

$$E_B = \frac{1}{2\pi} \int_{-B}^{B} |\hat{s}(\omega)|^2 \mathrm{d}\omega \ ,$$

and the energy fraction $\beta = E_B/E$ equals

$$\beta = \frac{\sum_{n=0}^{\infty} \lambda_n b_n^2}{\sum_{n=0}^{\infty} b_n^2} \ .$$

As before, the energy fraction is maximized by setting all b_n, except b_0, equal to 0. Thus, the optimum energy fraction $b_{\max}$ in the frequency band $-B < \omega < B$ equals λ_0.

How close does the famous Hamming window

$$s(t) = 0.54 + 0.46 \cos\left(\pi \frac{t}{T} \right) \quad \text{for } |t| < T \tag{10.96}$$

$$s(t) = 0 \text{ otherwise}$$

come to optimizing the energy fraction in the frequency range $|\omega| < \pi/T$?

In some problems, limits are imposed on both α and β. In such cases the optimum pulse shape is a linear combination of $\varphi_0(t)$ and a time-gated $\varphi_0(t)$. Given the time–bandwidth product TB and thus the eigenvalue λ_0, a noteworthy trading relation between α and β rules the realizable energy concentrations:

$$\arccos \sqrt{\alpha} + \arccos \sqrt{\beta} = \arccos \sqrt{\lambda_0} \ .$$

The largest possible *product* of energy fractions, $\alpha\beta$, is obtained for $\alpha = \beta$ resulting in

$$(\alpha\beta)_{\max} = \left(\frac{1 + \sqrt{\lambda_0}}{2} \right)^2 \ .$$

For $\lambda_0 = 0.6$ ($BT \approx 1$), this gives $(\alpha\beta)_{\max} = 0.787\ldots$, a remarkable degree of energy concentration. By comparison, for the Gaussian window, setting $T = \sigma_t$ and $B = \sigma_\omega = 1/\sigma_t$, the product $(\alpha\beta)$ is only about 0.466.

10.12 Time and Frequency Windows

As we remarked before, the Gaussian pulse shape of infinite length is optimum for minimizing the time–bandwidth product if measured by standard deviations. But signals in the real world have *finite* durations and a gated Gaussian is often not a good choice. Also, any discontinuity in a signal results in a power spectrum proportional to ω^{-2} for large ω. This means that the standard deviation, which is based on the second moment of the power spectrum, does not exist. Thus, other criteria for designing pulse shapes and windows are needed.

One such criterion is convenience, and the most convenient procedure is simply to limit the signal to a finite window interval $(-T, T)$ by gating with a rectangular function:

$$s_{\mathrm{r}}(t) = \begin{cases} 1 & \text{for } |t| < T \\ 0 & \text{otherwise .} \end{cases}$$

The corresponding Fourier transform

$$\hat{s}_{\mathrm{r}}(\omega) = 2\frac{\sin \omega T}{\omega}$$

has so much spectral energy splatter (the second moment of the energy spectrum is infinite!) that the rectangular window is unacceptable in many applications.

More generally, any discontinuity in the signal has a Fourier transform that, asymptotically, is proportional to $1/\omega$ and thus decays relatively slowly with increasing frequency (namely, with 6 dB/octave). This follows from the fact that a discontinuous function, when *differentiated*, has delta functions at the discontinuities which have *flat* Fourier transforms (independent of frequency) and the inverse operation, integration, multiplies the Fourier transform by $1/i\omega$.

Similarly, a continuous signal with a discontinuous first derivative has a Fourier transform that, asymptotically, is proportional to $1/\omega^2$. In general, a continuous signal that has continuous derivatives up to and including the nth derivative has a Fourier transform that, asymptotically, is proportional to $1/\omega^{n+2}$. This law also applies to discontinuous functions whose integral is continuous if we count an integration as a "negative" differentiation ($n = -1$).

Another simple shape is the triangular window

$$s_\Delta(t) = \begin{cases} T - |t| & \text{for } |t| < T \\ 0 & \text{otherwise .} \end{cases}$$

Because a triangular window of length $2T$ is the convolution of two rectangular windows of length T, its Fourier transform is the square of that of such a rectangular window (divided by a scale factor T):

$$\hat{s}_\Delta(\omega) = 4\frac{\sin^2(\omega T/2)}{\omega^2 T} .$$

For the triangular window the standard deviation of the energy spectrum does exist and equals $\sigma_\omega^{(E)} = \sqrt{3}/T$. Together with the standard deviation in the time domain $\sigma_t^{(E)} = T/\sqrt{10}$, the uncertainty product for the energy $\sigma_t^{(E)} \cdot \sigma_\omega^{(E)}$ equals $\sqrt{3/10} \approx 0.548$, which compares quite well with the *energy* uncertainty product 0.5 for a Gaussian window.

Still another simple window is the raised-cosine window called "Hanning" by J. W. Tukey [10.29] and which should perhaps be called *Tukey window* in honor of the statistician who gave us such enduring (and endearing) terms as *bit, byte, cepstrum* and *quefrency*. The Hanning/Tukey window

$$s_T(t) = \begin{cases} 0.5 + 0.5\cos(\pi t/T) & \text{for } |t| < T \\ 0 & \text{otherwise} \end{cases}$$

has a Fourier transform

$$\hat{s}_T(t) = \frac{\pi^2 \sin(\omega T)}{\omega(\pi^2 - \omega^2 T^2)}$$

with a standard deviation of it energy spectrum $\sigma_\omega^{(E)} = \pi\sqrt{3}/T$.

Another well-known window was designed by R. W. Hamming and is now called *Hamming window*, see (10.96). Hamming added a "pedestal" to the raised-cosine window to minimize the magnitude of largest spectral side-lobe.

The Fourier transform of the Hamming window,

$$\hat{s}_H(\omega) = \frac{(1.08\pi^2 - 0.16T^2\omega^2)\sin(\omega T)}{\omega(\pi^2 - \omega^2 T^2)} \ ,$$

has an infinite second spectral moment (because of the discontinuities at $|t| = T$), but its largest sidelobe is down by more than 43 dB from the main spectral peak (as opposed to 31 dB) for the Hanning/Tukey window.

10.13   The Wigner–Ville Distribution

One way to tackle the time-frequency resolution problem is the Wigner–Ville distribution (WVD) of a signal $s(t)$:

$$W(t,\omega) := \frac{1}{2\pi} \int s^*\left(t - \frac{\tau}{2}\right) s\left(t + \frac{\tau}{2}\right) \exp(-\mathrm{i}\omega\tau)\, d\tau \ ,$$

which depends both on time and frequency [10.30].

The WVD was originally proposed around 1932 by the Hungarian physicist Eugene P. Wigner in connection with the new quantum mechanics and Heisenberg's uncertainty relation [10.31]. It has the following highly desirable properties for signal and system analyses:

Integrating $W(t,\omega)$ over frequency gives the signal energy density as a function of time. Integrating $W(t,\omega)$ over time gives the energy density as a function of frequency. Thus, $W(t,\omega)$ contains both the full, unsmoothed time and frequency information. It is a kind of precursor to the Fourier transformation in that a simple projection onto the frequency axis (integrating over time) yields the spectral energy distribution. In fact, $W(t,\omega)$ can be interpreted as an energy distribution in time and frequency – somewhat like a running spectrogram ("voice print"), yet without the application of a window function. The Fourier transformation of $W(t,\omega)$ with respect to t yields (to within a constant factor) the Fourier transform of the signal. Similarly, the Fourier transform of $W(t,\omega)$ with respect to ω recovers the signal (to within a constant factor). Thus, the WVD does not discard any information; both the signal and its Fourier transform can be completely recovered. It is interesting to note that the WVD can also be defined by an integral over frequency (instead of time) in which the signal is replaced by its Fourier transform. Thus, the WVD "plays no favorites;" it treats time and frequency on an equal footing [10.32].

Other helpful properties of the WVD are that if the signal $s(t)$ has bounded support, i.e. vanishes outside a finite time interval, then so does the WVD (for the same time interval). Similarly, if the Fourier transform of the signal has bounded support in frequency space, so does the WVD (for the same frequency interval). Hence, the WVD does not cause spectral or temporal "splatter." If the signal is the product of two time functions, its WVD is the convolution of the two original WVDs with respect to the frequency variable. If the signal is a convolution of two time functions, its WVD is a convolution with respect to its time variable. The time course of instantaneous frequency, $\dot{\varphi}(t)$, of a signal $a(t)\exp(i\varphi(t))$ is given by the mean frequency ω obtained with $W(t,\omega)$ as a weighting function. The frequency-dependent centroid of the signal, $\bar{t}(\omega)$, obtained with $W(t,\omega)$ as a weighting function, is given by the (negative) derivative of the Fourier phase, $-\psi'(\omega)$. The WVD has been widely used in system analysis, especially loudspeaker responses [10.33]. Various discrete time forms of the WVD are discussed in [10.34].

The WVD is closely related to another function of time and frequency. It is in fact the Fourier transform of the "ambiguity function," known from radar technology. During World War II the Allied air forces used aluminum foil strips ("chaff"), tuned to the wavelength of the enemy radar, to "swamp" their monitors with false targets. Thereupon the enemy started using chirped pulses in their radars, which – courtesy of the Doppler effect – allowed them to distinguish fast moving objects (planes) from the stationary chaff. However, chirp pulses introduce an undesirable ambiguity between target range and target velocity. Thus, the search was on for radar signals with a low ambiguity (which a chirp lacks). The ideal ambiguity function is the "thumb-tack" function, a function that has only a single high peak in the time-frequency plane. It is interesting to note that some of the best ambiguity functions are supplied by number theory [10.13].

10.14 The Cepstrum:
Measurement of Fundamental Frequency

One of the most difficult problems in speech analysis is the accurate measurement of the fundamental frequency, especially if the Fourier component at the fundamental frequency itself is missing, as is often the case in telephone signals. The problem is aggravated by the fact that speech synthesis requires an accurate reproduction of the natural fundamental frequency. While the human ear is somewhat tolerant to errors in the formant frequencies (and relatively insensitive to formant bandwidth), even minute deviations from the pitch contour of natural speech can be quite objectionable. Often synthetic pitch contours are too smooth compared to real speech. But introducing randomness *artificially* into the pitch almost always reduces speech quality rather than improving it. Natural pitch does fluctuate, but it does so in a nonrandom manner resulting from subtle linear and nonlinear interactions between the vocal cords and the vocal tract. In speech compression systems that include a pitch parameter, accurate measurement of successive fundamental periods is therefore a prime requirement.

Thus it is not surprising that a great many schemes for extracting pitch from running speech – even in the absence of the fundamental frequency component – have been proposed and tested. The simplest among these are the so-called *peak pickers* that determine the location of the prominent peaks of the signal or its envelope, hoping that they reflect successive pitch periods. But even if they do, formant-frequency shifts affect the location of these peaks within the fundamental period, leading to a "quavery" voice in the resynthesized speech signal.

Another approach to fundamental-frequency measurement is the short-time autocorrelation function (ACF) of the speech signal. For a periodic signal, the ACF has a large maximum at a delay of one pitch period. But, unfortunately, there are secondary maxima in the ACF that reflect the *formant* frequencies. During rapid phoneme transitions, these formant peaks sometimes exceed in magnitude the pitch-period maximum, leading to sizeable errors. It is in fact this interference from the formants of speech that bedevils most pitch extractors. But how can we suppress the formants to facilitate pitch extraction?

At very high signal-to-noise ratios, inverse filtering would remove the formant resonances and yield the glottal waveform, which is of course ideal for pitch measurements.

At more realistic signal-to-noise ratios, *spectrum flattening* can reduce the influence of the formants on the spectrum. Spectrum flatteners were originally proposed in connection with voice-excited vocoders (VEVs) to generate excitation signals for the high speech frequencies from a baseband by means of nonlinear distortion [10.35]. A very effective method of nonlinear distortion for spectral flattening uses *center* clipping. (While *peak* clipping does little harm to the formant structure, severe center clipping effectively remove the formants.) Effective center clipping depends of course on a well-chosen *adaptive* clipping threshold. Another method for emphasizing the peaks of a signal, one that doesn't require touchy threshold adjustments, is taking the third (or fifth) power of the signal.

But the most effective method of removing the bothersome formant structure from a speech spectrum is the so-called *cepstrum* method [10.36]. The cepstrum, originally conceived to distinguish underground nuclear explosions from earthquakes, is defined as the Fourier transform of the *logarithm* of the power spectrum. Without the logarithm, one would obtain the autocorrelation functions with the formant-peak problems already mentioned. In the cepstrum, by contrast, formant effects are almost completely removed from the pitch representation. To see this, we model a voiced speech signal $s(t)$ as a convolution of periodic excitation pulses $p(t)$ and the response $h(t)$ of the vocal tract (including the glottal waveform and radiation from the lips):

$$s(t) = p(t) \star h(t) \ .$$

Fourier transformation turns the noisesome convolution (which "mixes up the formant and pitch information") into a simple product:

$$\hat{s}(\omega) = \hat{p}(\omega) \cdot \hat{h}(\omega) \ . \tag{10.97}$$

Taking logarithms turns the simple product into an even simpler sum:

$$\log \hat{s}(\omega) = \log \hat{p}(\omega) + \log \hat{h}(\omega) \ . \tag{10.98}$$

The effects of pitch, $\hat{p}$, and vocal tract, $\hat{h}$, are now simply additive and can be clearly separated by a further Fourier transformation:

$$c(q) = \log \widehat{\hat{s}}(q) = \log \widehat{\hat{p}}(q) + \log \widehat{\hat{h}}(q) \ , \tag{10.99}$$

where q is the new Fourier variable having the dimension of time and called *quefrency* by Tukey (and almost everyone else). The function $c(q)$ is called the complex cepstrum, which has found many applications in "homomorphic filtering" and homomorphic vocoders [10.37, 10.38]. If $\hat{c}$ is replaced by its magnitude, the regular cepstrum results.

Figure 10.1 shows the cepstra for an utterance containing voiced speech. The left half of Fig. 10.1 shows a sequence of logarithmic spectra for the utterance and the right half shows the corresponding cepstra. The sharp peaks on the right, at high quefrencies, corresponds to the lengths of the pitch periods; it is caused by the high-quefrency "ripple" visible in the power spectra of the voiced sound. The formants lead to a smooth frequency variation in the power spectrum and show up near the origin of the cepstrum. Thus, pitch and formant effects are completely separated by the cepstrum, at least for voices whose pitch is not so high that the corresponding spectral ripple has too low a quefrency.

For an even better pitch detection method see Appendix B, Sect. B.7.

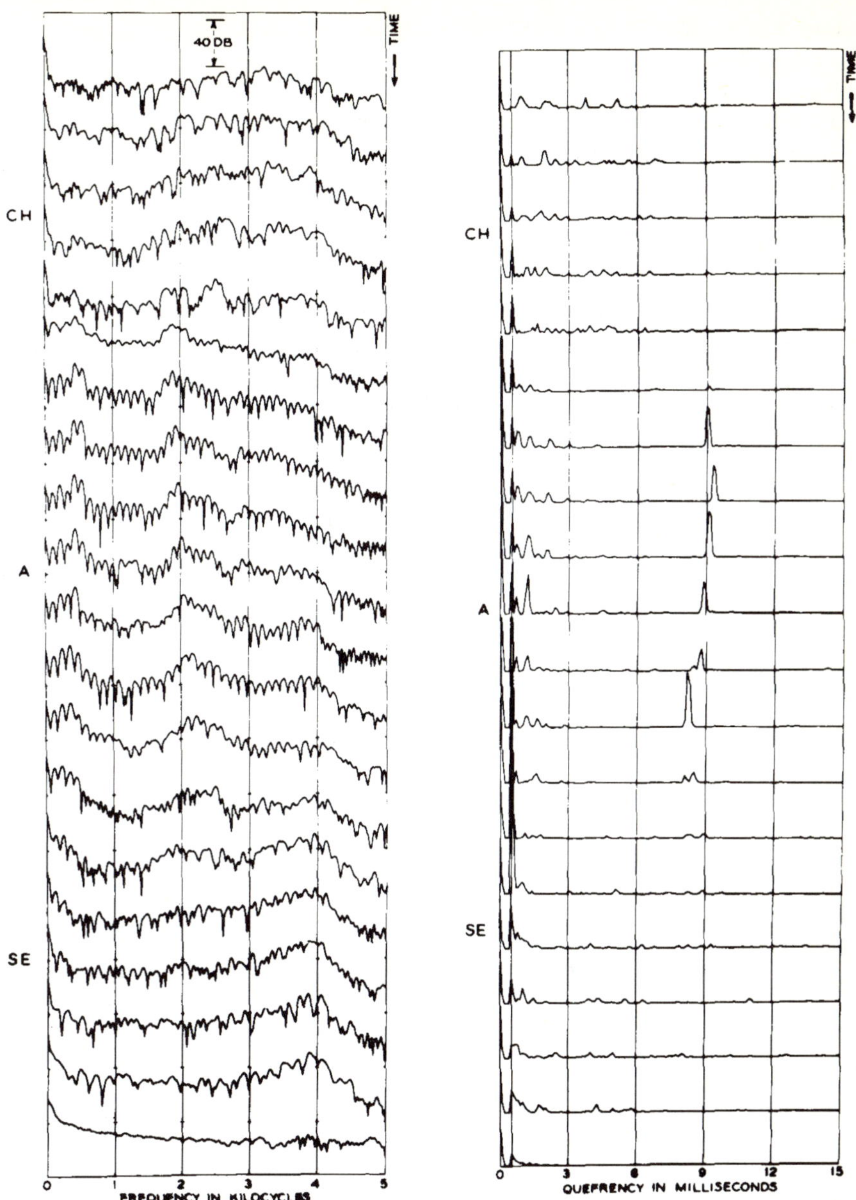

Fig. 10.1. *Left:* a sequence of logarithmic short-time spectra of a partly voiced utterance (/chase/). Note the harmonic ripple of the spectra during the voiced portion (/a/). *Right:* sequence of *cepstra*. The cepstrum is defined as the magnitude of the Fourier transform of the logarithmic power spectrum. Note the prominent peaks around *quefrencies* of 9 ms, corresponding to fundamental frequencies near 110 Hz, during the voiced vowel sound. The low-quefrency clutter (below 3 ms) represents formant and other information in the logarithmic power spectra that change smoothly along the frequency axis. This is the information in the spectral *envelope* (as opposed to the spectral *fine structure* represented by the harmonic ripples)

10.15 Line Spectral Frequencies

While the cepstrum has proved very useful to characterize the spectral *fine* structure of a periodic signal, the so-called "line spectral frequencies" are an efficient means to represent spectral *envelopes* and filter responses.

Let $P(z)$ be the z-transform of an all-zero filter with all its zeros z_k inside the unit circle. For example, $P(z)$ could be the reciprocal of a stable all-pole filter, such as a linear prediction filter. Such filters are usually characterized by the locations of their complex zeros z_k inside the unit circle – angles corresponding to the frequencies of the filter's resonances and magnitudes to their bandwidths. To quantize these locations efficiently has sometimes proved difficult.

As an alternative we introduce a new concept, the *line spectral frequencies* [10.39]. They are defined as follows. First, we introduce the of *reciprocal polynomial* of $P(z)$:

$$\tilde{P}(z) := z^{-n} P\left(\frac{1}{z}\right) , \tag{10.100}$$

where n is the degree of $P(z)$. It follows that

$$L(z) := \frac{\tilde{P}(z)}{P(z)} \tag{10.101}$$

has an allpass response, i.e. $|L(\mathrm{e}^{\mathrm{i}\omega})| = 1$.
The *symmetric polynomial*

$$A(z) := \frac{1}{2}(P(z) + \tilde{P}(z)) \tag{10.102}$$

has zeros for $L(z) = -1$. On the unit circle, $z = \mathrm{e}^{\mathrm{i}\omega}$, we have

$$L(z) = \mathrm{e}^{\mathrm{i}z\varphi(\omega)} ,$$

where $\varphi(\omega)$ is the phase of $P(z)$ (to within a constant phase). Thus, the zeros of $A(z)$ occur for

$$\varphi(\omega_k) = \left(k + \frac{1}{2}\right)\pi , \quad k = 0, 1, \cdots, n-1 \tag{10.103}$$

and there are exactly n such frequencies in the interval $0 \le \omega \le \pi$. (This is not necessarily true if some zeros of $P(z)$ fall outside the unit circle.) The frequencies ω_k are called *line spectral frequencies*.
Similarly, for the *anti*symmetric polynomial

$$B(z) := \frac{1}{2}(P(z) - \tilde{P}(z)) \tag{10.104}$$

the zeros occur for

$$\varphi(\omega_m) = m\pi, \quad m = 0, 1, \cdots, n-1 . \tag{10.105}$$

Thus, the zeros of $A(z)$ and $B(z)$ fall on the unit circle and are interleaved with each other.

The line spectral frequencies are not necessarily close to the zeros of $P(z)$ and they are easier to quantize than predictor coefficients.

A. Acoustic Theory
and Modeling of the Vocal Tract

by H.W. Strube, Drittes Physikalisches Institut, Universität Göttingen

A.1 Introduction

This appendix is intended for those readers who want to inform themselves about the mathematical treatment of the vocal-tract acoustics and about its modeling in the time and frequency domains. Apart from providing a fundamental understanding, this is required for all applications and investigations concerned with the relationship between geometric and acoustic properties of the vocal tract, such as articulatory synthesis, determination of the tract shape from acoustic quantities, inverse filtering, etc.

Historically, the formants of speech were conjectured to be resonances of cavities in the vocal tract. In the case of a narrow constriction at or near the lips, such as for the vowel [u], the volume of the tract can be considered a Helmholtz resonator (the glottis is assumed almost closed). However, this can only explain the first formant. Also, the constriction – if any – is usually situated farther back. Then the tract may be roughly approximated as a cascade of two resonators, accounting for two formants. But all these approximations by discrete cavities proved unrealistic. Thus researchers have have now adopted a more reasonable description of the vocal tract as a nonuniform acoustical transmission line. This can explain an infinite number of resonances, of which, however, only the first 2 to 4 are of phonetic importance. Depending on the kind of sound, the tube system has different topology:

- for vowel-like sounds, pharynx and mouth form one tube;
- for nasalized vowels, the tube is branched, with transmission from pharynx through mouth and nose;
- for nasal consonants, transmission is through pharynx and nose, with the closed mouth tract as a "shunt" line.

The situation becomes even more complicated for plosive and fricative consonants, where one must further take into account different places and kinds of excitation. Instead of – or in addition to – glottal oscillation, there is a turbulent-noise source at any narrow constriction, and for plosives, a sudden pressure release after opening a closure.

In this appendix, we will present a fundamental description of a one-dimensional tube in the time and frequency domains, show the connection between tube shape and formants, and present methods for time-domain modeling of sound propagation as well as frequency-domain computation of transfer functions and impedances. The "inverse problem" of how to estimate the tract shape from acoustical data will also be discussed briefly.

A.2 Acoustics of a Hard-Walled, Lossless Tube

To keep the formulas simple, we will present the fundamental equations for the hard-walled, lossless tube only, but first allowing time-varying tube shape. The more general case will only be described in the frequency domain for a time-invariant tube shape. In addition to the well-known representation by pressure and volume velocity, less familiar representations will be introduced that are useful for modeling and computation or show analogies to other fields of physics.

A.2.1 Field Equations

The acoustic field equations are derived from the Navier–Stokes flow equations by linearization, assuming that flow velocity is small compared to the speed of sound, c. Furthermore, the non-zero average (dc) air flow in the vocal tract is neglected (its effects on the formants would be of second order only). But keep in mind that at narrow constrictions, nonlinear effects can become important, e.g. when whistling or in the glottis. Additional approximations are:

(1) The curved vocal tract is treated like a straight tube.
(2) The waves propagate one-dimensionally along the tube axis x and are approximately plane. This requires that the slope of the tube walls be small.
(3) No higher modes with nodes over the cross-section are taken into account [they are removed by the integrals in (A.1) below]. In the vocal tract, higher modes cannot propagate below about 4 kHz.

Thus the tube is entirely described by its "area function" $A(x,t)$. Let y, z be the coordinates in the cross-section plane. The appropriate field quantities are the alternating (ac) pressure averaged over the cross-section, $p(x,t)$, and the volume velocity $q(x,t)$, defined as

$$p(x,t) = \frac{1}{A(x,t)} \iint\limits_{A} p_\sim(x,y,z,t)\,\mathrm{d}y\,\mathrm{d}z \;,$$
$$q(x,t) = \iint\limits_{A} v_x(x,y,z,t)\,\mathrm{d}y\,\mathrm{d}z \;. \tag{A.1}$$

Here $p_\sim$ is the three-dimensional ac pressure field and v_x the x component of the velocity field. The ac density $\varrho(x,t)$ is defined analogously to $p(x,t)$ and proportional to it (state equation); the constant average density will be denoted by ϱ_0. The motion is then described by "Newton's law", the (one-dimensional) continuity equation, and the state equation:

$$\varrho_0(q/A)^{\cdot} = -p' , \tag{A.2}$$

$$(\varrho A)^{\cdot} + \varrho_0 \dot{A} = -\varrho_0 q' , \tag{A.3}$$

$$p = c^2 \varrho . \tag{A.4}$$

Here, a dot denotes $\partial/\partial t$, a prime means $\partial/\partial x$. The proportionality factor c^2 in (A.4) will in fact turn out to be the speed of sound (phase velocity). The second term in (A.3) represents a flow source due to the motion of the tube walls. Since in the vocal tract these move too slowly to generate audible sound, this term will henceforth be neglected. Then the last two equations can be combined into

$$(pA)^{\cdot}/\varrho_0 c^2 = -q' . \tag{A.5}$$

Obviously, the two field equations (A.2), (A.5) are of a form analogous to those of a lossless electrical transmission line, if p is identified with voltage and q with current and

$$L' = \varrho_0/A , \qquad C' = A/\varrho_0 c^2 \tag{A.6}$$

correspond to an inductance and capacitance density, respectively. These are not independent, since $L'C' = c^{-2}$ is constant. Thus the tube may be completely described by the *characteristic impedance*:

$$Z = \sqrt{L'/C'} = \varrho_0 c/A ; \tag{A.7}$$

then $L' = Z/c$, $C' = 1/Zc$, and for any derivative or variation "∂" we have

$$\partial A/A = \partial C'/C' = -\partial L'/L' = -\partial Z/Z . \tag{A.8}$$

Equations (A.2), (A.5) are rewritten as

$$-p' = (L'q)^{\cdot} = c^{-1}(qZ)^{\cdot} , \tag{A.9a}$$

$$-q' = (C'p)^{\cdot} = c^{-1}(p/Z)^{\cdot} . \tag{A.9b}$$

The infinitesimal transmission-line element is then that shown in Fig. A.1. Note that in the time-varying case, L' contains a quasi-resistive and C' a quasi-conductive component, since $(L'q)^{\cdot} = L'\dot{q} + \dot{L'}q$, etc.

The energy balance of the tube can be derived by multiplying (A.9a) and (A.9b) with q and p, respectively, and adding them, leading to the continuity equation

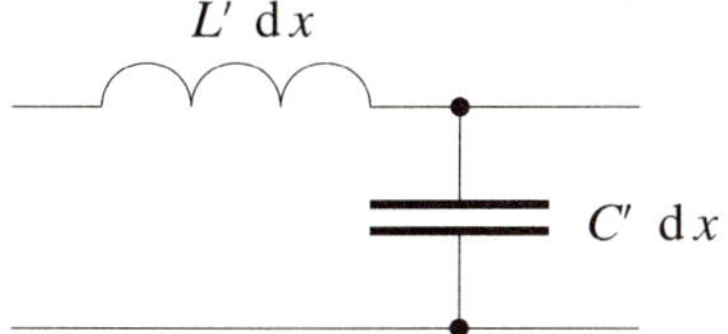

Fig. A.1. Electrical equivalent circuit of the infinitesimal lossless transmission-line element

$$(w_p + w_q)^{\cdot} + P' = (w_p - w_q)\dot{Z}/Z \,,$$
$$w_p = C'p^2/2 \,, \quad w_q = L'q^2/2 \,, \quad P = pq \,, \tag{A.10}$$

where w_p and w_q are the potential and kinetic energy densities and P is the power (energy flow). The right-hand side represents an energy source density due to work of the moving walls against the radiation pressure in the tube. This term vanishes in the time-invariant case, so that energy is then conserved.

Note that all equations are invariant under the *duality transformation*

$$p \leftrightarrow q \,, \qquad L' \leftrightarrow C' \,, \qquad Z \leftrightarrow 1/Z \,. \tag{A.11}$$

Another familiar representation uses the velocity potential Φ, related to p and q according to

$$p = \varrho_0 \dot{\Phi} \,, \qquad q = -A\Phi' \,. \tag{A.12}$$

These equations imply (A.2) or (A.9a) automatically. Inserting them in (A.5) now yields a second-order wave equation, namely Webster's horn equation, generalized for time-varying A:

$$c^{-2}(\dot{\Phi}A)^{\cdot} = (\Phi'A)' \,, \tag{A.13}$$

which has a completely symmetric form in the space and time derivatives. Another similar form with A replaced by $1/A$ – again corresponding to the duality transformation (A.11) – can be obtained by using the volume displacement $\int q \, dt$ instead of Φ.

When A and thus L', C', Z are constant in time, Webster's horn equation can be written in its familiar form, not only for velocity potential and volume displacement but also for pressure and volume velocity themselves:

$$p'' + (A'/A)p' - c^{-2}\ddot{p} = 0 \,, \tag{A.14}$$
$$q'' - (A'/A)q' - c^{-2}\ddot{q} = 0 \,. \tag{A.15}$$

Other Representations.

a) Square root of energy density. By replacing p and q with the corresponding square-root-of-energy-density components,

$$\psi = p\sqrt{C'/2} \,, \qquad \varphi = q\sqrt{L'/2} \,, \tag{A.16}$$

the field equations now read

$$c^{-1}(Z^{1/2}\varphi)^{\cdot} = -(Z^{1/2}\psi)' \,, \qquad c^{-1}(Z^{-1/2}\psi)^{\cdot} = -(Z^{-1/2}\varphi)' \,, \tag{A.17}$$

or equivalently,

$$c^{-1}(\dot{\varphi} + Q\varphi) = -\psi' - W\psi \,, \qquad c^{-1}(\dot{\psi} - Q\psi) = -\varphi' + W\varphi \,, \tag{A.18a}$$
$$\text{with} \quad Q = \dot{Z}/2Z = -\dot{A}/2A \,, \qquad W = Z'/2Z = -A'/2A \,. \tag{A.18b}$$

In the time-invariant case ($Q = 0$), this representation removes the first-order derivatives of the fields from the Webster horn equations (A.14), (A.15), yielding Schrödinger (or rather, Klein–Gordon) type equations instead:

$$-\psi'' + V_p\psi + c^{-2}\ddot{\psi} = 0 \ , \tag{A.19}$$

$$-\varphi'' + V_q\varphi + c^{-2}\ddot{\varphi} = 0 \ , \tag{A.20}$$

with potentials

$$\begin{aligned}
V_p &= (\sqrt{A})''/\sqrt{A} &&= W^2 - W' \ , \\
V_q &= (1/\sqrt{A})'' \sqrt{A} &&= W^2 + W' \ .
\end{aligned} \tag{A.21}$$

This representation may be useful for eigenvalue problems and inverse problems. In the quantum-mechanical terminology, V_p and V_q have the form of supersymmetric partner potentials with W as superpotential.

b) Wave quantities. As will become apparent in Sect. A.3 below, it is often advantageous to transform p and q to an equivalent representation by "right" and "left" traveling waves, whose dimension may be pressure, volume velocity, or square root of power. With Z from (A.7), these waves are defined as

$$p_\pm = (p \pm qZ)/2 \ , \tag{A.22}$$

$$q_\pm = (p/Z \pm q)/2 \ , \tag{A.23}$$

$$\psi_\pm = (p/\sqrt{Z} \pm q\sqrt{Z})/2 = (\psi \pm \varphi)c/\sqrt{2} \ . \tag{A.24}$$

The field equations for pressure and volume-velocity waves are, with Q and W as in (A.18b),

$$c^{-1}\dot{p}_+ + p'_+ = \quad c^{-1}\dot{p}_- - p'_- = (Q-W)p_- + (Q+W)p_+ \ ; \tag{A.25}$$

$$c^{-1}\dot{q}_+ + q'_+ = -c^{-1}\dot{q}_- + q'_- = (Q-W)q_- - (Q+W)q_+ \ ; \tag{A.26}$$

those for square-root-of-power waves are

$$c^{-1}\dot{\psi}_+ + \psi'_+ = (Q-W)\psi_- \ , \qquad c^{-1}\dot{\psi}_- - \psi'_- = (Q+W)\psi_+ \ . \tag{A.27}$$

From this is it obvious that W represents a reflection-factor density due to a spatially changing Z. This is also clear since $Z'/2Z$ is the infinitesimal form of the well-known expression $(Z_2 - Z_1)/(Z_2 + Z_1)$ for the reflection factor at a discontinuity of the characteristic impedance. Time variation ($Q \neq 0$) causes special additional reflections.

However, the reader should be warned that these waves have only a formal meaning. They are not really unidirectionally traveling waves, except in the constant, uniform tube ($Q = W = 0$). The idea behind this representation is to consider the nonuniform tube as a sequence of infinitely short uniform segments with infinitesimal reflections at their boundaries (similarly for temporal changes), which will be explicitly used for discrete modeling in Sect. A.3.

The energy balance can be written in terms of the powers $\psi_\pm^2$ of the right and left traveling waves:

$$c^{-1}(\psi_+^2 + \psi_-^2)^{\cdot} + (\psi_+^2 - \psi_-^2)' = 2Q\psi_+\psi_- \ . \tag{A.28}$$

Thus the energy density is $w = c^{-1}(\psi_+^2 + \psi_-^2)$ and the power is $P = \psi_+^2 - \psi_-^2$. The source term on the right-hand side again vanishes in the time-invariant case.

A.2.2 Time-Invariant Case

The vocal-tract motions are rather slow compared with acoustic frequencies, $|\dot{A}/A| \ll |\omega|$, except in the oscillating glottis and perhaps during plosive bursts. Thus the assumption of time-invariance is usually justified. Under this condition, the time derivatives of the field quantities can be eliminated, transforming all the partial differential equations into ordinary ones. This is achieved by Fourier transforming with respect to time. Since the field equations are linear, they hold for each Fourier component separately. For any field quantity $f(x,t)$ the component with angular frequency ω is $\hat{f}(x,\omega)\,\mathrm{e}^{\mathrm{i}\omega t}$, $\mathrm{i} = \sqrt{-1}$, where $\hat{f}(x,\omega)$ is the (complex) Fourier transform of $f(x,t)$. (We are using the "engineering" convention here. Theoretical physicists prefer $\mathrm{e}^{-\mathrm{i}\omega t}$, making all quantities their complex conjugates.) Thus, any time derivative is turned into a multiplication by $\mathrm{i}\omega$. For example, (A.9a), (A.9b) become

$$-\hat{p}' = \mathrm{i}\omega L'\hat{q}\,, \qquad -\hat{q}' = \mathrm{i}\omega C'\hat{p}\,. \tag{A.29}$$

In the remainder of this section, we will always restrict ourselves to the time-invariant case with $\mathrm{i}\omega$ replacing time derivatives. To avoid complication of the formulas, the field quantities will be written without "hats" again, equivalent to a pure $\mathrm{e}^{\mathrm{i}\omega t}$ time dependence with fixed ω. Also, the argument t, not explicitly occurring any more, will be omitted.

However, since the fields are now complex rather than real, *nonlinear* expressions such as energies and powers must be reformulated. The energy densities and the power from (A.10) are replaced by

$$w_p = C'|p|^2/2\,, \quad w_q = L'|q|^2/2\,, \quad P = \mathrm{Re}\{p^*q\}\,, \tag{A.30}$$

where the asterisk denotes the complex conjugate. For a single $\mathrm{e}^{\mathrm{i}\omega t}$ component, all three are independent of time. Consequently, in the lossless case, P is constant in space according to (A.10).

"Uniform" Waves. In uniform tubes, all solutions are linear combinations of the two unidirectional traveling waves $\exp(\mathrm{i}\omega t \mp \mathrm{i}kx)$, with a *dispersion relation* connecting ω and k (here $|\omega/c| = |k|$). For the square-root-of-energy-density fields ψ, φ, such waves – let us call them "uniform" – even exist in some nonuniform tubes, since only V_p or V_q in (A.19), (A.20) need be constant. For ψ, this is the case if $\sqrt{A(x)}$ is constant or linear ($V_p = 0$) or of the form $a\mathrm{e}^{\alpha x} + b\mathrm{e}^{-\alpha x}$ or $a\cos(\alpha x) + b\sin(\alpha x)$ (a, b, α real so that these expressions are > 0 in the considered interval), $V_p = \alpha^2$. For φ, the same forms hold for $1/\sqrt{A(x)}$ and $V_q = \alpha^2$. The dispersion relation is

$$k^2 = (\omega/c)^2 - \alpha^2\,, \tag{A.31}$$

so that no wave-like propagation is possible for $|\omega/c| < |\alpha|$; instead there is exponential decay $\exp(\mathrm{i}\omega t \pm \kappa x)$, $\kappa^2 = \alpha^2 - (\omega/c)^2$. Only for the constant or exponential area functions do both ψ and φ have uniform-wave solutions, and then $V_p = V_q$, $|\alpha| = |W| = |A'/2A|$.

As mentioned above, these uniform waves are not identical with the formal waves $\psi_\pm$ etc., except for the uniform tube.

A.2.3 Formants as Eigenvalues

The formants can be defined as the resonances of the tube, given certain boundary conditions at the glottis and at the lips. The glottal excitation flow is disregarded, the treatment being based on *free* oscillations. The glottis (situated at $x = 0$) is of rather high impedance compared to the tract, whereas the lips (at $x = l$) have a relatively low radiation impedance, especially at low frequencies. Thus the crudest approximation of the boundary conditions would be $Z(0) = \infty$ ("hard"), equivalent to $q(0) = 0$ or $p'(0) = 0$ or $\varphi(0) = 0$ or $\psi'(0) - W(0)\psi(0) = 0$, and $Z(l) = 0$ ("soft"), meaning $p(l) = 0$ or $q'(l) = 0$ or $\psi(l) = 0$ or $\varphi'(l) + W(l)\varphi(l) = 0$. A somewhat better approximation would use an inductive lip termination, $Z(l) = i\omega L_{\mathrm{rad}}$, representing the radiation mass load but still neglecting the energy loss due to radiation. However, we do not consider losses at this stage.

Under these conditions, our problem can be treated as an eigenvalue problem of the Webster horn equations (A.14), (A.15)

$$p" + (A'/A)p' + (\omega/c)^2 p = 0 \,, \tag{A.32}$$

$$q" - (A'/A)q' + (\omega/c)^2 q = 0 \,, \tag{A.33}$$

or the corresponding Schrödinger equations (A.19), (A.20)

$$-\psi" + V_p\psi - (\omega/c)^2\psi = 0 \,, \tag{A.34}$$

$$-\varphi" + V_q\varphi - (\omega/c)^2\varphi = 0 \,. \tag{A.35}$$

All these equations with their boundary conditions are of Sturm–Liouville type. Their solutions fulfil the boundary conditions only for a discrete set of ω values, which give us the formant frequencies. This was first done for (A.14) by Ungeheuer [A.1] based on plaster casts of actual vocal tracts, using the simplest boundary conditions above. The solutions were obtained iteratively by perturbation methods, e.g., treating (A'/A) as a small quantity.

Note that the above-mentioned inductive termination would work only for the volume-velocity equations (A.33), (A.35) in the form of $L_{\mathrm{rad}}q' + L'q = 0$. For the pressure equations, the corresponding boundary condition would itself depend on ω^2, presenting a generalized eigenvalue problem. The same holds for capacitive termination in the opposite case, which, however, plays no role in the vocal tract.

In the case of ideal "hard" and "soft" termination, the eigenvalues depend on $\ln A(x)$ only; there is no absolute area scale. But in the general case this holds only if the terminating impedances are scaled in proportion to $1/A$, otherwise they fix the scale.

Unfortunately the Schrödinger forms of the equations have very different boundary conditions from those in quantum mechanics. If we digress from the vocal tract for a while and assume the tube to be terminated equally hard or soft at both ends, these equations show an interesting invariance with respect to area-function transformations: V_p is not changed if

$$A \longrightarrow A \left(\alpha \int_0^x A^{-1}(\xi)\, \mathrm{d}\xi + \beta \right)^2 , \tag{A.36}$$

with α, β arbitrary but so that the parenthesized expression has no zeros in $0 \le x \le l$. (Note that α has the dimension of a length.) Consequently, if $p = 0$ at both ends, the eigenvalues and even the potential-energy distribution $w_p = |\psi|^2$ remain unchanged! The corresponding holds in the dual case for V_q with $q = 0$ at both ends, and

$$A \longrightarrow A \left(\alpha \int_0^x A(\xi)\, \mathrm{d}\xi + \beta \right)^{-2} . \tag{A.37}$$

(Here α has the dimension of length^{-3}.) As special cases, a soft-terminated conical tube ($\sqrt{A}$ = linear function of x) and a hard-terminated hyperbolic tube ($1/\sqrt{A}$ = linear function of x) have the same resonances as a uniform tube of equal length and termination. However, the application of (A.36) to a hard termination changes this termination to an inductance, and the application of (A.37) to a soft termination changes this to a capacitance.

Area Perturbations. Given the solution for a specific eigenvalue (formant frequency), how is this frequency affected by infinitesimal perturbations δA of the area function? Starting from (A.32), it can be shown that the Webster operator $\mathcal{W} = \frac{\mathrm{d}^2}{\mathrm{d}x^2} + (A'/A)\frac{\mathrm{d}}{\mathrm{d}x}$ is self-adjoint with respect to the scalar product $\langle f|g \rangle = \int_0^l A f^* g\, \mathrm{d}x$: $\langle p|\mathcal{W}p \rangle = \langle \mathcal{W}p|p \rangle = -(\omega/c)^2 \langle p|p \rangle$. Variation of this expression yields

$$\delta(\omega/c)^2 = - \int_0^l A\, p^*\, \delta\left(\frac{A'}{A}\right) p'\, \mathrm{d}x \Big/ \int_0^l A\, |p|^2\, \mathrm{d}x ,$$

from which, by partial integration and substitution of (A.29) and noting further that potential energy $\int_0^l w_p\, \mathrm{d}x$ = kinetic energy $\int_0^l w_q\, \mathrm{d}x = \frac{1}{2}$ total energy E, we obtain

$$\frac{\delta\omega}{\omega} = \frac{1}{E} \int_0^l (w_q - w_p)\frac{\delta A}{A}\, \mathrm{d}x . \tag{A.38}$$

This is a well-known result obtained by Schroeder [A.2] and, for a discrete LC line, by Fant [A.3]. The integral is δE, in accordance with Ehrenfest's theorem; it is also the work done against the radiation pressure in the tube [A.2].

In the special case of a uniform tube with $q(0) = 0$ and $p(l) = 0$, the solutions for the nth eigenvalue ($n = 1, 2, \dots$) are $q(x) = \sin\left((n - \frac{1}{2})\pi x/l\right)$, $p(x) = \cos\left((n - \frac{1}{2})\pi x/l\right)$, so that $w_q - w_p = -\cos\left((2n - 1)\pi x/l\right)$. This is an antisymmetric function about the tube center $x = l/2$. Consequently, if $\delta A/A$ is symmetric, it cannot contribute to the perturbation. More specifically, because cosines of different n are orthogonal, only the odd spatial cosine-series component of form $\cos\left((2n - 1)\pi x/l\right)$ will contribute to the perturbation of the nth formant frequency. This is also a well-known result from [A.2].

Length Perturbations. Consider monotonic perturbations of the x axis, $x \to x + \delta x(x)$, $\delta x(0) = 0$, $\delta x' > -x'$. This can be reduced to the previous case by setting $\delta A = -A' \delta x$. Partial integration in (A.38) then yields, with $w = w_q + w_p$:

$$\frac{\delta\omega}{\omega} = -\frac{1}{E} \int_0^l w\, \delta x'(x)\, \mathrm{d}x \;. \tag{A.39}$$

Linear variation of the total length gives $\delta\omega/\omega = -\delta l/l$, as it trivially should. The corresponding result for a discrete LC line is also contained in [A.3].

A.2.4 Losses and Nonrigid Walls

Linear losses within the vocal tract have two main sources: viscosity and heat conduction. (In constrictions, there may be additional, nonlinear losses due to turbulence.) At speech-acoustic frequencies, both occur in a narrow layer at the tube wall, whose thickness is proportional to $1/\sqrt{\omega}$. If this is small compared to the tube radius, the viscous losses can be represented by an impedance density in series with $\mathrm{i}\omega L'$, given by $(S/A^2)(\mathrm{i}\omega\varrho\mu)^{1/2}$, where S is the circumference of the tube cross-section and μ is the viscosity. Since $\sqrt{\mathrm{i}\omega} = (1 + \mathrm{i}\,\mathrm{sgn}\,\omega)\sqrt{|\omega|/2}$, this adds both an inductive and a resistive term of equal sizes. For a derivation of this and the following expressions, see [A.4]. *Note that in complex square roots, we always use the solution with positive real part.*

Likewise, the losses due to heat conduction add an admittance in parallel to $\mathrm{i}\omega C'$, given by $S(\eta - 1)\varrho^{-1}c^{-2}(\mathrm{i}\omega\lambda/c_p\varrho)^{1/2}$, where η is the adiabatic exponent, λ the heat conductivity, and c_p the specific heat at constant pressure.

Thus we have to substitute

$$\mathrm{i}\omega L' \longrightarrow \mathrm{i}\omega L' + R' = \mathrm{i}\omega L_0' + (1 + \mathrm{i}\,\mathrm{sgn}\,\omega)R', \quad L' = L_0' + R'/|\omega| \;,$$
$$\mathrm{i}\omega C' \longrightarrow \mathrm{i}\omega C' + G' = \mathrm{i}\omega C_0' + (1 + \mathrm{i}\,\mathrm{sgn}\,\omega)G', \quad C' = C_0' + G'/|\omega| \;,$$

where L_0', C_0' now denote the original, frequency-independent L', C' and R', G' are proportional to $\sqrt{|\omega|}$. This extends the circuit of Fig. A.1 into that shown in Fig. A.2. The L', C', R', G' in this figure do not actually correspond to such electronic components because of their $\sqrt{|\omega|}$ dependence; they just indicate imaginary and real parts of the longitudinal impedance and transversal admittance. Moreover, these impedances are of a very unpleasant form, because $\sqrt{|\omega|}$ does not correspond to any closed-form or finite-order differential or convolutional operator in the time domain. This precludes any exact time-domain simulation of the lossy vocal tract on the computer!

The characteristic impedance and phase velocity now also become complex and frequency dependent. Instead of the phase velocity, we give the propagation "constant" $\gamma = \mathrm{i}\omega/c$. For small losses, i.e. $R'/|\omega|L' \ll 1$, $G'/|\omega|C' \ll 1$, we have, with $Z_0 = \sqrt{L_0'/C_0'}$,

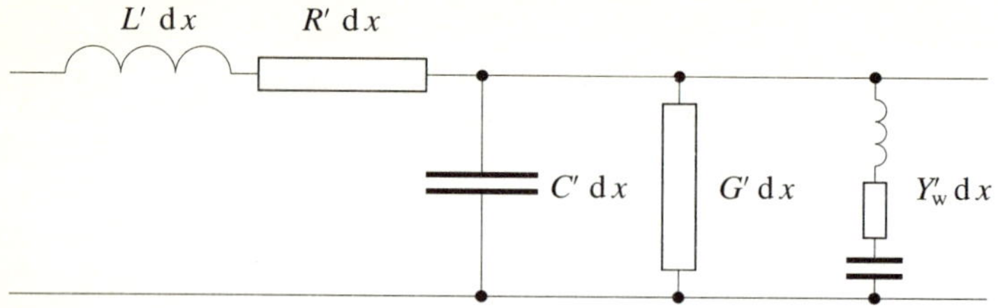

Fig. A.2. Infinitesimal element of a transmission line with losses due to viscosity and heat conduction; a wall admittance Y'_{w} is also included

$$Z = \left((\mathrm{i}\omega L' + R')/(\mathrm{i}\omega C' + G')\right)^{1/2}$$
$$\approx Z_0\left(1 + (1 + \mathrm{i}\,\mathrm{sgn}\,\omega)(R'/L'_0 - G'/C'_0)/2\mathrm{i}\omega\right), \tag{A.40}$$
$$\gamma = \left((\mathrm{i}\omega L' + R')(\mathrm{i}\omega C' + G')\right)^{1/2}$$
$$\approx \mathrm{i}\omega\sqrt{L'_0 C'_0} + (1 + \mathrm{i}\,\mathrm{sgn}\,\omega)(R'/Z_0 + G'Z_0)/2 . \tag{A.41}$$

Thus, apart from adding a damping term $\mathrm{Re}\{\gamma\}$, R' and G' also slightly change the phase propagation, $\mathrm{Im}\{\gamma\}$. However, the modification of L', C' by the $\sqrt{|\omega|}$ terms can often be neglected, except at very low frequencies.

Nonrigid walls. It is also possible to approximate the effect of nonrigid walls. We assume the walls to be locally reacting (i.e. there is no lateral coupling along the tube) and of constant characteristics around the circumference of one cross-section; moreover radiation through the walls is neglected – surely daring assumptions! Then the wall impedance may be represented as a mass-spring-damping combination, electrically expressed by an LRC series resonance circuit. In Fig. A.2, this circuit must be inserted in parallel with C' and G' as a shunt admittance density $Y'_{\mathrm{w}} = 1/(\mathrm{i}\omega L_{\mathrm{w}} + R_{\mathrm{w}} + 1/\mathrm{i}\omega C_{\mathrm{w}})$, thus changing Z and γ again.

The series-resonance frequency of Y'_{w} is very low, e.g. 30 Hz, so that the spring C_{w} can often be neglected. The mass, however, shifts the formant frequencies upwards, also their damping increases due to wall losses. For example, when a constriction at the lips goes to zero, the first formant no longer approaches zero as it would in the hard-walled tube but remains bounded at, say, 170 Hz.

For certain distributions of the wall impedance the wave equation can be solved exactly [A.5]. However, since the effect is large only for the first formant, the wall impedance may often be represented by one or a few lumped LRC or LR shunts instead of by the above distributed shunts.

A.3 Discrete Modeling of a Tube

By "discrete modeling" we mean the spatial discretization of the area function for the purposes of simulating the sound transmission in the time domain, e.g.

for articulatory synthesis, or of computing transfer functions and impedances of the vocal tract in the frequency domain. The spatial segments may be of unequal length. Historically, there were analog hardware implementations by electronic components in the form of Figs. A.1 or A.2. But we will base our considerations only on the wave equations themselves. Under simplifying assumptions, these can be simulated efficiently on the computer in the time domain. Then the time axis must be also discretized, thus turning the whole system into a digital filter.

A.3.1 Time-Domain Modeling

As mentioned in Sect. A.2.4, no time-domain modeling of an actual lossy vocal tract is possible. We will restrict ourselves to the simplified case of nondispersive propagation and frequency-independent, real characteristic impedance, i.e., $L'C' = \text{const}$; $R'/L' = G'/C'$; R', G' frequency independent. At first we even give the equations for the lossless case only. Also the wall impedance will initially be neglected.

As the wave propagation is especially simple in uniform tubes, we will consider uniform segments, also piecewise constant in time. Then in intervals where $A(x,t) = \text{const}$, there is free propagation of left and right traveling waves along the characteristics $dx = \pm c\,dt$, whereas at the interval boundaries, reflections occur. Note that the spatial segmentation is at variance with our initial assumption that the slope of the tube walls is small: here it is infinite at the segment boundaries! Thus the approximation is physically good only for small relative area changes. (Other tube forms without discontinuities, for instance, composed of exponential or conical segments, have no time-domain representations by finite-order, causal, stable systems.)

We assume a minimal length d of which all spatial segments are integer multiples. As both x and t are discretized, there will be a relation between d and the sampling period $T = 1/f_\mathrm{s}$. Intuitively one would guess $d = cT$, but it turns out that $d = cT/2$, $f_\mathrm{s} = c/2d$ is sufficient, if the sampling epochs for adjacent segments are displaced by $T/2$. This is clear from Fig. A.3, where the spatiotemporal lattice of pulse propagation is shown. (The temporal area changes should occur at intervals $T/2$ or multiples thereof.) If instead $f_\mathrm{s} = c/d$ were chosen, two causally nonconnected pulse-trajectory lattices would be present. A sampling frequency of 10 kHz now corresponds to a segment length of 17 mm. Unfortunately, the computational expense increases with d^{-2} or f_s^2.

We use index n for space and k for time (k will never mean wave number here). However, to keep the indexing simple, we will index time at double rate, as if $f_\mathrm{s} = c/d$, but noting that in one of two adjacent segments, only the odd k occur and in the other one, only the even k. (Alternatively, we could use an oblique space–time coordinate system with space axis parallel to the right traveling waves, thus choosing different time zero points for each segment.) The continuous fields are replaced by pulse sequences of amplitudes

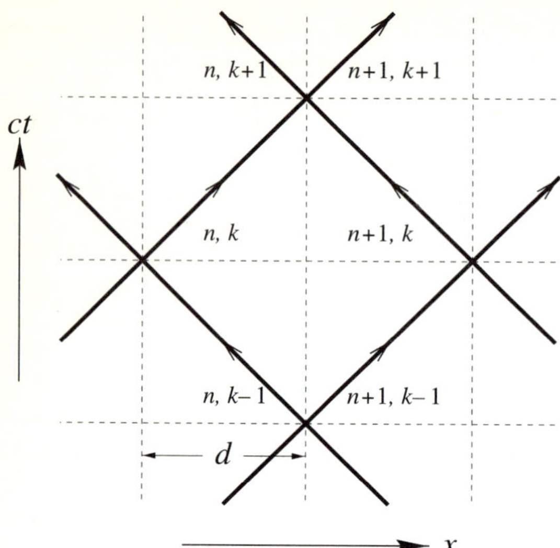

Fig. A.3. Spatiotemporal pulse trajectories in a segmented tube; temporal sampling interval $2d/c$; *dashed: regions of constant* $Z = Z_{n,k}$

$p_{n,k}$ etc. at the sampling frequency, traveling along the diagonals of the $d \times d/c$ rectangles of constant $Z = Z_{n,k}$. For the p, q samples, n, k refers to the lower left corner of this rectangle.

As vocal-tract motions are rather slow compared to acoustic frequencies, we give here only the formulas for the time-invariant case, neglecting reflections due to temporal area changes ($Q = 0$, $Z_{n,k} = Z_n$). Then it is known that p, q are continuous at the segment boundaries (ψ, φ are not!). The difference equations can best be derived from the constancy of the waves p_+, p_- (A.22) along the diagonals:

$$\begin{aligned}
p_{n+1,k+1} + Z_n q_{n+1,k+1} &= p_{n,k} \quad\; + Z_n q_{n,k} \;, \\
p_{n,k+1} \quad\; - Z_n q_{n,k+1} &= p_{n+1,k} - Z_n q_{n+1,k} \;.
\end{aligned} \tag{A.42}$$

These can be resolved for any two of the (p, q) pairs, given all the others, depending on the task, for instance, computing future from past values:

$$\begin{aligned}
p_{n,k+1} &= \frac{Z_{n-1}^{-1} p_{n-1,k} + Z_n^{-1} p_{n+1,k} + q_{n-1,k} - q_{n+1,k}}{Z_{n-1}^{-1} + Z_n^{-1}} \;, \\
q_{n,k+1} &= \frac{p_{n-1,k} - p_{n+1,k} + Z_{n-1} q_{n-1,k} + Z_n q_{n+1,k}}{Z_{n-1} + Z_n} \;.
\end{aligned} \tag{A.43}$$

However, it is computationally much more efficient to directly employ the wave representation. (The wave subscripts $+, -$ will now be written as superscripts because of the other subscripts n, k.) Here the outgoing waves are obtained by the scattering of the incoming waves at a boundary:

$$\begin{aligned}
p_{n+1,k+1}^{+} &= (1 + r_n) p_{n,k}^{+} \quad\; - r_n p_{n+1,k}^{-} \;, \\
p_{n,k+1}^{-} &= (1 - r_n) p_{n+1,k}^{-} + r_n p_{n,k}^{+} \;;
\end{aligned} \tag{A.44}$$

$$r_n = \frac{Z_{n+1} - Z_n}{Z_{n+1} + Z_n} = \frac{A_n - A_{n+1}}{A_n + A_{n+1}} \;, \qquad |r_n| < 1 \;, \tag{A.45}$$

which are the discrete form of (A.25) for $Q = 0$. These can be extended for the time-varying tube, see [A.6], needing two different reflection factors; but this is usually not required. In the (p, q)-representation, the time-varying case is more difficult to treat, because p and q are not continuous in space *and* time at the corners of the constant-Z rectangles and thus cannot be assigned unique values there!

For volume-velocity or square-root-of-power waves, the scattering equations differ from (A.44) only in the form of the transmission factors, if the same r_n from (A.45) is used here too (although the actual reflection factor for q is $-r_n$):

$$\text{for } q \text{ waves,} \quad (1 \pm r_n) \longrightarrow (1 \mp r_n)\,,$$
$$\text{for } \psi \text{ waves,} \quad (1 \pm r_n) \longrightarrow \sqrt{1 - r_n^2}\,.$$

The p and q waves have the advantage that they can be implemented with a single multiplier (and three adders), but may result in an unpleasantly large range of values when r_n approaches ± 1. The ψ waves require four multipliers, but their values, directly related to power, are less prone to become large. In the terminology of wave digital filters (WDF) [A.7], the scattering equations (A.44) describe a "two-port adaptor".

If the simulation is to include the nasal tract, at the branching the equations become more complicated, based on continuity of p and conservation of q. In the WDF terminology, this is described by a "three-port parallel adaptor", with r_n replaced by two parameters.

Damping. In the wave representation, a frequency-independent damping as mentioned above can easily be introduced: Simply multiply each wave quantity by a factor smaller than 1 between two time steps.

Termination and Wall Impedances. For the complete tract model, not only the tube but also the termination impedances at lips, nostrils, glottis, and possibly the wall impedances must be modeled. In most cases these impedances will first be represented by analog one-port networks, whose differential equations are then approximated by difference equations. These define a relation between the p and q signals or between the two wave signals at the connection. In the wave representation, it is natural to use the WDF formulation of these networks and attach them using the appropriate adaptors. For instance, if a is the incident and b the reflected wave, an inductance L is described as $b = -z^{-1}a$ or $b_k = -a_{k-2}$ with a port impedance $2f_sL$, a capacitance C as $b = z^{-1}a$ with a port impedance $1/(2f_sC)$, a resistance R as $b = 0$ with a port impedance R. But note that, whereas the wave representation of the segmented tube is exact, the WDF description of discrete components is equivalent to the bilinear z-transform, distorting the frequency scale according to $\omega \to 2f_s \arctan(\omega/2f_s)$. One has to choose a sufficiently high sampling rate, also desirable for fine segmentation.

Sources in the Tract. A noise source in the tract for fricative excitation is obtained by adding random numbers to the field quantities. Their standard deviation must depend on area and flow in the segment in an appropriate way. A plosion burst can be simulated by opening a closed tract after pressure buildup. Both these sources require the inclusion of a dc flow or subglottal pressure in the simulations. Also in narrow constrictions, the damping must become large to avoid the occurrence of unnaturally high field values.

A.3.2 Frequency-Domain Modeling, Two-Port Theory

In the time-invariant frequency-domain description of the vocal-tract model, we have full freedom with respect to dispersion and damping. The most convenient approach is the representation of segments by the chain or transmission matrices of the two-port theory, which are easily multiplied to yield the corresponding matrix of the whole tube. From these and the terminating impedances, the transfer functions and input impedances are obtained. Let the segments be uniform again, but we now allow the lengths to be arbitrary $(d \to d_n)$.

If no direct time-domain modeling is possible, the transfer functions computed in the frequency domain can be used to implement a digital filter, possibly by Fourier techniques (overlap-add).

(p,q)-Representation. The chain matrix of a segment connects the values at the segment input with those at the output:

$$\begin{bmatrix} p_n \\ q_n \end{bmatrix}_{\text{in}} = \begin{bmatrix} \cosh(\gamma_n d_n) & Z_n \sinh(\gamma_n d_n) \\ Z_n^{-1} \sinh(\gamma_n d_n) & \cosh(\gamma_n d_n) \end{bmatrix} \begin{bmatrix} p_n \\ q_n \end{bmatrix}_{\text{out}} ; \qquad (A.46)$$

Without damping, $Z_n = \varrho_0 c / A_n$, $\gamma_n = i\omega/c$, $\cosh(\gamma_n d_n) = \cos(\omega d_n/c)$, $\sinh(\gamma_n d_n) = i \sin(\omega d_n/c)$; with damping, see (A.40), (A.41). Even with finite wall impedance, the form of the matrix remains the same. Because p and q are continuous, $(p_n, q_n)_{\text{out}}^{\mathsf{T}} = (p_{n+1}, q_{n+1})_{\text{in}}^{\mathsf{T}}$, and so the matrices from (A.46) can simply be multiplied to give the total chain matrix; let us call it $\begin{bmatrix} \mathcal{A} & \mathcal{B} \\ \mathcal{C} & \mathcal{D} \end{bmatrix}$. Obviously the determinant is $\mathcal{A}\mathcal{D} - \mathcal{B}\mathcal{C} = 1$, so that the inverse matrix is $\begin{bmatrix} \mathcal{D} & -\mathcal{B} \\ -\mathcal{C} & \mathcal{A} \end{bmatrix}$. This means, *reciprocity* is fulfilled:

$$\left(\frac{p_{\text{out}}}{q_{\text{in}}} \right)_{q_{\text{out}}=0} = - \left(\frac{p_{\text{in}}}{q_{\text{out}}} \right)_{q_{\text{in}}=0} , \qquad (A.47a)$$

$$\left(\frac{q_{\text{out}}}{p_{\text{in}}} \right)_{p_{\text{out}}=0} = - \left(\frac{q_{\text{in}}}{p_{\text{out}}} \right)_{p_{\text{in}}=0} . \qquad (A.47b)$$

In the (ψ, φ) representation, the matrix in (A.46) contains no Z_n; instead each of the segment boundaries also has a chain matrix $\operatorname{diag}(\sqrt{Z_{n+1}/Z_n}, \sqrt{Z_n/Z_{n+1}})$ connecting $(\psi_n, \varphi_n)_{\text{out}}^{\mathsf{T}}$ with $(\psi_{n+1}, \varphi_{n+1})_{\text{in}}^{\mathsf{T}}$. In the lossless case, the segment matrices are unitary.

Let the tube be terminated by a radiation impedance Z_{rad}. Then the transfer function for volume velocity is

$$H_q = q_{\text{out}}/q_{\text{in}} = 1/(\mathcal{C}Z_{\text{rad}} + \mathcal{D}) \, . \tag{A.48}$$

The far-field sound pressure in front of the mouth is proportional to $i\omega q_{\text{out}}$. The input impedance of the tract "seen" by the glottis is

$$Z_{\text{in}} = p_{\text{in}}/q_{\text{in}} = (\mathcal{A}Z_{\text{rad}} + \mathcal{B})/(\mathcal{C}Z_{\text{rad}} + \mathcal{D}) \, . \tag{A.49}$$

In this manner, all quantities of interest can be calculated. When the tube is branched, the parallel combination of the input impedances of two branches is taken as the output impedance of the third branch.

Radiation Impedance. The radiation impedance of the actual mouth cannot be written in closed form. The simplest approximation (beyond short-circuit or inductance) using constant components will be a parallel combination of inductance and conductance,

$$Z_{\text{rad}} = 1/\big((1/i\omega L_{\text{rad}}) + G_{\text{rad}}\big) \, , \quad L_{\text{rad}} \propto A^{-1/2}, \quad G_{\text{rad}} \propto A \, , \tag{A.50}$$

where A ist the lip-opening area. This would hold exactly for a pulsating sphere, with $L_{\text{rad}} = \varrho/\sqrt{4\pi A}$, $G_{\text{rad}} = A/\varrho c$. The proportionality factors are often derived from a piston in a plane baffle or a piston in a sphere of the size of the head. But in the frequency domain, there is actually no need to consider discrete-component circuits; arbitrary functions are possible.

The following trick can facilitate the modeling of the radiation impedance [A.8]. The spherical waves outside the mouth are approximately described in an extended tube model with quadratically increasing area. At its end, the radiation impedance for the larger area is less critical to model. This extended tube also allows the modeling of lip protrusion without changing the total number of segments.

Wave Representation. The chain matrices are here replaced by transmission matrices:

$$\begin{bmatrix} p_n^+ \\ p_n^- \end{bmatrix}_{\text{in}} = \begin{bmatrix} \exp(\gamma_n d_n) & 0 \\ 0 & \exp(-\gamma_n d_n) \end{bmatrix} \begin{bmatrix} p_n^+ \\ p_n^- \end{bmatrix}_{\text{out}} ; \tag{A.51}$$

and likewise for the q or ψ waves. The segment boundaries also have transmission matrices, representing reflection and transmission:

$$\begin{bmatrix} p_n^+ \\ p_n^- \end{bmatrix}_{\text{out}} = \begin{bmatrix} 1/(1+r_n) & r_n/(1+r_n) \\ r_n/(1+r_n) & 1/(1+r_n) \end{bmatrix} \begin{bmatrix} p_{n+1}^+ \\ p_{n+1}^- \end{bmatrix}_{\text{in}} \, . \tag{A.52}$$

For q waves, $(1 + r_n)$ is replaced by $(1 - r_n)$, and for ψ waves, by $\sqrt{1 - r_n^2}$. In order to obtain the total transmission matrix, these matrix pairs have to be multiplied up again. With the ψ waves and no losses, the transmission matrix is $\in$ SU(1,1), preserving the power $|\psi^+|^2 - |\psi^-|^2$.

An impedance, e.g. Z_{rad}, connected to the output of the last (Nth) segment is represented by a complex reflection factor $r_{\text{rad}} = (Z_{\text{rad}} - Z_N)/(Z_{\text{rad}} +$

$Z_N)$, so that $p_{n\,\text{out}}^- = r_{\text{rad}} p_{n\,\text{out}}^+$ and likewise for the q and ψ waves. If the total transmission matrix is $\begin{bmatrix} \mathcal{P} & \mathcal{Q} \\ \mathcal{R} & \mathcal{S} \end{bmatrix}$, the reflection factor at the tube input and the input impedance are obtained:

$$r_{\text{in}} = p_{\text{in}}^-/p_{\text{in}}^+ = (\mathcal{R} + \mathcal{S}r_{\text{rad}})/(\mathcal{P} + \mathcal{Q}r_{\text{rad}})\,, \qquad Z_{\text{in}} = Z_1 \frac{1 - r_{\text{in}}}{1 + r_{\text{in}}}\,, \qquad (A.53)$$

where Z_1 ist the characteristic impedance of the first segment. The volume-velocity transfer function is, for p waves,

$$H_q = Z_1 / \big((\mathcal{P} - \mathcal{R})(Z_{\text{rad}} + Z_N) + (\mathcal{Q} - \mathcal{S})(Z_{\text{rad}} - Z_N)\big)\,. \qquad (A.54)$$

(For q waves, replace Z_1 by Z_N in this equation, and for ψ waves, by $\sqrt{Z_1 Z_N}$.)

Time Discretization and z-Transform. From the frequency-domain equations for the lossless (or at least dispersion-free) case and common segment length $d_n = d$, we can immediately derive the z-transform equivalents with respect to the sampling frequency $f_s = c/2d$. Simply set $z = \exp(i\omega/f_s)$. Then the chain matrix and the transmission matrix of a segment become, for the lossless case,

$$\begin{bmatrix} (z^{1/2} + z^{-1/2})/2 & Z_n(z^{1/2} - z^{-1/2})/2 \\ Z_n^{-1}(z^{1/2} - z^{-1/2})/2 & (z^{1/2} + z^{-1/2})/2 \end{bmatrix}$$

$$\text{and} \quad \begin{bmatrix} z^{1/2} & 0 \\ 0 & z^{-1/2} \end{bmatrix}, \qquad\qquad (A.55)$$

respectively. Thus the elements of the total matrices are polynomials in z^{-1} times a total advance factor $z^{N/2}$. The matrix multiplication gives recursion formulas for their coefficients. It is further easily verified that the total lossless transmission matrix shows the time-reversal symmetry

$$\mathcal{P}(z) = \mathcal{S}(z^{-1}), \qquad \mathcal{Q}(z) = \mathcal{R}(z^{-1})\,. \qquad\qquad (A.56)$$

This means the polynomial coefficients of $\mathcal{P}$, $\mathcal{Q}$ are those of $\mathcal{S}$, $\mathcal{R}$ in reverse sequence, which halves the computational expense in computing the transmission matrix. If there is a common constant wave damping factor $a < 1$ per segment, $z^{-1/2}$ needs simply be replaced by $az^{-1/2}$.

Whereas the z representation of the tube itself is exact, the forms for attached discrete impedances must be approximated by the usual methods. For wave quantities, the wave-digital-filter approach is the most natural one, as stated in Sect. A.3.1.

From the z-transform expressions, we can immediately go back to the time domain by interpreting $z^{-1/2}$ as a delay by d/c, i.e. $k \to k-1$ using the double-rate time indexing of Sect. A.3.1, and get the difference equations in space and time again.

A.3.3 Tube Models and Linear Prediction

It is well known from linear-prediction theory [A.9] that a discrete-time all-pole filter $H(z) = 1/A(z)$, $A(z) = \sum_{k=1}^{N} a_k z^{-k}$, $a_0 = 1$, can be realized, up to gain and delay factors, as the transfer function of a segmented lossless tube as used in the previous sections. This can be seen from the relations between "PARCOR" coefficients k_m and the predictor coefficients a_k, which lead to a realization of $A(z)$ as a nonrecursive lattice filter and of $1/A(z)$ as a recursive one. Define auxiliary signals e_m^+, e_m^- (called forward and backward prediction errors). The lattice filter is then recursively defined as

$$
\begin{aligned}
e_m^+ &= e_{m-1}^+ - k_m z^{-1} e_{m-1}^- \, , \\
e_m^- &= z^{-1} e_{m-1}^- - k_m e_{m-1}^+ \, ,
\end{aligned}
\qquad m = 1, \ldots, N; \quad e_0^- = e_0^+ . \tag{A.57}
$$

If e_N^+ is the input and e_0^+ the output (e_N^- discarded), this implements $1/A(z)$. Now compare this to the transmission in a tube. Combining (A.52) and (A.55), this reads for the p waves at the segment *out*puts:

$$
\begin{aligned}
(1 + r_n) p_n^+ &= z^{1/2} p_{n+1}^+ + r_n z^{-1/2} p_{n+1}^- \, , \\
(1 + r_n) p_n^- &= z^{-1/2} p_{n+1}^- + r_n z^{1/2} p_{n+1}^+ \, .
\end{aligned}
\tag{A.58}
$$

We now make the following identifications:

$$
m = N - n \, , \quad e_m^\pm = \pm p_n^\pm \, z^{n/2} \prod_{\nu=n}^{N-1} (1 + r_\nu) \, , \quad k_m = r_n \, , \tag{A.59}
$$

and assume a short-circuit at the tube output ($p_N^- = -p_N^+$) and a source of real, constant impedance Z_0 at the input. This is equivalent to inserting a segment 0 of impedance Z_0 before segment 1 whose p_0^- is absorbed. The p_0^+ is taken as the input signal, p_N^+ as the output signal. It is then obvious that (A.57) and (A.58) become identical. [For q or ψ waves, the factors $(1 + r_n)$ have to be replaced as mentioned after (A.52).] Note that the factors $z^{n/2}$ in (A.58) mean that for the signals e_m^+, e_m^-, an oblique space–time coordinate system (as briefly mentioned in Sect. A.3.1) has been used, where right-traveling waves have a constant time coordinate. This combines a pair of $z^{-1/2}$ delays in the right and left traveling waves into ordinary z^{-1} delays in the left wave only, as known from the lattice filter.

But this way to identify (A.57) and (A.58), originally proposed by Wakita [A.10], is not the only one. An earlier but less well known interpretation using different boundary conditions was given by Atal and Hanauer [A.11]. Here we assume a "hard" input of the tube with a volume-velocity source q_{in}. The radiation impedance at the output is real and constant, so that formally a segment $N + 1$ of this impedance with reflection factor $r_N \equiv r_{\text{rad}}$ can be inserted, with $p_{N+1}^- = 0$ and $p_{N+1} = p_{N+1}^+$ as the output signal of the total system. Instead of deriving the formulas from the matrices, we can obtain the result from the previous analogy, employing the reciprocity relations (A.47b)

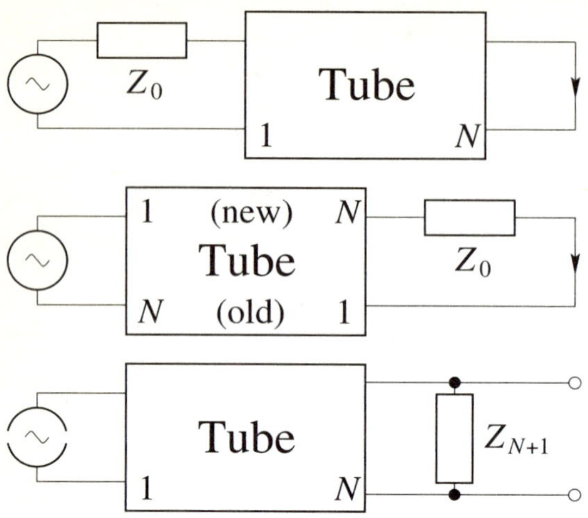

Fig. A.4. Reciprocity and duality transformation between tube models related to the PARCOR lattice. *Top:* Wakita's boundary conditions; *middle:* reciprocity applied and tube mirrored; *bottom:* duality applied, giving Atal's boundary conditions ($Z_{N+1} \propto Z_0^{-1}$). Source is always left, output right

and duality (A.11), as visualized by the electrical equivalent circuits in Fig. A.4.

To describe the Wakita system in the (p, q) domain, we replace the formal segment 0 by a pressure source $p_0 = 2p_0^+$ in series with a resistance Z_0 and assume a volume-velocity output $q_N = (p_N^+ - p_N^-)/Z_N = 2p_N^+/Z_N$ (Fig. A.4, top), just scaling the transfer function by Z_N. According to the reciprocity theorem, the transfer function is then identical to that of a volume-velocity output in (formal) segment 0 with respect to a pressure source in segment N (Fig. A.4, middle). Now we can invert the segment numbering, $n \to N+1-n$, so that $r_n \to -r_{N-n}$. Next, we apply the duality transformation, changing the zero-impedance pressure source into an infinite-impedance current source and the volume-velocity output into a pressure output (Fig. A.4, bottom); furthermore, this transformation inverts all areas, whereby the r_n change sign again and are identical to the original ones, apart from numbering. The total area transformation is consequently $A_n \to A_{N+1-n}^{-1}, \quad n = 1, \ldots, N$.

Thus the PARCOR lattice filter can be identified with an acoustic tube in two different ways, depending on the physical boundary conditions assumed.

A.4 Notes on the Inverse Problem

By inverse problem we mean, generally speaking, the determination of geometric properties of the vocal tract from acoustic data. The former can be detailed area values, but also the values of articulatory parameters. The acoustic data may comprise formant frequencies and bandwidths, spectra, autocorrelation or LPC coefficients, or impedance data. We can only briefly present some selected approaches. Area values are directly related to the transfer properties of the tract and therefore people have tried to determine them on theoretical grounds, whereas articulatory data require empirical mapping methods.

A.4.1 Analytic and Numerical Methods

It is easily imaginable that any knowledge related to a finite frequency range will not give information about arbitrarily fine structure of the area function. But even if we knew all the (infinitely many) formant frequencies of the tube, this would only provide half the information required. This is easily seen from the area-perturbation results for a lossless tube [A.2] as described in Sect. A.2.3. Only the odd cosine-series components of the logarithmic area function can be determined from the formant frequencies for small deviations from a uniform tube. Consequently, two sets of data are needed. These may be

(1) formant frequencies for different boundary conditions – hardly available in the vocal tract;
(2) poles and zeros of an input impedance, for instance, measured at the lips from outside [A.2], although this impedes articulation and forbids phonation;
(3) formant frequencies *and* bandwidths for a lossy termination of known form – difficult to measure exactly enough;
(4) a piece of the autocorrelation function of the impulse response of the tract with lossy termination (or the corresponding LPC coefficients), approximated by analysis of actual speech with proper preemphasis.

In fact, these possibilities are essentially equivalent. For (3) and (4), this is clear, both expressing the transfer function of the tube with lossy termination. As for (1) and (2), the poles and zeros of the input impedance correspond to the resonances for hard and soft termination. Furthermore, the input impedance is related to the transfer or autocorrelation function, as will be shown below.

Let us start with approach (2), the construction of the area function from the input impedance. This is feasible in the frequency domain, but requires knowledge about length and termination at the other end. By identifying the poles and zeros with the formants for hard and soft termination, perturbation methods as in [A.2] are applicable. The missing higher formants can be filled in using the asymptotic eigenvalue theorems for Sturm–Liouville systems and choosing the unknown length so that $\log A(x)$ deviates minimally from a uniform tube [A.12]

However, the reconstruction from the input impedance is much more comprehensive in the time domain. We consider the lossless tube only. At time $t = 0$, apply a volume-velocity delta pulse to the tube input and record the pressure response. This is the inverse Fourier transform (or z-transform, respectively) $\zeta_{\mathrm{in}}(t)$ of the impedance $Z_{\mathrm{in}}(\omega)$ or $Z_{\mathrm{in}}(z)$. For reasons of causality, the interval $[0, \tau]$ of this impulse response contains information about the length interval $[0, c\tau/2]$; in discrete time, the samples $0, \ldots, n$ contain information about the first $n + 1$ segments. In the continuous case, the solution uses integral equations [A.13], whereas in the discrete case, the segment areas are obtained by a simple recursion derived from (A.42). Even the length of the tube need not be known. It might be estimated from the derived tract shape itself.

Instead of using the input impulse response directly, we can (for the discrete lossless tube) employ the linear-predictive tube model from Sect. A.3.3 to compute the area function. Since a current source was assumed, Atal's boundary conditions apply. For a tube of at least M segments to be determined, formally assume termination of the Mth segment by an arbitrary real constant conductance G_{trm}, where the pressure is $p_{\mathrm{trm}} = p_{M\mathrm{out}}$. The equality of input and output powers reads, in the frequency domain,

$$\mathrm{Re}(Z_{\mathrm{in}})|q_{\mathrm{in}}|^2 = G_{\mathrm{trm}}|p_{\mathrm{trm}}|^2 \; . \tag{A.60}$$

Note that for a unit pulse, $|q_{\mathrm{in}}|^2 = 1$. Transforming back to the time domain, this yields

$$\zeta_{\mathrm{in}}(t) + \zeta_{\mathrm{in}}(-t) = 2G_{\mathrm{trm}}R_{p_{\mathrm{trm}}}(t) \; , \tag{A.61}$$

where $R_{p_{\mathrm{trm}}}(t)$ is the autocorrelation function of $p_{\mathrm{trm}}(t)$. Thus – in discrete time – the samples $2\zeta_{\mathrm{in}}(0)$, $\zeta_{\mathrm{in}}(1), \ldots, \zeta_{\mathrm{in}}(M-1)$ (independent of the *actual* termination of segment M) can be identified with a piece of a formal ACF, from which then $M - 1$ reflection coefficients are obtained by the usual LPC techniques. This yields Z_n or A_n, $n = 1, \ldots, M$, up to an unknown factor, which may be determined from $Z_{\mathrm{in}}(t = 0) = Z_1$.

Now let us consider approach (4), the well-known construction of a segmented tube model by linear prediction, already described in Sect. A.3.3. We can start with an autocorrelation function (ACF) or a covariance matrix of the speech output, from which the PARCOR coefficients are derived [A.9] and then interpreted as reflection factors between the segments of a tube. However, the sequence of these reflection factors depends on the assumed boundary conditions, as described above! Only if the logarithmic area function is antisymmetric about its midpoint, do the two cases considered yield the same result. In fact, Atal's boundary conditions of a hard glottis and constant real termination (Z_{N+1} in Fig. A.4, bottom) can be generalized to a more realistic radiation admittance with constant real part and arbitrary imaginary part without changing the result. Look at (A.61) with $M = N+1$, $G_{\mathrm{trm}} = Z_{N+1}^{-1}$. Equation (A.61) still holds if G_{trm} is the constant real part of some complex admittance Y_{trm}. The conductance–inductance parallel model of the radiation admittance mentioned in Sect. A.3.2 is of just this form! As the termination does not influence the initial portion of the impulse response $Z_{\mathrm{in}}(t)$ at the glottal end and (A.61) is independent of the imaginary part of Y_{trm}, the latter does not affect the initial portion of the ACF of the output pressure and thus the PARCOR coefficients. These can still be interpreted as the same reflection coefficients. But the absolute area scaling remains unknown, because G_{trm} of the radiation load is itself approximately proportional to the lip area. The relations between input impulse response and output ACF were first presented by Atal [A.14].

As nice as these relations look, they have not led to a reliable determination of the vocal-tract shape from the speech output. We have mentioned the extreme sensitivity of the results to the physical boundary conditions. Further, the actual transfer function of the vocal tract is not measurable, since its excitation is not a sequence of delta pulses. The glottal pulse shape or its spectrum show considerable variation. Moreover, the source-filter approximation is not exact; the oscillating glottis acts as a time-varying source impedance. Attempts to use adaptive preemphasis or LPC analysis on closed-glottis intervals (which are already difficult to determine) may yield reasonable-looking results. Another unknown factor is the distribution of losses and wall admittance, not accounted for in the above approaches. For specific simplifying assumptions a solution based on integral equations has been achieved [A.5].

A.4.2 Empirical Methods

These difficulties have led researchers to deliberately renounce reliance on complete acoustic data or analytic methods. Even in analytic approaches, incomplete information is often replaced by ad hoc assumptions; for instance, assume the logarithmic area function to be odd [A.2], assume minimum least-squares deviation from a uniform tube [A.12], guess the formant bandwidths according to empirical relations, etc.

Instead of trying to reconstruct the area function directly, one can decrease the number of unknowns by expressing the area function by some parameters. The cosine series of [A.2] is a simple example; but more promising appears to be the use of parameters from an articulatory model. This might automatically restrict the possible area functions to anatomically reasonable ones. However, such parameters cannot be determined by closed-form algorithms any more. Instead, empirical tables, vector quantizers, or neural networks must be employed to "learn" the relation between acoustic and articulatory data for the model by presenting many (synthetic) examples. An early large investigation, also considering nonuniqueness, was given in [A.15]. Accounting for temporal continuity constraints of the parameter trajectories might be helpful. Since such methods are not directly related to the acoustic theory of the vocal tract, they are beyond the scope of this appendix.

B. Direct Relations
Between Cepstrum and Predictor Coefficients[1]

Here we derive direct, i.e., nonrecursive, relations for the cepstrum in terms
of the predictor coefficients and vice versa. Connections with algebraic roots,
symmetric functions, statistical moments, and cumulants are pointed out.
Some implications for pitch detection are also discussed.

Recursive relations between cepstrum and predictor coefficients [B.1] have
long been known [B.2]. For some purposes, knowledge of *direct* relations between these two sets of important parameters characterizing sources and signals is desirable.

B.1 Derivation of the Main Result

Let

$$A(z) = \sum_{k=0}^{p} a_k z^{-k} \; ; \quad a_0 = 1 \; ; \quad a_p \neq 0 \tag{B.1}$$

be an "inverse filter" polynomial [B.2] of order p whose roots are inside the
unit circle. The a_k are the predictor coefficients. Then $1/A(z)$ is a (stable)
all-pole filter whose cepstrum coefficients c_n are customarily defined by

$$\ln\left[1/A(z)\right] =: \sum_{n=1}^{\infty} c_n z^{-n} \; . \tag{B.2}$$

The well-known recursion relation between the a_k and c_n is obtained by
differentiating (B.2) with respect to z^{-1} and equating equal powers of z^{-1},
yielding [B.3]

$$c_n = -a_n - \frac{1}{n}\sum_{k=1}^{n-1} k c_k a_{n-k} \; . \tag{B.3}$$

A direct (nonrecursive) relation can be obtained by applying a formula [B.4]
for the division of two power series to the ratio $-A'(z)/A(z)$ obtained after
differentiating the left side of (B.2). This gives

[1] Adapted from *IEEE Trans. Acoustics, Speech and Signal processing*, **ASSP-29**,
297–301 (1981).

$$c_n = \frac{1}{n}(-1)^n \begin{vmatrix} a_1 & 1 & 0 & \cdots & 0 \\ 2a_2 & a_1 & 1 & 0 & \cdots & 0 \\ \vdots & & & & \\ na_n & a_{n-1} & & \cdots & a_1 \end{vmatrix} . \tag{B.4}$$

Unfortunately, this determinant is somewhat unwieldy. An alternative direct form is, therefore, desirable and can be derived as follows. From (B.1) and (B.2) we have

$$\ln\left(1 + \sum_{k=1}^{p} a_k z^{-k}\right) = -\sum_{n=1}^{\infty} c_n z^{-n} . \tag{B.5}$$

Using the well-known power series expansion for $\ln(1+x)$ yields

$$\sum_{m=1}^{\infty} \frac{1}{m} \left(-\sum_{k=1}^{p} a_k z^{-k}\right)^m = -\sum_{n=1}^{\infty} c_n z^{-n} \tag{B.6}$$

or [B.5]

$$\sum_{m=1}^{\infty} \frac{1}{m} m! \sum_{n=m}^{\infty} z^{-n} \sum \frac{(-a_1)^{k_1} \cdots (-a_p)^{k_p}}{k_1! \cdots k_p!} = -\sum_{n=1}^{\infty} d_n z^{-n} , \tag{B.7}$$

where the third sum has to be taken over all

$$k_1 + 2k_2 + \ldots + pk_p = n \tag{B.7a}$$

and

$$k_1 + k_2 + \ldots + k_p = m . \tag{B.7b}$$

Because m is summed over all positive integers, the condition (B.7b) can be dropped if m in (B.7) is replaced by $k_1 + k_2 + \ldots + k_p$.

Equating equal powers of z^{-1} in (B.7) then yields the desired *direct* relation between cepstrum and predictor coefficients

$$c_n = \sum \frac{(k_1 + k_2 + \ldots + k_p - 1)!}{k_1! \ldots k_p!} (-a_1)^{k_1} \ldots (-a_p)^{k_p} \tag{B.8}$$

where the sum is to be taken over all k_r that fulfill (B.7a).

What does the restriction (B.7a) on the sum in (B.8) mean? Assume that $n = 4$ and $p \geq 4$. Then (B.7a) can be satisfied by the following five choices of the k_i

k_1	k_2	k_3	k_4
4	0	0	0
2	1	0	0
1	0	1	0
0	2	0	0
0	0	0	1 .

In addition, all k_i with $i > 4$ must equal zero.

Since k_i is multiplied by i in (B.7a), we can also say that the different k_i are "counted" i times in adding up to n. In other words, each row of the above table corresponds precisely to one *decomposition* of n into positive integers:

$$
\begin{array}{cccccll}
\text{number of} & \text{1's} & \text{2's} & \text{3's} & \text{4's} & & \\
\hline
& 4 & 0 & 0 & 0 & (1 + 1 + 1 + 1 & = 4) \\
& 2 & 1 & 0 & 0 & (1 + 1 + 2 & = 4) \\
& 1 & 0 & 1 & 0 & (1 + 3 & = 4) \\
& 0 & 2 & 0 & 0 & (2 + 2 & = 4) \\
& 0 & 0 & 0 & 1 & (4 & = 4) \,.
\end{array}
\tag{B.8a}
$$

Thus, the number of terms in (B.8) equals the number of partitions $P(n)$ of n into positive integers not exceeding p. The generating function for $P(n)$ is

$$
\prod_{n=1}^{p} (1 - x^n)^{-1} \,,
\tag{B.8b}
$$

a result that can be verified by expanding each term of the product into a geometric series.

The restricted partitions $P(n)$ are related to the unrestricted partitions $p(n)$ [B.6] by the formula

$$
P(n) = p(n) - \sum_{i=0}^{n-p-1} p(i)
\tag{B.8c}
$$

where $p(0)$ is defined to equal 1 and the empty sum is considered to be zero, i.e. for $n \le p$, $P(n) = p(n)$. Equation (B.8c) is proved by observing that for $n = p + 1$, $P(n) = p(n) - 1$ and by complete induction.

B.2 Direct Computation of Predictor Coefficients from the Cepstrum

From (B.1) and (B.2) we have

$$
\sum_{n=0}^{p} a_n z^{-n} = \exp \left[- \sum_{k=1}^{\infty} c_k z^{-k} \right] \,.
\tag{B.9}
$$

Expanding the exponential function into a power series results in

$$
\sum_{n=0}^{p} a_n z^{-n} = \sum_{m=0}^{\infty} \frac{1}{m!} \left(- \sum_{k=1}^{\infty} c_k z^{-k} \right)^m \,.
\tag{B.10}
$$

Evaluation of the mth power [B.5] yields

$$\sum_{n=0}^{p} a_n z^{-n} = \sum_{m=0}^{\infty} \sum_{n=m}^{\infty} z^{-n} \sum \frac{(-c_1)^{k_1} \cdots (-c_n)^{k_n}}{k_1! \cdots k_n!} \tag{B.11}$$

where the third sum on the right is to be taken over

$$k_1 + 2k_2 + \cdots + nk_n = n \tag{B.11a}$$

and

$$k_1 + k_2 + \cdots + k_n = m . \tag{B.11b}$$

Because of the sum over m in (B.11), the subsidiary condition (B.11b) is obviated. Equating equal powers of z^{-1} gives the desired direct relation for the predictor coefficients in terms of the cepstrum

$$a_n = \sum \frac{(-c_1)^{k_1} \cdots (-c_n)^{k_n}}{k_1! \cdots k_n!} , \tag{B.12}$$

where the sum is to be taken over all k_r subject to (B.11a).

B.3 A Simple Check

With $c_k = -1/k$, the third sum in (B.11), summed according to (B.11a) and (B.11b), equals [B.7] $1/(n!)$ times the number of permutations of n objects which have exactly m cycles [B.8]. Thus, the sum over m in (B.11) must equal 1 for *all* n. Hence,

$$a_n = 1 \ (n = 1, \cdots, p) \ \text{ if } \ c_k = -\frac{1}{k} \ (k = 1, \cdots, p) . \tag{B.13}$$

Equation (B.13) and its (generalized) inverse

$$c_n = -\frac{q^n}{n} \ (n = 1, \cdots, p) \ \text{ if } \ a_k = q^k \ (k = 1, \cdots, p) \tag{B.14}$$

also follow directly from applying the summation formula for geometric series to $A(z)$,

$$A(z) = 1 + qz^{-1} + \cdots + q^p z^{-p} = \frac{1 - q^{p+1} z^{-(p+1)}}{1 - qz^{-1}}$$

and expanding $\ln A(z)$ into a power series.

B.4 Connection with Algebraic Roots and Symmetric Functions

Equation (B.8) can also be derived as follows. If z_r are the roots of $A(z)$, then

$$A(z) = \prod_{r=1}^{p}(1 - z_r z^{-1}) \tag{B.15}$$

and

$$\ln[1/A(z)] = \sum_{r=1}^{p}\sum_{m=1}^{\infty} \frac{1}{m} z_r^m z^{-m} . \tag{B.16}$$

By inverting the order of summation one has (for uniform convergence of the sum over m, i.e., for $|z_r z^{-1}| < 1$)

$$\ln[1/A(z)] = \sum_{m=1}^{\infty} \frac{1}{m} R_m z^{-m} , \tag{B.17}$$

where the

$$R_m = \sum_{r=1}^{p} z_r^m \tag{B.17a}$$

are the "root-power sums" of $A(z)$.

By equating equal powers of z^{-1} in (B.2) and (B.17) one obtains a relation between cepstrum and root-power sums,

$$c_n = \frac{1}{n} R_n . \tag{B.18}$$

Equation (B.8) then results from Warring's formula [B.9] for the root-power sums R_m in terms of the polynomial coefficients a_k.

It is interesting to note that the recursive relation (B.3), when the cepstrum coefficients c_n are replaced by the root-power sums R_n using the identity (B.18), was already known to Newton [B.10].

According to Vieta's root theorem (see p. 102 of [B.8]), the relation between the predictor coefficients a_k and the roots z_r is as follows,

$$\begin{aligned}
z_1 + z_2 + \cdots + z_p &= -a_1 \\
z_1 z_2 + z_1 z_3 + \cdots + z_{p-1} z_p &= a_2 \\
&\vdots \\
z_1 z_2 \cdots z_p &= (-1)^p a_p .
\end{aligned} \tag{B.19}$$

Here the left-hand sides are the complete set of *elementary symmetric functions* of the roots z_r and, as (B.19) shows, they are equal, to within a factor of ± 1, to the predictor coefficients a_k. (Symmetric functions are defined as functions that do not change when the variables are arbitrarily interchanged; see p. 138 of [B.8].)

On the other hand, the root-power sums

$$z_1^m + z_2^m + \cdots + z_p^m = R_m \tag{B.19a}$$

are also symmetric functions of the roots z_r, albeit not of the elementary type. All symmetric functions can be expressed in terms of the elementary functions (p. 138 of [B.8]) and, in fact, we find our result (B.8) in the literature on symmetric functions [B.11].

B.5 Connection with Statistical Moments and Cumulants

Let $f(x)$ be a probability density function. Its characteristic function $F(y)$ is then defined as

$$F(y) = \int f(x)e^{ixy}\,dx , \tag{B.20}$$

or, by expanding the exponential,

$$F(y) = 1 + \sum_{k=1}^{\infty} \mu'_k \frac{(iy)^k}{k!} , \tag{B.21}$$

where the μ'_k are the "moments" of $f(x)$. The "cumulants" κ_n are then defined as the coefficients in the power series expansion of $\ln F(y)$ as follows:

$$\ln F(y) = \sum_{k=1}^{\infty} \kappa_k \frac{(iy)^k}{k!} . \tag{B.22}$$

If we identify iy with z^{-1} and $F(y)$ in (B.21) with $A(z)$ in (B.1), then we see that the predictor coefficients correspond to $\mu'_k/k!$ and the cepstrum coefficients to $-\kappa_n/n!$. Our main result (B.8) is then deduced by invoking the relation between statistical moments and cumulants [B.12].

B.6 Computational Complexity

The number of terms to compute c_n directly from the a_k equals $P(n)$, the number of restricted partitions of n (see above). This number may be further reduced by the following observation. It is known in probability theory that the number of terms needed to represent the cumulant κ_n by *central* moments μ_k (moments about the mean) is much smaller than the number of terms required by ordinary moments μ'_k. In fact, all terms containing μ'_1 disappear (because $\mu_1 = 0$).

How can we translate this saving to the direct computation of the cepstrum coefficients c_n from the predictor coefficients a_k? We need a transformation that makes a_1 (which corresponds to μ'_1) equal to zero. In probability theory, the required operation is a shifting of the distribution function $f(x)$ by $-\mu'_1$ or, equivalently, a multiplication of the characteristic functions $F(y)$ by $e^{-i\mu'_1 y}$. Since $F(y)$ corresponds to $A(z)$ and iy to z^{-1}, the modified predictor "polynomial" is

$$\tilde{A}(z) = A(z)\,e^{-a_1/z} \tag{B.23}$$

or by expanding the exponential

$$\tilde{A}(z) = \sum_{k=0}^{p} a_k z^{-k} \sum_{m=0}^{\infty} \frac{(-a_1)^m}{m!} z^{-m} . \tag{B.24}$$

Introducing "modified predictor coefficients" $\tilde{a}_k$ defined by

$$\tilde{A}(z) = \sum_{k=0}^{\infty} \tilde{a}_k z^{-k} \tag{B.25}$$

one obtains, by multiplying the two sums in (B.24),

$$\tilde{a}_k = \sum_{m=0}^{p} a_m \frac{(-a_1)^{k-m}}{(k-m)!} \, , \tag{B.26}$$

with $\tilde{a}_0 = 1$ and $\tilde{a}_1 = 0$, as expected.

The saving in computation, once this transformation has been performed, can be substantial. The number of terms required to express c_n in terms of the $\tilde{a}_k$ equals $p(n) - p(n-1)$, where $p(n)$ is the number of *unrestricted* partitions of n. (Because the degree of $\tilde{A}(z)$ is unlimited, the partitions become unrestricted and precisely $p(n-1)$ of the $p(n)$ partitions of n contain the integer 1 corresponding to the vanishing $\tilde{a}_1$.) For example, for a predictor polynomial $A(z)$ of order $p \geq 9$, c_9 is given by 30 terms in the a_k but requires only eight terms in the $\tilde{a}_k$. By contrast, the recursive computation of c_9 involves 45 terms. However, if *all* cepstrum coefficients up to n have to be calculated, the recursive formula becomes advantageous for $n \geq 13$. (That a crossover in efficiency occurs for some finite n follows from the fact that the number of partitions grows exponentially as n goes to infinity whereas the number of recursive terms grow only polynomially.)

The change from a_k to $\tilde{a}_k$ has a very simple effect on the logarithm of the Fourier transform or "log-spectrum" $L(\omega)$ defined by

$$L(\omega) = \ln[A(\mathrm{e}^{\mathrm{i}\omega T})] \, . \tag{B.27}$$

With (B.23) the new log-spectrum is

$$\tilde{L}(\omega) = L(\omega) - a_1 \mathrm{e}^{-\mathrm{i}\omega T} \, , \tag{B.28}$$

which is just the original log-spectrum minus its fundamental "quefrency".

Thus, to compute the cepstrum, one can use (B.8) as before, with the $\tilde{a}_k$ replacing the a_k and remembering that $c_1 = -a_1$. Since $\tilde{a}_1 = 0$, most terms drop out – which was the purpose of the transformation.

Because of Vieta's theorem and $\tilde{a}_1 = 0$, the modified polynomial $\tilde{A}(z)$ has a vanishing sum of roots. This (or the fact that $\tilde{L}(\omega)$ has no fundamental "quefrency") may be useful for signal spectrum preemphasis.

B.7 An Application of Root-Power Sums to Pitch Detection

Several years ago, Atal [B.13] proposed a method for pitch detection (fundamental frequency measurement of a speech signal) that is closely related to the root-power sums. In this method, one determines the predictor coefficients a_k for a speech segment (low-pass filtered at $1\,\mathrm{kHz}$, say) of ca. $40\,\mathrm{ms}$ duration. The order of the predictor is relatively high ($p \approx 40$). As a result, for voiced speech sounds, the linear-prediction spectrum approximates the harmonic *fine* structure of the spectrum. In other words, the pole frequencies of the predictor polynomial represent the fundamental frequency and its harmonics – and not primarily the formant frequencies as in low-order linear prediction.

If we write

$$z_r = \mathrm{e}^{\mathrm{i}\omega_r T} , \tag{B.29}$$

where T is the sampling time interval and ω_r the complex frequency of the rth root of $A(z)$, then the root-power sums are

$$R_m = \sum_{r=1}^{p} \mathrm{e}^{\mathrm{i}\omega_r mT} . \tag{B.30}$$

Thus, if the index m is considered as representing time, the R_m are the sums of p sampled complex exponentials, all being added with *equal* weight and *zero* phase at time zero (corresponding to $m = 0$).

Because the significant terms in (B.30) represent the harmonic frequencies, the magnitude of R_M, if MT equals the pitch period, will be relatively large. The reason is that for $m = M$ all such terms in (B.30) add in phase again (the way they started out at $m = 0$). If p exceeds the number of harmonics, then the excess terms in (B.30) will not necessarily coincide with any harmonic frequency but such excess terms will also have large imaginary parts of ω_r (i.e., will be highly damped) so that they contribute little to the value of R_M. This method has been included in a comparative study of various pitch detectors [B.14].

There are similarities between pitch detectors based on root-power sums and those based on *autocorrelation* ("matched filter") analysis. However, an important distinction between the two is that in the autocorrelation function individual components ("harmonics") are added with their amplitudes *squared* while in the root-power sums, the amplitudes of all terms are equal. Thus, root-power sums act as *spectrum flatteners* ("inverse filters"), thereby avoiding the problems in pitch detection resulting from nonflat spectra due to formant structure, vocal source spectrum, lip radiation, etc. [B.15].

How do *cepstrum* pitch detectors fit into this picture? Because of the identity $c_m = R_m/m$, pitch detectors based on the cepstrum and root-power sums are very similar. In fact, they are identical except for the weighting factor m. Both eliminate the formant (and spectrum envelope) structure from the signal spectrum and thereby enhance the spectrum fine structure that contains the pitch information. But in the cepstrum the higher "quefrencies" are attenuated by a factor $1/m$. This is not necessarily advantageous. In fact, it was found that multiplying the cepstrum c_m by the "quefrency" m

often gives better results. It is, therefore, legitimate to say that cepstrum pitch detectors work well, especially when a quefrency weighting factor m is included because of the close connection with root-power sums which act as an inverse filter flattening the spectrum and setting the phases of all components to zero.

References

Chapter 1 — Introduction

1.1 H.W. Dudley: Remaking Speech. J. Acoust. Soc. Am. **11**, 169–177 (1939)

1.2 M.D. Fagen (ed.): *A History of Engineering and Science in the Bell System: National Service in War and Peace (1925–1975)* Sect. IV. Secure Speech Transmission (pp. 291–317) (Bell Telephone Laboratories, Murray Hill, New Jersey, 1978)

1.3 M.R. Schroeder: *Speech and Speaker Recognition* (Karger, Basel 1985)

1.4 R.H. Bolt, F.S. Cooper, E.E. David, Jr., P.B. Denes, J.M. Pickett, K.N. Stevens: Speaker identification by speech spectrograms: A scientists' view of its reliability for legal purposes. J. Acoust. Soc. Am. **47**, 597–612 (1970)

1.5 J.C.R. Licklider: The intelligibility of amplitude-dichotomized, time-quantized, speech waves. J. Acoust. Am. **22**, 820–823 (1950)

1.6 M.R. Schroeder: Improved quasi-stereophony and "colorless" artificial reverberation. J. Acoust. Soc. Am. **33**, 1061–1064 (1961)

1.7 P. Marcou, New methods for speech transmission. In J. Daguet: New methods for speech transmission. In E.C. Cherry (ed.): *Proc. 3rd Symp. on Info. Theory* (Butterworth, London 1956)

1.8 B.P. Bogert: The vobanc – a two-to-one speech bandwidth reduction scheme. J. Acoust. Soc. Am. **28**, 399–404 (1956)

1.9 M.R. Schroeder, B.F. Logan, A.J. Prestigiacomo: New methods for speech analysis, synthesis and bandwidth compression. *Proc. Stockholm Speech Comm. Seminar* (Royal Institute of Technology, Stockholm 1962)

1.10 M.R. Schroeder: Correlation techniques for speech bandwidth compression. J. Audio Eng. Soc. **10**, 163–166 (1962)

1.11 M.R. Schroeder, S. Hanauer: Interpolation of data with continuous speech signals. Bell Syst. Tech. J. **46**, 1931–1933 (1967)

1.12 J.E. Miller: Decapitation and recapitation, a study of voice quality. J. Acoust. Soc. Am. **36**, 2002 (1964)

1.13 N. Guttman, J.R. Nelson: An instrument that creates some artificial speech spectra for the severely hard of hearing. Am. Ann. Deaf **112**, 295–302 (1968)

1.14 M.R. Schroeder: unpublished memorandum

1.15 S.F. Boll: Speech enhancement in the 1980s: Noise suppression with pattern matching. In S. Furui, M.M. Sondhi (eds.): *Advanced Speech Signal Processing* (Marcel Dekker, New York 1992) pp. 309–325

1.16 H.W. Strube: Separation of several speakers recorded by two microphones (cocktail-party processing). Signal Processing **3**, 355–364 (1981)

1.17 M.R. Schroeder: Improvement of feedback stability of public address systems by frequency shifting. J. Audio Eng. Soc. **10** (2), 108–109 (1962)

1.18 M.R. Schroeder: Electronic suppression of reverberation. J. Acoust. Soc. Am.
41, 1579 (1967)

Chapter 2 — A Brief History of Speech

2.1 H. Dudley, T.H. Tarnocy: The speaking machine of Wolfgang von Kempelen.
J. Acoust. Soc. Am. **22**, 151–166 (1950)
2.2 W. von Kempelen: *Mechanismus der menschlichen Sprache nebst der
Beschreibung seiner sprechenden Maschine* (Wien 1791)
2.3 M.R. Schroeder, H.W. Strube: Flat-Spectrum Speech. J. Acoust. Soc. Am.
79, 1580–1583 (1986)
2.4 H. v. Helmholtz: *Die Lehre von den Tonempfindungen als physiologische
Grundlage für die Theorie der Musik.* (F. Vieweg & Sohn, Braunschweig
1870), English translation by A.J. Ellis: *On the Sensations of Tone* (Dover,
New York 1954) pp. 103–123
2.5 J.W.S. Rayleigh: *The Theory of Sound.* **Vol. II** (Dover, New York 1945)
2.6 A.M. Bell: *Visible Speech – The Sciences of Universal Alphabetics* (Van Nostrand, New York 1867)
2.7 J. Brooks: *Telephone: The First Hundred Years.* (Harper & Row, New York
1975)
2.8 A.G. Bell: *Mechanisms of Speech,* 2nd ed. (1907)
2.9 J.E. Hyde: *The Telephone Book.* (Henry Regnery, Chicago 1976)
2.10 A.G. Bell: Prehistoric telephone days. Natl. Geographic **14**, 223–242 (1922)
2.11 J.L. Flanagan: *Speech Analysis Synthesis and Perception,* 2nd ed. (Springer,
Berlin, Heidelberg 1972)
2.12 J.L. Kelly, C. Lochbaum: Speech Synthesis in *Proc. Speech Comm. Seminar*
(Royal Inst. Tech., Stockholm 1962)
2.13 G. Ungeheuer: *Elemente einer akustischen Theorie der Vokalartikulation.*
(Springer, Berlin 1962)
2.14 C. Stumpf: *Die Sprachlaute.* (Springer, Berlin 1926)
2.15 E.A. Meyer: *Untersuchungen über Lautbildung.* (Marburg 1910), Vietor
Festschrift
2.16 O.G. Russel: *The Vowels.* (Ohio State Univ. Press, Columbus 1928)
2.17 O.G. Russel: The mechanisms of speech. J. Acoust. Soc. Am. **1**, 83–109 (1929)
2.18 G. Fant: *Acoustic Theory of Speech Production,* 2nd ed. (Mouton, The Hague
1970)
2.19 R. Paget: *Human Speech.* (Hartcourt, London 1930)
2.20 A.M. Noll, M.R. Schroeder: Short-time 'cepstrum' pitch detection. J. Acoust.
Soc. Am. **36**, 1030(A) (1964). See also A.M. Noll, M.R. Schroeder: *Real
Time Cepstrum Analyzer* (U.S. Patent 3,566,035, filed July 19, 1969, issued
February 23, 1971)
2.21 J. Obata, T. Teshima: On the properties of Japanese vowels. Jap. J. Physics
8 (1932)
2.22 E. Thienhaus: Neuere Versuche zur Klangfarbe und Lautstärke von Vokalen.
Zeitschrift f. Physik **15**, 637 (1934)
2.23 M. Grützmacher: Eine neue Methode zur Klanganalyse. ENT 4, 533 (1927)
2.24 W. Apel (ed.): *Harvard Dictionary of Music* (Harvard University Press, Cambridge, Massachusetts, 1970)
2.25 F.S. Cooper, P.C. Delattre, A.M. Liberman, J.M. Borst, L.J. Gerstman: Some
experiments on the perception of synthetic speech sounds.
2.26 R.K. Potter, G.A. Kopp, H.G. Kopp: *Visible Speech* (Dover, New York 1966)

2.27 R.H. Bolt, F.S. Cooper, Jr., E.E. David, Jr., P.B. Denes, J.M. Pickett, K.N. Stevens: Speaker identification by speech spectrograms: A scientists' view of its reliability for legal purposes. J. Acoust. Soc. Am. **47**, 597–612 (1970)

2.28 S. Kiritani, O. Fujimura, H. Ishida: Computer controlled radiography for observation of articulatory movement. *Proc. 3rd Symp. Information Theory* paper 21–C–13 (Budapest 1971)

2.29 G. Borg: Acta Math. **78**, 1–96 (1946)

2.30 M.R. Schroeder: Determination of the geometry of the human vocal tract by acoustic measurements. J. Acoust. Soc. Am. **41**, 1002–1010 (1967)

2.31 K. Ishizaka, J.L. Flanagan: Synthesis of voiced sounds from a two-mass model of the vocal cords. Bell Systems Tech. J. **51**, 1233–1269 (1962). See also M.M. Sondhi: Measurement of the Glottal Waveform. *J. Acoust. Soc. Am.* **57** 228–232 (1975)

2.32 T. Houtgast, H.J.M. Steeneken: The modulation transfer function in room acoustics as a predictor of speech intelligibility. Acustica **28** 66 (1973)

2.33 M.R. Schroeder: Modulation transfer functions: Definition and measurement. Acustica **49** 179–182 (1981)

2.34 H.P. Kramer, M.V. Mathews: A linear coding for transmitting a set of correlated signals. IRE Trans. Inform. Theory **IT-2**, 41–46 (1956)

2.35 M.R. Schroeder: New results concerning monaural phase sensitivity. J. Acoust. Soc. Am. **31**, 1579(A) J5 (1959), more details on this work can be found in J.R. Pierce, "Some work on hearing", Amer. Scientist **48**, 40-45 (1960)

2.36 W. Hess: *Pitch Determination of Speech Signals. Algorithms and Devices.* (Springer, Berlin, Heidelberg 1983)

2.37 J.L. Flanagan, R.M. Golden: Phase vocoder. Bell Syst. Tech. J. **45**, 1493–1509 (1966)

2.38 J.L. Flanagan: A difference limen for vowel formant frequencies. J. Acoust. Soc. Am. **27**, 613–617 (1955)

2.39 E.S. Weibel: Vowel synthesis by means of resonant circuits. J. Acoust. Soc. Am. **27**, 858 ff (1955)

2.40 M.R. Schroeder: Correlation techniques for speech bandwidth compression. J. Audio Eng. **10**, 163–166 (1962)

2.41 M.R. Schroeder, E.E. David, Jr.: A vocoder for transmitting 10 kc/s speech over a 3.5 kc/s channel. Acustica **10**, 35–43 (1960)

2.42 M.R. Schroeder, J.L. Flanagan, E.A. Lundry: Bandwidth compression of speech by analytic signal rooting. Proc. IEEE **55**, 396–401 (1967)

2.43 M.R. Schroeder, B.F. Logan, A.J. Prestigiacomo: New methods of speech analysis–synthesis and bandwidth compression. *Proc. 4th Internat. Congress. Acoustics* (Copenhagen 1962)

2.44 B.S. Atal, M.R. Schroeder: Predictive coding of speech signals. *Proc. IEEE Conf. on Communication and Processing* 360–361 (1967)

2.45 B.S. Atal, M.R. Schroeder: Adaptive predictive coding of speech signals. Bell Syst. Tech. J. **49**, 1973–1986 (1970)

2.46 F. Itakura, S. Saito: Speech analysis–synthesis system based on the partial autocorrelation coefficient. Presented at Acoust. Soc. of Japan Meeting (1969)

2.47 M.R. Schroeder, B.S. Atal, J.L. Hall: Optimizing digital speech coders by exploiting masking properties of the human ear. J. Acoust. Soc. Am. **66**, 1647–1652 (1979)

2.48 B.S. Atal, M.R. Schroeder: Predictive coding of speech signals and subjective error criteria. IEEE Trans. Acoust., Speech, Signal Processing **ASSP-27**, 247–254 (1979)

2.49 M.R. Schroeder, B.S. Atal: Stochastic coding of speech signals at very low bit rates: the importance of speech perception. Speech Communication **4**, 155–162 (1985)

2.50 M.G. Rahim, C.C. Goodyear, W.B. Kleijn, J. Schroeter, M. Sondhi: On the use of neural networks in articulatory speech synthesis. J. Acoust. Soc. Am. **93**, 1109–1121 (1993)

2.51 M. Paping, H.W. Strube, T. Gramss: Modulation-frequency encoding of speech with application to neural speech recognizers. in *Proc. Int. Conf. Applications of Neural Networks (ICANN'93*, Amsterdam), ed. by S. Gielen, B. Kappen, 422 (Springer, London 1993)

2.52 L.R. Rabiner, B.H. Juang: An introduction to hidden Markov models. IEEE ASSP Magazine **3** (1), 4–16 (1986)

2.53 C.K. Chui: *An Introduction to Wavelets.* (Academic Press, Boston 1992)

2.54 M.R. Schroeder: *Fractals, Chaos, Power Laws: Minutes from an Infinite Paradise* (Freeman, New York 1991)

Chapter 3 — Speech Recognition

3.1 C.-H. Lee, F.K. Soong, K.K. Paliwal: *Automatic Speech and Speaker Recognition* (Kluwer, Boston 1996)

3.2 K.H. Davis, R. Biddulph, S. Balashek: Automatic recognition of spoken digits. J. Acoust. Soc. Am. **24**, 637–642 (1952)

3.3 L.R. Rabiner, B.-H. Juang: *Fundamentals of Speech Recognition* (Prentice–Hall, Englewood Cliffs, New Jersey, 1993)

3.4 S.E. Levinson, L.R. Rabiner: A Task-Oriented Conversational Mode Speech Understanding System, in M.R. Schroeder (ed.): *Speech and Speaker Recognition* (Karger, Basel 1985)

3.5 R.K. Potter, G.A. Kopp, H.C. Green: *Visible Speech* (D. van Nostrand Co., New York 1947)

3.6 R.H. Bolt, F.S. Cooper, E.E. David, Jr., P.B. Denes, J.M. Pickett, K.N. Stevens: Speaker identification by speech spectrograms: A scientists' view of its reliability for legal purposes. J. Acoust. Soc. Am. **47**, 597–612 (1970)

3.7 S. Furui: An Overview of Speaker Recognition Technology, in [3.1] pp. 31–56

3.8 H.W. Strube, D. Helling, A. Krause, M.R. Schroeder: Word and Speaker Recognition Based on Entire Words, in M.R. Schroeder (ed.): *Speech and Speaker Recognition* (Karger, Basel 1985)

3.9 E.J. Gumbel (ed.): *The Emil J. Gumbel Collection: Political Papers of an Anti-Nazi Scholar in Weimar and Exile, 1914–1966* (1990). See also S. Fleishman: *Gumbel, the Fire-Breathing Dragon* (1970)

3.10 L.R. Rabiner, B.H. Juang: An introduction to hidden Markov models. IEEE ASSP Magazine (January 1986)

3.11 J. Glimm, J. Impagliazzo, I. Singer (eds.): *The Legacy of John von Neumann* (Proceedings of Symposia in Pure Mathematics), **50** (American Mathematical Society, Washington 1988)

3.12 T. Gramss, S. Borholdt, M. Gross, M. Mitchell, T. Pellizzari (eds.): *Non-Standard Computation* (Wiley–VCH, Weinheim 1998.)

3.13 W.S. McCulloch: *The Complete Works of Warren S. McCulloch* (Intersystems Publications, Salinas, California, 1993)

3.14 F. Rosenblatt: *Principles of Neurodynamics* (Spartan Books, New York 1962)

3.15 D.E. Rumelhart, J.L. McClelland: *Parallel Distributed Processing* (MIT Press, Cambridge, Massachusetts, 1986)

3.16 T. Kohonen: *Self-Organizing Maps*, 2nd ed. (Springer, Berlin, Heidelberg 1995)

3.17 J.J. Hopfield: Neural networks and physical systems with emergent collective computational abilities. Proc. Nat. Acad. Sciences, USA **79** 2554–2558 (1982)

3.18 L.P. Yaroslavsky: *Digital Picture Processing: An Introduction* (Springer, Berlin, Heidelberg 1985)

3.19 J.-C. Junqua, J.-P. Haton (eds.): *Special Issue on Robust Speech Recognition.* Speech Communication **25**, 1–192 (1998)

3.20 B.E.D. Kingsbury, N. Morgan, S. Greenberg: Robust speech recognition using the modulation spectrogram. Speech Communication (Special Issue on Robust Speech Recognition) **25**, 3–27 (1998)

3.21 H. Hermansky: Should recognizers have ears? Speech Communication (Special Issue) **25**, 3–27 (1998)

3.22 B. Kollmeyer, R. Koch: Speech enhancement based on physiological and psycoacoustic models of modulation perception and binaural ineraction. J. Acoust. Soc. Am. **95**, 1593–1602 (1994)

3.23 T. Houtgast, H.J.M. Steeneken: A review of the MTF concept in room acoustics and its use for estimating speed intelligibility. J. Acoust. Soc. Am. **77**, 1069–1077, (1985)

3.24 M.R. Schroeder: Modulation transfer function: definition and measurement: Acustica **49**, 179–182 (1980)

Chapter 4 — Speech Compression

4.1 H.W. Dudley: Remaking speech. J. Acoust. Soc. Am. **11**, 169–177 (1939)

4.2 M.D. Fagen (ed.): *A History of Engineering and Science in the Bell System: National Service in War and Peace (1925–1975)* Sect. IV. Secure Speech Transmission (pp. 291–317) (Bell Telephone Laboratories, Murray Hill, New Jersey, 1978)

4.3 R.L. Miller: personal communication.

4.4 B.M. Oliver, J.R. Pierce, C.E. Shannon: The philosophy of PCM. Proc. IEEE **36**, 1324–1331 (1948)

4.5 N.J.A. Sloane, A.D. Wyner: *Claude Elwood Shannon – Collected Papers* (IEEE Press, New York 1993)

4.6 C.E. Shannon: Communication theory of secrecy systems. Bell Syst. Tech. J. **28**, 656–715 (1949)

4.7 R.L. Miller, personal communication.

4.8 L.R. Rabiner, M.J. Cheng, A.E. Rosenberg, C.A. McGonegal: A comparative performance study of several pitch detection algorithms. IEEE Trans. Acoust. Speech, and Signal Proc. **ASSP-24**, 399–418 (1976)

4.9 A.M. Noll, M.R. Schroeder: Short time 'cepstrum' pitch detection. J. Acoust. Soc. Am. **36**, 1030 (1967). See also: A.M. Noll, M.R. Schroeder: *Real Time Cepstrum Analyzer* (U.S. Patent 3,566,035, filed July 17, 1969, issued February 23, 1971)

4.10 M.R. Schroeder (unpublished)

4.11 M.R. Schroeder: Period histogram and product spectrum: New methods for fundamental frequency detection. J. Acoust. Soc. Am. **43**, 829–834 (1968). See also R.L. Miller: Performance characteristic of an experimental harmonic identification pitch extraction (HIPEX) system. J. Acoust. Soc. Am. **47**, 1593–1601 (1970)

4.12 J.L. Flanagan: Bandwidth and channel capacity necessary to transmit the formant information of speech. J. Acoust. Soc. Am. **28**, 592–596 (1956)

4.13 M.R. Schroeder, B.F. Logan, A.J. Prestigiacomo: New methods for speech analysis–synthesis and bandwidth compression. Proc. Stockholm Speech Comm. Seminar, Royal Institute of Technology (KTH), Stockholm 1962.

4.14 M.R. Schroeder: Correlation techniques for speech bandwidth compression. J. Audio Eng. Soc. **10**, 163–166 (1962)

4.15 J.L. Flanagan, R.M. Golden: Phase vocoder. Bell Syst. Tech. J. **45**, 1493–1509 (1966)

4.16 M.R. Schroeder: Vocoders: Analysis and synthesis of speech. Proc. IEEE **55**, 396–401 (1967)

4.17 J.L. Flanagan: *Speech Analysis, Synthesis and Perception*, 2nd ed. (Springer, Berlin, Heidelberg 1972)

4.18 E.E. David, Jr., M.V. Mathews, H.S. McDonald: Description of results of experiments with speech using digital computer simulation. Proc. Natl. Elect Conf. pp. 766–775 (1958)

4.19 J.L. Kelly, Jr., C. Lochbaum, V.A. Vyssotsky: A block diagram compiler. Bell System Tech. J. **40**, 669–676 (1961)

4.20 M.V. Mathews: Extremal coding for speech transmission. IRE Trans. Inform. Theory **IT-5**, 129–136 (1959)

4.21 M.R. Schroeder, B.S. Atal: Computer simulation of sound transmission in rooms. IEEE Internatl. Convention Record, Part 7 (1963)

4.22 B.S. Atal, M.R. Schroeder: Predictive coding of speech signals. Proc. Sixth Internatl. Congr. of Acoustics, Tokyo, paper C-5-4 (1968). Originally published in *Proc. 1967 IEEE Conf. on Communication and Processing*, pp. 360–361 (1967)

4.23 B.S. Atal, M.R. Schroeder: Adaptive predictive coding of speech signals. Bell Syst. Tech. J. **49**, 1973–1986 (1970)

4.24 M.R. Schroeder, B.S. Atal, J.L. Hall: Optimizing digital speech coders by exploiting masking properties of the human ear. J. Acoust. Soc. Am. **66**, 1647–1652

4.25 B.S. Atal, M.R. Schroeder: Predictive coding of speech signals and subjective error criteria. IEEE Trans. Acoust., Speech, Signal Processing **ASSP-27**, 247–254 (1979)

4.26 B.S. Atal, M.R. Schroeder: Stochastic coding of speech signals at very low bit rates. *Proc. Internatl. Conf. on Communication* (North–Holland, Amsterdam 1984, pp. 1610–1613). See also A. Gersho, R.M. Gray: Vector Quantization and Signal Compression (Kluwer Academic, Boston 1992)

4.27 D. Sinha, J.D. Johnson, S. Dorward, S.R. Quackenbush: The perceptional audio coder. In V.K. Machisetti, D.B. Williams: *The Digital Signal Processing Handbook* pp. 42-1 to 42-17. (IEEE Press, New York 1998)

4.28 J.D. Markel, A.H. Gray, Jr.: *Linear Prediction of Speech* (Springer, Berlin, Heidelberg 1976)

4.29 F. Itakura, S. Saito: Speech analysis–synthesis systems based on the partial correlation coeficients (Acoustic Soc. of Japan Meeting, Tokyo 1969)

4.30 B.S. Atal, S.L. Hanauer: Speech analysis and synthesis by linear predition of the speech wave. J. Acoust. Soc. Am. **50**, 637–655 (1971)

4.31 M.R. Schroeder, B.S. Atal: Rate distortion theory and predictive coding. *Proc. IEEE Internatl. Conf. on Acoustics, Speech and Signal Processing* pp. 201–204 (Atlanta 1981)

4.32 W. Hess: *Pitch Determination of Speech Signals* (Springer, Berlin, Heidelberg 1983)

4.33 M.R. Schroeder, E.E. David, Jr.: A vocoder for transmitting 10 kc/s speech over a 3.5 kc/s channel. Acustica **10**, 35–43 (1960)

4.34 M.M. Sondhi: New methods for pitch extraction. *Proc. Conf. on Speech Communication and Processing* (IEEE Audio and Electoacoustics Group, Cambridge, Massachusetts, 1967)

4.35 B.S. Atal, J.R. Remde: A new model of LPC excitation for producing natural-sounding speech at low bit rates. Proc. IEEE Internatl. Conf. on Acoustics, Speech and Signal Processing **1**, 614–617 (1982)

4.36 M.R. Schroeder: Die statistischen Parameter der Frequenzkurven von grossen Räumen. Acustica **4**, 594–600 (1954). English translation: M.R. Schroeder: Statistical parameters of the frequency response of large rooms. J. Audio Eng. Soc. **35**, 299–306 (1987)

4.37 J.B. Anderson, J.B. Bodie: Tree encoding of speech. IEEE Trans. Inform. Theory **IT-21**, 379–387 (1975). See also [4.31] and M.R. Schroeder, B.S. Atal: Speech coding using efficient block codes. Proc. IEEE Internatl. Conf. on Acoustics, Speech and Signal Processing. **3**, 1668–1671 (1982)

4.38 M.R. Schroeder, B.S. Atal: Code-excited linear prediction (CELP) – high quality speech at very low bit rates. *Proc. IEEE Internatl. Conf. on Acoustics, Speech, and Signal Processing* (1985) pp. 937–940. See also M.R. Schroeder, B.S. Atal: Code-excited linear prediction. Speech Communication **4**, 155–162 (1985)

4.39 M.R. Schroeder, N.J.A. Sloane: New permutation codes using Hadamard unscrambling. IEEE Trans. on Inform. Theory IT-33, 144–146 (1987)

4.40 J.L. Flanagan, M.R. Schroeder, B.S. Atal, R.E. Crochiere, N.S. Jayant, J.M. Tribolet: Speech coding. IEEE Trans. on Communications **COM-27**, No. 4 (1979)

4.41 J. Max: Quantizing for minimum distortion. IRE Trans. Inform. Theory **IT-6**, 7–12 (1960). See also S.P. Lloyd: Least squares quantization in PCM: IEEE Trans. on Information Theory **IT–28**, 127–135 (1982)

4.42 F. DeJager: Delta modulation: A method of PCM transmission using a one-unit code. Philips Res. Rep. **7**, 442–466 (1952)

4.43 C.C. Cutler: Differential Pulse Code Modulation. (U.S. Patent 2,605,361, filed June 29, 1950, patented July 29, 1952)

4.44 N.S. Jayant: Adaptive quantization with a one-word memory. Bell Syst. Tech. J. **52**, 1119–1144 (1973)

4.45 D.J. Goodman, J.L. Flanagan: Direct digital conversion between linear and adaptive delta modulation formats. *Proc. IEEE Int. Commun. Conf.*, Montreal, Canada, (1971)

4.46 P. Cummiskey, N.S. Jayant, J.L. Flanagan: Adaptive quantization in differential PCM coding of speech. Bell Syst. Tech. J. **52**, 1105–1118 (1973)

4.47 R.E. Crochiere, S.A. Webber, J.L. Flanagan: Digital coding of speech in subbands. Bell Syst. Tech. J. **55**, 1069–1085 (1976)

4.48 M. Bosi, K. Brandenburg, S. Quackenbush, L. Fielder, K. Akagiri, H. Fuchs, M. Dietz, J. Herre, G. Davidson, Y. Oikawa: ISO/IEC MPEG-2 Advanced Audio Coding. J. Audio Eng. Soc. **45**, 789–814 (1997)

4.49 J.S. Byrnes, B. Saffari, H.S. Shapiro: Energy spreading and data compression using the Prometheus orthogonal set. *Proc. IEEE DSP Conf.* Locn, Norway (1996)

4.50 M.R. Schroeder: *Number Theory in Science and Communication*, 3rd ed. (Springer, Berlin, Heidelberg 1997)

4.51 J.S. Byrnes: A low complexity energy spreading transform coder. Proc. Conf. Haifa (1995)

4.52 A. Gersho: Advances in Speech and Audio Compression. Proc. IEEE **82**, 900–918 (1994)

Chapter 5 — Speech Synthesis

5.1 J.P.H. van Santen, W. Sproat, J. Olive (eds.): *Progress in Speech Synthesis* (Springer, New York 1996)

5.2 C.E. Shannon: Prediction and entropy of printed English. Bell Syst. Tech. J. **30**, 50–64 (1951)

5.3 S.G. Nooteboom: Text and prosody. In [5.1], pp 431–434 ff See also M.E. Beckman: Speech models and speech synthesis. In [5.1], pp 185–209 ff

5.4 T. Sejnowski, C.R. Rosenberg: Parallel networks that learn to pronounce English text. Complex Systems **1**, 145–168 (1986)

5.5 D. Kahn, M.J. Macchi: Recent approaches to modeling the glottal source. In [5.1] pp 3–7 ff

5.6 J.P. Olive: Concatenative synthesis. In [5.1], pp 261–262 ff

5.7 J. Schroeter: Articulatory synthesis and visual speech. in [5.1], pp 179–184 ff

5.8 O. Fujimura: An analysis of English syllables as cores and affixes. Zeitschrift für Phonetik **4/5** 471–476 (1979)

5.9 L.H. Nakatani, K.D. Dukes: Sensitive test of speech communication quality. J. Acoust. Soc. Am. **53**, 1083 ff (1973)

Chapter 6 — Speech Production

6.1 S. Pinker: *The Language Instinct: How the Mind Creates Language* (William Morrow, New York 1994)

6.2 M.E. Beckman: Speech models and speech synthesis. In [6.15], pp 185–209 (1996)

6.3 T. Guiard-Marigny, A. Adjoudani, C. Benoît: 3D models of the lips and jaw. In [6.15], pp 247–258 (1996)

6.4 A. Rosenberg: Effect of pulse shape on the quality of natural sounds. J. Acoust. Soc. Am. **49**, 583–590 (1971)

6.5 J. Sundberg: *The Science of the Singing Voice* (Northern Illinois University Press, DeKalb 1987)

6.6 See Ref. [6.5] pp 35 ff

6.7 R.L. Miller: Nature of the vocal cord wave. J. Acoust. Soc. Am. **31**, 667–677 (1959)

6.8 I. Steineke, H. Herzel: Bifurcations in an asymmetric vocal-fold model. J. Acoust. Soc. Am. **97**, 1874–1884 (1995)

6.9 H. Herzel, C. Knudsen: Bifurcations in a vocal fold model. Nonlinear Dynamics **7**, 53–64 (1995)

6.10 G. Fant: *Acoustic Theory of Speech Production* (Mouton, The Hague 1969)

6.11 J.L. Flanagan: *Speech Analysis, Synthesis, and Perception*, 2nd ed. (Springer, Berlin, Heidelberg 1972)

6.12 G.E. Peterson, H.L. Barney: Control methods in a study of vowels. J. Acoust. Soc. Am. **24**, 175–184 (1952)

6.13 J.P. Olive, A. Greenwood, J. Coleman: *Acoustic Phonetics of American English* (Springer, New York 1993)

6.14 D.H. Whalen: Coarticulation is largely planned. J. of Phonetics **18**, 3–35 (1990)

6.15 J.P.H. van Santen, W. Sproat, J. Olive (eds.): *Progress in Speech Synthesis* (Springer, New York 1996)

6.16 S.E.G. Öhman: Coarticulation in VCV utterances: spectrographic measurements. J. Acoust. Soc. Am. **39**, 151–168 (1965)

6.17 L.L. Beranek: *Acoustics* (McGraw–Hill, New York 1954)

6.18 E.S. Weibel: personal communication

6.19 A.G. Webster: Acoustical impedance and the theory of horns. Proc. National Academy of Sciences, U.S. **5**, 275–289 (1919)

6.20 G. Ungeheuer: *Elemente einer akustischen Theorie der Vokalartikulation* (Springer, Berlin, Heidelberg 1962). Ein Stein, ein *Meilen*stein.

6.21 M.R. Schroeder: Determination of the geometry of the human vocal tract by acoustic measurements. J. Acoust. Soc. Am. **41**, 1002–1010 (1967)

6.22 B.S. Atal, J.J. Chang, M.V. Mathews, J.W. Tukey: Inversion of articulatory-to-acoustic transformation in the vocal tract by a computer sorting technique. J. Acoust. Soc. Am. **63**, 1535–1555.

6.23 L.R. Rabiner, R.W. Schafer: *Digital Processing of Speech Signals* (Prentice Hall, Englewood Cliffs, New Jersey, 1978)

Chapter 7 — The Speech Signal

7.1 J.P. Olive, A. Greenwood, J. Coleman: *Acoustic Phonetics of American English* (Springer, New York 1993)

7.2 R. Jacobson, G. Fant, M. Halle: *Preliminaries to Speech Analysis: The Distinctive Features and Their Correlates* (MIT Press, Cambridge, Massachusetts, 1951)

7.3 N. Chomsky, M. Halle: *The Sound Pattern of English* (Harper and Row, New York 1968)

Chapter 8 — Hearing

8.1 W.M. Hartmann: *Signals, Sound, and Sensation* (Springer, New York 1996)

8.2 E. Zwicker, H. Fastl: *Psychoacoustics* (Springer, Berlin, Heidelberg 1990)

8.3 M.R. Schroeder, B.S. Atal, J.L. Hall: Optimizing digital speech coders by exploiting masking properties of the human ear. J. Acoust. Soc. Am. **66**, 1647–1652 (1979)

8.4 M.R. Schroeder, B.S. Atal: Stochastic coding of speech signals at very low bit rates: the importance of speech perception. Speech Communication **4**, 155–162 (1985)

8.5 T. Lucretius: *The Nature of the Universe*, book IV (Penguin, Baltimore, Maryland, 1952)

8.6 G. Tartini: *Trattato di Musica Seconda la Vera Scienza dell'Armonia* (Padua, Italy, 1754)

8.7 T. Seebeck: Über die Definition des Tones. Ann. Phys. Chem. **63**, 353–368 (1844)

8.8 J.F. Schouten: The perception of pitch. Phillips Tech. Rev. **5**, 286–294 (1940)

8.9 J.F. Schouten, R.J. Ritsma, B.L. Cardozo: Pitch of the residue. J. Acoust. Soc. Amer. **34**, 1418–1424 (1962)

8.10 H. Helmholtz: *On the Sensation of Tone* (Dover, New York 1954)

8.11 G. von Békésy: *Experiments in Hearing* (McGraw–Hill, New York 1960)

8.12 W.S. Rhode: Observations of the vibration of the basilar membrane in squirrel monkeys using the Mössbauer technique. J. Acoust. Soc. Amer. **49**, 1218–1231 (1971)

8.13 H. Levitt: Transformed up-down methods in psychophysics. J. Acoust., Soc. Am. **49**, 167–177 (1971)

8.14 B.C.J. Moore: *An Introduction to the Psychology of Hearing*, 2nd ed. (Academic Press, London 1989)

8.15 J. Blauert: *Spatial Hearing* (MIT Press, Cambridge, Massachusetts 1983)

8.16 E.F. Evans, J.P. Wilson (eds.): *Psychophysics and Physiology of Hearing* (Academic Press, London 1977). International symposium.

8.17 R.M. Warren: *Auditory Perception* (Pergamon Press, New York 1982)

8.18 E. Zwicker, E. Terhardt: Analytical expression for critical baudrate and critical bandwidth as a function of frequency. J. Acoust. Soc. Am. **68**, 1523–1525 (1980)

8.19 M.R. Schroeder: An integrable model for the basilar membrane. J. Acoust. Soc. Amer. **53**, 429–434 (1973)

8.20 H. Traunmüller: Analytical expression for the tonotopic sensory scale. J. Acoust. Soc. Am. **88**, 97–100 (1990). See also [8.18]

8.21 J.P. Wilson, J.R. Johnstone: Capacitive probe measures of basilar membrane vibration. In B.L. Cardozo (ed.): *Hearing Theory* (Institute for Perception Research, Eindhoven, the Netherlands, 1972) pp. 172–181

8.22 D.T. Kemp: Stimulated acoustic emissions from within the human auditory system. J. Acoust. Soc. Am. **64**, 1386–1391 (1978)

8.23 E. Zwicker: "Otoacoustic" emissions in a nonlinear hardware model with feedback. J. Acoust. Soc. Am. **80**, 146–153 (1986)

8.24 A. Flok: Excitatory and inhibitory events in hair cells. J. Acoust. Soc. Am. **54**, 293 (1973)

8.25 M.R. Schroeder, J.L. Hall, Jr.: A model for mechanical to neural transduction in the auditory receptor. J. Acoust. Soc. Am. **55**, 1055–1060 (1974)

8.26 M.R. Schroeder: Vocoders: Analysis and synthesis of speech. Proc. IEEE **54**, 720–734 (1966)

8.27 M.R. Schroeder: Synthesis of low-peakfactor signals and binary sequences with low autocorrelation. IEEE Trans. Inform. Theory **IT-16**, 85–89 (1970)

8.28 M.R. Schroeder: New results concerning monaural phase sensibility. J. Acoust. Soc. Am. **31**, 1579 (1959)

8.29 J.H. Craig, L.A. Jeffress: Effect of phase on the quantity of a two-component tone. J. Acoust. Soc. Am. **34** 1752–1760 (1962)

8.30 S.S. Stevens: *Psychophysics* (Wiley, New York 1975)

8.31 M.R. Schroeder: *Fractals, Chaos, Power Laws: Minutes from an Infinite Paradise* (W.H. Freeman, New York 1991)

Chapter 9 — Binaural Hearing

9.1 D. Lehnhardt: *Physiologie der Schalleitung* (G. Thieme, Stuttgart 1979)

9.2 J. Blauert: Sound localization in the median plane. Acustica **22**, 205–213 (1969)

9.3 M.B. Gardner: Distance estimation of $0°$ or apparent $0°$-oriented speech signals in anechoic space. J. Acoust. Soc. Am. **45**, 47–53 (1969)

9.4 M.B. Gardner: Historical background of the Haas and/or precedence effect. J. Acoust. Soc. Am. **43**, 1243–1248 (1968)

9.5 J. Blauert: *Spatial Hearing* (MIT Press, Cambridge, Massachusetts 1983)

9.6 V. Mellert, K.F. Siebrasse, S. Mehrgardt: Determination of the transfer function of the external ear by impulse response measurements. J. Acoust. Soc. Am. **56**, 1913–1915 (1974)

9.7 W.M. Hartmann, A. Wittenberg: On the externalization of sound images. J. Acoust. Soc. Am. **99**, 3678–3688 (1996). See also P. Laws: *Zum Problem des Entfernungshörens und der Im-Kopf-Lokalisation von Hörereignissen* (Ph.D. thesis, Technische Hochschule Aachen, Germany, 1972)

9.8 M.R. Schroeder, B.S. Atal: Computer simulation of sound transmission in rooms. IEEE International Conventive Record, Part 7 (1963)

9.9 M.R. Schroeder: Computers in acoustics: Symbiosis of an old science and a new tool. J. Acoust. Soc. Am. **45**, 1077–1088 (1969)

9.10 N.I. Durlach: Binaural signal detection: Equalization and cancellation theory. In J.V. Tobias (ed.): *Foundations of modern auditory theory*, Vol. 2 (Academic Press, New York 1972)

9.11 M.R. Schroeder: *Speech Privacy System* (U.S. Patent 3,328,526, filed December 20, 1963, issued June 27, 1967)

9.12 A.J. Fourcin: Central pitch and auditory lateralization. In R. Plomp, G.F. Smoorenburg (eds.): *Frequency Analysis and Periodicity Detection in Hearing* 319–328 (Sijthoff, Leiden 1970)

9.13 D. Deutsch: The octave illusion and auditory perceptual integration. In J.V. Tobias, E.D. Schubert (eds.): *Hearing Research and Theory*, Vol. 1 (Academic Press, New York 1981) pp. 99–142

9.14 J.C.R. Licklider: Periodicity pitch and related auditory process models. Intern. Audiol. **1**, 11–36 (1962). See also J.C.R. Licklider: A duplex theory of pitch perception. Experientia **7**, 128–134 (1951).

9.15 H. Lauridsen: Some experiments on a system of stereophonic sound (in Danish with English summary). Ingeniören **47**, 906 (December 1954)

9.16 M.R. Schroeder: An artificial stereophonic effect obtained from a single audio signal. J. Audio Eng. Soc. **6**, 74–79 (1958)

9.17 M.R. Schroeder: Improved quasi-stereophony and "colorless" artificial reverberation. J. Acoust. Soc. Am. **33**, 1061–1064 (1961)

9.18 M.R. Schroeder: Computer models for concert hall acoustics. Am. J. Physics **41**, 461–471 (1973)

9.19 J. Chowning: Methods of synthesizing a musical sound. J. Acoust. Soc. Am. **63**, 1002 (1978)

9.20 M. Barron, A.H. Marshall: Spatial impression due to early lateral reflections in concert halls: The derivative of a physical measure. J. Sound & Vibrations **77**, 211–232 (1981)

9.21 M.R. Schroeder, D. Gottlob, K.F. Siebrasse: Comparative study of European concert halls. J. Acoust. Soc. Am. **56**, 1195–1201 (1974). See also P. Damaske: Head-related two-channel stereophony with loudspeaker reproduction. J. Acoust. Soc. Am. **50**, 1109–1115 (1971)

9.22 M.R. Schroeder: Binaural dissimilarity and optimum ceilings for concert halls: More lateral diffusion. J. Soc. Acoust. Am. **65**, 958–963 (1979)

9.23 M.R. Schroeder: *Number Theory in Science and Communication*, 3rd ed. (Springer, Berlin, Heidelberg 1997)

9.24 M.R. Schroeder: *Fractals, Chaos, Power Laws: Minutes from an Infinite Paradise* (W.H. Freeman, New York 1992)

9.25 P. D'Antonio: A new 1- or 2-dimensional fractal sound diffusor. J. Acoust. Soc. Am. **87**, suppl. 1, S10 (1990)

Chapter 10 — Basic Signal Concepts

10.1 J.R. Pierce, A.M. Noll: *Signals: The Science of Telecommunications* (W.H. Freeman, New York 1990)

10.2 A. Papoulis: *The Fourier Integral and its Applications* (McGraw–Hill, New York 1962). See also [10.8]

10.3 D.C. Champeney: *Fourier Transforms and their Applications* (Academic Press, London 1973)

10.4 B.B. Mandelbrot: *The Fractal Geometry of Nature*, updated and augmented (W.H. Freeman, New York 1983)

10.5 M.R. Schroeder: *Fractals, Chaos, Power Laws: Minutes from an Infinite Paradise* (W.H. Freeman, New York 1991)

10.6 B.B. Mandelbrot: *Fractals in Scaling and Finance* (Springer, New York 1997)

10.7 N. Wiener: *The Extrapolation and Smoothing of Stationary Time Series with Engineering Applications* (John Wiley, New York 1949)

10.8 A. Papoulis: *Signal Analysis* (McGraw–Hill, New York 1984)

10.9 W. Hess: *Pitch Determination of Speech Signals: Algorithms and Devices* (Springer, Berlin, Heidelberg 1983)

10.10 S.O. Rice: Mathematical Analysis of random noise. Bell Syst. Tech. J. **23**, 282–332 (1944), and **24**, 46–156 (1945)

10.11 S.W. Golomb: *Shift Register Sequences* (Holden–Day, San Francisco 1967)

10.12 F.J. MacWilliams, N.J.A. Sloane: *The Theory of Error Correcting Codes* (North–Holland, Amsterdam 1977)

10.13 M.R. Schroeder: *Number Theory in Science and Communication*, 3rd ed. (Springer, Berlin, Heidelberg 1997)

10.14 B.F. Logan, M.R. Schroeder: *Compatible Single-Sideband Transmission* (U.S. Patent 3,085,203, filed August 8, 1960, issued April 9, 1963)

10.15 M.R. Schroeder: Improved acoustic feedback stability by frequency shifting. J. Acoust. Soc. Am. **36**, 1718–1724 (1964)

10.16 M.R. Schroeder: Die statistischen Parameter der Fequenzkurven von großen Räumen. Acustica **4**, 594–600, Beiheft 2, (1954). English translation: M.R. Schroeder: Statistical parameters of the frequency response curves of large rooms. J. Audio Eng. Soc. **35**, 299–305 (1987)

10.17 T. Gramss, S. Bornholdt, M. Gross, M. Mitchell, T. Pellizzari (eds.): *Non-Standard Computing* (Wiley–VCH, Weinheim 1998)

10.18 M.R. Schroeder: Synthesis of low peak-factor signals and binary sequences with low autocorrelation. IEEE Trans. Inform. Theory **IT 13**, 85–89 (1970)

10.19 M.R. Schroeder: Peak factor in vocoders.

10.20 M.R. Schroeder: Normal frequency and excitation statistics: Model experiments with electrical waves. J. Audio Eng. Soc. **35**, No. 5 (1987)

10.21 M.R. Schroeder: Measurement of reverberation time by counting phase coincidences. In L. Cremer (ed.): *Proc. 3rd Internatl. Congress on Acoustics* (Elsevier, Amsterdam 1959)

10.22 J.L. Flanagan, L. Landgraf, D.J. MacLean: Matched-filter processing of hydrophone arrays. J. Acoust. Soc. Am. **42**, 1165 (1967)

10.23 M.R. Schroeder: *Multipath Focussing Signal Processor* (U.S. Patent 3,424,269, filed September 30, 1966, issued January 28, 1969)

10.24 J.W. Goodman: *Introduction to Fourier Optics* (McGraw–Hill, New York 1988)

10.25 L.R. Rabiner, R.W. Schafer: *Digital Processing of Speech Signals* (Prentice–Hall, Englewood Cliffs, New Jersey, 1978)

10.26 D. Bouwmeester, J.-W. Pau, K. Mattle, M. Eibl, H. Weinfurter, A. Zeilinger: Experimental quantum teleportation. Nature **390**, 575–579 (1997)

10.27 H.O. Pollak, D. Slepian: Prolate spheroidal wave functions. Fourier analysis and uncertainty I. Bell Syst. Tech. J. **40**, 43–64 (1961)

10.28 H.J. Landau, H.O. Pollak: Prolate spheroidal wave functions. Fourier analysis and uncertainty II, III. Bell Syst. Tech. J. **40**, 65–84 (1961) and **41**, 1295–1336 (1962). See also D. Slepian: Prolate spheroidal wave functions. Fourier analysis and uncertainty IV, V. Bell Syst. Tech. J. **43**, 3009–3057 (1964) and **57**, 1371–1430 (1978)

10.29 R.B. Blackman, J.W. Tukey: *The Measurement of Power Spectra* (Dover, New York 1958)

10.30 V.A. Topkar, S.K. Mullick, E.L. Titlebaum: Invariant transformations of the t–ω plane with respect to Wigner Distribution. Signal Processing **22**, 127–137 (1991)

10.31 T.A.C.M. Claasen, W.F.G. Mecklenbräuker: The Wigner distribution – a tool for time–frequency signal analysis. Part I: Continuous-time signals. Philips J. Res. **35**, 217–250 (1980)

10.32 T.A.C.M. Claasen, W.F.G. Mecklenbräuker: The aliasing problem in discrete–time Wigner distributions. IEEE Trans. Acoust., Speech and Signal Processing **ASSP-31**, 1067–1072 (1983)

10.33 C.R. Janse, A.J.M. Kaizer: Time–frequency distributions of loudspeakers: The application of the Wigner distribution. J. Audio. Eng. Soc. **31**, 198–223 (1983)

10.34 T.A.C.M. Claasen, W.F.G. Mecklenbräuker: The Wigner distribution – a tool for time–frequency signal analysis. Part II: Discrete-time signals. Philips J. Res. **35**, 276–300 (1980)

10.35 M.R. Schroeder, E.E. David, Jr.: A vocoder for transmitting 10 kc/s speech over 3.5 kc/s channel. Acustica **10**, 35–43 (1960)

10.36 A.M. Noll: Short-time spectrum and 'cepstrum' technique for vocal-pitch detection. J. Acoust. Soc. Am. **36**, 296–302 (1964)

10.37 A.V. Oppenheim, R.W. Schafer, T.G. Stockham: Nonlinear filtering of multiplied and convolved signals. Proc. IEEE **56**, 1264–1291 (1968)

10.38 A.V. Oppenheim: Speech analysis-synthesis system based on homomorphic filtering. J. Acoust. Soc. Am. **45**, 459–462 (1969)

10.39 F. Itakura: Line spectral representation of linear predictor coefficients of speech signals. J. Acoust. Soc. Am. **57**, Suppl. 1, S35 (1975). See also C.S. Liu, M.-T. Wang, H.-C. Wang: Study of line spectrum pair frequencies for speaker recognition. Proc. IEEE Internatl. Conference Acoustics, Speech, and Signal Processing (ICASSP 90), 277–280 (1990)

Appendix A — Acoustic Theory and Modeling of the Vocal Tract

A.1 G. Ungeheuer: *Elemente einer akustischen Theorie der Vokalartikulation* (Springer, Berlin, Heidelberg 1962)

A.2 M.R. Schroeder: Determination of the geometry of the human vocal tract by acoustic measurements. J. Acoust. Soc. Am. **41**, 1002–1010 (1967)

A.3 G. Fant: Vocal-tract area and length perturbations. Speech Transmission Lab. – Quarterly Progress and Status Report **4/1975**, 1–14 (KTH, Stockholm 1976)

A.4 J.L. Flanagan: *Speech Analysis Synthesis and Perception* (Springer, Berlin, Heidelberg 1965, 2nd ed. 1972)

A.5 M.M. Sondhi: Model for wave propagation in a lossy vocal tract. J. Acoust. Soc. Am. **55**, 1070–1075 (1974)

A.6 H.W. Strube: Time-varying wave digital filters for modeling analog systems. IEEE Trans. Acoust., Speech, Signal Processing **ASSP-30**, 864–868 (1982)

A.7 A. Fettweis: Wave digital filters: theory and practice. Proc. IEEE **74**, 270–327 (1986)

A.8 B.S. Atal: private communication (1970)

A.9 J.D. Markel, A.H. Gray, Jr.: *Linear Prediction of Speech* (Springer, Berlin, Heidelberg 1976)

A.10 H. Wakita: Direct estimation of the vocal tract shape by inverse filtering of acoustic speech waveforms. IEEE Trans. Audio Electroacoustics **AU-21**, 417–427 (1973)

A.11 B.S. Atal, S.L. Hanauer: Speech analysis and synthesis by linear prediction of the speech wave. J. Acoust. Soc. Am. **50**, 637–655 (1971), Appendix F

A.12 A. Paige, V.W. Zue: Computation of vocal tract area function. IEEE Trans. Audio Electroacoustics **AU-18**, 7–18 (1970)

A.13 M.M. Sondhi, B. Gopinath: Determination of vocal-tract shape from impulse response at the lips. J. Acoust. Soc. Am. **49**, 1867–1873 (1971)

A.14 B.S. Atal: Determination of the vocal-tract shape directly from the speech wave. 78th ASA Meeting, San Diego 1969, paper 4K1. Abstract: J. Acoust. Soc. Am. **47**, 65(A) (1970)

A.15 B.S. Atal, J.J. Chang, M.V. Mathews, J.W. Tukey: Inversion of articulatory-to-acoustic transformation in the vocal tract by a computer sorting technique. J. Acoust. Soc. Am. **47**, 1535–1555 (1978)

Appendix B — Direct Relations
Between Cepstrum and Predictor Coefficients

B.1 B.S. Atal, M.R. Schroeder: Adaptive coding of speech signals. Bell Syst. Tech. J. **49**, 1973–1986 (1970)

B.2 J.D. Markel, A.H. Gray, Jr.: *Linear Prediction of Speech* (Springer, New York 1976) p. 130

B.3 B.S. Atal: Linear prediction for speaker identification. J. Acoust. Soc. Am. 1304–1312 **55** (1974)

B.4 I.S. Gradstein, I.M. Ryzhik: *Table of Integrals, Series and Products* (Academic, New York 1965) p. 14

B.5 M. Abramowitz, I.A. Stegun: *Handbook of Mathematical Functions* (Dover, New York 1965) p. 823

B.6 *Ibid.* p. 825.

B.7 *Ibid.* pp. 823-824.

B.8 W. Gellert, H. Küstner, M. Hellwich, H. Kästner (eds.): *The VNR Concise Encyclopedia of Mathematics* (Van Nostrand Reinhold, New York 1977) p. 343

B.9 O. Perron: *Algebra I* (W. de Gruyter, Berlin 1951) p. 154

B.10 I. Newton (D.T. Whiteside with M.A. Hoskin, ed.): *Mathematical Papers* (University Press, Cambridge, Massachusetts, 1967) p. 517. See also G.A. Korn, T. Korn: *Mathematical Handbook for Scientists and Engineers* (McGraw–Hill, New York 1961)

B.11 F.N. David et al: *Symmetric Functions and Allied Tables* (University Press, Cambridge, Massachusetts, 1966) p. 4

B.12 M.G. Kendall, A. Stuart: *Advanced Theory of Statistics*, Vol. 1 (MacMillan, New York 1977)

B.13 B.S. Atal: personal communication. See [B.14], Fig. 7, for a block diagram of Atal's pitch detector.

B.14 L.R. Rabiner, M.J. Cheng, A.E. Rosenberg, C.A. McGonegal: A comparative performance study of several pitch detection algorithms. IEEE Trans. Acoust., Speech, Signal Processing **ASSP-24**, 399–418 (1976)

B.15 M.R. Schroeder: Vocoders: analysis and synthesis of speech. Proc. IEEE, **54**, 728–734 (1966)

General Reading

Within the various subject categories, the references are listed in order of *publication date*

Speech Analysis and Processing
K. Johnson, J.W. Mullenix (eds.): *Talker Variability in Speech Processing* (Academic Press, San Diego 1997)

J.P.H. van Santen, W. Sproat, J. Olive, J. Hirschberg (eds.): *Progress in Speech Synthesis* (Springer, New York 1996)

A. Gersho: Advances in Speech and Audio Compression. *Proc. IEEE* **82**, 900–918 (1994)

M.G. Rahim: *Artificial Neural Networks for Speech Analysis/Synthesis* (Chapman & Hall, London 1994)

V. van Heuvel, L. Pols: *Analysis and Synthesis of Speech: Strategic Research towards High-Quality Text-to-Speech Generation* (Mouton, Berlin 1993)

S. Furui, M.M. Sondhi (eds.): *Advances in Speech Processing* (Marcel Dekker, New York 1992)

B.S. Atal, J.L. Miller, R.D. Kent (eds.): *Papers in Speech Communication: Speech Processing* (Acoustical Society of America, Woodbury, New York, 1991)

A. Cutler, D.R. Ladd: *Prosody: Models and Measurements* (Springer, Berlin, Heidelberg 1983). Volume 14 of Springer Series in Language and Communication.

W. Hess: *Pitch Determination of Speech Signals: Algorithms and Devices* (Springer, Berlin, Heidelberg 1983)

J.-P. Haton (ed.): *Automatic Speech Analysis and Recognition* (D. Reidel, Dordrecht, Holland 1982). Proceedings of NATO Advanced Study Institute.

R.W. Schafer, J.D. Markel (eds.): *Speech Analysis* (IEEE Press, New York 1979)

L.R. Rabiner, R.W. Schafer: *Digital Processing of Speech Signals* (Prentice–Hall, Englewood Cliffs, New Jersey, 1978)

J.D. Markel, A.H. Gray, Jr.: *Linear Prediction of Speech* (Springer, Berlin, Heidelberg 1976)

J.L. Flanagan: *Speech Analysis, Synthesis, and Perception, 2nd ed.* (Springer, Berlin, Heidelberg 1972). Indispensable.

V.K. Chew: *Talking Machines 1877–1914* (Her Majesty's Stationery Office, London 1967). Early history of the gramophone.

R.K. Potter, G.A. Kopp, H.G. Kopp: *Visible Speech* (Dover, New York 1966)

General Signal Analysis and Processing
H. Feichtinger, T. Strohmer: *Gabor Analysis and Algorithms* (Birkhäuser, Boston 1998)

V.K. Machisetti, D.B. Williams (eds.): *The Digital Signal Processing Handbook* (IEEE Press, New York 1998)

S. Mallat: *A Wavelet Tour of Signal Processing* (Academic Press, San Diego 1998)

F. Nebeker: *Signal Processing: The Emergence of a Discipline 1948–1998* (IEEE History Center, New Brunswick 1998)

H.L. Resnikoff, R.O. Wells, Jr.: *Wavelet Analysis: The Scalable Structure of Information* (Springer, New York 1998). Introduction to wavelets in digital signal processing.

B.W. Suter: *Multirate and Wavelet Signal Processing* (Academic Press, San Diego 1997)

M.R. Schroeder: *Number Theory in Science and Communication, 3rd ed.* (Springer, Berlin, Heidelberg 1997). Contains finite field methods for digital signal processing.

W.M. Hartmann: *Signals, Sound, and Sensation* (Springer, New York 1996)

G. Wornell: *Signal Processing with Fractals – A Wavelet Based Approach* (Prentice–Hall, Englewood Cliffs, New Jersey, 1996)

M. Vetterli, J. Kovacevic: *Wavelets and Subband Coding* (Prentice–Hall, Englewood Cliffs, New Jersey, 1995)

A. Gersho, R.M. Gray: *Vector Quantization and Signal Compression* (Kluwer Academic, Boston 1992)

R.E. Blahut: *Algebraic Methods for Signal Processing and Communications Coding* (Springer, New York 1992)

C.K. Chui, G. Chen: *Signal Processing and Systems Theory* (Springer, Berlin, Heidelberg 1992)

I. Daubechies: *Ten Lectures on Wavelets* (Society for Industrial and Applied Mathematics (SIAM) 1992). Great listening.

K. Huber: Some comments on Zech's Logarithms. IEEE Transactions on Information Theory 946–950 (July 1990)

J.R. Pierce, A.M. Noll: *Signals: The Science of Telecommunications* (Scientific American Library, W.H. Freeman, New York 1990). Past, present, and future. Lucid.

R.W. Lucky: *Silicon Dreams: Information, Man, and Machine*. Great style. Covers most aspects of information.

P. Strobach: *Linear Prediction Theory* (Springer, Berlin, Heidelberg 1990)

P.A. Ruymgaart, T.T. Soong: *Mathematics of Kalman–Bucy Filtering* (Springer, Berlin, Heidelberg 1988)

R. Bracewell: *The Hartley Transform* (Oxford University Press, Oxford 1986)

M. Heideman, D. Johnson, C. Burrus: Gauss and the history of the fast Fourier transform. IEEE Transactions on Acoustics, Speech, and Signal Processing Magazine **34**, 265–267 (1985)

A. Papoulis: *Signal Analysis* (McGraw–Hill, New York 1984)

R.E. Crochiere, L.R. Rabiner: *Multirate Digital Signal Processing* (Prentice–Hall, Englewood Cliffs, New Jersey, 1983)

J.R. Pierce: *An Introduction to Information Theory: Symbols, Signals, and Noise* (Dover, New York 1980). Broad coverage, by the father of communication satellites.

J.H. McClellan, C.M. Rader: *Number Theory in Digital Signal Processing* (Prentice Hall, Englewood Cliffs, New Jersey, 1979)

D.G. Childers: *Modern Spectrum Analysis* (IEEE Press, New York 1978)

N.S. Jayant (ed.): *Waveform Quantization and Coding* (IEEE Press, New York 1976). Still very useful.

Digital Signal Processing Committee: *Selected Papers in Signal Processing II* (IEEE Press, New York 1976)

H.D. Helms, J.F. Kaiser, L.R. Rabiner (eds.): *Literature in Digital Signal Processing, Revised and Expanded Edition* (IEEE Press, New York 1975)

J.F. Kaiser, H.D. Helms: *Supplement to Literature in Digital Signal Processing, Author and Permuted Title Index* (IEEE Press, New York 1979)

L.R. Rabiner, B. Gold: *Theory and Application of Digital Signal Processing* (Prentice–Hall, Englewood Cliffs, New Jersey, 1975)

D.C. Champeney: *Fourier Transforms and Their Physical Applications* (Academic Press, London 1973)

B. Gold, C.M. Rader, A.V. Oppenheim, T.G. Stockham: *Digital Processing of Signals* (McGraw–Hill, New York 1969)

E.I. Jury: *Theory and Application of the z-Transform Method* (John Wiley & Sons, New York 1964)

A. Papoulis: *The Fourier Integral and Its Applications* (McGraw–Hill, New York 1962)

D. Gabor: Theory of communication. J. Inst. Elect. Eng. **93**, 429–457 (1946)

Speech Recognition

F. Jelinek: *Statistical Methods for Speech Recognition. Language, Speech, and Communication* (MIT Press, Cambridge, Massachusetts, 1997)

R. Kompe: *Prosody in Speech Understanding Systems* (Springer, Berlin, Heidelberg 1997)

S. Furui: An Overview of Speaker Recognition Technology, pp. 31–56. In C.-H. Lee, F.K. Soong, K.K. Paliwal: *Automatic Speech and Speaker Recognition* (Kluwer, Boston 1996)

D.B. Roe, J.G. Wilpon (eds.): *Voice Communication between Humans and Machines* (National Academy Press, Washington 1994)

L.R. Rabiner, B.-H. Juang: *Fundamentals of Speech Recognition* (Prentice–Hall, Englewood Cliffs, New Jersey, 1993)

S. Furui, M. Sondhi (eds.): *Advances in Speech Signal Processing* (Marcel Dekker, New York 1991)

K.-F. Lee: *Automatic Speech Recognition* (Kluwer, Boston 1989)

A. Waibel, K.-F. Lee (eds.): *Readings in Speech Recognition* (Morgan Kaufmann, San Mateo, California, 1989). Excellent selection.

D. O'Shaughnessy: *Speech Communication – Human and Machine* (Addison Wesley, Reading, Massachusetts, 1987)

L.R. Rabiner, B.H. Juang: An introduction to hidden Markov models. IEEE ASSP Magazine (January 1986)

A. E. Rosenberg, F.K. Soong: Recent Research in Automatic Speaker Recognition. pp. 701–737. In S. Furui, M. Sondhi (eds.): *Advances in Speech Signal Processing* (Marcel Dekker, New York 1991) pp. 701–737

S.E. Levinson, L.R. Rabiner: A Task-Oriented Conversational Mode Speech Understanding System. In M.R. Schroeder (ed.): *Speech and Speaker Recognition* (Karger, Basel 1985)

M.R. Schroeder: *Speech and Speaker Recognition* (Karger, Basel 1985). Great cover.

J.-P. Haton (ed.): *Automatic Speech Analysis and Recognition* (D. Reidel, Dordrecht, Holland 1982). Proceedings of NATO Advanced Study Institute.

M.M. Marcus: *A Theory of Syntactic Recognition for Natural Language* (MIT Press, Cambridge, Massachusetts, 1980)

N.R. Dixon, T.B. Martin (eds.): *Automatic Speech & Speaker Recognition* (IEEE Press, New York 1979). Now mostly of historical interest.

W.A. Ainsworth: *Mechanisms of Speech Recognition* (Pergamon Press, Oxford 1976)

Neural Networks and Nonstandard Computing

J.A. Anderson, E. Rosenfeld (eds.): *Talking Nets* (MIT Press, Cambridge, Massachusetts, 1998). With contributions by G. Carpenter, L. Cooper, J. Cowan, S. Grossberg, R. Hecht-Nielsen, G. Hinton, T. Kohonen, J. Lettvin, D. Rumelhart, T. Sejnowski.

M.A. Arbib: *The Handbook of Brain Theory and Neural Networks*, new paperback edition (The MIT Press, Cambridge, Massachusetts, 1998). How does the brain work? Can we build intelligent machines? Hundreds of expert articles and overviews.

C. Koch, I. Segev (eds.): *Methods in Neural Modeling: From Ions to Networks, 2nd ed.* (MIT Press, Cambridge, Massachusetts, 1998)

T. Gramss, S. Bornholdt, M. Gross, M. Mitchell, T. Pellizzari (eds.): *Non-Standard Computation* (Wiley–VCH, Weinheim 1998). Includes molecular and quantum computers.

R. Kurzweil: *When Computers Exceed Human Intelligence* (Viking, New York, 1998). *Kurzweilig*

K. Mehrota, C.K. Mohan, S. Ranka: *Elements of Neural Networks* (MIT Press, Cambridge, Massachusetts, 1996)

T. Kohonen: *Self-Organizing Maps, 2nd ed.* (Springer, Berlin, Heidelberg 1995)

M.G. Rahim: *Artificial Neural Networks for Speech Analysis/Synthesis* (Chapman & Hall, London 1994)

P. Wasserman: *Advanced Methods of Neural Computing* (Van Nostrand Reinhold, New York 1993)

E. Domany, J.L. van Hemmen, K. Schulten: *Models of Neural Networks* (Springer, New York 1991)

H. Haken: *Synergetic Computers* (Springer, Berlin, Heidelberg 1991)

T. Kohonen: *Self-Organization and Associative Memory* (Springer, Berlin, Heidelberg 1988)

T. Kohonen: *Content-Addressable Memories* (Springer, Berlin, Heidelberg 1987)

T.J. Sejnowski, C.R. Rosenberg: Parallel networks that learn to pronounce English text. Complex Systems **1**, 145–168 (1987)

D.E. Rumelhart, J.L. McClelland, PDP Research Group: *Parallel Distributed Processing: Explorations in the Microstructure of Cognition Volume I: Foundations* (MIT Press, Cambridge, Massachusetts, 1986)

D.E. Rumelhart, J.L. McClelland, PDP Research Group: *Parallel Distributed Processing: Explorations in the Microstructure of Cognition Volume II: Psychological and Biological Methods* (MIT Press, Cambridge, Massachusetts, 1986)

S. Grossberg: *The Mind's New Science* (Basic Books, New York 1985)

A. Newell, H.A. Simon: *Human Problem Solving* (Prentice–Hall, Englewood Cliffs, New Jersey, 1972)

D.O. Hebb: *The Organization of Behavior* (Wiley, New York 1948)

Speech Production and Synthesis

J.P.H. van Santen, W. Sproat, J. Olive, J. Hirschberg (eds.): *Progress in Speech Synthesis* (Springer, New York 1996). With CD-ROM. Up-to-date and comprehensive.

R. De Mori (ed.): *Spoken Dialogues with Computers* (Academic Press, San Diego 1998)

K. Johnson, J.W. Mullenix (eds.): *Talker Variability in Speech Processing* (Academic Press, San Diego 1997)

M.G. Rahim: *Artificial Neural Networks for Speech Analysis/Synthesis* (Chapman & Hall, London 1994)

D.B. Roe, J.G. Wilpon (eds.): *Voice Communication between Humans and Machines* (National Academy Press, Washington 1994)

U.R. Titze: *Principles of Voice Production* (Prentice–Hall, Englewood Cliffs, New Jersey, 1994)

H. Fujisaki: The role of quantitative modeling in the study of intonation. In Proc. International Symp. on Japanese Prosody, Nara, Japan 163–174 (1992)

R.D. Kent, B.S. Atal, J.L. Miller (eds.): *Papers in Speech Communication: Speech Production* (Acoustical Society of America, Woodbury, New York 1991)

A. Fourcin, G. Harland, W. Barry, V. Hazan: *Speech Input and Output Assessment* (Ellis Horwood, Chichester, England, 1989)

W.J.M. Levelt: *Speaking: From Intention to Articulation* (MIT Press, Cambridge, Massachusetts, 1989). Excellent exposition.

K.N. Stevens: On the quantal nature of speech. J. Phonetics **17**, 3–45 (1989)

J. Allen, S. Hunicutt, D.H. Klett: *From Text to Speech: The MITalk System* (Cambridge University Press, Cambridge, Massachusetts, 1987)

P.F. MacNeilage (ed.): *The Production of Speech* (Springer, New York 1983). Top authors in the field.

W.E. Cooper: *Speech Perception and Production* (Ablex, Norwood, New Jersey, 1979). Studies in selective adaptation.

W.J. Hardcastle: *Physiology of Speech Production* (Academic Press, London 1976). An introduction.

B.R. Fink: *The Human Larynx* (Raven Press, New York 1975). A functional study.

J.L. Flanagan, L.R. Rabiner: *Speech Synthesis* (Dowden, Hutchinson & Ross, Stroudsberg, Pennsylvania, 1973)

J.L. Flanagan: *Speech Analysis, Synthesis, and Perception*, 2nd ed. (Springer, Berlin, Heidelberg 1972)

P.B. Denes, E.N. Pinson: *The Speech Chain* (Bell Telephone Laboratories, Murray Hill, New Jersey, 1970)

G. Fant: *Acoustic Theory of Speech Production* (Mouton, The Hague 1970)

V.K. Chew: *Talking Machines 1877–1914* (Her Majesty's Stationery Office, London 1967). Early history of the gramophone.

G.A. Miller, G.A. Heise, W. Lichten: The intelligibility of speech as a function of the context of the test material. J. Experimental Psychology **41**, 329–335 (1951)

Language and Linguistics

K.N. Stevens: *Acoustic Phonetics* (to be published, 1998)

C. Fellbaum (ed.): *Wordnet: An Electrical Lexical Database* (MIT Press, Cambridge, Massachusetts, 1998). Preface by G.A. Miller. Comes also as a CD ROM: *Wordnet 1.6 CD-ROM*.

C. Gussenhofen and J. Haike: *Understanding Phonology* (Arnold Publishing, London 1998)

J. McWhorter: *The Word on the Street: Fact and Fable about American English* (Plenum, New York 1998)

J. Miller, R. Weinert: *Spontaneous Spoken Language: Syntax and Discourse* (Oxford University Press, Oxford 1998)

S. Savage-Rumbaugh, S.G. Shanker, T.J. Taylor: *Apes, Language, and the Human Mind* (Oxford University Press, Oxford 1998)

F. de Waal: *Chimpanzee Politics*, revised ed. (Johns Hopkins University Press, Baltimore 1998). Recommended by Newt Gingrich for members of the U.S. Congress.

S. Pinker: *The Language Instinct: How the Mind Creates Language* (William Morrow and Company, New York 1994)

P. Ladefoged: *A Course in Phonetics* (Harcourt, Fort Worth 1993)

J.P. Olive, A. Greenwood, J. Coleman: *Acoustics of American English Speech* (Springer, New York 1993)

G.A. Miller: *The Science of Words* (W.H. Freeman, New York 1991)

D. Bollinger: *Intonation and its Uses* (Edward Arnold, London 1989)

G.A. Miller: *Language and Speech* (W.H. Freeman, San Francisco 1981)

M.M. Marcus: *A Theory of Syntactic Recognition for Natural Language* (MIT Press, Cambridge, Massachusetts, 1980)

J. Pierrehumbert: *The Phonology and Phonetics of English Intonation* (MIT Press, Cambridge, Massachusetts, 1980)

V. Teller, S.J. White: *Studies in Child Language and Multilingualism* (The New York Academy of Sciences, New York 1980)

L.M. Hyman: *Phonology: Theory and Analysis* (Holt, Rinehart, and Winston, New York 1975)

N. Chomsky, M. Halle: *The Sound Patterns of English* (Harper and Rowe, New York 1968)

P. Lieberman: *Intonation, Perception, and Language* (MIT Press, Cambridge, Massachusetts, 1968)

B. Malmberg: *Manual of Phonetics* (North–Holland, Amsterdam 1968)

I. Lehiste: *Readings in Acoustic Phonetics* (MIT Press, Cambridge, Massachusetts, 1967)

B. Malmberg: *Structural Linguistics and Human Communication* (Springer, Berlin, Heidelberg 1963)

M. Halle (ed.): *For Roman Jacobson* (Mouton, The Hague 1956)

Hearing and Perception

E. Terhardt: *Akustische Kommunikation: Grundlagen mit Hörbeispielen* (Springer, Berlin, Heidelberg 1998). Cuts a wide swath; includes over 200 illustrations and tables and an audio compact disc.

B.C.J. Moore: *An Introduction to the Psychology of Hearing*, 4th ed. (Academic Press, San Diego 1997)

W.M. Hartmann: *Signals, Sound, and Sensation* (Springer, New York 1996)

J.B. Allen (ed.): *Harvey Fletcher. Speech and Hearing in Communication* (Acoustical Society of America, Am. Inst. of Physics, Woodbury, New York, 1995). Includes biography and annotated bibliography of Harvey Fletcher.

J.L. Miller, R.D. Kent, B.S. Atal (eds.): *Papers in Speech Communication: Speech Perception* (Acoustical Society of America, Woodbury, New York, 1991)

A.S. Bregman: *Auditory Scene Analysis: the Perceptual Organization of Sound* (The MIT Press, Cambridge, Masssachussetts, 1990)

S.A. Gelfand: *Hearing,* 2nd ed. (Dekker, New York 1990) An introduction.

E. Zwicker, H. Fastl: *Psychoacoustics.* 2nd edn. (Springer, Berlin, Heidelberg 1999). Focus on Zwicker's school.

R. Parncutt: *Harmony: A Psychoacoustical Approach* (Springer, Berlin, Heidelberg 1989)

H. Duifhuis, J.W. Horst, H.P. Witt (eds.): *Basic Issues in Hearing* (Academic Press, London 1988). Proceedings of a symposium.

H.C. Longuet-Higgins: *Mental Processes: Studies in Cogninive Science* (MIT Press, Cambridge, Massachusetts, 1987). Covers artificial intelligence, language, music, vision, and memory.

A. Michelson (ed.): *Time Resolution in Auditory Systems* (Springer, Berlin, Heidelberg 1985)

J. Blauert: *Spatial Hearing* (MIT Press, Cambridge, Massachusetts, 1983)

R. Klinke, R. Hartman (eds.): *Hearing – Physiological Bases and Psychophysics* (Springer, Berlin, Heidelberg 1983). Contains list of five preceding symposia on hearing.

R. Carlson, B. Granström (eds.): *The Representation of Speech in the Peripheral Auditory System* (Elsevier, Amsterdam 1982)

R.M. Warren: *Auditory Perception* (Pergamon Press, New York 1982)

W.E. Cooper: *Speech Perception and Production* (Ablex, Norwood, New Jersey, 1979). Studies in selective adaptation.

E.C. Carterette, M.P. Friedman (eds.): *Handbook of Perception* (Academic Press, New York 1978)

E.F. Evans, J.P. Wilson (eds.): *Psychophysics and Physiology of Hearing* (Academic Press, London 1977). International symposium.

D.M. Green: *An Introduction to Hearing* (John Wiley, New York 1976)

R. Plomp: *Aspects of Tone Sensation* (Academic Press, London 1976) A psychophysical study.

A. Cohen, S.G. Nooteboom (eds.): *Structure and Process in Speech Perception* (Springer, Berlin, Heidelberg 1975). Dynamics of speech perception.

S.S. Stevens: *Psychophysics* (Wiley, New York 1975)

P. Dallos: *The Auditory Periphery* (Academic Press, New York 1973)

A.R. Møller (ed.): *Basic Mechanisms in Hearing* (Academic Press, New York 1973)

J.L. Flanagan: *Speech Analysis, Synthesis, and Perception,* 2nd ed. (Springer, Berlin, Heidelberg 1972)

J.V. Tobias: *Foundations of Modern Auditory Theory* (Academic Press, New York 1972)

P. Lieberman: *Intonation, Perception, and Language* (MIT Press, Cambridge, Massachusetts, 1968)

D.M. Green, J.A. Swets: *Signal Detection Theory and Psychophysics* (Wiley, New York 1966)

G. von Békésy: *Experiments in Hearing* (McGraw–Hill, New York 1960)

W.A. van Bergeijk, J.R. Pierce, E.E. David, Jr.: *Waves and the Ear* (Doubleday, Garden City, New York, 1960). A work of love.

D.E. Broadbent: *Perception and Communication* (Pergamon Press, New York 1958)

H. Helmholtz: *On the Sensations of Tone* (Dover, New York 1954). Includes Helmholtz' bibliography.

I.J. Hirsch: *The Measurement of Hearing* (McGraw–Hill, New York 1952). Still very useful.

H. Fletcher: *Speech and Hearing* (D. Van Nostrand Co., New York 1929). The Old Testament.

Music

D. Deutsch (ed.): *The Psychology of Music*, 2nd ed. (Academic Press, San Diego 1999)

N.H. Fletcher: *The Physics of Musical Instruments* (Springer, New York 1998)

T. Winkler: *Composing Interactive Music* (MIT Press, Cambridge, Massachusetts, 1998)

E. Selfridge-Field: *Beyond MIDI: The Handbook of Musical Codes* (MIT Press, Cambridge, Massachusetts, 1997)

A. Hirschberg, J. Kergomard, G. Weinreich (eds.): *Mechanics of Musical Instruments* (Springer, Vienna 1995)

J.G. Roederer: *The Physics and Psychophysics of Music* (Springer, New York 1995)

T. Umemoto, E.C. Carterette (eds.): *The First International Conference on Music Perception and Cognition* (The Japanese Society for Music Perception & Cognition, Kyoto 1989)

J. Sundberg: *The Science of the Singing Voice* (Northern Illinois University Press, DeKalb, Illinois, 1987)

W. Apel: *Harvard Dictionary of Music*, 2nd ed. (Harvard University Press, Cambridge, Massachusetts, 1970)

Communication and Statistical Methods

W. Pedrycz, F. Gomide: *An Introducion to Fuzzy Sets: Analysis and Design* (MIT Press, Cambridge, Massachusetts, 1998). Covers fuzzy neurocomputation, fuzzy evolutionary computing, and fuzzy modeling.

N. Wu: *The Maximum Entropy Method* (Springer, Berlin, Heidelberg 1997)

C.E. Shannon: *Collected Papers* (IEEE Press, New York 1993). A treasure trove.

J.R. Pierce, A.M. Noll: *Signals: The Science of Telecommunications* (Scientific American Library, New York 1990). A well written introduction, profusely illustrated.

A. Papoulis: *Probability, Random Variables, and Stochastic Processes* (McGraw–Hill, New York 1986)

D.E. Rumelhart, J.L. McClelland, PDP Research Group: *Parallel Distributed Processing: Explorations in the Microstructure of Cognition Volume I: Foundations* (MIT Press, Cambridge, Massachusetts, 1986)

D.E. Rumelhart, J.L. McClelland, PDP Research Group: *Parallel Distributed Processing: Explorations in the Microstructure of Cognition Volume II: Psychological and Biological Methods* (MIT Press, Cambridge, Massachusetts, 1986)

A. Cutler, D.R. Ladd: *Prosody: Models and Measurements* (Springer, Berlin, Heidelberg 1983). Volume 14 of Springer Series in Language and Communication.

R. Carlson, B. Granström: *The Representation of Speech in the Peripheral Auditory System* (Elsevier, Amsterdam 1982)

P. McCorduck: *Machines Who Think* (W.H. Freeman, San Francisco 1979)

L. Lindblom, S. Öhman: *Frontiers of Speech Communication Research* (Academic Press, London 1979). A Festschrift for Gunnar Fant.

P.B. Denes, E.N. Pinson: *The Speech Chain* (Bell Telephone Laboratories, Murray Hill, New Jersey, 1970). Recently revised.

C. Cherry: *On Human Communication: A Review, Survey, and Criticism* (MIT Press, Cambridge, Massachusetts 1966)

D.E. Broadbent: *Perception and Communication* (Pergamon Press, New York 1958)

Selected Journals and Research Reports

Computer Speech and Language

Computational Linguistics (MIT Press)

Speech Communication (Elsevier).

Journal of the Acoustical Society of America.

Journal of the Audio Engineering Society.

Acustica / acta acustica. The Journal of the European Acoustics Association (S. Hirzel).

Acoustical Physics (Translation of *Akusticheskii Zhurnal*, Russian Academy of Sciences, Moscow)

Phonetica: International Journal of Speech Sciences. (Karger, Basel)

IEEE Transactions on Signal Processing.

IEEE Transactions on Speech and Audio Processing.

IEEE Signal Processing Magazine.

Neural Networks.

Hearing Research (Elsevier).

Artificial Intelligence.

Journal of Speech and Hearing Research.

Journal of Phonetics.

Biological Cybernetics. Contains papers on hearing.

Physical Review Letters. Contains articles on neural networks and nonstandard computing (Am. Phys. Soc.).

Computer (IEEE Computer Society).

Signal Processing (Elsevier).

Computer Music Journal (MIT Press).

IEEE Proceedings.

Quarterly Progress and Status Reports, Department of Speech, Music, and Hearing, Royal Institute of Technology, Stockholm, Sweden.

Scientific Reports: Human–Machine Communication Department, Laboratoire d'Informatique, Centre National de la Recherche Scientifique, Orsay, France.

Annual Bulletin, Research Institute of Logopedics and Phoniatrics, University of Tokyo.

Annual Report, Parmly Hearing Institute, Loyola University, Chicago.

Speech, Hearing and Language. Work in Progress, University College, London.

Annual Progress Report, IPO, Technische Universiteit Eindhoven, The Netherlands.

Publication Reports, Institute of Hearing Research, Medical Research Council, Nottingham, U.K.

Jahresberichte, Institut für Übertragungstechnik und Elektrotechnik, Technische Universität Darmstadt, Germany.

Research Reports, Panasonic Technologies, Speech Technology Laboratory, Santa Barbara, California.

A Sampling of Societies and Major Meetings

Eurospeech. European conferences on speech communication and technology, organized by the European Speech Communication Association (ESCA).

ICASSP. IEEE International Conferences on Acoustics, Speech, and Signal Processing.

AES Conventions. Meetings of the Audio Engineering Society.

ICA. International congresses on acoustics, held every three years, organized by the International Commission on Acoustics (United Nations).

ASA Meetings of the Acoustical Society of America, held twice a year, with extensive coverage of speech and hearing.

ICPhS. International Congresses of Phonetic Sciences.

ICSLP. International Conferences on Spoken Language Processing.

Conferences of the International Neural Networks Society.

DAGA. Annual meetings of the German Acoustical Society (DEGA).

DAD. Danish Acoustical Days, organized by the Danish Acoustical Society (DAS).

SFA. Société Française d' Acoustique, holds frequent meetings.

IOA. (British) Institute of Acoustics.

EEAA. East-European Acoustical Societies.

EEIG. European Acoustics Association.

Annual meetings of the Association for Computational Linguistics.

ELSNET. European Network for Language and Speech. Maintains a WWW page containing a list of Speech and Natural Language events with contact addresses. http://www.elsnet.org/conferences/

EUSIPCO. European Signal Processing Conferences.

ICANN. International Conferences on Applications of Neural Networks.

IEEE Workshops on Interactive Voice Technology.

SPECOM. International Workshops "Speech and Computer."

KONVENS. Conferences on Natural Language Processing.

International Workshops on Speech Synthesis.

Glossary of Speech and Computer Terms

The beginning of wisdom is the definition of terms.

Socrates (470?–399 BC)

This is not the end. It is not even the beginning of the end.
But it is perhaps the end of the beginning.

Winston Churchill (10 November 1942, after the victory at El Alamein)

Terms in *italics* are explained in their respective alphabetical entries.

ACELP adaptive *code-excited linear prediction.*
A/D *analog*-to-*digital* converter.
adaptive differential pulse code modulation *differential pulse code modulation* in which the quantizing steps adapt to the signal.
adaptive predictive coding (APC) early name for *linear predictive coding* emphasizing the adaptive nature of the *predictor* for speech signals (as opposed to the fixed predictors used for image coding).
ADPCM *adaptive differential pulse code modulation.*
Advanced Encryption Standard a new standard that uses flexible, larger block- and key sizes than its predecessor, the *DES.*
Advanced Research Project Agency agency of the U.S. Defense department supporting research in speech and other fields.
AES *Advanced Encryption Standard.*
AI artificial intelligence.
algorithm an explicit, step-by-step program or set of instructions for getting the solution to some problem.
algorithmic computing see *programmed computing.*
aliasing generating extraneous frequency components by *undersampling* a signal.

allpass filter mechanical or electrical device that transmits all frequencies of a signal equally well and therefore does not change its *amplitude spectrum*.

allpole transmission medium, such as a filter, that has no zeroes in its *transfer function*.

America Online (AOL) an *Internet service provider*.

amplitude range (of a signal) difference between highest and lowest amplitude values of a signal.

amplitude spectrum magnitude (absolute value) of the Fourier transform, also called *spectrum*.

analog capable of assuming a continuous range of values (such as the hands of a clock) — as opposed to *digital*.

analysis-by-synthesis the synthesis of several trial versions of a signal and choosing the best match to a given signal.

anechoic room an acoustic space without echoes or reverberation, used for acoustic tests.

angular frequency frequency multiplied by 2π.

anti-causal passive device that produces an output only before an input is applied and zero output thereafter. The inverse of an *allpass* filter is anti-causal.

any key any one of the keys of a (computer) keyboard. Not a special key called "Any."

APC *adaptive predictive coding*.

APCM adaptive *pulse code modulation*.

aphasia the loss or impairment of language abilities usually following brain damage.

Apple Macintosh computer.

applet literally: little application. A small program which may be started through an applet viewer or web browser, and which has strictly limited access (e.g. read/write restriction on hard disk) to the host system.

application a computer program designed for a specific task or use, like word processing, accounting etc.

AR *autoregression*.

ARMA *AR* followed by *MA*: autoregressive analysis combined with moving average of data.

ARPA *Advanced Research Project Agency*.

ARPANET forerunner of the *Internet*, linking military sites, defense contractors and universities. After 1983 mostly nonmilitary uses.

articulation the movements of speech organs involved in producing a (speech) sound.

articulator movable organs (tongue, lips etc.) involved in the production of speech sounds.

articulatory feature property of speech sound such as voicing, nasality, bilabial, and place of articulation in the *vocal tract*.

artificial intelligence the attempt to program computers to carry out intelligent tasks such as learning, reasoning, recognizing objects, understanding speech, and moving arms and legs.

ASL American Sign Language, the primary sign language for the deaf in the United States.

ASR *automatic speech recognition.*

asynchronous transfer mode a standard that allows the transmission of data, voice and video in *real time.*

ATM *asynchronous transfer mode.*

AT&T American Telephone and Telegraph Company, the former mother company of the defunct *Bell System.*

auto-correlation normalized average of signal multiplied by the delayed signal.

automatic speech recognition automatic recognition (usually by computer) of speech signals for speech-to-text systems.

autoregression (statistical) linear regression analysis based on prior data values.

back door a secret way to enter a computer that bypasses normal security procedures.

backpropagation through time a popular algorithm to train recurrent *spatiotemporal neural networks*, an extension of the standard *backpropagation algorithm.*

backup copy of a file that is kept in case the original is lost.

back(ward) propagation algorithm adjustment of weights in a multilayer *neural network* beginning with the output layer and working backward to the input layer.

bandpass filter a mechanical or electronic device that lets only intermediate frequencies pass through and blocks lower and higher frequencies.

bandwidth the width in frequency of a communication channel or filter that, together with the *signal-to-noise ratio*, characterizes its information carrying capacity.

Bark unit of a frequency scale based on subjective pitch. 1 Bark, named after Heinrich Barkhausen (1881–1956), corresponds to a *bandwidth* of about 100 Hz below 600 Hz and about 1/6 of the (center) frequency above 600 Hz. The frequency range of normal human hearing (20 Hz to 20 000 Hz) corresponds to 24 Bark. The Bark scale is linear along the *basilar membrane* in the inner ear, 1 Bark corresponding to 1 mm.

baseband low-frequency components of a signal. For speech, typically, the frequency components below 2000 Hz.

basilar membrane membrane in the inner ear along which sound waves travel.

baud bits per second: rate of information transmission. A 56-kbaud *modem* can handle information up to 56 000 bits per second.

Bell (Telephone) Laboratories the research laboratories of *AT&T*, later of *Lucent Technologies*.

binaural masking level difference ability of human hearing to perceive tones that are up to 20 dB weaker than in the corresponding monaural situation. See also *cocktail-party effect*.

bit basic unit of binary information, a simple alternative, such as yes/no, 0/1, on/off etc. (Pun created by J.W. Tukey.)

BMLD *binaural masking level difference*.

boot to start a computer.

Bronx cheer a loud, spluttering noise made with the lips and tongue to express contempt.

browser *web browser*.

bug a defect or imperfection in a machine or computer program.

bundling a marketing strategy to promote weak or new products by shipping them with a popular, established or essential product.

bus circuit that connects the *central processing unit* with other devices in a computer. (From "bus bar" in electrical power engineering: heavy-duty conductor to distribute electrical currents.)

byte eight bits, corresponding to $2^8 = 256$ possibilities, such as the 256 different characters ("letters") of a computer font. One byte therefore corresponds to one character. (Another pun, this time based on bite: a big bit).

cache *cache memory*.

cache memory a portion of memory in which frequently used information is duplicated for quick access.

CAD computer aided design.

Caltech California Institute of Technology at Pasadena. Home of the Jet Propulsion Laboratory.

causal passive physical device that does not produce an output before an input is applied.

CD *compact disc*.

CD-ROM *read-only memory* on a *compact disc*.

CELP *code-exited linear prediction*.

center clipping setting the smallest values of a signal equal to zero. Center clipped speech is difficult to understand. See also *peak clipping*.

central processing unit main component of a computer that interprets and executes program instructions.

cepstrum *Fourier transform* of the logarithm of the *spectrum* of a signal.

chord a combination of usually three or more musical tones sounded simultaneously.

coarticulation the change in phoneme *articulation* caused by the effect of neighboring sounds.

cochlea spiral-shaped structure in the inner ear where frequency discrimination ("Fourier analysis") and transduction from sound wave to nerve impulses take place.

cochlear implant microelectrodes, implanted in the *cochlea*, that deliver electrical stimuli to the auditory nerve to alleviate sensorineural deafness.

cocktail-party effect binaural ability of human listeners to suppress unwanted sounds (such as the speech babble during a noisy cocktail party) and concentrate on a single voice.

code-excited linear prediction (CELP) *linear prediction* coder in which the excitation function for synthesis is derived from a pre-existing code-book.

coding representation of data, usually in *digital* form, for purposes of *data compression, encryption* etc.

comb filter electrical or mechanical filter with periodically spaced transmission peaks.

combination tone a tone perceived but not physically present in an auditory stimulus, such as the difference tones $f_2 - f_1$ and $2f_1 - f_2$ resulting from nonlinear (quadratic and cubic, respectively) distortion in the middle or inner ear.

compact disc optical recording medium, read out by a laser beam.

computer simulation mimicking of real-world process (such as flying an airplane) on a computer.

consonance correspondence of sounds; harmony of sounds. In music: a simultaneous combination of tones conventionally accepted as being in a state of repose. See also *dissonance*.

consonant (of speech) a *phoneme* produced by diverting (m, n, ng), obstructing (f, v, z etc), or occluding (p, b, t, d, k, g) the flow of air in the *vocal tract* — as opposed to *vowel*.

constant-Q of a set of resonances (such as the *formants* of a speech signal): all having the same Q or *relative bandwidth*.

continuity effect the appearance of continuity of an interrupted visual or auditory stimulus.

convolution integral of a function multiplied by delayed, time-inverted version of another function.

CPU *central processing unit*.

cross-correlation normalized average of signal multiplied by another signal.

cyberspace environment created by *virtual reality*.

D/A *digital*-to-*analog* converter.

daemon an automatic utility program that runs in the background of a computer.

DARPA Defense *Advanced Research Project Agency*.

data-base management *software* for storing, manipulating and accessing large amounts of data.

data compression *coding* of data in a more efficient manner.

Data Encryption Standard a popular standard that breaks the data into 64-bit blocks and uses a 56-bit key to encrypt messages. Soon to be replaced by *AES*.

dB *decibel.*

DCT *discrete cosine transform.*

decibel ten times the logarithm to the base 10 of the ratio of two intensities or powers. For a ratio equal to 2, the decibel difference is 6 decibels.

delta modulation *coding* of a signal by positive and negative pulses representing the sign of the difference between a current signal value and its expectation.

demisyllable part of a syllable obtained by cutting it in the middle of its steady (*vowel*) part.

DES *Data Encryption Standard.*

desktop a display that arranges *icons* and menus to make the screen look like the top of a desk. Popularized by the *Apple* Macintosh and then by Microsoft *Windows.*

DFT *discrete Fourier transform.*

differential pulse code modulation *pulse code modulation* applied to signal differences. Akin to *delta modulation.*

digital having only discrete values (such as the displayed numbers on a cash register).

digital certificate digital encryption method that guarantees the legitimacy of the transmitted information.

ditgital signatures digital encryption method that guarantees the signature under a letter, order, or contract to be authentic.

digital simulation *computer simulation.*

diphones *vowel* plus postvocalic transition.

diphthong gliding speech sound, such as *ai* in my, *oi* in boy, *au* in how, *ou* as in low. In English many vowels are diphtongized that are pronounced as pure vowels in Italian, Hungarian, German and other languages.

discrete cosine transform (DCT) Fourier-like transform based on cosine functions.

discrete Fourier transform *Fourier transform* for time-discrete ("sampled") data.

Disk Operating System (DOS) venerable computer operating system to run programs.

dissonance inharmonious or harsh sound. In music: a simultaneous combination of tones conventionally accepted as being in a state of unrest and needing completion.

distinctive feature crucial distinguishing mark (voicing, nasality etc.) between two *phonemes.*

dongle piece of *hardware* that must be attached to a computer to make certain *software* work. A dongle, also known as hardware key, prevents illegal access to software. (The origin of dongle, a neologism, is uncertain.)

DOS *Disk Operating System.*

download to receive a file from another computer via *modem.*

DPCM *differential pulse code modulation.*

DRAM *Dynamic Random Access Memory.*

driver a piece of software that controls a hardware device. Usually, drivers are written by the hardware manufacturer and then integrated into the *operating system.*

DSP *digital* signal processing or processor, often realized by an *integrated circuit.*

DVD Digital Versatile (or Video) Disk, resembles a *compact disc.* New high-density standard for optically recording images, music, and other data on a disk.

dynamic programming an algorithm for finding the "best" path through a grid of data.

Dynamic Random Access Memory a *RAM* chip that stores information in small capacitors. DRAMs have high storage capacity due to their simple, small design, but the information must be refreshed periodically (approximately every 2 ms) as stored charge tends to leak.

dyslexia difficulty in reading, often caused by brain damage or inherited factors.

e-lancer free (unaffiliated employed) agent who is electronically linked. (A rhyming play on free-lancer, originally a medieval mercenary soldier.)

electronic of or pertaining to processes involving electrons.

electronic commerce *web sites* that generate revenue through online sales of products or services.

electronic mail messages sent via the *Internet* between computers.

e-mail *electronic mail.*

e-mail software *software* for sending and receiving electronic messages over the *Internet.*

e-money electronic money transmitted by the *Internet.* Similar formations: e-bucks, e-credit, e-commerce, e-tailing (a play on retailing).

emulate imitate *software* by another type of software (the "emulator" or "emulation program").

encryption process for making data inaccessible for unauthorized users. Modern encryption methods are typically based on number-theoretic algorithms, such as exponentiation in *finite fields.*

entropy measure of randomness.

entropy coding source coding based on probability distribution of the source symbol.

envelope curve tangent to each member of a set of curves. Also: curve connecting the peaks of a *waveform*.

error signal usually: *prediction residual*.

Ethernet *software* protocol for building networks.

Exclusive Or one or the other but not both.

expert systems an information processing system that is knowledge based and uses *programmed computing*.

fast Fourier transform algorithm that reduces the computing time of an N-point *Fourier transform* by a factor up to $N/2 \log_2 N$. For $N = 2^{10} = 1024$ the reduction factor exceeds 50.

FAQ frequently asked question.

fax facsimile. To transmit a facsimile (of printed text, photographs, or the like) electronically. Originally used by Interpol and other police agencies for the distribution of photographs ("mug shots") of criminals. Long ignored for nonforensic applications.

FFT *fast Fourier transform*.

file transfer protocol a type of *Internet* site for file *downloading*.

filter mechanical or electrical device with input and output terminals that changes the amplitude spectrum and/or the *phase spectrum* of a signal applied to its input.

finite (number) field mathematical structure having a finite number of members that permits adding, subtracting, multiplying and dividing. Also called *Galois field*.

FIR finite *impulse response* (of a filter). FIRs have zeroes in their *transfer functions*.

firewall defensive *software* that protects a computer system from unauthorized intruders.

FIR neural network an implementation of a *time-delay neural network* where each synapse (link between neurons) is represented as a linear, time-invariant (lti) filter. Thus, the input received from each synapse can be described as the convolution sum of a finite impulse (the delayed inputs) and the impulse response of the lti filter.

floppy *floppy disk*.

floppy disk a flexible magnetic disk for storing digital data.

FM synthesis a simple way to generate sounds by frequency modulation of a sine wave.

formant *resonance* of the *vocal tract*. From musicology where a formant is one of the resonances of a musical instrument. Different formant frequencies distinguish different *vowel* sounds of human speech.

Fourier transform mathematical transformation (of a time signal such as speech) that picks out the individual frequency components ("harmonics," "overtones").

freeware free *software*.

frequency channel a slice of a speech *spectrum* with a bandwidth between 100 and 300 Hz.

frequency diversity method of communication in which the signal is transmitted over several frequency channels to combat interference from other sources. Similar formations: time diversity and space diversity (the use of several transmitting or receiving antennas). See also *spread spectrum*.

frequency hopping a combination of *frequency diversity* and time diversity to reduce interference from other sources occupying the same frequency band. Frequency hopping is also used to reduce range and velocity ambiguity in radar. Some optimal hopping schemes are based on number theory.

frequency warping transformation of the frequency scale to the *Bark* scale to conform to the frequency analysis in the inner ear.

fricative speech sound with audible friction produced by forcing air through a constriction in the *vocal tract* (*f, v*; *s, z*; *sh, zh*; *th* as in thin, *th* as in they).

FTP *file transfer protocol*

function word preposition, article, auxiliary or pronoun such as an, the and, in, etc. — as opposed to context words.

fundamental frequency for a periodic signal the fundamental frequency is the greatest common divisor of its *harmonic* frequencies. The fundamental frequency of a sound signal (if it exceeds 20 Hz) determines the perceived *pitch*, even if it is physically absent. The pitch percept in the case of the "missing fundamental" is called *residue pitch*.

Furby a furry toy, stuffed with electronics. A purported threat to the *National Security Agency* (see p. 45).

fuzzy logic logic based on *fuzzy sets*.

fuzzy sets a generalization of a classical set with the property that each member of a population of objects has associated with it a number, usually from 0 to 1, that indicates the degree to which the object belongs to the set.

f_0 *fundamental frequency*.

Galois field *finite field* of numbers based on the power of a prime number.

Gaussian variable random variable with Gaussian ("normal") probability distribution such as many hiss-like noises.

GB *gigabyte*.

generative grammar a set of rules that determines the form and meaning of words and sentences in a given language.

GHz one billion *Hertz*.

GIF graphic image format, based on lossless *entropy coding*.

Gigabyte one billion *bytes*. Modern computers have hard discs with typically several gigabytes of memory.

glottal wave air flow emanating from the vocal cords. For *voiced sounds* the glottal wave consists of quasiperiodic puffs of air.

Graphical User Interface computer *operating system* that uses *icons* and symbols to launch and operate programs.

group delay delay of the *envelope* of a group of frequencies.

GUI *Graphical User Interface.*

hacker person who intrudes a computer system; also someone who writes programs of a somewhat routine nature.

Hadamard transform binary transform based on *orthonormal* Hadamard matrices. Hadamard matrices of order 2^n, like the *fast Fourier transform*, permit a fast algorithm.

Hamming distance number of *bits* that are different in two binary code words.

Hamming window function of time (or frequency or space) which, used as a *window* function, causes a low amount of *spectral splatter*.

hands-free telephone *speakerphone.*

handshake initial exchange of information between two *modems* to establish an electronic link on the *Internet* or between two *fax* machines.

hard disk a digital mass storage device consisting of one or more rigid magnetic disks rotating at high speed.

hard limiter nonlinear electronic device that reduces all input values to two fixed output levels.

hardware physical (computer) devices (as opposed to *software*).

harmonic pertaining to, or denoting a series of oscillations in which each oscillation has a frequency that is an integral multiple of the same basic or *fundamental frequency.*

hash algorithm in encryption: Method that arranges fixed-length pieces of a message into blocks before encryption and yields a distinct output (the digest, or "hash"). Used as a digital fingerprint to detect forgeries.

Heisenberg uncertainty product of standard deviations of energy distributions in time and frequency (or any other Fourier conjugate variables). In quantum mechanics conjugate variables are position and momentum, angle and angular momentum, energy and time, etc.

hidden Markov model statistical model that describes input–output relations of sequentially occurring signals (such as phonemes in a speech sample) using internal, "hidden" states and transition probabilities between them. One of the most powerful tools in speech recognition.

highpass filter a mechanical or electronic device that lets only high frequencies pass through and blocks out low frequencies.

Hilbert envelope *envelope* obtained with the help of the *Hilbert transform.*

Hilbert transform integral transform corresponding to a 90°-phase shift in the *Fourier transform* ("frequency domain").

HMM *hidden Markov model* (for *automatic speech recognition*).

homepage the *web site* of a person, institution, company or other entity rather than a site dedicated to an abstract topic.

homomorphic filtering nonlinear filtering of signals utilizing the complex *cepstrum*.

HTML hypertext markup language.

HTTP hypertext transfer protocol.

hyperlink a technology that lets users jump from one item to another by clicking with a *mouse* on a word or *icon* that points to some other part of the network.

hypertext a computer text document that is connected to others through *hyperlinks*.

Hz Hertz, formerly "cycles per second," measure of frequency or *bandwidth*.

IBM International Business Machines Corporation introduced first *personal computer* (PC) in 1981.

IC *integrated circuit.*

icon a small image that represents a file, program or location on the Internet.

IIR infinite *impulse response* (of a filter). *Minimum-phase* or *allpole* filters have IIRs and stable inverses.

infinite clipping setting all positive values of a signal equal to $+1$ and all negative values equal to -1. Center clipping leaves a speech signal moderately intelligible. See also *hard limiter*.

integrated circuit solid-state circuit consisting of interconnected semiconductor devices like transistors, capacitors and resistors that form a logical unit on a small chip.

Intel manufacturer of *microchips*.

interactive (with regard to computers) interacting with a human user to obtain data or commands and to give immediate results.

Internet a decentralized collection of networks that connects dissimilar computers around the world and allows them to send and receive data by following a set of global communications rules. The Internet is the platform for *e-mail*, the *World Wide Web*, file transfers and chat programs, among other technologies.

Internet Explorer *web browser* by Microsoft.

Internet protocol a low-level convention that allows computers to move packets of data across the *Internet*.

Internet service provider organization as America Online (AOL) that allows you to connect your computer to the *Internet*.

intonation the melody or *pitch* contour of speech.

inverse filter filter with a *transfer function* that is the reciprocal of that of a given filter. Inverse filtering of a speech signal with the inverse of the *vocal tract transfer function* produces the *glottal wave*.

I/O input/output.

IP *Internet protocol.*

IRCAM Institut de Récherche et de Coordination Acoustique Musique, a
   department of the Centre Pompidou, Paris, established by Pierre Boulez
   to foster modern music research. Originally conceived as a Max Planck
   Institute, it was rejected – in no uncertain terms – by Werner Heisenberg
   who could not see *modern music* as a proper concern of the august German body. (IRCAM was briefly called IRAM before the C was inserted to
   avoid – given the singularities of French pronunciation – confusion with
   Iran.)
is third person singular of the present tense indicative of the verb "to be."
ISP *Internet service provider.*

JAVA a computer language developed by Sun Microsystems that produces
   programs that run on almost any computer or operating system. Its com-
   patibility and ease of use make it an increasingly popular language for
   developing *applets*, tiny applications that can be sent quickly over the
   World Wide Web.
JPEG Joint Photographic Expert Group which sets the standards for image
   coding and transmission over the *Internet.*

kHz one thousand *Hertz.*

LAN *local area network.*
larynx the valve at the top of the windpipe.
LaTeX a set of high level commands that allows one to take advantage of
   TeX's text formatting capabilities in a more comfortable way.
limiter see *hard limiter.*
linear predictive coding (LPC) predicting a present value of a signal (a
   speech signal, for example) by linearly combining past values.
links (not the German left.) Connections between *hypertext* documents,
   soundfiles, software etc. that can be activated by clicking on a symbol like
   an icon or highlighted text. These links allow one to connect hypertexts
   with related topics by a mouse click, even when the systems where the
   documents are stored are thousands of miles apart.
Linux simplified clone of *Unix.*
liquid frictionless speech sound, with partly obstructed air flow from the
   lungs, that can be held steady like a *vowel* (especially *l* and *r*).
local area network a small computer network, e.g. in an office building.
lossless coding method of *coding* that permits the complete reconstruction
   of the original data. (Lossless coding of English text can save about half
   the necessary *bits.*)
lowpass filter a mechanical or electronic device that lets only low frequencies pass through and blocks high frequencies.
LPC *linear predictive coding.*

Lucent Technologies research and manufacturing company, including Bell Laboratories, split off from AT&T in 1994.

MA moving average: process for smoothing data.

Ma Bell Ma as in Mama: the Bell Telephone System consisting (before the break up of AT&T in 1984) of *AT&T, Western Electric, Bell (Telephone) Laboratories* and 23 "operating companies."

Mac OS the operating system that runs the *Apple* Macintosh computer.

mainframe computer large computer, often the hub of a system serving many users.

masked threshold threshold of hearing in the presence of a masking noise.

masking in hearing: a strong sound (the "masker") making a "weaker" sound inaudible.

matched filter mechanical or electrical *filter* with *transfer function* that is the complex conjugate of the *Fourier transform* of the signal to be detected.

MB *megabyte.*

megabyte one million *bytes.* Top laptops have typically 32 to 128 Megabyte of random access memory.

mel subjective scale characterizing the "tone height" or *pitch* of a sound, similar to the *Bark* scale.

memory organ to forget with.

MHz one million *Hertz.*

microchip a semiconductor device that serves as an *integrated circuit.*

microcomputer compact computer with lower capabilities than a *minicomputer.*

microprocessor *integrated circuit* (e.g. in a computer or appliance) etched on layers of silicon that organizes the central electronics of a computer on a chip.

Microsoft software developer, best known for its *Windows* operating systems.

MIDI *Musical Instruments Digital Interface.*

millennium bug *year 2000 problem* or year 2000 *bug.*

minicomputer computer with processing capabilities smaller than those of a *mainframe computer.*

MIT Massachusetts Institute of Technology.

modem modulator-demodulator: device for converting *digital* data to *analog* data and vice versa.

modulation transfer function factor with which different modulation frequencies of a signal are multiplied.

module part of a computer program that performs a distinct function
or
an interchangeable, plug-in *hardware* unit.

monitor device with a screen for viewing data at a computer terminal.

morphemes the smallest meaningful pieces into which words can be cut.

mouse a palm-size computer input device that is moved on a flat surface to change the position of the cursor on the screen, to open menus, enter data etc.

MPEG Motion Picture Expert Group, which sets standards for picture coding for the Internet. The latest standard, MPEG 4, includes motion compensation and object recognition.

MS-DOS Microsoft *disk operating system.*

multimedia integration of still images, videos and sound (music and speech).

multimedia software *software* that enables audio and video content on computers.

multimedia publishing computer *software* that combines text with video, animated graphics and sound.

Musical Instruments Digital Interface *serial bus* to connect electronic musical instruments; file standard which stores musical information efficiently as codebook entries.

nasal speech sound emanating partly (as in French nasal *vowels*) or entirely through the nose (*m, n,* and *ng* as in sing).

National Security Agency government agency, headquartered in Ft Meade, Maryland, charged with the design and breaking of secrecy codes.

net the *Internet.*

netiquette rules for good behavior on the *Internet.*

Netscape Navigator *web browser* by Netscape.

neural net(work) mathematical model simulating the behavior of biological neural networks for *pattern recognition, speech processing* and self-directed problem solving.

neurocomputing an alternative to *programmed computing.* An approach to develop information processing capabilities for tasks where the *algorithms* or rules are not known or cannot be implemented. This is achieved with parallel, distributed, adaptive information processing systems such as *neural networks,* genetic or fuzzy learning systems, and learning automata.

nonstandard computing computing, usually in a highly parallel mode, making use of molecules (e.g. DNA and RNA), cellular automata, or quantum mechanical states.

NSA *National Security Agency.*

NSFnet high-speed backbone network established by the National Science Foundation (1987–1995).

Nyquist rate The smallest possible *sampling rate* that avoids *aliasing.*

Nyquist theorem see *sampling theorem.*

Office Suite a collection of *software applications* that can share data.

offline operating independently of an associated computer (as opposed to *online*).

one-time pad encryption method that uses a key only once and then discards it for better protection against decryption.

online operating under direct control of a main computer (as opposed to *offline*).

online publishing publishing on the *Internet*.

online service a business that provides dial-up access to information, entertainment, e-mail and chat groups, among other features.

operating system the software that allows users and application programs to interact with and control a computer or microprocessor and its peripheral devices. Examples include *Mac OS, Windows*, and *Unix*.

orthonormal system of functions or sequences that are orthogonal ("linearly independent") to each other and normalized to have unit energy.

OS computer *operating system*.

oversampling sampling at a rate above the *Nyquist rate*.

overtone an acoustical frequency that is higher in frequency than the fundamental.

packet a package of data that travels together on the *Internet*.

parallel bus computer *bus* that transmits several bits simultaneously (in parallel) as opposed to a *serial bus*.

parsing one of the mental processes in sentence comprehension in which the listener (or reader) determines the syntactic categories of words.

partial masking in hearing: a strong sound reducing the loudness of another, usually weaker, sound.

partial tone one of the pure tones forming a part of a complex tone. Also called partial.

PC *personal computer*.

PCM *pulse code modulation*.

peak clipping limiting the *amplitude range* of a signal. See also *infinite clipping*.

peak factor ratio of the *amplitude range* of a signal to its *root-mean-square* value. For a sine wave the peak factor equals $2\sqrt{2} \approx 2.8$.

peak value highest value of a signal.

pel picture element (before 1970), now called *pixel*.

perceptron historically, a single-layer *neural network*. The perceptron is incapable of executing the *Exclusive Or* or XOR function.

personal computer desktop or laptop computer compatible with IBM computers (as opposed to *Apple*/Macintosh).

PGP *Pretty Good Privacy*.

phase delay phase shift, expressed as a time.

phase spectrum phase angles as a function of frequency (as in the *Fourier transform* of a signal).

phon unit of loudness level of a sound, obtained by comparison with a 1-kHz tone.

phone speech sound.

phoneme any of the 15 to 70 distinctive speech sounds of a language.

phonetic pertaining to the production and transcription of speech sounds.

phonetic spelling Dutch spelling is largely phonetic. English is decidedly not. (Think of the "spelling" of *fish* as *ghoti*: *gh* as in enough, *o* as in w*o*men, *ti* as in na*ti*on.)

phonology the part of grammar that determines the sound pattern of a language.

phonotopic map mapping from a speech signal or its *spectrum* to a two-dimensional space in which adjacent *formant* frequencies are adjacent.

photonic of or pertaining to processes involving photons.

phrase a group of words that behaves as a unit in a sentence and has some coherent meaning.

pitch subjective height of a tone.

pixel smallest element of an image that can be individually processed and displayed.

place of articulation location in the *vocal tract* at which two speech organs (such as tongue tip and teeth or tongue body and palate) approach each other or come together.

plain old telephone service (POTS) service of the kind that old *Ma Bell* provided.

platform a fundamental layer of *software* required to make other programs run. The word is used interchangeably with operating system, which is the most common type of platform. The *Internet* is another, and local networks, web browsers and *Java* are all frequently viewed as platforms.

plosive stop *consonant* characterized by sudden air pressure release (p, b; t, d; k, g).

point of articulation *place of articulation*.

pole a resonance in a signal or *transfer function*.

PONS^{TM} Prometheus OrthoNormal System, a binary coding scheme that minimizes *Heisenberg uncertainty*.

port a connection, or channel, into a computer.

PostScript a popular, flexible printing and plotting language for ready-to-print files that allows electronic file transfer to other institutions.

POTS *plain old telephone service*.

power spectrum squared magnitude of the *Fourier transform*.

prediction error *prediction residual*.

prediction residual remaining error in a predictive analysis system such as *linear predictive coding*.

predictive coding predicting a present value of a signal (a speech signal, for example) from its past values.

predictor coefficient coefficient in a *predictor polynomial*.

predictor polynomial polynomial that predicts a present signal value from its past values.

presentation software *software* for creating business presentations on computer screens.

pretty good privacy a simplified version of a fully secure encryption system.

programmed computing problem-solving by devising an *algorithm* and/ or a set of rules and then coding these in software. So far the most common software design approach. Less flexible than *neurocomputing*.

prosody the stress and intonation patterns of an utterance.

protocol rules and standards for information transfer between computers.

psychoacoustics the study of sound perception, a subfield of *psychophysics*.

psychophysics the branch of psychology that describes the relation between physical stimuli and the resulting sensations.

public key cryptosystems system for encrypting data, using generally accessible ("public") keys and mathematical functions that are easy to execute in one direction (such as multiplying) but very difficult in the opposite direction (factoring).

pulsation threshold the level at which an interrupted stimulus (a tone or speech) in the presence of an alternating noise sounds continuous as a result of the auditory *continuity effect*.

pulse code modulation replacing an *analog* signal by a sequence of discrete or *digital* values.

Q also Q-factor: the resonance frequency of a resonance (such as a *formant* of speech) divided by its *bandwidth*.

quantizing converting an *analog* value into a discrete or *digital* one.

quantizing noise signal residues remaining as imprecisions when converting an analog signal to discrete (digital) values. The higher the time resolution (*sampling rate*) and amplitude resolution (*wordlength*) the better the *signal-to-noise ratio*.

quantum computer (so far nonexistent) computer exploiting the very high degree of parallelism implicit in quantum mechanical systems and therefore promising extremely high computing speeds (e.g. for factoring large composite numbers in cryptography).

quefrency independent variable of the *cepstrum*. If the signal is a function of time (such as speech), then quefrency also has the dimension of time.

radian frequency *angular frequency*.

random access memory (RAM) fast storage device used by computers during calculation. A top laptop has 64 Megabyte of memory at the time of writing (1998).

read-only memory a *random access memory* whose content is fixed during manufacture and cannot be changed subsequently.

RealAudio radio programs distributed over the *Internet*. Made possible by speech and music *compression*.

real-time a computer processing mode in which incoming data is processed instantaneously, without interrupting the data stream. (In television real-time is referred to as "live.")

recurrent backpropagation neural network a recurrent *spatiotemporal neural network* that feeds back the delayed outputs of all the top-level's neurons to all the neurons in the lowest level. At each time step, an external input vector is supplied to some of the lowest-level neurons and an output vector is received from some of the highest-level neurons.

relative bandwidth *bandwidth* divided by resonance frequency. The relative bandwidth equals the reciprocal of Q.

residual *prediction residual.*

residue pitch pitch percept engendered by the higher harmonics of a periodic or nearly periodic sound.

resonance concentration of energy in the *spectrum* (of a sound).

ROM *read-only memory.*

root-mean-square square root of the average of the squared signal amplitude.

rough in phonetics: uttered with aspiration, aspirated. In music: a dissonant sound.

RSA R.L. **R**ivest, A. **S**hamir, and L.A. **A**dleman, inventors of *public key cryptosystems.*

sample instantaneous value of a signal.

sampling noise see *quantizing noise.*

sampling rate rate of data samples. For 4 kHz-*bandwidth* speech, for example, the sampling rate is typically somewhat above 8 kHz. See also *Nyquist rate.*

sampling theorem also called Nyquist theorem, states the fact that the *sampling rate* (*Nyquist rate*) needs to be higher than twice the highest frequency component of the sound to be discretized in order to prevent *aliasing.*

scanner photoelectric device for scanning and digitizing a picture or text (e.g. for further processing by a computer).

or

a program that attempts to learn about the weaknesses of a victim computer by repeatedly probing it with requests for information.

segmentation cutting up of words into *syllables* and *phonemes.*

self-steering array array of microphones (hydrophones or loudspeakers) that homes in on a target automatically.

semantics the rules that specify the meaning of words and sentences.

semi-vocoder *vocoder* in which only part of the spectrum is coded. The *voice-excited vocoder* is a semi-vocoder.

sensor microphone, hydrophone or other device sensing physical data.

serial bus computer *bus* that transmits data bits one after another (serial) as opposed to a *parallel bus.*

server a data processing unit linked to a large computer. Serves as a large data buffer and distributor.

shareware *software* that can be *download*ed from the *Internet.*

shell a software layer that provides the interface between a user and the *operating system* of a computer.

short-time spectrum *Fourier transform* based on a short time segment of a signal (such as speech).

sibilant *fricative.*

signal-to-noise ratio ratio of signal power to noise power on a communication channel. Together with the *bandwidth* of the channel, the signal-to-noise ratio determines its information carrying capacity.

simulation *computer simulation.*

sine wave a signal having a sinusoidal dependence of its amplitude as a function of time, such as a pure tone.

sleep mode permits the reduction of the amount of power consumed by a computer while it is not in use.

sniffer a program that records computer and network activity.

SNR *signal-to-noise ratio.*

soft palate the posterior soft portion of the palate that separates the oral cavity from the nasal cavity.

software computer program.

sone unit of subjective loudness. By definition, 1 sone is the loudness of a binaural 1-kHz tone at a sound pressure of 40 dB above the threshold of hearing. A sound that is perceived as twice as loud has a loudness of 2 sone.

sonogram *spectrogram* of sound signal.

soundcard computer component generating and processing sounds. Soundcards contain *A/D* and *D/A* converters and use *FM* or *wavetable synthesis.*

spam (e-mail) junk e-mail.

spatiotemporal neural network a *neural network* that can deal with inputs and outputs that are explicit functions of time, such as in *real-time* speech processing. To obtain these dynamic properties, the network must be given memory, either as time delay or feedback (recurrent network).

speakerphone telephone with loudspeaker.

spectrogram two-dimensional graphic representation of spectral energy distribution over time and frequency.

spectrum magnitude of *Fourier transform,* also *amplitude spectrum.*

spectrum (or spectral) flattener device that flattens the *spectrum* of a signal, thereby suppressing any resonance (*formant*) structure.

spreadsheet *software* for analyzing and modeling financial and other numerical data.

spread spectrum method of communication in which the signal is spread over a wide spectrum to combat multipath and other interference.

square wave a signal having only two distinct amplitude values.

stop consonant a *consonant* in which the air flow is completely blocked (p, t, k; b, d, g).

syllable uninterrupted segment of speech comprising a "center" of relatively great sonority. Examples of one-syllable English words are man, wolf, sheep etc. Human, mankind, kindness etc. have two syllables.

syntax rules for the formation of grammatical sentences in a language. (Not a misspelled tax.)

TCP transmission control protocol, the set of communications conventions that enable the sending and receiving of data over the Internet.

TEX read: [tek] or [teχ] (χ as in Scottish *loch*). A powerful programming language for text formatting; popular because of its ability to produce book quality text, especially for scientific and technical works. As opposed to a word processor with which text can be entered, formatted, displayed and printed, TEX only assumes the role of a formatter/typesetter.

telemedicine delivery of healthcare, especially medical diagnosis, over the *Internet*.

Telnet network for exchanging data (excluding graphics) between computers. Introduced in the 1970s, it is still popular because of its speed.

tense relative time of occccurrence of the event described by the sentence, the moment at which the speaker utters the sentence, and, often, some third reference point.

timbre sound quality (as opposed to *pitch*) such as the different sound qualities of different musical instruments or human vowel sounds.

time-delay neural network (TDNN) a *spatiotemporal neural network* whose hidden and output units receive not only the present input value but also one or more of the previous ones. Originally devised to capture the concept of time symmetry as encountered in phoneme recognition from a spectrogram.

time warping changing the time scaling in a nonlinear manner.

tonotopic mapping adjacent frequencies and modulation frequencies are represented in the cortex ("brain") by adjacent areas.

transfer function the (complex) ratio of output voltage or pressure of a linear system (such as an electrical filter or the coval tract) to the input quantity.

TTS text-to-speech synthesis.

tuning curve the firing rate of an acoustic neuron as a function of frequency.

Turing machine a simple computer consisting of an infinite strip of paper, and a processor that moves along the paper and prints or erases symbols on it in a sequence that depends on which symbol the processor is currently reading and which of several states it is in.

uncertainty *Heisenberg uncertainty*.

undersampling taking samples at a *sampling rate* that is too small to cover a given bandwidth, causes aliasing and/or sampling noise.

universal resource locator Internet address, usually starting with *http://*.

Unix a powerful *operating system* especially suited for *servers*, the large computers that power networks or data bases. Invented at Bell Laboratories in 1969, Unix is now a splintered family of operating systems that includes IBM's AIX, Sun Microsystems' Solaris, and the public domain platform Linux.

unvoiced *voiceless* speech sound.

upload to place a file on another computer system via *modem*.

upward spread of masking in hearing: the fact that the *masking* or *partial masking*, by a given masking sound, of a higher-frequency sound is more pronounced than that of a lower-frequency sound. This frequency-asymmetry of masking stems from the fact that low frequency waves pass the region of high-frequency detection on the basilar membrane in the inner ear, whereas high-frequency waves hardly reach the regions of low-frequency detection.

URL *universal resource locator*.

USB universal serial bus.

utilities *software* that performs maintenance, diagnostics or repairs on computer hardware or software.

vaporware computer jargon: a product, especially software, that is promoted or marketed while it is still in development and that may never be produced.

vector quantizing simultaneous *quantizing* of several signal samples such as successive speech *samples*.

velum the *soft palate*.

VEV *voice-excited vocoder*.

virtual memory way of extending the main memory by allowing the programmer to access slower backing storage (normally the hard disk) in the same way as immediate access store (*RAM* chips).

virtual reality realistic simulation of an environment, including three-dimensional graphics and sound.

virus a set of *software* instructions that damage or erase information, work files, or programs on a computer.

visible speech *spectrogram* of speech signal.

vocal cords the elastic bands near the "Adam's apple" of a human that vibrate during voiced (not whispered) speech.

vocal tract the "cavity" in the human head between the *vocal cords* and the lips. Its resonances determine the acoustic quality and phonetic value of a speech sound.

vocoder (also channel vocoder) from *voice coder*. Electronic device that analyzes a speech signal in terms of its amplitude spectrum, separating the *spectral envelope* from its *spectral fine structure (pitch)* and synthesizing an artificial speech signal from the pitch information and the spectral envelope. The latter information is carried by typically 6 to 16 *frequency channel* signals. The total *bandwidth* for transmitting this spectral information is roughly 1/10 of the bandwidth of the speech signal itself.

voiced speech sound produced with vibrations of the *vocal cords* — as opposed to *voiceless speech sound*.

voice-excited vocoder *vocoder* in which the excitation signal is obtained from the low-frequency components (the *baseband*) of a speech signal.

voiceless speech sound produced by air friction without vibration of the *vocal cords* — as opposed to *voiced speech sound*.

voiceprint graphic representation of a person's voice showing energy as a function of time and frequency.

volume focussing *matched filters* applied to an array of *sensors* (hydrophones in the ocean, for example). In multipath transmission media, this results in an array focussed on a limited volume in three-dimensional space rather than just a directed beam.

Voronoi cell region in multi-dimensional (signal) space where each point inside a given cell is closer to its quantized value than to any other quantized value.

vowel speech sound, such as *ah, eh, ee, oh, oo*, produced without obstructing or diverting the flow of air from the lungs — as opposed to *consonant*.

WAN *wide area network*.

war dialer a program that will automatically dial a range of telephone numbers.

waveform the shape of a signal. A speech waveform (in air) is the sound pressure as the function of time.

wavelet literally: little wave, a *waveform* used in signal analysis and synthesis. Compactly supported wavelets have limited extent. Scaling wavelets are derived by scaling and shifting the independent variable of a "mother wavelet."

wavetable synthesis a process where sound samples (often of real instruments) are digitally stored and then manipulated for playback.

.wav file waveform file, a computer file for storing sound.

web *World Wide Web*.

web browser a program that enables users to navigate the *World Wide Web*, interact with other programs and users on the *Internet*, and call up and display *multimedia* files.

web page a quantity of information on the *web* that has one *URL* and can be watched in one frame of a *web browser*.

web site a source of information on the *web* consisting of one or an ensemble of *web pages* usually dealing with one specific topic.

Western Electric former manufacturing arm of *AT&T*.

wide area network an extensive computer network connecting machines over a longer distance than in a *LAN*.

window function of time through which only a portion of a running signal is seen.

Windows an integrated family of operating systems developed by *Microsoft* to bring a common look and feel to computers spanning a wide range of capabilities. They include *Windows 95* and *Windows 98*, which generally run on the Intel Corporation's *microprocessors*; *Windows NT*, which is generally found on more powerful *Unix*-class machines, and *Windows CE*, for small electronic devices.

Windows 95/98 operates *personal computers.*

Windows CE operates handheld computers, consumer electronics devices.

Windows NT operates *workstations* and large servers for networking.

Wine Windows emulator: Software designed to imitate the Microsoft *Windows* operating system.

wintel a term for the combination of *Windows* operating systems and Intel microprocessors found on more than 80 percent of all computers sold today.

wordlength number of bits per sample value. The wordlength determines the precision of a value.

word processor *software* for creating text documents.

word spotting automatic recognition of selected words (such as "wheat") usually in a large amount of data such as obtained from the tapping of thousands of telephone lines.

workstation powerful *microcomputer* used in *computer-aided design*, electronic publishing, or other graphics intensive processing.

World Wide Web a vast, disparate network of pages of data and programs on the Internet, connected to one another via *hyperlinks* — a technology that lets users jump from one item to another by clicking with a *mouse* on a word or *icon* that points to some other part of the network. The web is the *platform* for most electronic commerce and publishing on the *Internet*.

WWW *World Wide Web* (also, sarcastically, World Wide Wait).

XOR the *Exclusive Or* or XOR function.

year 2000 problem the book-keeping problem resulting from the fact that most computer programs did not envisage intelligent life after the year 1999. As a result, the year 2000 is interpreted as the year 1900 with

disastrous consquences in commerce, banking, health care, and almost every other kind of human activity. (Of course the use of just two digits to designate a year in a given century far antedates computers.)

Y2K the *year 2000 problem*.

zero an antiresonance in a signal or *transfer function*.

Zip drive a drive that reads and writes zip diskettes. A single zip diskette can store up to 100 megabytes of data.

Name Index

Page numbers in *italics* refer to author citations in the References

Subject Index

The Author

Manfred Schroeder studied mathematics and physics at the University of Göttingen in Germany. In his thesis he investigated the distribution of resonances in concert halls using microwave cavities as models. The chaotic distribution he found is now recognized as characteristic for complex dynamical systems.

In 1954 Schroeder joined the research department of AT&T's Bell Laboratories in Murray Hill, New Jersey. From 1958 to 1969 he directed research on speech compression, synthesis, and recognition. Since 1969 he has also served as a Professor of Physics at Göttingen, commuting between the university and Bell.

Schroeder is also a founding member of the Institut de Recherche et Coordination Acoustique/Musique of the Centre Pompidou in Paris. In the late 1950s he helped to formulate the U.S. standards for stereophonic broadcasting, now used worldwide. Schroeder holds 45 U.S. Patents in speech processing and other fields.

In 1991 Schroeder was awarded the Gold Medal of the Acoustical Society of America for "theoretical and practical contributions to human communication through innovative application of mathematics." He also received the Rayleigh Medal of the British Institute of Acoustics, the Helmholtz Medal of the German Acoustical Society, and the Gold Medal of the Audio Engineering Society.

Schroeder is a Fellow of the American Academy of Arts and Sciences and the New York Academy of Sciences. He is also a member of the National Academy of Engineering in Washington and the Göttingen Academy.

Schroeder's hobbies are languages, bicycling, down-hill skiing, and computer graphics.

Springer Series in Information Sciences

Editors: Thomas S. Huang Teuvo Kohonen Manfred R. Schroeder

Springer and the environment

At Springer we firmly believe that an international science publisher has a special obligation to the environment, and our corporate policies consistently reflect this conviction.
We also expect our business partners – paper mills, printers, packaging manufacturers, etc. – to commit themselves to using materials and production processes that do not harm the environment. The paper in this book is made from low- or no-chlorine pulp and is acid free, in conformance with international standards for paper permanency.

Springer

Druck: Strauss Offsetdruck, Mörlenbach
Verarbeitung: Schäffer, Grünstadt